The Life and Music of Elizabeth Maconchy

Portrait of Maconchy by Kitty Church, 1931 (reproduced by permission of the Maconchy Estate).

The Life and Music of Elizabeth Maconchy

Erica Siegel

THE BOYDELL PRESS

First published 2023
The Boydell Press, Woodbridge

ISBN 978 1 83765 051 4

The Boydell Press is an imprint of Boydell & Brewer Ltd
PO Box 9, Woodbridge, Suffolk IP12 3DF, UK
and of Boydell & Brewer Inc.
668 Mt Hope Avenue, Rochester, NY 14620–2731, USA
website: www.boydellandbrewer.com

A CIP catalogue record for this book is available
from the British Library

This publication is printed on acid-free paper

FSC www.fsc.org MIX Paper from responsible sources FSC® C013056

Printed and bound in Great Britain by TJ Books Limited, Padstow, Cornwall

For Byron Adams

Contents

Illustrations

Figures

Musical Examples

Full credit details are provided in the captions to the images in the text. The author and publisher are grateful to all the institutions and individuals listed for permission to reproduce the materials in which they hold copyright. Every effort has been made to trace the copyright holders; apologies are offered for any omission, and the publisher will be pleased to add any necessary acknowledgement in subsequent editions.

Acknowledgements

This book would have been impossible to complete without the help and support of many individuals. I owe a particular debt to Nicola LeFanu for her incredible kindness, generosity, and assistance. I am also indebted to the scholars who have come before me, as the works of Jenny Doctor, Sophie Fuller, Rhiannon Mathias, Catherine Roma, and Ailie Blunnie, among others, have greatly enhanced my own understanding of Maconchy and her music. I'm incredibly grateful to Sophie for her insightful feedback on drafts of this book.

I'd especially like to thank Nicolas Bala, Anna Dunlop, Erika Fox, Anthony Gilbert, Giles Swayne, David Lumsdaine, as well as the late Jane Manning and Anthony Payne, who were all incredibly generous with their time and recollections of the past. Many thanks are also due to the following individuals who offered advice and/or assistance throughout various stages of this project: Hugh Cobbe, Thierry Burger-Helmchen, Meredith Graham, Daniel Grimley, Stephen G.F. Hall, Nicola Hyman, Jaclyn Howerton, Rachel Howerton, Philip Rupprecht, and Dave Volpe.

In 2014, I was fortunate to receive a dissertation fellowship from the Mellon Foundation that enabled me to spend a year at the Institute of Historical Research at the University of London. This fellowship enabled me to undertake much of the initial research for this project. I remain grateful for the encouragement and perceptive advice I received from the IHR's then-director, Lawrence Goldman, as well as the support of Vanessa Rockel.

Enormous thanks are due to Oliver Mahony, the archivist at St Hilda's College, who put up with my near-constant presence over the course of countless weeks with unfailing kindness over the years. I also wish to thank Elizabeth Boardman, the former archivist at St Hilda's, as well as Maira Canzonieri and Peter Horton at the RCM. Thanks are also due to the staff of the BBC Written Archives Centre, the Victoria & Albert Theatre and Performance Archives, and the British Library.

I would also like to thank the following copyright holders for generously granting permission to reproduce various letters, writings, and photographs: Hugh Cobbe (on behalf of the Vaughan Williams Charitable Trust), Ruth Farcas (on behalf of the Gordon Jacob Estate), Nicola LeFanu (on behalf of the Maconchy Estate), Clare Monro (on behalf of the Cecil Armstrong Gibbs Estate), and Ben Ridler (on behalf of the Anne Ridler Estate). BBC copyright content is reproduced by courtesy of the British Broadcasting Corporation. All rights reserved. Thanks are also due to Faber Music, Oxford University Press, and Hal Leonard Europe (on behalf of Chester Music and Alfred Lengnick & Co.) for their permission to reproduce musical examples.

Above all, this book owes an insurmountable debt to Byron Adams, who first suggested that I take a look at some of Maconchy's works in January 2011. I am forever grateful for his unwavering encouragement and resolute belief in this project, particularly when its future at times seemed uncertain.

I also owe a tremendous debt to the editorial team at Boydell for believing in this project and their extraordinary patience.

Last but not least, I'd especially like to thank my family for their support, and Daniel Selifonov, for helping me see flickers of schematic light at the end of the tunnel.

Abbreviations

Societies and Organisations

BBC	British Broadcasting Corporation
CEMA	Council for the Encouragement of Music and the Arts
CPNM	Committee for the Promotion of New Music
ICA	Institute of Contemporary Arts
ISCM	International Society for Contemporary Music
LCMC	London Contemporary Music Centre
RCM	Royal College of Music
SPNM	Society for the Promotion of New Music
SWM	Society of Women Musicians
WMA	Workers' Music Association

Sources

BBC WAC	British Broadcasting Corporation Written Archives Centre
BL	British Library
MLCT	Sophie Fuller and Jennifer Doctor (eds), *Music, Life, and Changing Times: Selected Correspondence Between British Composers Elizabeth Maconchy and Grace Williams* (Abingdon: Routledge, 2019)
OUP	Oxford University Press
SHC	Maconchy Archive, St Hilda's College, Oxford
VWL	The Letters of Ralph Vaughan Williams: https://vaughanwilliams.uk/

Note: For brevity, letters exchanged between Maconchy and Williams are referenced by their date. Most of the letters and their contents can be found in *MLCT*.

Introduction

For many, the name of Anglo-Irish composer Elizabeth Maconchy (1907–94) is completely unknown. In others, her name sparks some faint recollection, namely in connection to the musicians and composers she came into contact with, or in reference to her cycle of thirteen string quartets for which she remains best known. For those more familiar with her life and story, it remains a cautionary tale of the uphill battle facing women in male-dominated professions: regarded as one of the most brilliant students at the Royal College of Music (RCM) in the late 1920s, she rose to great acclaim in the early 1930s. The première of her orchestral suite, *The Land*, conducted by Sir Henry Wood at the Proms in 1930, was a smashing success and seemed destined to catapult her to stardom. But instead of opening further doors, what she encountered was discouraging in the extreme: no publisher was willing to consider publishing orchestral music by a woman composer; they would only consider songs, as the composition of miniatures better befitted her gender.

Maconchy came of age during a period of rapid change and transformation for women. The grant of partial enfranchisement in 1918, followed by The Representation of the People (Equal Franchise) Act in 1928, which extended the right to vote to women over the age of twenty-one, ushered in a period that some deemed a 'watershed' for improving the status of women. In the press, the argument that women had achieved equality with men was bolstered by the chronicling of 'women's firsts', insinuating that gender-based discrimination had become a thing of the past. Yet, as women gained entrance into professions from which they had hitherto been barred through the passage of The Sex Disqualification (Removal) Act in 1919, which allowed women to hold civil and judicial appointments, in many other professions, marriage bars remained in full force.[1] Of the position of women composers, in *A Room of One's Own* (1929), Virginia Woolf stated the following in her poignant critique of the widespread belief that enfranchisement had placed women on equal terms with men:

> The woman composer stands where the actress stood in the time of Shakespeare. Nick Greene, I thought, remembering the story I had made about Shakespeare's sister, said that a woman acting put him in mind of a dog dancing. Johnson repeated the phrase two hundred years later of women preaching. And here, I said, opening a book about music, we have the very words used again in this year

1 See Martin Pugh, *Women and the Women's Movement in Britain, 1914–1999*, 2nd edn (London: Macmillan, 2000); Adrian Bingham, *Gender, Modernity, and the Popular Press in Inter-War Britain* (Oxford: Oxford University Press, 2004); and Julie V. Gottlieb and Richard Toye (eds), *The Aftermath of Suffrage: Women, Gender, and Politics in Britain, 1918–1945* (Basingstoke: Palgrave Macmillan, 2013).

of grace, 1928, of women who try to write music. 'Of Mlle. Germaine Tailleferre one can only repeat Dr. Johnson's dictum concerning a woman preacher, transposed into terms of music. "Sir, a woman's composing is like a dog's walking on his hind legs. It is not done well, but you are surprised to find it done at all."' So accurately does history repeat itself.[2]

The book on music to which Woolf refers is Cecil Gray's *A Survey of Contemporary Music*. First published in 1924 by Oxford University Press, followed by a second edition in 1928, Tailleferre (1892–1983) was not the only woman composer to be included in Gray's examination of contemporary composers, as Cécile Chaminade (1857–1944) receives a brief, but disparaging mention. For a period in which one could name many established women composers of renown, such as Amy Beach (1867–1944), Lili Boulanger (1893–1918), Régine Wieniawski (1879–1932), known professionally by the pseudonym Poldowski, Ethel Smyth (1858–1944), and Maude Valérie White (1855–1937), to name but a few, Gray's assertion of the inferiority of women composers, as well as their rarity, was a stark distortion of reality.[3]

By the time Maconchy arrived at the RCM in 1923, many women had already begun to make some cracks in the proverbial glass ceiling. She received an education that was equal to her male peers. Instead of being restricted to songs, women were encouraged to compose orchestral works that were beginning to be performed in greater numbers on the public stage. But, as Maconchy's experience after the successful debut of *The Land* demonstrates, many barriers remained, particularly in the realm of publishing. Though Maconchy never liked the term 'woman composer', it remained a label from which she could never escape.

Nevertheless, Maconchy persisted. Over the course of her professional career, which spanned over five decades, she composed a prodigious number of works, gaining accolades from not only her peers, but also established musical figures of the day. As compelling as Maconchy's story indeed is, she led a life that was not always conducive to building up the kind of public admiration and veneration amassed by some of her colleagues. Despite taking up public-facing roles at various points during her career, she never sought out the limelight and remained a deeply private person and modest to a fault. Following her death, music critic Hugo Cole remarked, 'She was not an easy person to interview. There were no glib answers; every response had to be exact and if she had nothing to say, nothing was said. She was incapable of small-talk or gossip.'[4]

When Maconchy died, she did not leave behind a meticulously curated life. She never kept a journal. Of her childhood, little is known. Though she kept appointment diaries, the earliest one known to survive is from 1953. While a modest amount of correspondence survives, the overwhelming majority of it

[2] Virginia Woolf, *A Room of One's Own* (New York: Harcourt, Brace, & Co., 1963), 56.

[3] See Sophie Fuller, 'Women Composers during the British Musical Renaissance, 1880–1918' (PhD thesis, King's College, University of London, 1998); and Paula Gillett, *Musical Women in England, 1870–1914* (New York: St. Martin's Press, 2000).

[4] Hugo Cole, 'Music of honest passion', *Guardian*, 14 November 1994.

is one-sided. There are, nevertheless, two notable exceptions: her correspondence with Grace Williams, as well as her letters to the BBC. Many of the talks she delivered to various organisations survive as well, in addition to her vast output of music. With a corpus of well over 200 extant works, only a minuscule fraction can be discussed here. In discussing her music, my aim has been to highlight works that embody Maconchy's musical style, tracing its development and transformation over the years. From wars to fame, illness, motherhood, and critical acclaim, this biography traces Maconchy's life and music from the fragments that remain.

1

An Unexpected Talent, 1907–23

Elizabeth Violet Maconchy was born on 19 March 1907. The second of three daughters of Violet Mary, née Poë (1878–1940), a homemaker, and Gerald Edward Campbell Maconchy (1875–1922), a solicitor, Maconchy's birth took place at the family's home at Silverleys, St Catharine's Estate in Hoddesdon, Hertfordshire.

Of her paternal lineage, Maconchy's roots can be traced to Scotland. Sometime in the late seventeenth century, a move to Ireland took place, with Maconchy's ancestors eventually settling in the county of Longford. According to records published in 1878, Maconchy's grandfather, George Maconchy (1818–89), possessed 10,319 acres, making him one of the largest land owners in the county.[1] After receiving his Bachelor of Arts from Trinity College, Dublin in 1838, George embarked on a career as a solicitor, later serving as a magistrate in the counties of Longford and Wexford, as well as High Sheriff for the county of Longford in 1846. In addition to a home in Rathmore, North Longford, the family also owned a home called Edenmore in Raheny, Dublin, as well as a home called Corrinagh in Torquay, Devonshire, where George relocated his family around the latter half of the 1850s. After the death of his first wife, Louisa Elizabeth Richards (1824–64), with whom he had had ten children, George married Janet Hamilton (Campbell) Middleton (1835–1910) on 2 July 1867.[2]

Gerald, who was the youngest of Janet and George's children, was born on 21 June 1875 in Torquay. He spent part of his childhood living in Clifton, Gloucestershire and was later sent to Charterhouse school, where he boarded at Pageites House.[3] In 1894, Gerald matriculated at Trinity College, Oxford, graduating with a 4th Class Juris and Bachelor of Arts in 1897. In 1901, he passed his qualifications to become a solicitor, basing his practice in London. Given his familial ties to Ireland, Gerald appears to have visited the country with some

1 See Bernard Burke, *A genealogical and heraldic history of the landed gentry of Great Britain & Ireland.* 6th edn with supplement, vol. II (London: Harrison and Sons, 1882), 1041–2; U. H. Hussey De Burgh, *The Landowners of Ireland* (Dublin: Hodges, Foster, and Figgis, 1878), 299; and Frank Columb, *The Lough Gowna Valley* (Oxford: Gasan Academic Publishing Company, 2002), 161–7.

2 'Marriages', *Western Daily Press*, 5 July 1867. Born in Glasgow, Janet was the daughter of Colin Murdoch Campbell of Colgrain and his wife Janet, née Miller. Prior to George and Janet's marriage, in 1857 Janet married Major William Middleton, who died in 1859.

3 Gerald left Charterhouse in 1892. See *Charterhouse Register, 1872–1910,* vol. I (London: Proprietors at the Chiswick Press, 1911), 387.

frequency. A keen amateur golfer, in the summertime he often took part in amateur golf tournaments.[4]

Of Maconchy's maternal lineage, Violet was the eldest of four children born to George Leslie Pöe (1846–1934) and his wife Mary, née Caldecott (c. 1855–1924). While little is known of Mary's family history, George counted among his descendants an officer in Cromwell's army, who, after the siege of Limerick, was granted land in the county of Tipperary.[5] In 1860, George embarked on what would become a long and distinguished naval career spanning over thirty years, rising to the rank of captain before retiring in 1891. In addition to his military career, Captain Poë, as he was commonly known, was also involved in banking, serving as a director of the Provincial Bank of Ireland.[6]

Captain Poë and his family resided at Santry Court, a vast eighteenth-century Jacobean mansion in Santry, Co. Dublin, for which he served as agent-in-residence after the bankruptcy of its owner, Sir Charles C.W. Domvile in 1875, to whom the Poë family was related by marriage.[7] Violet was raised at Santry Court and educated at Alexandra College in Milltown, Dublin, where she excelled in drama, with details of her performances appearing in the likes of the *Gentlewoman*, and *The Queen: The Lady's Newspaper and Court Chronicle*.

While exact details pertaining to how Gerald became acquainted with Violet are unclear, the families tended to move in the same social circles in Dublin through which they presumably met. Gerald and Violet's marriage took place on 29 January 1902 at Santry Church with a reception held for 200 guests at Santry Court.[8] The newlyweds honeymooned in Paris before settling into their home in Hertfordshire with Maconchy's elder sister, Mary (Maureen) Barbara, arriving later in the year on 4 November.

Although a great many details of Maconchy's childhood are unknown, she grew up primarily in Buckinghamshire where her father purchased the Tile House in Chalfont St Giles for £2,225 in 1908. Set on four acres of land, Gerald purchased an additional two acres of property, later making renovations to the tile and brick home to accommodate their growing family, with the addition of Maconchy's younger sister, Sheila, who was born on 12 March 1910. By 1913, the property purportedly featured three living rooms and seven bedrooms in addition to a garden and summer house, as well as a tennis lawn and motor shed.[9] While Gerald commuted to his office in London at 15 Arundel Street,

4 Many of his results appeared in the *Freeman's Journal*.

5 'Obituary: Captain Poë, R.N.', *Times*, 10 May 1934.

6 Ibid.

7 Nick Kingsley, '(418) Barry of Santry Court, Barons Barry of Santry', *Landed families of Britain and Ireland* (blog), 27 May 2020, https://landedfamilies.blogspot.com/2020/05/418-barry-of-santry-court-barons-barry.html [accessed 5 June 2019].

8 'Mr. G.E.C. Maconchy to Miss V.M. Poë', *Gentlewoman*, 8 February 1902.

9 See http://www.chalfonthistory.co.uk/pollards_wood_recent_history.html [accessed 30 March 2021].

Figure 1. Maconchy and her older sister, Maureen, 1907 (reproduced by permission of the Maconchy Estate).

Violet presumably managed the household with the aid of the family's parlour maid, nursery maid, and cook.[10]

Maconchy's education was facilitated through a series of governesses shared with other nearby families. It was a haphazard education with only one of the governesses possessing adequate proficiency in mathematics. Maconchy

[10] These details are according to England's census records for 1911.

Figure 2. Maconchy with her parents and sisters, 1911
(reproduced by permission of the Maconchy Estate)

reportedly enjoyed doing sums and also became proficient in French through a French governess.[11] An interest in poetry also appears to have taken root with a poem she wrote at the age of ten titled 'The New Year' awarded a prize in a literary competition in the children's magazine *Little Folks* in 1918:

The wind came skimming o'er the sea,
She seemed to whisper things to me,
She seemed to bring in softest tones
Some message from other zones.

A song of hope she seem'd to sing;
"The bells for Victory will ring,
This year will be a happy year,
And none of us will shed a tear.

"The earth it will be strewn with dow'es,
The cry will be 'Vict'ry is ours,'
And all will sing a song of praise
For peace 'twill be in future days."

[11] See Anna Dunlop, 'Personal Recollections of my mother, Elizabeth Maconchy', in Christa Brüstle and Danielle Sofer (eds), *Elizabeth Maconchy: Music as Impassioned Argument* (Vienna: Universal Edition, 2018), 14; and Ailie Blunnie, 'Passion and Intellect in the Music of Elizabeth Maconchy' (master's thesis, National University of Ireland, Maynooth, 2010), 10.

I woke to find myself alone,
To hear no more that cheering tone;
And there before me was the sea,
From whence the wind had come to me.[12]

Throughout her childhood, holidays were often spent in Ireland visiting her maternal grandparents at Santry Court. Around 1917 or 1918, the family decided to relocate to Ireland, settling in the seaside village of Howth, outside Dublin.[13] The decision to settle near the sea may have been prompted by Gerald's health as he had contracted tuberculosis during his service in the First World War.[14]

The Maconchy family's return to Ireland occurred during a tumultuous period in the fractured country's history. In 1916, Gerald's half-brother, Brigadier General Ernest William Stuart King Maconchy (1860–1945), led the Sherwood Forester Brigade during the Easter Rising, later presiding over some of the subsequent trials of captured insurgents.[15] Violence and unrest continued with the Irish War of Independence from 1919 to 1921, with the Anglo-Irish Treaty and the establishment of the Irish Free State offering a brief respite before the Irish Civil War which raged for ten months between June 1922 and May 1923. In contrast to the unionist views of her maternal grandparents, Maconchy was a supporter of the republican cause.[16]

In spite of the political turmoil and social unrest permeating much of her early life, Maconchy's childhood and adolescence appears to have been a happy one. Ireland was the country closest to her heart and she cherished the time she spent with her maternal grandparents, even if it required some strategic planning to avoid having to learn to play bridge with her grandfather so that

[12] Betty Maconchy, 'The New Year', *Little Folks* 21/1 (May 1918): 13.

[13] The exact date of this move is unclear. While Maconchy stated in later years that the family moved to Ireland when she was twelve, which would suggest that the move occurred sometime after March 1919, she told her daughters that she was around ten at the time the move took place. As Gerald sold the family's home in Buckinghamshire in 1918, the family's move likely occurred prior to the sale of the home.

[14] The earliest known surviving record of Gerald's wartime service dates from October 1918 in which he is listed as a 2nd Lieutenant in the newly formed Royal Air Force's administrative branch. It is believed that Gerald also served in the Royal Army Medical Corps sometime prior to his transfer. As over half of the army's service records were destroyed during bombings in the Second World War, further details regarding Gerald's service remain unknown. 'Maconchy, Gerald Edward Campbell', Air Ministry: Department of the Master-General of Personnel: Officer's Service Records, AIR 76/328/173, The National Archives; William Spencer, *First World War Army Service Records*, 4th edn (Kew: National Archives, 2008); Blunnie, 9.

[15] For details of the trials, see Seán Enright, *Easter Rising 1916: The Trials* (Sallins: Merrion, 2014).

[16] Blunnie, 9–10.

she would have enough time to practise piano.[17] Fortunately for Maconchy, her younger sister, Sheila, was able to make up the fourth.[18]

While music never played a prominent role in the household, at the age of six, Maconchy had been 'found at the piano, picking out tunes',[19] an impulse that soon expanded to the composing of small piano pieces. Of these early pieces, Maconchy later stated, 'There was nothing remarkable about my first essays except perhaps the fact that in an unmusical family, I should write music at all.'[20] Exactly how unmusical Maconchy's family truly was, however, remains uncertain: Gerald reportedly had some familiarity with the piano, and Violet played the organ at church.[21] Despite this ambiguity, the apparent indifference to formal musical training until Maconchy had reached approximately twelve years of age appears to confirm her own recollections of music's lowly status within the household during her early formative years.

However, once settled in Ireland, Maconchy was enrolled in piano lessons in Dublin with a Mrs Boxwell, who was presumably Edith Boxwell (1876–1937), as well as lessons in theory with Dorothy Stokes (1898–1982) who taught harmony and counterpoint at the Royal Irish Academy of Music.[22] Maconchy also had some composition lessons with Irish composer John Larchet (1884–1967). For one interested in art music, conditions in Ireland were far from ideal, as long-standing tensions between nationalist ideologies and British colonialism ensured there was little in the way of infrastructure to offer adequate support for classical music endeavours, despite periodic attempts at intervention.[23] Nevertheless, there were some organisations, such as the Royal Dublin Society (RDS), that did a great deal to foster classical music in Ireland, and it was through the RDS that Maconchy attended a recital by pianist Myra Hess (1890–1965). Yet, even in Dublin, opportunities were severely limited. As the family did not own a gramophone, aside from attending a performance of Beethoven's Seventh Symphony by the visiting Hallé Orchestra at the age of fifteen, and a production of *Carmen* by the touring British National Opera Company,

[17] Anna Dunlop, interview by author.

[18] Ibid.

[19] Nicola LeFanu, 'Elizabeth Maconchy DBE (1907–1994): some biographical and musical notes by her daughter Nicola LeFanu', https://www.nicolalefanu.com/resources/writings/EVM-biogcomplete.pdf [accessed 25 September 2020].

[20] Elizabeth Maconchy, draft of contribution to an article for *Hibernia*, June 1967, SHC. A revised version was published later in the year. See 'Music in Ireland: Leading Irish Composers', *Hibernia* (September 1967): 14.

[21] See Anne Macnaghten, 'Elizabeth Maconchy', *Musical Times* 90/1348 (June 1955): 298; and Dunlop, 14.

[22] Both Boxwell and Stokes had studied with pianist Margaret O'Hea (1843–1938) who taught at the Royal Irish Academy of Music. See Jennifer O'Connor, 'Women and Music in Nineteenth-Century Dublin', *Journal of the International Alliance for Women in Music* 15/1 (2009): 12–17.

[23] For detailed discussion of this topic, see Harry White, *The Keeper's Recital: Music and Cultural History in Ireland, 1770–1970* (Notre Dame: University of Notre Dame Press, 1998).

Maconchy's musical world was largely confined to what she could play herself: Beethoven's less challenging sonatas, Mendelssohn's *Songs Without Words*, and the works she composed herself.[24]

In 1922, Gerald's health declined and he returned to England, seeking treatment at Mundesley Sanatorium in Norfolk. While Violet spent time visiting her husband, Maconchy and her sisters remained in Ireland with family. Tragically, Gerald died later that year on 21 December. In spite of her sorrow, Maconchy continued with her musical studies, and in May 1923, she received a score of highly commended in a local Feis Coeil competition.[25] With the support and encouragement of Maconchy's teachers, following a summer holiday in France, Violet moved her family to London, where her daughter would embark on a new and glorious chapter in her life at the Royal College of Music.

[24] Elizabeth Maconchy, draft of talk titled 'Retrospective Concert', 3 January 1977, SHC. According to Dunlop, one of the works Maconchy composed during her childhood was based on a Psalm that referred to 'lions roaring', which was presumably Psalm 104:21. See Dunlop, 14.

[25] The Feis Coeil was formed in 1897 to cultivate music in Ireland.

2

The Royal College of Music, 1923–9

If there was one place that proved vital to Maconchy's development as a composer, it was the Royal College of Music (RCM). Shortly after moving to London and eventually settling in Paddington, Maconchy began her studies at the College in the Christmas term of 1923.[1] Initially, her principal study was piano and she was assigned to Arthur Alexander (1891–1969) for lessons. For her second study, she elected to study composition and was assigned to Irish composer Charles Wood (1866–1926). Maconchy also enrolled in lessons in harmony and counterpoint with Charles Herbert Kitson (1874–1944).[2] Life in London was a dramatic change from Ireland, and it took Maconchy some time to adjust, as she recalled: 'I was a shy and unsophisticated schoolgirl … [s]o this plunge into the musical life of London was thrilling but also overwhelming, and it took me a year or two to surface'.[3]

In the 1920s, the RCM was going through an adjustment of its own as it adapted to the dramatic increase of students after the war, as well as a whirlwind of change ushered in by Hugh Allen (1869–1946), who had been appointed Director of the College in 1919 after the death of Sir Hubert Parry in October 1918. While the most visible change to the College after the war was the abolition of sex-segregated staircases, Allen also made a number of alterations to the institution that included a complete reorganisation of the teaching staff, as well as reforms to its curriculum, and an expansion of performance opportunities for students.[4] Guy Warrack (1900–86), who both studied and later taught at

1 The earliest known address for Maconchy during her years of study at the RCM is 42 Westbourne Terrace, Hyde Park, W8. By 1925, the Maconchy family had moved to 188c Gloucester Terrace, Hyde Park, W2, which served as Maconchy's London address for the remainder of her studies at the College.

2 All RCM students were required to have a first and second study. The primary difference between the two was the amount of time allocated for lessons: first study lessons were forty minutes in length, while second study lessons were twenty minutes in length. See Guy Warrack, 'The Royal College of Music: The First Eighty-five Years' (typescript draft, BL, c. 1977), 23–4; and Christopher Grogan and Rosamund Strode, *Imogen Holst: A Life in Music*, revised edn (Woodbridge: Boydell, 2010), 41.

3 Maconchy, 'Retrospective Concert'.

4 While Allen is often credited for being responsible for the demise of the sex-segregated staircases, this issue has at times been disputed. Frank Howes (1891–1974), who studied at the RCM after the First World War and became a music critic at the *Times* in 1925, and later a lecturer at the RCM in 1938, observed 'When he came to the College in 1919 he found a certain number of conventions to break, e.g. the sexual

the RCM in the 1920s, aptly characterised the College's growth under Allen's leadership as 'a period of vigorous and almost breathless creation, revival and expansion. There was any amount of music to be absorbed on every side.'[5] Contrary to the popular image of the College in the 1920s as an inherently conservative institution where, according to Elisabeth Lutyens (1906–83), 'Brahms was the god of *new* music', an examination of College concert programmes reveals that this period was in fact much more diverse, with a heavy influx of French and Russian repertoire as works by Debussy, Franck, Saint-Saëns, Ravel, Borodin, Rachmaninoff, and Tchaikovsky were routinely performed at the College, with even composers such as Stravinsky and Schönberg making appearances in programmes.[6]

Surviving records indicate that Maconchy excelled as a student, making steady progress each term over the course of her first year despite being somewhat younger than the average RCM pupil.[7] In the Christmas term of 1924, she was awarded a Council Exhibition in pianoforte to the amount of £5. This term also included the first performance of one of her compositions, with her Suite for Strings in E Minor featured in an Informal Concert on 25 November, performed by her fellow RCM students Mary Gladden, Mabel Weller, Gwendolen Windsor, and Ruth Riley.[8]

Although Maconchy studied piano with Alexander for four years, she appears never to have discussed her studies with him publicly. Born in New Zealand, Alexander trained at the Royal Academy of Music (RAM), where he studied piano with Tobias Matthay (1858–1945) and composition with Frederick Corder (1852–1932).[9] According to pianist Angus Morrison

---

segregation of the staircases'. Warrack, however, has suggested that the liberation of the staircases was primarily a result of the retirement of Mrs Bindon, the Lady Superintendent. See Frank Howes, 'Sir Hugh Allen, 1869–1946', *R.C.M. Magazine* 65/3 (1969): 25–6; and Warrack, 60, 140.

5 Warrack, 196.

6 Elisabeth Lutyens, *A Goldfish Bowl* (London: Cassell, 1972), 38. Other notable composers making appearances in College programmes between 1923 and 1929 included Albéniz, Arensky, Bax, Bliss, Bruch, Chaminade, Dohnányi, Dvořák, Falla, Granados, Holst, Liapounov, Rimsky-Korsakov, Sibelius, Smyth, Tailleferre, and Vaughan Williams, among others.

7 Records of Maconchy's academic progress over the course of her first two years of study at the RCM are limited to those contained within the RCM's Roll of Studies that note Maconchy received marks of four in both Paper Work and Music Class in the Christmas term of 1923, which improved to marks of five in both subjects in the Easter term of 1924. In the Midsummer term, she received a mark of six in Music Class; however, no mark is indicated for Paper Work. A Teacher's Terminal Report, which was sent to students at the end of each term, would yield more information regarding Maconchy's studies during this period, but unfortunately the earliest one known to survive is from the Christmas term of 1925.

8 RCM Informal Concert (No. 72) programme, SHC.

9 Maisie Aldridge, 'Arthur Alexander, 1891–1969', *R.C.M. Magazine* 65/3 (1969): 33–5.

(1902–89), Alexander's appointment to the teaching staff at the RCM in 1920 proved controversial:

> Sir Hugh felt that the Matthay influence, then so strong at the Academy, should be represented at the College as well. Unfortunately, what was regarded as almost sacred in Marylebone Road was viewed with considerable suspicion in Prince Consort Road, and I think because of that Arthur suffered quite a lot of veiled, if not open, hostility from some of his older colleagues when he was first appointed. However it was not long before Arthur's fine gifts as a teacher silenced all criticism, and the subsequent record of his wonderful work for the College … justified to the fullest degree the far-sighted wisdom of Sir Hugh's original choice.[10]

As a teacher, Alexander adhered closely to Matthay's pedagogy, which, physiologically, focused on muscular relaxation, but also argued for an emphasis to be placed on psychology.

Alexander loathed the title 'piano teacher', as his former pupil Michael Talbot recalled that 'in his own words, he [Alexander] does not teach "the piano", but music, through the medium of the piano'.[11] Maisie Aldridge's recollections of her lessons with Alexander at the RCM in the early 1930s offer further testimony to his idiosyncrasies:

> Alexander was an inspired teacher and a complex and interesting character as well. He was intensely stimulating, very outspoken and took a great interest not only in his pupils' musical progress but in their personal development as well. … He was sometimes in a good mood, sometimes not, so that one pupil would say to another: 'Have you had your lesson yet? What mood is he in today?' He was sparing in his praise, so that a very grudging 'That's better!' after half a term of endeavour would be enough to send one away walking on air.[12]

Alexander appears to have thought highly of Maconchy. In his term reports, he frequently remarked upon her industry and studious nature.[13] He also appears to have supported Maconchy's interest in modern music, as she played Bartók's Suite for Piano, op. 14 at an Informal Concert on 1 March 1927.[14] In a testimonial submitted to the College the following month, Alexander offered further praise, highlighting steady progress as well as her interests in piano

[10] Angus Morrison, 'Personal Appreciation', *R.C.M. Magazine* 65/3 (1969): 36. For further details regarding 'the Matthay Method', see W.R. Anderson, 'Tobias Matthay (1858–1945)', *Musical Times* 87/1235 (January 1946): 9–13; and Stephen Siek, *England's Piano Sage: The Life and Teachings of Tobias Matthay* (Lanham: The Scarecrow Press, 2012).

[11] Michael Talbot, 'Farewell to Arthur Alexander…', *R.C.M. Magazine* 57/2 (May 1961): 39.

[12] Aldridge, 35.

[13] RCM Teacher's Terminal Report, Christmas term 1925, SHC.

[14] RCM Informal Concert (No. 105) programme, SHC. The Informal Concert series was implemented by Allen to give less experienced students an opportunity to gain experience performing.

literature.[15] In the Midsummer term of 1927 – her final term of study with Alexander – he noted that while progress continued unabated, she needed to be careful not to ruminate on particular technical problems that he felt were at times inhibiting her development.[16]

Maconchy's studies with Kitson were limited to her first year at the College. Though at times she found him to be 'a dry old stick', she nevertheless enjoyed her lessons in strict counterpoint with him.[17] Barbara Banner, who studied with Kitson at the RCM, aptly described him as:

> a shy, retiring man who had a genius for imparting knowledge. He never spoke much during lessons, but worked swiftly and quietly, his keen and methodical mind adjusting mistakes with unfailing speed and precision. His lessons were periods of hard study and concentration; he did a great deal of work during them and expected a great deal to be brought in return.[18]

Kitson evidently thought highly of Maconchy and declared her to be one of the best pupils he had had the pleasure of teaching.[19]

Like Kitson, Charles Wood was a highly skilled technician. Described by former pupils as shy and kind, he instilled a 'hatred of bad workmanship and false style which was in him an inevitable instinct'.[20] Wood had a passion for chamber music, especially Beethoven's quartets, which had inspired him in his youth. Over the course of his career, Wood composed eight string quartets, six of which were published posthumously. One of his greatest skills as a teacher was his uncanny ability to identify weaknesses in a composition almost at once.[21] While Wood was often described as a brilliant instructor, his teaching did have its limitations. Ralph Vaughan Williams (1872–1958), who studied with Wood while preparing for his Mus. Bac. degree at Cambridge, opined,

> Charles Wood was the finest technical instructor I have ever known. I do not say necessarily the greatest teacher. I do not think he had the gift of inspiring enthusiasm or of leading to the higher planes of musical thought. Indeed, he was rather prone to laugh at artistic ideals and would lead one to suppose that composing music was a trick anyone might learn if he took the trouble. But for the craft of composition he was unrivalled[.][22]

15 Arthur Alexander, testimonial letter, 10 April 1927, SHC.

16 RCM Teacher's Terminal Report, Midsummer term 1927, SHC.

17 John Skiba, 'Elizabeth Maconchy in Conversation with John Skiba', *Composer* 63 (1978): 7.

18 Barbara Banner, 'Charles Herbert Kitson', *R.C.M. Magazine* 40/2 (1944): 57.

19 Charles Herbert Kitson, testimonial letter, 30 March 1927, SHC.

20 'The Late Dr. Charles Wood: An Appreciation by a Friend', *R.C.M. Magazine* 22/3 (1926): 77. Also see Ian A. Copley, *The Music of Charles Wood: A Critical Study* (London: Thames, 1978); and Jeremy Dibble, 'Wood, Charles', *Grove Music Online*, 2001, https://doi.org/10.1093/gmo/9781561592630.article.30536 [accessed 15 July 2010].

21 'An Appreciation by a Friend', 73–4.

22 Ralph Vaughan Williams, 'A Musical Autobiography', in *National Music and Other Essays* (London: Oxford University Press, 1963), 183.

Wood's precise teaching, combined with Kitson's strict counterpoint and harmony lessons, nevertheless provided Maconchy with the crucial grounding in technique from which she would be able to develop and explore her own ideas in greater depth. Aside from the string quartet Maconchy composed in 1924 – a work that was certainly influenced by Wood's own interest in the genre – the majority of her works from her first two years at the RCM consist of songs and works for solo piano.[23] While many of her early piano pieces were likely technical exercises, the skilful craftsmanship of some of her early songs, notably her strophic setting of *There is a lady sweet and kind* (1924–5), reflects her deep love of poetry, revealing a marked level of technical and artistic prowess beyond her years.

In the Christmas term of 1925, Maconchy began studying composition with Vaughan Williams. Working with Vaughan Williams proved to be transformative, as Maconchy recalled: 'everything suddenly opened out to me: it was a whole new World when I became a pupil of his, not so much from his teaching as just from him as a person, his attitude to music, he was a tremendously inspiring person'.[24] Vaughan Williams began his teaching career at the RCM in 1919 at the invitation of Allen, who was a close friend. Like many of Allen's new hires, Vaughan Williams had been a former pupil at the College and was determined to improve both its social environment and level of training. Of his approach to teaching, Vaughan Williams later reflected: 'With my own pupils now I always try to remember the value of encouragement. Sometimes a callow youth appears who may be a fool or may be a genius, and I would rather be guilty of encouraging a fool than of discouraging a genius.'[25]

As a teacher, Maconchy found Vaughan Williams's approach to be haphazard. He refused to teach from textbooks, preferring to have his students learn directly from the music itself. Bach was a particular favourite of his, and he often illustrated his discussion of a particular work on the piano. Maconchy recalled, 'He liked to play the works he was discussing on the piano, often as piano duets: and very odd they sounded at times.'[26] In a tribute to Vaughan Williams after his death in 1958, Maconchy wrote the following:

> He somehow imparted to his pupils his own attitude to composition, a complete and uncalculating devotion to music. His teaching was not conventional. He fully recognized the importance of an adequate technique, but for him the

[23] Rhiannon Mathias, *Lutyens, Maconchy, Williams and Twentieth-Century British Music: A Blest Trio of Sirens* (Farnham: Ashgate, 2012), 16–17.

[24] Skiba, 7.

[25] Vaughan Williams, 'A Musical Autobiography', 187.

[26] Elizabeth Maconchy, 'Vaughan Williams as a Teacher', *Composer* 2 (March 1959): 18–19. Also see Jennifer Doctor, 'Intersecting Circles: The Early Careers of Elizabeth Maconchy, Elisabeth Lutyens, and Grace Williams', *Women & Music* 2 (1998): 90–109; and Jennifer Doctor '"Working for her own salvation": Vaughan Williams as teacher of Elizabeth Maconchy, Grace Williams, and Ina Boyle', in Lewis Foreman (ed.), *Vaughan Williams in Perspective* (London: Albion Press, 1998), 181–201.

> purpose of technique was how best to enable each of us to express his own ideas in his own way. He had no use for ready made solutions: he had worked out his own salvation as a composer and he encouraged his pupils to do the same. Technical brilliance for its own sake he despised, and this perhaps made him rather too distrustful of brilliance in any form – though he overcame this distrust to some extent later. … His criticism came slowly; but I always found, when I thought it over, that what he said was right, even if I did not like it at first. And if, as sometimes happened, he said: 'This is a great work' it was praise worth having indeed.[27]

By all accounts, Vaughan Williams appeared to have taken an instant liking to his new pupil: at the beginning of Maconchy's first term of study with Vaughan Williams, she played the piano for some of the RCM Chorus rehearsals in preparation for the première of his new work titled *Flos campi* – a suite for viola, small orchestra, and wordless choir – and was asked to listen to the balance at the orchestral rehearsals at Queen's Hall. Instead of giving his manuscript to the work's dedicatee, as was his usual practice, Vaughan Williams instead elected to give his manuscript to Maconchy after the final rehearsal.[28]

In his report for the Christmas term, Vaughan Williams noted that Maconchy's progress had been 'excellent'; however, he added '[she] must not be allowed to overwork her plenty of ideas and knowledge'.[29] In lessons, Vaughan Williams frequently discussed his own compositions, and Maconchy became well acquainted with many of her teacher's works that were composed in the mid-to-late twenties which included his ballet *Job*, the operas *Sir John in Love* and *Riders to the Sea*, as well as his Concerto in C Major for Pianoforte and Orchestra.[30] Under Vaughan Williams's tutelage Maconchy's compositional output increased exponentially in 1926, and in addition to composing several songs, she began work on several orchestral and chamber works, as well as an opera.

Like many of Vaughan Williams's pupils, Maconchy initially began to compose in a style similar to her teacher.[31] Stylistically, she characterised these works as 'middle-period Vaughan Williams'.[32] This influence is readily apparent in the modal writing in *Allegro for Flute and Strings*, which is built upon the Phrygian mode (Example 2.1). Another example is *Ophelia's Song*, which, like

[27] Elizabeth Maconchy, 'Ralph Vaughan Williams', *R.C.M. Magazine* 55/1 (1959): 33–4.

[28] The work was premièred on 10 October 1925. Maconchy details this information in a note that accompanies the manuscript, which is held at the BL (Add MS 57294). Violist Lionel Tertis (1876–1975) was the featured soloist for the work's première. Also see footnote three in Oliver Neighbour, 'Ralph, Adeline, and Ursula Vaughan Williams: Some Facts and Speculation (with a note about Tippett)', *Music & Letters* 89/3 (2008): 337. As Maconchy did not begin studying with Vaughan Williams until 1925, Neighbour is incorrect in his suggestion that Maconchy may have been a source of inspiration for the work.

[29] RCM Teacher's Terminal Report, Christmas term 1925, SHC.

[30] Rhiannon Mathias, *Lutyens, Maconchy, Williams and Twentieth-Century British Music*, 18.

[31] Skiba, 8.

[32] Elizabeth Maconchy, draft of talk titled 'Composer's Concourse – Comments on Bartók', 8 March 1956, SHC.

Figure 3. Studio portrait, 1925 (reproduced by permission of the Maconchy Estate).

Example 2.1. Maconchy, *Allegro for Flute and Strings*, opening. Reproduced by permission of the Maconchy Estate.

Allegro, was completed in April 1926. Set to the famous text from Shakespeare's *Hamlet*, the song, which is in binary form, is built upon a melody in Dorian mode (Example 2.2).

By 1926, Maconchy's compositions were starting to be performed at the College with some regularity. On 11 March, Muriel Nixon performed three of Maconchy's songs at a College Chamber Concert, and in the Midsummer term, two of her orchestral works – *Fantasy for Flute, Harp, and String Orchestra*, and *Elegy for Flute, Horn, and String Orchestra* – were scheduled for inclusion at a College Orchestral Concert on 23 July, conducted by W.H. Reed. For reasons

Example 2.2. Maconchy, *Ophelia's Song*, opening. © Oxford University Press 1983. Reproduced by permission. All rights reserved.

unclear, however, only the *Fantasy* was performed.[33] The concert was reviewed in both the *Daily Telegraph* and the *Monthly Musical Record*. The critic in the *Daily Telegraph* was unimpressed by the work, remarking,

> the 'Fantasy' for string orchestra, flute, and harp, by Miss Elizabeth Maconchy, sounded more ill-balanced than they might have done. Unquestionably the first cause of this lay in the writing, which, especially in the 'Fantasia', is, at times, somewhat eccentric. But more adequate playing might have done something towards cloaking over Miss Maconchy's obvious want of experience[.][34]

[33] Nixon performed *The Call* (1926), *There is a lady sweet and kind* (1924–5), and *My sweet sweeting* (1926). A proof of the College Orchestral Concert programme lists both the *Elegy* and *Fantasy*; however, the final programme, which is included in Maconchy's first scrapbook, held at SHC, only lists the *Fantasy for Flute, Harp, and String Orchestra*.

[34] 'Royal College of Music', *Daily Telegraph*, 26 July 1926. It is curious that the critic appears to suggest that both works were performed by criticising Maconchy's writing,

In the *Monthly Musical Record*, the criticism levelled at Maconchy was based solely on speculation as to why her *Elegy* had been omitted:

> Of Elizabeth Maconchy's Two Pieces for Small Orchestra only one could be performed. We hear a rumour that the time-signatures in the second piece were too alarming even for a modern orchestra. It seems a pity that young composers should take advantage of the amazing reading-powers of these musicians, as complex and subtle rhythmic effects depend very little on bar divisions.[35]

In the Christmas term, Maconchy's *Elegy* finally received its first performance in a College Orchestral Concert on 3 December that also featured her *Fantasy*. Both pieces were also performed a week later at a Patron's Fund orchestral rehearsal for composers on 10 December with the London Symphony Orchestra, conducted by Adrian Boult (1889–1983). Established in 1903 with financial support from Ernest Palmer, the aim of the Patron's Fund was to encourage native talent by funding performance opportunities. For young composers, the opportunity to hear their works rehearsed and performed by professional musicians and conductors was invaluable.[36]

Sadly, Patron's Fund examiner reports, which would have yielded insight into the opinion of the examiners, do not exist for the works that were programmed at this concert. A review of the concert did, however, appear in the *Times*. In contrast to the opinion of the critic[s] of the July concert, the unnamed critic in the *Times*, who discussed Maconchy's works alongside a score by one of her peers, Marjory Harrison, opined, 'In the work of Marjory Harrison and Elizabeth Maconchy we had more technical skill expended over slight ideas. The style of both is tinged with the folk-song flavour, and one did not feel that it had been assimilated in either case.'[37]

Although the manuscripts of Maconchy's *Fantasy* and *Elegy* have been lost, the *Daily Telegraph* critic's use of the term 'eccentric', as well as the attention paid to the alleged rhythmic complexity of the *Elegy* in the *Monthly Musical Record* raise intriguing questions about Maconchy's compositional development during this period. It was sometime most likely around the early Midsummer term that Maconchy made her fateful visit to Chester's lending library, where she first came across a copy of Bartók's Suite for Piano, op. 14.[38] Maconchy

---

'especially in the "Fantasia"'.

35 'Royal College of Music', *Monthly Musical Record* 56/669 (1 September 1926): 268. Both the review in the *Monthly Musical Record* and the *Daily Telegraph* share a similarity in tone that suggests they may have been written by the same critic.

36 Despite being administered by the RCM, the Patron's Fund was open to all British citizens. See Warrack, 80–1, 152.

37 'New British Music', *Times*, 11 December 1926.

38 Maconchy has cited the period that she first encountered Bartók's music as occurring about a year after she began studying with Vaughan Williams (Skiba, 8). However, on 1 July 1926, Vaughan Williams sent a letter to E.J. Dent noting that Maconchy had been 'badly bitten by Bartók', suggesting that Maconchy had become interested in Bartók's music prior to July. Leoine Gershon writes in her thesis on Maconchy that 'a visit to

recalled, 'I discovered Bartók almost by chance – I found some piano-pieces ...This was a revelation – it seemed to open up a new world of rhythm, harmony, everything; and to release a sort of spring inside me that had not been touched before.'[39] Like Alexander, Vaughan Williams was a strong supporter of his pupil's interest in the composer's works, advising her to 'Study Purcell or Bartok' with Maconchy evidently selecting the latter.[40] The earliest surviving manuscript to reflect a shift in Maconchy's compositional style is *Four Pieces for String Quartet* (1926–7). The opening bars of the first piece, which she completed in November 1926, show Maconchy beginning to experiment with the inversion of transpositionally related pitch class sets (Example 2.3).

While Maconchy was busy with her studies at the RCM, the life of a composition student was often a solitary one. As Warrack observed,

> Perhaps the student who knew least about what others in the same field were doing was the composition student. He would bring his weekly work to his Professor, when it would be looked over, perhaps tried over and probably smoked over for forty minutes. He might have arranged that his other commitments happened on the same day and so he would depart having derived some benefits from his Professors, but nothing from the College.[41]

During his years of study at the RCM, Vaughan Williams had benefitted from the feedback he received from his peers, particularly Gustav Holst (1874–1934), whom Vaughan Williams credited as having the greatest influence on his music. The two would show each other the sketches of compositions they were working on and offer advice and criticism, as well as encouragement. Vaughan Williams was eager to encourage his own students to do the same, as Grace Williams (1906–77), recalled: 'He always arranged for us to have play-throughs and to discuss our works with each other.'[42]

Of the friendships Maconchy developed at the College, the most profound was undoubtedly her friendship with Grace Williams. Born and raised in Wales, Williams arrived at the RCM in 1926 and the two quickly established a close and lifelong friendship. Of her impressions of Maconchy, Williams described her at the time as 'very young, very sensitive', further adding 'she was full to the brim with musical creativeness'.[43]

In the Christmas term of 1926, Maconchy, Williams, and Imogen Holst (1907–84) decided to form a club for composers to hear each other's works, as well as to discuss contemporary music. According to Imogen Holst, 'It was Bartok's music

---

Chester's Library in the 1920s gave her a chance acquaintance with a newly imported, hitherto unknown work – the "Suite", op. 14, by Bela Bartok'. See Leoine Gershon, 'The String Quartets of Elizabeth Maconchy C.B.E.' (thesis, University of Bristol, 1983–4), 3.

39 Maconchy, 'Composer's Concourse – Comments on Bartók'.

40 Ralph Vaughan Williams to Elizabeth Maconchy, 20 December [1943?], VWL 1822.

41 Warrack, 199–200.

42 A.J. Heward Rees, 'Views and Revisions. The Composer Grace Williams talks with A.J. Heward Rees', *Welsh Music* 5/4 (Winter 1976–7): 7–8.

43 Grace Williams, draft of Third Programme talk on Maconchy's quartets, 13 February 1955, SHC.

Example 2.3. Maconchy, *Four Pieces for String Quartet*, mvt. I, bars 1–2. Reproduced by permission of the Maconchy Estate.

that we particularly wanted to hear, and we were overjoyed when Bartok himself came to London to play his recent *Sonata for Pianoforte* and *Three Open Air Pieces* as well as the *Rumanian Folkdances from Hungary*.'[44] Though the club was open to all students, its core members – in addition to Maconchy, Williams, and Imogen Holst – included Maconchy's close friend Dorothy Gow (1892–1982), as well as Mary Chater, Leonard Isaacs (1909–97), and David Moule-Evans (1905–88).[45]

Over the course of 1927, Maconchy continued to make strides towards developing an individual voice. In addition to composing several new songs, she began to explore choral writing in greater depth, completing a work inspired by Shakespeare's *King Lear* titled *He that hath a little tiny wit* for SATB, as well two works for double chorus. Her instrumental works during this period included *Andante con moto for Flute and Strings*, a violin sonata, and a ballet titled *Bluebeard and Fatima*, based upon the French folk tale by Charles Perrault (1628–1703).[46] Maconchy also began work on a composition for small orchestra titled *Fantasy for Children* that she would later complete in 1928.

After passing her ARCM examination in piano in the Easter term of 1927, Maconchy began to focus more heavily on composition, which would officially become her primary subject of study in the Christmas term.[47] In his Mid-

[44] Imogen Holst, 'Grace Williams: A Symposium (Part I)', *Welsh Music* 5/6 (1977): 19. Also quoted in Mathias, *Lutyens, Maconchy, Williams and Twentieth-Century British Music*, 20.

[45] Warrack, 200.

[46] See Mathias, *Lutyens, Maconchy, Williams and Twentieth-Century British Music*, 21.

[47] According to the RCM's Roll of Studies, the official switch occurred in the Christmas term, with Gordon Jacob listed as her primary instructor. Her second study was piano accompaniment with Charles Thornton Lofthouse (1895–1974).

summer report, Vaughan Williams noted that while she continued to make progress in her technique, '[she] is going through rather an experimental stage at present'.[48] During this period, Maconchy also began to study orchestration with Gordon Jacob (1895–1984).[49] Jacob had been one of Vaughan Williams's early pupils at the RCM, and after completing his studies in 1924, he began teaching at the College. Vaughan Williams frequently suggested that his pupils take lessons in orchestration from Jacob. Of her lessons with Jacob, Maconchy recalled, 'I enjoyed our sessions very much, & learned a great deal from him.'[50]

On 15 September – four days before the official start of the Christmas term – Maconchy was awarded the newly established Blumenthal Scholarship, which funded her final two years of study at the RCM.[51] Though none of her compositions were performed at the RCM in 1927, her *Andante con moto* and *Allegro for Flute and Strings* were featured in a School Subscription concert by the Guildford Orchestra, conducted by Claud Powell on 7 May. Tenor Steuart Wilson (1889–1966) included three of Maconchy's songs in a recital on 13 October, and on 10 November, an orchestral arrangement that Maconchy made of the folk song *Ward the Pirate* was featured in the children's portion of the Kensington Musical Competition Festival. Maconchy also submitted *Bluebeard and Fatima* to the Patron's Fund, and it was reviewed by S.P. Waddington and Eric Coates. Coates rejected it outright, with his examiner's report suggesting that he found the work deeply unattractive, contrived, and overly complicated.[52] Waddington, on the other hand, was more open-minded, marking the work as a possibility despite his reservations about its overabundance of dissonance.[53] Unfortunately, the work was not selected for further consideration.

While the rejection of *Bluebeard and Fatima* by the Patron's Fund adjudicators was surely a disappointment, Maconchy's hard work was beginning to pay off, as Vaughan Williams wrote in his report for the Easter term of 1928 that she was at last 'finding her feet'.[54] Though another work she submitted to the Patron's Fund – an orchestral work titled *Theme and Variations* – received slightly

[48] RCM Teacher's Terminal Report, Midsummer term 1927, SHC.

[49] While Maconchy's record in the RCM's Roll of Studies only lists Jacob as her composition teacher for her final two years of study, surviving term reports held at SHC include progress reports from Vaughan Williams, suggesting that she studied with both.

[50] Elizabeth Maconchy, handwritten biographical note, May 1986, SHC.

[51] The Blumenthal Composition Scholarship was established in 1927 by bequest of Léonie Blumenthal in memory of her late husband, German pianist and composer Jacques Blumenthal (1829–1908). Blumenthal had been a member of the RCM Council. The annual amount of the scholarship was £135. Royal College of Music Report of the Council, Statement of Accounts, &c. for the year ending 31 August 1926, RCM Archive.

[52] Eric Coates, Patron's Fund Examiner's Report, 29 January 1928, Patron's Fund: adjudicator's reports on compositions submitted 1925–35, RCM Archive.

[53] S.P. Waddington, Patron's Fund Examiner's Report, 16 January 1928, RCM Archive.

[54] RCM Teacher's Terminal Report, Easter term 1928, SHC.

more favourable evaluations, with both Waddington and Coates marking it as a possibility, the work was ultimately rejected.[55] Jacob, however, noted in his Easter term report that he found her *Theme and Variations* to be 'a sound piece of work'.[56]

Maconchy's success did not go unnoticed by her peers. According to Lutyens, Maconchy was the 'star pupil' at the College in the 1920s and even her friends such as Gow and Chater couldn't help but find themselves a bit envious of both their friend's evident skill, but also the number of performances her works received at the College.[57] During this period, Maconchy also began two ambitious new projects: an opera titled *The Knight's Tale*, based upon the first tale of the same title in Chaucer's *The Canterbury Tales*, and a piano concerto she initially titled Concertino for Piano and Chamber Orchestra.[58] Further recognition of her talent in spite of previous snubs by the Patron's Fund adjudicators arrived in the Midsummer term of 1928 when she was awarded the Sullivan Prize for composition.

In October, Maconchy completed her Concerto (Concertino) for Piano and Chamber Orchestra.[59] On the advice of Allen, who, in addition to his role as Director at the RCM, also served on the BBC's Music Advisory Committee, she sent the work to the BBC so that it could be considered for a run-through with the BBC Orchestra. The work was initially reviewed by Victor Hely-Hutchinson (1901–47), who wrote the following in a memo:

> This looks jolly, particularly the second movement – I can't give any definite opinion about it without hearing it, but as far as I can judge it is the work of a student with plenty of rigour and ideas, but who has not yet found her feet – & who has moreover been brought up on the strong waters of modern music more than on the milk of classical music.
>
> I think Mr Clark should see it; & with his approval I suggest it should be put into a 'try over' rehearsal – Perhaps miss Maconcky [*sic*] could suggest someone to play it.[60]

55 Eric Coates, Patron's Fund Examiner's Report, 23 May 1928; and S.P. Waddington, Patron's Fund Examiner's Report, 11 April 1928, RCM Archive.

56 RCM Teacher's Terminal Report, Easter term 1928, SHC.

57 Elisabeth Lutyens, *A Goldfish Bowl* (London: Cassell, 1972), 49; and Dorothy Gow to Elizabeth Maconchy, undated, private collection.

58 In regards to *The Knight's Tale*, Maconchy also corresponded with Proctor Gregg, who handled opera productions at the College. Gregg sent Maconchy some sketches for a few of the opera's scenes, which suggests that there may have been some idea towards performing it at the College; however, no further documentation indicating whether or not this was indeed the case has been found.

59 Sometime around late 1928 or early 1929, Maconchy decided to change the title from Concertino to Concerto for Piano and Chamber Orchestra. She continued to refer to the work as a concerto for several decades before reverting back to the title of Concertino for Piano and Chamber Orchestra. For clarity, this work is referred to as a concerto throughout the remainder of the book.

60 Victor Hely-Hutchinson to Kenneth Wright, undated, BBC WAC RCONT1: Maconchy, E. Composer: File 1, 1928–39 (hereafter BBC WAC EM1). Also quoted in

On 17 November, the BBC returned the score and parts to Maconchy, as Allen had arranged for the work to be included in a Patron's Fund Orchestral Rehearsal with the New Symphony Orchestra, conducted by Adrian Boult, on the 30th. A review of the concert appeared the following day:

> Miss Maconchy's Concerto showed evident traces of the influence of contemporary composers, particularly that of Vaughan Williams in the second movement, and of the modern Russians and Hungarians in the first and last. Although derivative in style, the work possesses considerable fertility of invention, both thematic and orchestral, and is incidentally interesting in showing the remarkable degree of liberty permitted to present-day students of the college. Only a few years ago a student writing as Miss Maconchy does would perhaps have been reprimanded rather than encouraged. Such tolerance and broadmindedness in an official institution cannot be sufficiently praised.[61]

After the concert, Maconchy decided to withdraw the work in order to make revisions. As Doctor has noted, the BBC was still prepared to give the work a run-through and a memo sent from Kenneth Wright (1899–1975), then the BBC's Music Executive, to Roger Eckersley (1892–1963), Assistant Controller of Programmes, on 10 December confirms this promise, while also elaborating upon some concerns that had been expressed about the work:

> I am not certain whether Mr. Pitt told you about his visit to the College. Sir Hugh admitted on hearing the work that it wanted a good deal of re-writing, which was precisely the opinion given here by the people who had seen the score, although we were prepared when it came to give it a play through. Miss Maconcky [*sic*] herself has written to-day saying that she will submit the new score when it is completed.[62]

In 1929, Maconchy focused on revisions to the concerto and also began work on an orchestral suite titled *The Land*. In the spring she was informed that she had been selected as a finalist for the prestigious Mendelssohn Scholarship, which was administered by the Royal Academy of Music.[63] The scholarship was awarded to David Moule-Evans, with Imogen Holst ranked second, and Maconchy third.[64] The day following her interview, Maconchy ran into Allen at the RCM. Maconchy recalled,

> I had the interview, and the next day, Sir Hugh Allen, who was head of the college came up to me and congratulated me on getting the scholarship and I said, 'but I didn't get it, you gave it to David Evans'. He said, 'Oh, they must have

Doctor, 'Intersecting Circles', 96.

[61] C.G., 'Royal College of Music', unidentified review in Maconchy's first scrapbook, SHC.

[62] Kenneth Wright to Roger Eckersley, 10 December 1928, BBC WAC EM1. Also see Doctor, 'Intersecting Circles', 96–7.

[63] Though the Mendelssohn Scholarship was administered by the Royal Academy of Music, the interviews took place at the RCM. See J.F.R. Stainer to Imogen Holst, 2 June 1929, HO/2/6/2, Imogen Holst Scrapbook, August 1928 – November 1929, Britten-Pears Archive.

[64] 'Occasional Notes', *Musical Times* 70/1037 (1 July 1929): 631.

changed it after I left. Anyway if we'd given it to you you'd have only got married and never written another note'.[65]

Though Maconchy was subsequently awarded an Octavia Travelling Scholarship, which enabled her to travel abroad for further study, Allen's remark hit Maconchy particularly hard as she was secretly engaged to be married at the time to William Richard LeFanu (1904–95) – the brother of Lucie LeFanu, who was a close friend of Maconchy's elder sister, Maureen.[66]

Tall, blonde, and effortlessly charming, LeFanu, or Billy, as he was known to his friends, was the second child of Irish civil servant Thomas LeFanu (1858–1945) and his wife Florence, née Sullivan. Born and raised in Ireland, LeFanu was of Huguenot descent, counting the famed Irish writer Sheridan Le Fanu among his distinguished ancestors. LeFanu was educated in England, attending Eton where he was a King's Scholar, followed by King's College, Cambridge, graduating with first-class honours in the Classical Tripos in 1926. Following his studies at Cambridge, LeFanu worked briefly as a teacher before finding employment as a second librarian at the Hellenic Society in London in 1927.[67] Early in their relationship, the two would meet around lunchtime in Kensington Gardens to avoid raising the suspicions of her mother.[68]

While Maconchy never had any intention of letting marriage get in the way of her burgeoning professional career, Allen's tactless remarks nevertheless reflected a long-standing prejudice from which Maconchy had been sheltered by Vaughan Williams, Jacob, and Alexander. With teachers such as Vaughan Williams, who treated his students equally regardless of gender, Maconchy never felt as though she had faced any discrimination, as she recalled, 'there was no discrimination against us as women while we were students at the RCM – this came afterwards'.[69]

65 *Elizabeth Maconchy*, documentary directed by Margaret Williams, 1985. Produced by the Arts Council of Great Britain. Transcription by author.

66 In a letter to Grace Williams dated 3 December 1929, Maconchy reveals that she had been engaged for approximately a year at that point.

67 See Alan Webster, 'Obituary: William LeFanu', *Independent*, 7 April 1995; Tina Craig, Eustace Cornelius, and Ian Lyle, 'Obituary: William Richard Lefanu (1904–1995)', *Health Libraries Review* 13 (1996): 179–81; and Front matter, *Journal of Hellenic Studies* 47/2 (1927): xiii.

68 Dunlop, 15.

69 Elizabeth Maconchy, draft of talk titled 'Women in the Arts', July 1973, SHC.

Figure 4. Maconchy with her grandfather, Captain Poë, mother Violet, aunt Muriel Poë, sister Maureen, Bill Dawson (Maureen's fiancé), sister Sheila, and William LeFanu at Santry Court, 1929 (reproduced by permission of the Maconchy Estate).

3

Prague, Paris, Vienna, and London, 1929–31

The years between 1929 and 1931 were a period of transition for Maconchy. Though she was still officially a student of the RCM while she held the Octavia Scholarship, her development – both musically and professionally – took place outside its supportive and inclusive environment.

It was not long after Maconchy began her studies with Vaughan Williams that she voiced a desire to study abroad. As Vaughan Williams had benefitted tremendously from his studies with Ravel in Paris, he was keen to help his own pupils to do the same. Initially, however, Vaughan Williams had been unsure about where to send Maconchy, and in 1926 – approximately a year after Maconchy had begun studying with him – he sought out the advice of E.J. Dent, professor of music at Cambridge University, writing in a letter dated 1 July 1926,

> May I ask you for some advice? A composition pupil of mine at the R.C.M. whom I consider very gifted is anxious to go abroad and study music, especially composition, for 6 months, or possibly longer.
>
> I also think it would be very good for her. Who do you consider the best composition teacher in Europe at present? And which centre do you consider the best for a young student to receive a 'finishing' musical education and generally to improve their musical culture. I expect you will say that the two queries are incompatible, in which case we shall have to make a compromise.
>
> Miss Maconchy is just 19 – plays the piano quite well and has had a thorough grounding at the hands of Kitson and Charles Wood. She has – as I say – in my opinion decided inventive powers but is of course at present like all young people going through a new phase every month. At present she has been badly bitten by Bartok and is of course anxious to study with him, but I rather doubt the wisdom of this.
>
> I feel possibly that Respighi or Casella might be good for her – if they ever take pupils. On the other hand neither Rome nor Buda-Pesth would I imagine be good from the point of view of general musical atmosphere and the hearing of plenty of good music etc. Also of course we must consider a place where we could find a nice family for her to live with and so on.
>
> Are Leipzig or Dresden any good nowadays? Prague has been suggested to me – what do you think of that? or [*sic*] I thought of sending her to Ravel but I doubt if he would take any pupils now.[1]

Though it remains unclear as to whether it was Dent who suggested the noted Czech composer and conductor Karel Boleslav Jirák (1891–1972) to Vaughan

[1] Ralph Vaughan Williams to Edward Joseph Dent, 1 July 1926, VWL 632.

Williams, Jirák was well known to Dent from his involvement with the ISCM.[2] As Vaughan Williams had travelled to Prague for the ISCM Festival in 1925, one may wonder whether Vaughan Williams encountered Jirák there as well.[3]

Despite Maconchy's eagerness to study abroad, by 1929 the prospect of leaving her family and fiancé had made this a much more challenging decision to make. Nevertheless, she set off for Prague, arriving at the end of September 1929. Initially she was incredibly homesick as this was the first time she had been away from her family and she soon began to doubt the wisdom of her decision, which was motivated in part by the rationale that spending time abroad would be the best use of her time until she and LeFanu had enough money to get married.[4] Maconchy also found the musical environment in Prague to be rather insular, describing it as 'a small, independent sort of place. Everybody was very much working on their own.'[5] As Maconchy did not speak Czech and her German was limited, the language barrier, combined with her shyness, only added to her difficulties. In a letter to Vaughan Williams sent soon after her arrival, she expressed doubts as to whether Prague had been the right choice. Vaughan Williams responded,

> Dearest Betty,
>
> I'm so sorry for you. […]
>
> For artistic reasons … it seems a pity not to follow up your success in Prague & set one out a career & hear your work – (I feel thoroughly ashamed that you should have to go to Prague to hear your work – but we did try hard, didn't we?) Also it seems to me that your lessons from Jirak … won't do you much good unless you can continue … a little longer. Don't you think you c^{d} bear to stay in Prague (with perhaps a visit to Vienna) … till Xmas holidays & then come home & we will make a new plan.
>
> I know it's easy to give good advice – & to be logical – but try & make up your mind whether your proposed Paris vision is really because you think it good for you musically – try not to deceive yourself. Personally I don't think the musical life in Paris w^{d} be half so much worth having for you as in Prague or Vienna or Berlin or Cologne – I'm sure I could get you to Ravel – (he would love to teach you – who w^{d} not?) I wonder if it would be useful to you? […]
>
> Dear Betty this is a horrid priggish letter full of good advice, which is so easy to give and wherever you go & whatever you do we shall all love you for it – and as to the musical side – I want you to be first rate & I believe you will be – but after all that depends eventually on your own inside and not on any outside influences.[6]

2 Milan Kuna, 'Jirák, K(arel) B(oleslav)', *Grove Music Online*, 2001, https://doi.org/10.1093/gmo/9781561592630.article.14315 [accessed 5 September 2020].

3 Mathias, *Lutyens, Maconchy, Williams and Twentieth-Century British Music*, 28. In 1925, the ISCM held festivals in both Prague and Venice.

4 Elizabeth Maconchy to Grace Williams, 3 December 1929.

5 Elizabeth Maconchy, 'Third Ear', Radio 3, 29 March 1990. Also quoted in Mathias, *Lutyens, Maconchy, Williams and Twentieth-Century British Music*, 35.

6 Ralph Vaughan Williams to Elizabeth Maconchy, c. October 1929, SHC. Unfortunately, the whereabouts of Maconchy's letter to Vaughan Williams is unknown, thus making

While the exact date the letter was sent is unclear, approximately a week after her arrival, her situation began to improve when she attended a performance of Janáček's opera *Jenůfa* (1904). It proved to be a turning point for Maconchy, as she recalled '[*Jenůfa*] transformed things'.[7] Deeply inspired, she purchased a copy of the score soon thereafter.[8]

In spite of the rough start to her studies in Prague, Maconchy adapted quickly, and it soon proved to be a productive period for her: in addition to her lessons with Jirák, whom she found an expert teacher, she also met with the composer Josef Suk (1874–1935), who was impressed with her orchestral suite, *The Land*.[9] Maconchy also became acquainted with the music critic Jan Löwenbach and his wife, Vilma. Like Jirák, the Löwenbachs played a critical role in introducing Maconchy to musical circles in Prague.[10] By the time Maconchy returned to England at the end of November, she had not only made substantial progress on a symphony and been asked by a chamber music society to write a quartet, but there were also plans to première her revised Piano Concerto with pianist Erwin Schulhoff (1894–1942) and Jirák conducting the Prague Philharmonic on her twenty-third birthday on 19 March 1930, as well as plans to broadcast her *Fantasy for Children* on 25 March, followed by her *Theme and Variations for Orchestra* in April or May.[11]

After a brief stay in London and discussions with Vaughan Williams, Maconchy travelled to Paris. Though details of her activities there are sparse, in a letter to Williams, she remarked on the many opportunities to hear a great deal of music, with Debussy's *Nocturnes* being a particular highlight. While she found the contemporary music scene less stimulating than she had initially hoped, confessing to Williams, '[I] was rather worried by feeling that perhaps I ought to … both[er] all sorts of people who didn't want to see me', she nevertheless made a great deal of progress on the quartet she had been asked to write, which

---

it impossible to know what she may have written regarding Paris. As Maconchy spoke French, one may wonder whether her desire to study in France was motivated by the language barrier she encountered in Prague.

7 LeFanu, 'Elizabeth Maconchy DBE (1907–1994)'.

8 Nicola LeFanu, interview by author. Maconchy's score of *Jenůfa* is inscribed with the date 6 October 1929.

9 Ibid. Anne Macnaghten also makes a reference to Maconchy's meeting with Suk in 'Elizabeth Maconchy', *Musical Times* 96/1348 (June 1955): 298. Maconchy had a total of seven lessons with Jirák during her first trip to Prague, which she mentions in her letter to Williams dated 3 December 1929.

10 In addition to his work as a music critic, Jan Löwenbach (1880–1972) was also a lawyer, specialising in copyright law. Like Jirák, he was also heavily involved in the ISCM administration. Fluent in several languages, Löwenbach's writings also appeared in the *Musical Times* as well as the *Chesterian* in the 1920s and 30s. See John Tyrrell, 'Löwenbach, Jan', *Grove Music Online*, 2001, https://doi.org/10.1093/gmo/9781561592630.article.17064 [accessed 5 September 2020].

11 Elizabeth Maconchy to Grace Williams, 3 December 1929. It remains unclear as to whether the planned performance of the *Theme and Variations* took place.

turned into a quintet.[12] After Paris, Maconchy spent a couple of days in London before travelling to Ireland to spend Christmas with her family. Maconchy also had further good news to celebrate as LeFanu began his new job at the Royal College of Surgeons, serving as an assistant to the Honorary Librarian, Sir D'Arcy Power. With LeFanu now earning £400 a year, they could at last begin to plan their long awaited nuptials.[13]

At the beginning of March, Maconchy set off for her second trip to Prague. This second trip proved to be more enjoyable than her first, with one notable exception: the dress she planned to wear to the première of her Piano Concerto was stolen from her suitcase during her journey.[14] Upon her arrival she received a warm welcome from her Czech friends, and quickly immersed herself in Prague's rich musical life with its many opportunities to hear a diversity of new music. Prior to the 19 March première, Maconchy travelled to Vienna to visit Williams, who had recently received an Octavia scholarship, and was studying with Egon Wellesz (1885–1974). With Williams, Maconchy attended performances of Wagner's *Die Meistersinger von Nürnberg*, Mozart's *Die Entführung aus dem Serail*, and Strauss's *Salomé*, and visited both the Kunsthistorisches Museum and the Albertina. Despite being on tight budgets, they did make one indulgence, as Maconchy recalled that they 'had coffee (we couldn't afford more) in the smartest Viennese café – where we smoked a cigar'.[15]

After a week in Vienna, Maconchy returned to Prague to attend rehearsals of her Piano Concerto. Williams, who was eager to support her friend, travelled to Prague ahead of the concert and was able to attend the second rehearsal. Williams wrote the following in an article titled 'A Letter from Vienna', which was published in the *R.C.M. Magazine* in June:

> The one occasion when I simply had to get away from Vienna was when Elizabeth Maconchy's Piano Concerto was being played in Prague; that was on 19th March. Prague is almost next door to Vienna (just as Budapest is next door on the other side). So of course I went to Prague, and arrived in time for the second rehearsal. Betty was quite happy after the first rehearsal, and at the end of the second things were going terribly well – the orchestra was the Prague Philharmonic, the Conductor Jirák, and the Soloist Erwin Schulhoff – but as the concert drew near we developed the usual fear that something would go wrong in the middle and spoil it. (I think I must have been more nervous than Betty; if appetites count for anything.) But the concert performance was even better than the rehearsal. They brought off the first and third movements (the quick ones) amazingly well; and they made the second movement sound almost as beautiful as it is; I think the second movement is one of the loveliest things I've ever heard; but then I've always thought the whole work astonishingly good, and I know it very well because, in the old days at the R.C.M. Betty and I used to play it on two

12 Elizabeth Maconchy to Grace Williams, 3 December 1929.

13 Ibid.

14 Elizabeth Maconchy to Grace Williams, [between 2 and 7] March 1930.

15 Elizabeth Maconchy, 'Grace Williams: A Symposium', *Welsh Music* 5/6 (Summer 1977): 18.

> pianos. The audience at Prague liked it tremendously, and all the critics said nice things about it.[16]

In spite of the Piano Concerto being written while Maconchy was still a student and experimenting with various techniques and procedures, it embodies several aspects of her emerging compositional style. The work is constructed out of a series of short motifs which serve as the basis for the melodic, harmonic, and rhythmic development within each movement, as Maconchy extends and varies the motific material by means of canonic reiteration, chromatic alteration, and inversion. The first movement opens with a motif consisting of C, F-sharp, and B that implies an octatonic collection. This motif is then expanded into theme 1 (Example 3.1). The second theme begins at rehearsal number 2 with a melody in the piano underpinned by the motif in the cello (Example 3.2). Theme 3, which is introduced by the clarinet at rehearsal number 3, features a melody comprising ascending and descending passages characterised by intervallic movement that alternates between a whole tone and semitone, linking it to the octatonicism implied in the opening motif (Example 3.3).

Following the introduction of each theme, it is expanded, varied, and developed contrapuntally. As each theme builds upon elements previously introduced, the interweaving of themes creates an intricate counterpoint, which leads to a dramatic build-up in bars 64–9 in which the opening motif, theme 1, theme 2, and theme 3 are combined. Following a brief cadenza, the opening four bars are restated, and elements of each theme are reintroduced as the density of the counterpoint is reduced, and the movement concludes with a chord comprising a perfect fifth from E to B alternating back and forth with a chord comprising a perfect fourth from C-sharp to F-sharp.

The second movement is one of rapturous lyricism during which a melody unfolds gradually over the course of the entire movement. The movement begins with a sustained F in the bass and cello, followed by the entrance of the soloist with a motific gesture consisting of two alternating perfect fourths separated by a whole tone. This pattern forms an ostinato that is sustained throughout the movement. The horn then enters with the same oscillating pattern, which expands into a melodic theme. A complementary theme in the flute follows directly after the horn, which is then reiterated in the piano (Example 3.4), concluding with a phrase reminiscent of the opening of Debussy's *La cathédrale engloutie* (Example 3.5). All the melodic and harmonic material in the second movement is derived from the stacked fourths which consist of the notes F, G, B-flat, and C, which Maconchy develops by means of inversion (placing emphasis on the interval of a perfect fifth, which is represented by F and C in the four-note motif) and chromatic alteration.

The third and final movement is a lively scherzo in which Maconchy combines elements of the thematic material introduced in the preceding movements. It begins with a variation of the opening motif of C, F-sharp, and B expressed as a series of chords, to which Maconchy adds an F-natural. This

[16] Grace Williams, 'A Letter from Vienna', *R.C.M. Magazine* 26/2 (June 1930): 66.

Example 3.1. Maconchy, Piano Concerto, mvt. I, bars 1–4.
Published by Alfred Lengnick & Co., a division of Universal Music Publishing Group.
Reproduced by permission of Hal Leonard Europe BV (Italy).

Example 3.2. Maconchy, Piano Concerto, mvt. I, rehearsal number 2.
Published by Alfred Lengnick & Co., a division of Universal Music Publishing Group.
Reproduced by permission of Hal Leonard Europe BV (Italy).

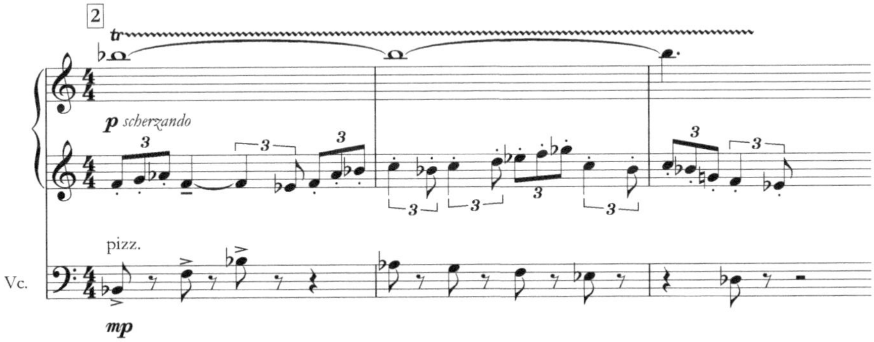

Example 3.3. Maconchy, Piano Concerto, mvt. I, rehearsal number 3.
Published by Alfred Lengnick & Co., a division of Universal Music Publishing Group.
Reproduced by permission of Hal Leonard Europe BV (Italy).

Example 3.4. Maconchy, Piano Concerto, mvt. II, bars 12–18. Published by Alfred Lengnick & Co., a division of Universal Music Publishing Group. Reproduced by permission of Hal Leonard Europe BV (Italy).

Example 3.5. Debussy, *La cathédrale engloutie*, opening. Paris: Durand et Cie, 1910.

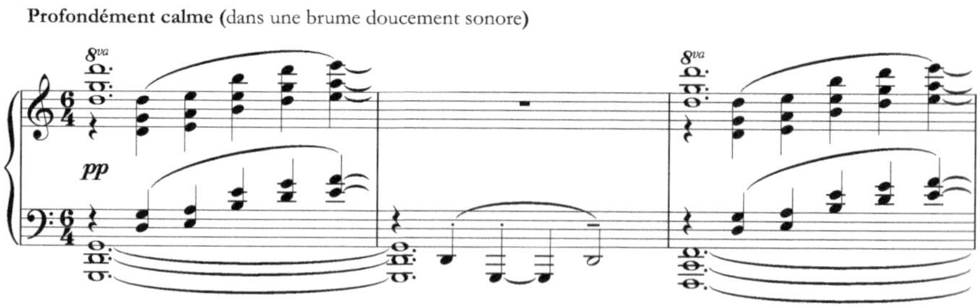

addition creates the interval of a perfect fourth, thus linking it to the second movement. This movement is characterised by a strong rhythmic drive, which persists up to the work's brusque conclusion.

As Williams noted, the work was well received by the press. In *Národni Osvobozeni*, the critic declared, 'It is decidedly one of the most attractive works by a woman composer.'[17] The critic in *Venkov* offered a more detailed assessment, observing '[the Piano Concerto] shows a remarkable creative genius both in the animation and sincerity of the first and third movements and in the individual temper and fine building up of the slow movement'.[18] Further positive notices appeared in *Bohemia*, *Prager Presse*, and the *Prager Tagblatt*, with the latter suggesting that the second movement evoked 'the eternal mood of the sea, and the melody above it seems to reflect the melancholy of her native land'.[19] Coverage of the concert was not limited to the Czech and German press, however, as it was covered in the British press as well, with the Prague correspondent in the *Times* writing, 'The first and third movements are definitely modern, and here the music seems to excel where so much modern music fails; it has strength not only in its thematic material, but also in its construction. The concerto was very favourably received.'[20]

Shortly after the première of her Piano Concerto, Maconchy returned to London, where she was now residing at 53 Campden Hill Square, W8, eager to follow up the success of her professional debut. Things got off to a promising start immediately: she received the Cobbett Prize at the RCM in the Easter term for her Quintet for Strings, and *The Land* was selected in March by the LCMC to be forwarded for consideration by the international jury for that year's ISCM Festival in Liège.[21] In April, the notoriety Maconchy's music continued to garner in Prague following the broadcast of her *Fantasy for Children* on 25 March gained the attention of the British press with both the *Daily Mail* and the *Daily Telegraph* offering commentary as to the significance of her growing reputation.[22] Maconchy had further good news to celebrate in May when she signed a contract with Oxford University Press (OUP) to publish three of her

17 'Z pražských koncertů', *Národni Osvobozeni*, 22 March 1930.

18 O.S., *Venkov*, 22 March 1930.

19 L.S., 'Konzerte', *Bohemia*, 20 March 1930; J.B., 'Bühne und Musik', *Prager Presse*, 21 March 1930; F.S., 'Konzerte', *Prager Tagblatt*, 3 March 1930.

20 'Englishwoman's Concerto', *Times*, 21 March 1930.

21 The notice in the *R.C.M. Magazine* lists the composition as 'Phantasy Quintet'. As the Cobbett Prize was specifically for phantasies, Maconchy presumably submitted her Quintet for Strings under this title. As she mentioned submitting the work for the Cobbett Prize in a letter to Williams on 3 December 1929, it seems logical to assume that the two are likely the same work. See 'The Term's Awards', *R.C.M. Magazine* 26/2 (June 1930): 72; and 'British Works for Liège Festival', *Times*, 8 March 1930.

22 See 'A Newcomer', *Daily Mail*, 17 April 1930; and 'A British Concerto in Prague: Tribute to Composer', *Daily Telegraph*, 26 April 1930.

songs: *Ophelia's Song*, *Have you seen a bright lily grow?* and *A Meditation for His Mistress*.

Although a disappointment occurred when she received word that *The Land* had been rejected by the ISCM's international jury, despondency soon turned to joy shortly after she submitted the score to Sir Henry Wood (1869–1944) for inclusion in the upcoming Proms season. In May, Maconchy received an encouraging letter from Wood stating that he had informed the BBC of his desire to programme the work. He also inquired after whether Maconchy wished to conduct it.[23] On the morning of 24 June, Maconchy received a call from the BBC confirming their intention to include *The Land* in a Proms concert on Saturday 30 August.[24]

On 31 July, Maconchy travelled to Ireland to spend a few weeks with her family ahead of her wedding to William LeFanu. Just before her departure, Maconchy sent a letter to Adrian Boult along with the score of her revised Piano Concerto in the hope that it might be considered for a BBC broadcast. Boult forwarded the work to the reading committee, and on 8 August, she received the following encouraging response:

> We have a favourable report from our readers concerning your Concerto for Pianoforte and Orchestra.
>
> We cannot yet say on what date we shall be able to include it in a programmes [*sic*], but we should like to retain it for inclusion when opportunity occurs. Meanwhile we should like you to send us the parts if you have them. Everything will then be in readiness.[25]

Maconchy arranged for the parts to be sent immediately to the BBC, along with an arrangement of the work for two pianos.

Maconchy's wedding to LeFanu took place at Santry Church on 23 August. For the ceremony, which was officiated by the Archbishop of Perth, Maconchy was walked down the aisle by her grandfather, Captain Poë. Given her family's social class, the wedding received substantial coverage in the *Irish Times*, including ample details of the bride's fashionable attire:

> [Maconchy] wore a graceful gown of flowered cream silk poplin, the long folds of the skirt falling to her feet, while the long-sleeved bodice fitted close to the figure. Her veil, which was arranged from a wreath of orange blossom, and also her train, was of old Honiton lace, and had been worn by the bride's great-grandmother. Her ornament was a pear and turquoise necklace, and she also carried a sheaf bouquet of lilies.[26]

Following the ceremony, a reception was held at Santry Court.[27] Their honeymoon in Connemara, however, would have to wait until after the Proms as

[23] Henry Wood to Elizabeth Maconchy, 22 May 1930, SHC.

[24] WWT (for Owen Mase, Director of Programmes) to Elizabeth Maconchy, 24 June 1930, BBC WAC EM1.

[25] Owen Mase to Elizabeth Maconchy, 8 August 1930, BBC WAC EM1.

[26] 'County Dublin Wedding', *Irish Times*, 25 August 1930.

[27] Ibid.

the couple returned to London shortly after their wedding, where they settled into a quaint flat at 28 Upper Addison Gardens, W14.

On Thursday, 28 August, Maconchy travelled to Hampstead to run through the score of *The Land* with Wood at his home. Two days later, on the morning of the 30th, she attended the final orchestral rehearsal at Queen's Hall before its performance that evening. *The Land* is based upon Vita Sackville-West's poem of the same title, which was published in 1926 and awarded the Hawthornden Prize in 1927. The poem is a georgic broken up into four parts, and arranged according to the seasons, beginning first with 'Winter', followed by 'Spring', 'Summer', and 'Autumn'. As research by Elizabeth Pomeroy and Ian Blyth has illustrated, Sackville-West's work draws heavily upon Virgil's *Georgics* (c. 29 BCE), with James Thomson's *The Seasons* (1726) likely serving as an influence as well.[28] Sackville-West's poem paints a vivid portrait of the Kentish countryside. In spite of its pastoral setting replete with vivid accounts of country life from shepherds to beekeeping, to the harvest in summer and cider-pressing in autumn, Sackville-West's work remains true to its georgic origins, as her son, Nigel Nicolson elaborates: 'Vita was determined not to sentimentalize the countryman or his unending combat with the soil. … [H]er purpose was to explain the alternating conflict and collaboration between man and nature which created it[.] … She looked Nature straight in the eye, reacting against the romanticism and prettiness of nineteenth-century poets and painters, and found the land spiteful.'[29]

Sackville-West's poem provided Maconchy with a powerful source of inspiration. Maconchy selected a quote to accompany each movement, and specifically requested that her suite be titled 'The Land – a suite for Orchestra, after the poem by V. Sackville-West',[30] in the Proms programme, along with the following verses from Sackville-West's poem:

> I. Winter
> Here is no colour, here but form and structure,
> The bones of trees, the magpie bark of birches,
> Apse of trees and tracery of network,
> Fields of snow and tranquil trees in snow
> Through veils of twilight, northern, still and sad,
> Waiting for the night, and for the moon.
>
> II. Spring
> Then broke the spring. The hedges in a day
> Burgeoned to green.
>
> III. Summer
> Jacob, seven years to win a maid

[28] See Elizabeth W. Pomeroy, 'Within Living Memory: Vita Sackville-West's Poems of Land and Garden', *Twentieth Century Literature* 28/3 (Autumn 1982): 269–89; and Ian Blyth, 'A Sort of English Georgics: Vita Sackville-West's *The Land*', *Modern Language Studies* 45/1 (2008): 19–31.

[29] Nigel Nicholson, 'Introduction', in Vita Sackville-West, *The Land & The Garden* (London: Webb & Bower, 1989), 8.

[30] Elizabeth Maconchy to BBC, 2 July 1930, BBC WAC EM1.

Drove out his flock into the stony place,
Ringstracked, speckled, pied;
Peeled the green poplar switch, and dreamed of Rachel's face.

IV. Autumn
The young men strained upon the crank
To wring the last reluctant inch.
They laughed together, fair and frank,
And threw their loins across the winch
...While round about the worthies stood,
... And still resolved, with maundering tongue,
That cider could not be the same
As once when they were young;
But still the young contemptuous men
Laughed kindly at their old conceit,
And strained upon the crank again.[31]

'Winter' opens with a motific theme in the cello, bass, and harp, followed by the addition of the violas in bar 3 and violins in bar 4. The opening four eighth notes form the basis of an ostinato pattern that pervades the entire movement (Example 3.6). This opening theme outlines the Phrygian scale beginning on E. The addition of a B-flat in bar 2 hints at the bitonality of the movement, which is revealed fully by the introduction of a contrasting theme in the clarinets in bar 7 (Example 3.7). This second theme clearly outlines an octatonic collection, beginning on D. The addition of an A-natural, which introduces the interval of a perfect fifth in theme 2, functions much like the intervallic relationship of the B-flat that introduced an augmented fourth in theme 1.

As the movement progresses, Maconchy develops themes 1 and 2 contrapuntally, adding tension by placing emphasis on augmented fourths and perfect fifths, such as in the build-up to rehearsal number 2, where she oscillates between augmented fourths and perfect fifths. The orchestration reflects the influence of Holst, with the melodic shape of the slow, ominous opening reminiscent of the first few bars of *Egdon Heath* (Example 3.8). During her studies at the RCM, Maconchy had occasional lessons with Holst, who thought highly of *The Land*.[32] As *Egdon Heath* (1927) received its first British performances in 1928, it is likely that Maconchy was familiar with the work.[33]

'Spring' offers a vivid contrast to its predecessor. The movement is a lively, fast-paced fugue. It begins with the violins and quickly builds into a dense polyrhythmic counterpoint. 'Summer' begins with a slow pattern of oscillating fifths (Example 3.9). As Rhiannon Mathias has illustrated, 'Summer' evinces many similarities to the opening of 'Saturn', from Holst's *The Planets*.[34] In addition

[31] Elizabeth Maconchy to BBC, 27 June 1930, BBC WAC EM1.

[32] Nicola LeFanu, 'Elizabeth Maconchy', *Contemporary Music Review* 11/1–2 (1994): 201.

[33] Though Holst started teaching at the RCM in 1919, he left the College in 1923 following a nervous breakdown. See Imogen Holst, *The Music of Gustav Holst* (Oxford: Oxford University Press, 1969), 89.

[34] Mathias, *Lutyens, Maconchy, Williams and Twentieth-Century British Music*, 37.

Example 3.6. Maconchy, *The Land*, mvt. I, 'Winter', opening.
Published by Alfred Lengnick & Co., a division of Universal Music Publishing Group.
Reproduced by permission of Hal Leonard Europe BV (Italy).

Example 3.7. Maconchy, *The Land*, mvt. I, 'Winter', bars 7–11.
Published by Alfred Lengnick & Co., a division of Universal Music Publishing Group.
Reproduced by permission of Hal Leonard Europe BV (Italy).

Example 3.8. Holst, *Egdon Heath*, op. 47, opening. London: Novello & Co., 1928.

to Holst, however, 'Summer' also reflects the influence of Vaughan Williams's *Flos campi*, as Maconchy makes a direct allusion to her erstwhile teacher's score (Examples 3.10 and 3.11). Whether or not this was a conscious decision on Maconchy's part is unclear. Nevertheless, as Maconchy quotes verses of Sackville-West's poem that specifically reference Jacob's marriages in Genesis 29, the quotation from the third movement of *Flos campi*, which Vaughan Williams based upon text from the Song of Solomon, is highly suggestive.

In the lively fourth movement, 'Autumn', Maconchy skilfully creates a dialogue between the woodwind, brass, and strings, as each part is given a distinct motific theme. This dialogue persists throughout the movement. Donald Tovey interpreted this movement to be the most literal musical translation of the text in Maconchy's suite. The persistent pattern of the eighth notes alongside the

Example 3.9. Maconchy, *The Land*, mvt. III, 'Summer', opening.
Published by Alfred Lengnick & Co., a division of Universal Music Publishing Group.
Reproduced by permission of Hal Leonard Europe BV (Italy).

text 'The young men strained upon the crank/To wring the last reluctant inch' certainly lends support to Tovey's claim.[35]

Overall, the reviews of *The Land* were highly favourable. In spite of the critic in the *Times* finding fault with what they perceived as too much repetition of thematic material, they ultimately concluded that 'a very favourable impression was created by its general style and character, for it successfully avoids the trivial and obvious. The greatest degree of imagination was discernible in the orchestration, which is compact, effective, and occasionally showing touches of freshness and originality.

35 See Donald Tovey, 'Elizabeth Maconchy', *The Classics of Music*, edited by Michael Tilmouth (Oxford: Oxford University Press, 2001), 133–4.

Example 3.10. Maconchy, *The Land*, mvt. III, 'Summer', bars 33–4. Published by Alfred Lengnick & Co., a division of Universal Music Publishing Group. Reproduced by permission of Hal Leonard Europe BV (Italy).

Example 3.11. Vaughan Williams, *Flos campi*, mvt. III, opening. © Oxford University Press 1928. Reproduced by permission. All rights reserved.

Altogether a very promising work.'[36] In the *Daily Express*, the unnamed critic stated that *The Land* was the only interesting work in that evening's programme that was able to distract the audience from the sweltering heat wave.[37]

Richard Capell offered further praise, as well as additional observations regarding the reaction of the audience in his review for the *Daily Mail*: 'The music excited, nonetheless, lively interest by reason of its boldness and directness. Miss Maconchy knows no timidity. She covers great, fresco-like surfaces with confidence and strength. … The audience on Saturday showed itself rather dull in not answering more generously to its stimulating rhythms.'[38] Eric Blom's lengthy review in the *Manchester Guardian* yielded additional observations regarding the audience:

> True, it [*The Land*] does not seem to have been properly appreciated by more than a handful of people, but then it was rather unfortunate that the work should have been included in a popular Saturday night programme. … There is an acrid quality about Miss Maconchy's music which must have struck many hearers as a sign of immaturity. It is fatally easy to fancy oneself discovering all sorts of crudities and callownesses in the work of a composer, and perhaps more especially in a woman composer whose age can be stated in a programme note without the least fear of indiscretion if not without the risk of engendering prejudice. But though

36 'Promenade Concert', *Times*, 1 September 1930.
37 'The Talk of London', *Daily Express*, 1 September 1930.
38 R.C. [Richard Capell], 'Miss E. Maconchy', *Daily Mail*, 1 September 1930.

> experience comes with years, talent is either there from the beginning or it is not. In Miss Maconchy's case, one has only to have an open mind while listening to be perfectly sure that it was talent that brought this suite into existence, and that the work is not the mere product of such skill as she has by this time acquired, which in itself is considerable. … One feels impelled to say of her, as of Vaughan Williams, that the management of her counterpoint justifies itself by aptness of result even where it offends against the injunctions of textbooks. In this respect she is truly that master's disciple, but in its actual quality her music differs almost as much from his as from anyone else's. She is clearly developing a personality of her own. All that she needs to overcome, one feels, is self-consciousness and a slight uncertainty in the handling of the orchestra which now and again betrays itself.[39]

Though the decision to place Maconchy's work in a programme usually reserved for popular works was certainly unconventional, its placement in the first half of the programme – which was broadcast – was more unusual, as novelties by less established composers were normally placed in the second half of programmes, which the BBC did not air.[40] The most enthusiastic praise, however, came from Herbert Hughes at the *Daily Telegraph*, whose review, titled, 'Girl Composer's Triumph', declared:

> Not only is this one of the best pieces of orchestral music written by any woman in recent years, but by far the most important and interesting work produced, so far, at the Promenade Concerts during the present season. … Modern it is, of course, in the plain meaning of that word; the method direct, terse, economical; the harmony at times acid and biting – never luxurious or sentimental or (in the pre-war sense) feminine. … A fine poem has been the inspiration of this music, and there is no doubt in my own mind, after this first hearing, that it is the music of a first-rate intelligence, sensitive and subtle, yet capable of creating things on big lines. One is not surprised to learn that Miss Maconchy is at work on a symphony.[41]

Considering the novelties that had been performed prior to 30 August, which included Grainger's *English Dance*, Krenek's *Potpourri*, Villa-Lobos's highly acclaimed *Chôros No. 8*, and Janáček's *Wallachian Dances*, Hughes's praise of Maconchy, in spite of its gendered language, is of the highest order.[42] At the conclusion of the Proms season, a review in the *Daily Telegraph* – again written by Hughes – went one step further, declaring, 'Most striking … was "The Land" Suite of Elizabeth Maconchy, by which, at one bold stroke, that young Irish lady immediately asserted her right to be regarded amongst the composers who count.'[43]

[39] E.B. [Eric Blom], 'New English Work for Orchestra', *Manchester Guardian*, 1 September 1930.

[40] See Jennifer Doctor, 'A New Dimension: The BBC Takes on the Proms, 1920–44', in Jennifer Doctor, David Wright, and Nicholas Kenyon (eds), *The Proms* (London: Thames & Hudson, 2007), 98.

[41] Herbert Hughes, 'Girl Composer's Triumph', *Daily Telegraph*, 1 September 1930.

[42] David Cox, *The Henry Wood Proms* (London: British Broadcasting Corporation, 1980), 274.

[43] Herbert Hughes, 'First Performances', *Daily Telegraph*, 4 October 1930. In addition to the works by Grainger, Krenek, Villa-Lobos, and Janáček, the 1930 Proms season

While the critical success of *The Land* seemed destined to catapult Maconchy to stardom, what she encountered was quite the opposite: 'It [*The Land*] received, though I say it, staggeringly good press notices – but that was all. No-one gave me a commission, or a grant, or a chatty interview, or another performance. It did not even seem strange at the time: it appeared that this was the composer's lot, and that writing music must be its own reward.'[44] This was a difficult period for Maconchy, as she came face-to-face with the realisation that despite her evident talent and skill, prejudice against women was still widespread as she struggled to find a publisher willing to consider *The Land*. Hughes, who read for Boosey & Hawkes in addition to his work as a critic, took it upon himself to lobby her case. His attempts, however, came to no avail, as Maconchy recalled: 'all [Leslie] Boosey would say was that he couldn't take anything except little songs from a woman'.[45]

The economy proved to be another impediment, as Britain was already in the throes of a depression. Unemployment was widespread, increasing from 10.4 percent in 1929 to 16.1 percent in 1930, further increasing to 21.3 percent in 1931, and reaching a peak of 22.1 percent in 1932.[46] For musicians, the figures were far more grim, with the 1931 census placing the unemployment rate at 38 percent for male musicians, and 32 percent for female musicians.[47] As Cyril Ehrlich has argued, the economy was only partly to blame, as shifts in patronage, combined with the adoption of new technology, substantially altered the balances of power.[48] In response to these conditions, musicians unions, as well as organisations such as the Society for Women Musicians (SWM) devoted their time and efforts to addressing the plight of British musicians.

Though the topic of unemployed musicians dominated many of the musical discussions concerning employment in the press, the issue of the lack of opportunities for young composers to hear their works performed was slowly beginning to gain some momentum. In addition to the SWM, there were smaller organisations, such as the London Contemporary Music Centre (LCMC) and The New English Music Society, that devoted substantial portions of their programmes to up-and-coming British composers; however, their programmes

---

included the following novelties: Frank Bridge's *Rhapsody for Orchestra* and *Enter Spring*, Marcel Dupré's Symphony for Orchestra and Organ, Eugene Goossens's Oboe Concerto, Honegger's Cello Concerto, John Ireland's Piano Concerto, Kodály's *Summer Evening*, and Ethel Smyth's *Ode anacréontique*. See Cox, *The Henry Wood Proms*, 274.

44 Maconchy, 'A Composer Speaks', 25.

45 Hugo Cole, 'Why can't a woman? Hugh Cole meets composer Elizabeth Maconchy, 70 today', *Guardian*, 19 March 1977.

46 W.R. Garside, *British Unemployment, 1919–1939: A Study in Public Policy* (Cambridge: Cambridge University Press, 1990), 5.

47 Cyril Ehrlich, *The Music Profession in Britain since the Eighteenth Century: A Social History* (Oxford: Clarendon Press, 1985), 210. Also see Sophie Fuller, '"Putting the BBC and T. Beecham to Shame": The Macnaghten-Lemare Concerts, 1931–7', *Journal of the Royal Musical Association* 138/2 (2013): 378.

48 Ehrlich, 209–11.

rarely extended beyond chamber works, as the high cost of mounting orchestral concerts was often beyond their financial resources. Among the larger and better-funded organisations and concert series, such as the Promenade Concerts, the BBC, the Courtauld-Sargent Concerts, and the Royal Philharmonic Society, only the BBC and the Promenade Concerts made a concerted effort to include contemporary works by young composers in Britain, as the Courtauld-Sargent Concerts and the Royal Philharmonic Society focused primarily on works by continental composers.[49]

Though Maconchy failed to receive further offers for *The Land*, its performance and broadcast did generate a certain amount of interest in her music. In September, conductor Anthony Bernard (1891–1963) wrote to Maconchy inquiring whether her Piano Concerto would be suitable for a programme in The New English Music Society's upcoming third season. As the score and parts were with the BBC, Maconchy suggested that Bernard contact them to arrange to borrow the score and parts. After reviewing the Piano Concerto, Bernard decided that a newer work, the Suite for Chamber Orchestra, which Maconchy was still in the process of writing, would be more suitable for the programme, and promised to return the borrowed score and parts promptly to the BBC.[50]

On 10 February 1931, Bernard conducted the première of Maconchy's Suite for Chamber Orchestra in a concert that included works by Dowland and Byrd, Lennox Berkeley's *Tombeaux*, Peter Warlock's *An Old Song*, five songs from Fauré's *La bonne chanson*, and Respighi's *Trittico Botticelliano*. The reviews of Maconchy's suite, which consists of five short movements, each characterised by a short motific theme, were largely mixed, and it was a work that Maconchy was not wholly satisfied with herself.[51] The anonymous critic in the *Morning Post* opined, 'There is so much freshness in such a movement as the fugal finale that one has hopes that the composer will in time cast off the manner in which she casts her thoughts.'[52] The review in the *Daily Telegraph* was not much kinder, noting that the Suite was 'distinguished by concise writing, essentially contrapuntal and paying as much respect to tonality as 1930 demands. She has a sense of orchestral colour, and uses her wood-wind with something more than mere skill. It is a work rather of promise than achievement.'[53] Capell contended in the *Daily Mail* that the work 'proved a lively talent'.[54]

49 See Fuller, '"Putting the BBC and T. Beecham to Shame"', 377–414. As Fuller notes, British music did make its way into the Courtauld-Sargent Series and the Royal Philharmonic Series; however, they were works by established composers.

50 Maconchy completed her Suite for Chamber Orchestra in December 1930. Information regarding the arrangements between Maconchy and Bernard are detailed in a letter to Owen Mase. Elizabeth Maconchy to Owen Mase, 28 May 1931, BBC WAC EM1.

51 Maconchy later withdrew this work.

52 'New English Music Society', *Morning Post*, 11 February 1931.

53 'New English Music Society', *Daily Telegraph*, 11 February 1931.

54 R.C. [Richard Capell], 'Musical Epigrams', *Daily Mail*, 12 February 1931.

In May, Maconchy followed up with the BBC about her Piano Concerto. She was informed that the BBC did not have the score, and that it was still with Bernard, who had failed to return it as Maconchy requested.[55] While the BBC still expressed an interest in the work, writing in a letter dated 26 May, 'If, however, you care to submit it again we will put it into the programmes when opportunity offers', Bernard's negligence could not have occurred at a worse time, as it coincided with programme planning for the fifth season of the BBC Concerts of Contemporary Music, which placed a particular emphasis on orchestral works by British composers.[56]

Maconchy experienced a further disappointment in June when she received word from the BBC that both her Symphony and Suite for Chamber Orchestra, which she submitted for consideration for the 1931 Proms season, had been rejected. Owen Mase, the BBC's Assistant Music Director, noted, however, that the BBC was still interested in the works, writing in a letter dated 17 June, 'We feel, however, that we should like to put them in a studio concert at a later date, and we should like to know if you have the parts. Meanwhile, we are retaining your scores and will get in communication with you again when we can find an opportunity to include them in a studio programme.'[57] Maconchy wrote back to inquire if the BBC might be able to give her a better idea as to when they intended to perform her Symphony, since, without a publisher, she would have to incur the costs of copying the parts. She received the following response from Arthur Wynn, on 22 June: 'although no definite date has yet been decided upon, we hope to give both the Symphony and "Suite for Chamber Orchestra" an early place in our programmes. We should be glad, therefore, if you could have the parts of the Symphony copied.'[58] Maconchy copied the parts as quickly as possible, and sent them off to the BBC in August.[59]

In July, the SWM included Maconchy's Quintet for Strings in a concert held on the afternoon of Saturday the 11th, in celebration of Walter Willson Cobbett's eighty-fourth birthday. In addition to Maconchy's Quintet for Strings, the

[55] Elizabeth Maconchy to Owen Mase, 20 May 1931, BBC WAC EM1. For details on Mase, see Jennifer Doctor, *The BBC and Ultra-Modern Music, 1922–1936* (Cambridge: Cambridge University Press, 1999), 403.

[56] Owen Mase to Elizabeth Maconchy, 26 May 1931, BBC WAC EM1. Jennifer Doctor suggests that the increase in the proportion of British works was due to Adrian Boult, who became the BBC's Music Director in 1930. The delay in programme planning for the 1930–1 season was likely attributable to Boult's transition into his new role, as well as the substantial amount of time programme builders needed to devote to the newly established BBC Symphony Orchestra and its programmes. The shift in emphasis from chamber music to orchestral music in the fifth season of the BBC's Concerts of Contemporary Music was strategic, as Doctor remarks: 'The new orchestra made it financially advantageous to plan orchestral concerts, since its members were on annual BBC contracts while chamber ensembles had to be hired specially for each appearance'. See Doctor, *The BBC and Ultra-Modern Music*, 198–9.

[57] Owen Mase to Elizabeth Maconchy, 17 June 1931, BBC WAC EM1.

[58] Arthur Wynn to Elizabeth Maconchy, 22 June 1931, BBC WAC EM1.

[59] Elizabeth Maconchy to Owen Mase, 19 August 1931, BBC WAC EM1.

programme included Katherine Eggar's String Quartet in C Major, Kalitha Dorothy Fox's *Five Pieces for Piano*, Simone Plé's *Chansons Franciscaines*, three songs by Fiona McCleary, a work for violin by Emilia Gubitosi, and a string quartet by Mabel Saumarez Smith. Like many women composers trying to make their way in the professional music world, Maconchy expressed some ambivalence about the organisation, namely in regard to its amateur emphasis.[60] In spite of any misgivings Maconchy had about the SWM, it nevertheless offered opportunities for performances that were much needed for young composers.[61]

Maconchy's quintet is in two movements; the first movement is highly lyrical with a dense contrapuntal texture that is contrasted by the rapid pace of the second movement in which the texture is largely homophonic. The work left the critics divided. Foss thought the work was too dissonant, arguing in his review in the *Sunday Times* that 'her *poco lento* did not fall agreeably on the ear, and hardly engaged the mind'. Foss conceded, however, that in the second movement, 'she seemed more at ease. There were ideas here, too, having a definite rhythmic basis.'[62] The critic in the *Daily Telegraph* was more impressed by the quintet, noting that it 'left the others far behind'. They noted, however, that the work was difficult to grasp: 'So hard is this nut to crack that it was considered advisable to give the audience another chance of extracting the kernel in a second performance.'[63] The most detailed review came from Blom who wrote in the *Manchester Guardian*:

> the new string quintet in two movements by Elizabeth Maconchy, who has already attracted attention once or twice by her unusual talent. The work, which is in two movements, one slow and one fast, is a genuine piece of contrapuntal writing, and, what is more, contrapuntal writing of a new kind. It is as much polyrhythmic as polymelodic. Rhythms as well as tunes assert themselves in each of the five parts with apparent independence, yet they conspire throughout towards the making of one consistent formal scheme. Often the parts clash crudely, but the crudity has a purpose, for the ear is able to seize on each separate strand in the web most easily where the tangle appears most inextricable. It would be too much to say that one could be at once convinced that every detail in this work bears closely upon the whole of it. It will need more than one hearing to decide that. But there is a distinct feeling of organic growth, and the fact that one is left with the strong desire for further performances testifies to the vitality of Miss Maconchy's music.[64]

In December, Maconchy was able to obtain a second performance of her Quintet for Strings in the second concert of a newly established concert series, advertised simply as 'Three Chamber Music Concerts (one with orchestra)

[60] Nicola LeFanu, interview by author. Also see Laura Seddon, *British Women Composers and Instrumental Chamber Music in the Early Twentieth Century* (Farnham: Ashgate, 2013), 73.

[61] Though Maconchy was never actively involved in the SWM's activities, she did later accept the title of Honorary Vice President of the society.

[62] H.F. [Hubert Foss], 'Yesterday's Music', *Sunday Times*, 12 July 1931.

[63] C.D.G., 'Women Musicians', *Daily Telegraph*, 14 July 1931.

[64] E.B. [Eric Blom], 'Women Composers: Unknown Music', *Manchester Guardian*, 13 July 1931.

at the Ballet Club Theatre'.[65] This concert series, which would be renamed the Macnaghten-Lemare Concerts in 1932, began as an experimental venture that emerged out of discussions between Elisabeth Lutyens, violinist Anne Macnaghten (1908–2000), and conductor Iris Lemare (1902–97) over the lack of opportunities for young composers and musicians. As Macnaghten later recalled, 'recognizing the common needs of young unknown composers and players, we set about making common cause'.[66] Though the series' early concerts were largely devoted to chamber music, as time progressed, they were able to expand the breadth of their concerts to feature more choral and orchestral works.[67]

Maconchy's Quintet was featured in a programme on 14 December that also included Lutyens's String Quartet in One Movement, three songs by Patrick Hadley, three songs by Philip Rosseter, Imogen Holst's Suite for Unaccompanied Viola, and Haydn's String Quartet in G Major, op. 77, No. 1.[68] The quintet, which was performed by the Macnaghten Quartet and aided by violist Joyce Cook, was played not once, but twice, as it was featured as an encore at the end of the programme. The music critic who reviewed the concert in the *Music Lover*, while noting the technical difficulty of the work, offered substantial praise, concluding that amongst that evening's programme, Maconchy's piece was '[t]he most significant work'.[69]

The accomplishments Maconchy was able to achieve in her transition from student to professional were nothing short of remarkable, especially considering that within the span of less than a year, she had made a critically successful debut at the Proms with *The Land*, published songs with the OUP, and established a favourable reputation abroad. The lack of support from a publisher for her orchestral works, however, created difficulties. Maconchy had to cover the costs of copying parts, as well as handling all negotiations for performances herself. Though she struggled to gain second hearings for her works, new ventures, such as the Macnaghten-Lemare Concerts series, created additional opportunities that would enable Maconchy to further develop her reputation as an increasingly prominent figure in modern music circles in Britain in the 1930s.

65 Anne Macnaghten, 'The Story of the Macnaghten Concerts', *Musical Times* 100/1399 (September 1959): 460.

66 Ibid. Also see Fuller, '"Putting the BBC and T. Beecham to Shame"'; and Lutyens, *A Goldfish Bowl*, 50–2.

67 Ibid.

68 For a full listing of the Macnaghten-Lemare programmes between 1931 and 1937, see Fuller's appendix in '"Putting the BBC and T. Beecham to Shame"', 407–14.

69 'At Other Concerts', *Music Lover*, 19 December 1931. At the time, the Macnaghten Quartet consisted of Anne Macnaghten (1st violin), Joan Worsdell (2nd violin), Violet Brough (viola), and Joan Bonner (cello).

4

An Expansion of Style, 1932–5

Just as Maconchy's career was about to take off in 1932, she was diagnosed with tuberculosis.[1] Though her doctors advised her to seek treatment in Switzerland, Maconchy, who was unwilling to abandon her burgeoning career, sought treatment in Brighton instead.[2] Although she found Brighton to be more pleasant than she had initially anticipated, as the weeks passed she grew weary of the monotony of her daily routine: waking at 11 in the morning, she would spend an hour in her bath-chair outside from approximately 11:30 to 12:30, followed by a brief respite for lunch before returning for more time in the bath-chair until tea time, after which she would spend the remainder of the day primarily on the sofa. For entertainment, there were frequent games of backgammon to be had with her mother, who had relocated to Brighton along with LeFanu, who commuted daily to London during the week. Despite feelings of perpetual idleness, she nevertheless managed to practise piano and revise her quintet, which Macnaghten planned to play at a private party later in the spring. By late February, she was feeling much improved; however, her doctors advised her that she would have to remain in Brighton for another couple of months. Of her frustration and growing strength, Maconchy recounted in a letter to Williams on 24 February, 'I went for a short walk this morning, & hope soon to be able to kick the bath-chair into the sea. It amused me so much at first – & Billy & I laughed a lot at ourselves when he pushed me along in it – but by now all the novelty has disappeared & I hate the thing.'[3]

Between 1932 and 1935, Maconchy struggled with poor health, and though she continued to compose a prodigious number of works, her isolation from London proved to be detrimental as she found it increasingly difficult to

[1] As Maconchy's father died from tuberculosis, it was thought by her doctors that Maconchy had developed latent TB that became active in 1932. Maconchy's younger sister, Sheila, also developed TB; however, she elected to seek treatment in Switzerland. See Macnaghten, 'Elizabeth Maconchy', 298; Mathias, *Lutyens, Maconchy, Williams and Twentieth-Century British Music*, 51–2; and LeFanu, 'Elizabeth Maconchy DBE (1907–1994)'.

[2] It is unclear as to the exact date Maconchy moved to Brighton; however, based on correspondence with Williams in late February, it appears that she had already been in Brighton for some weeks. Elizabeth Maconchy to Grace Williams, 24 February 1932. In a letter sent to the BBC on 4 March, Maconchy remarks that she will remain in Brighton until early April. Elizabeth Maconchy to ACB, 4 March 1932, BBC WAC EM1.

[3] Elizabeth Maconchy to Grace Williams, 24 February 1932.

advocate for her works from afar. During this period, she also began to shift away from composing orchestral works, which had dominated much of her earlier compositional output, and began to focus on chamber music. In spite of the challenges Maconchy faced during these years of precarious health, her works garnered high-profile performances, as interest in her music continued to grow both at home and abroad.

On 23 February, Wright wrote to Maconchy to inform her that the BBC had found a place for her Suite for Chamber Orchestra in their Regional Programme service on 21 March and that they intended to rehearse her Symphony as part of a 'New Works Play-Through' initiative.[4] With the permission of her doctor, Maconchy travelled to London to attend the rehearsal and studio concert at Savoy Hill. While the rehearsal and broadcast went well, Maconchy ultimately remained unsatisfied with the work, as she felt that the final movement needed revision.[5] Vaughan Williams arrived at a similar conclusion, as he wrote to Maconchy shortly after the studio concert: 'it was lovely – & the *sureness of touch* was wonderful – the 2 slow movements are the best I think – is the first a little too "chip chippy" – & I am old fashioned enough to want a coda to the last movement. … I thought they played v. well – & was a relief after the dreary Schumann'.[6] In spite of these reservations, the Suite received an encouraging review from Ferruccio Bonavia in the *Daily Telegraph*:

> The general impression went to confirm the favourable opinion one had formed of the composer's abilities from a work of hers given some time ago at the Queen's Hall.
>
> The texture of the suite points to a distinctly personal view of orchestration which in the first lively allegro is very effective. …
>
> The five short movements seem cast, apart from changes of tempo, in the same mould. This, in a young composer, is a distinctly encouraging feature, since it is a sure vindication of temperament and independence.[7]

Another admirer of the work was Gerald Finzi, whom Vaughan Williams had brought to the studio concert. Shortly after the concert, Finzi wrote to

4 Kenneth Wright to Elizabeth Maconchy, 23 February 1932, BBC WAC EM1. In a lecture on the topic of the BBC's rehearsals in relation to young composers, Boult was quoted in the *Sunday Times* stating, 'a certain number of border-line works, or works whose story does not readily give the judge an opportunity of hearing how it would come off are put down for some special rehearsals under the guidance of a competent conductor, and the decision taken after hearing them'. 'Young Composers and the B.B.C.', *Sunday Times*, 4 December 1932.

5 Elizabeth Maconchy to Grace Williams, 18 May 1932.

6 Ralph Vaughan Williams to Elizabeth Maconchy, [March 1932], VWL 1082. The suggested date listed in VWL is March 1933; however, given the content, which makes direct references to the broadcast of Maconchy's Suite and the rehearsal of her Symphony on 30 March, the letter is in fact from 1932.

7 F.B. [Ferruccio Bonavia], 'An English Suite', *Daily Telegraph*, 22 March 1932.

Maconchy to convey how much he enjoyed her Suite as well as his hopes that another performance of *The Land* would be forthcoming.[8]

Three days after the broadcast, Wright wrote to Maconchy as some additional space had opened up in the rehearsal on the 30th, and he was wondering if it would be possible to rehearse her Piano Concerto as well. Wright requested that Maconchy send the full score to the rehearsal's conductor, Aylmer Buesst.[9] Unfortunately, the letter was erroneously sent to Maconchy's London address and it did not reach her in Brighton until the 26th. As the score and parts were still in the possession of the BBC (as they had been since August), Maconchy immediately telephoned the BBC. As it was a Saturday, with Easter Monday falling on the 28th, she was informed that no one would be available in the Music Department until Tuesday. After getting off the telephone, Maconchy wrote a letter to Wright explaining the mix-up. Her letter arrived at the BBC on the 29th, but by then it was too late to alter arrangements for the rehearsal.

Maconchy travelled to London again on the 30th for the rehearsal of her Symphony, which was held in the BBC's famed Studio 10 under Waterloo Bridge. As she was permitted to bring guests, her mother, husband, two friends, and Vaughan Williams joined her.[10] Though Maconchy was disappointed by Buesst's stiff conducting, overall she felt that the rehearsal had gone well, and she was especially pleased with the intensely lyrical third movement, which is built around a poignant melody that unfolds and expands over the course of the movement.[11]

On 10 April, Maconchy wrote to Wright to inquire about the status of the symphony, and whether the BBC had made any plans for a future broadcast. Wright's response was disheartening:

> Now with regard to the symphony. We were all most interested to have a chance of hearing it, and we remarked next day on the extreme usefulness of devoting a session to a work of this kind, particularly when there is time to play it through twice. We hope that you yourself felt that the time was profitably spent, as we always think the composer stands to gain as much from these special rehearsals as do we ourselves.
>
> We did feel however, that though the symphony is extremely interesting in many ways, and is a highly creditable piece of work, we cannot foresee any possibility of our including it in an actual broadcast concert. As a matter of fact, we feel that your Chamber Suite which we have done, and the piano concerto which is still before us, are actually better works and are more useful to us, but the Symphony makes us look forward in keen anticipation to your next effort on this scale.

[8] Gerald Finzi to Elizabeth Maconchy, 22 March 1932, private collection.

[9] Kenneth Wright to Elizabeth Maconchy, 24 March 1932, BBC WAC EM1. Born and raised in Melbourne, Australia, Buesst (1883–1970) began his musical career as a budding violinist and studied with Joseph Joachim (1831–1907) before turning to conducting. Buesst was later promoted to the position of Assistant Music Director at the BBC in 1933.

[10] Elizabeth Maconchy to Kenneth Wright, 26 March 1932, BBC WAC EM1.

[11] Elizabeth Maconchy to Grace Williams, 18 May 1932.

> The news in this letter is bound to be somewhat disappointing to you, but I only hope that you will feel that the trouble you spent in getting the parts of the symphony ready was justified in the experience you enjoyed in hearing it played last month.[12]

Wright's letter contradicted correspondence Maconchy had with Mase, who had explicitly stated in a letter dated 17 June 1931 that the BBC intended to include both her Symphony and Suite for Chamber Orchestra in a studio concert.[13] Though Wright's letter offered little in the way of an adequate explanation for a reversal of the promises made by Mase, changes to the BBC's policies regarding contemporary music may have been a contributing factor.

As Doctor discusses in *The BBC and Ultra-Modern Music*, the increase in broadcasts of ultra-modern works in the months leading up to the ISCM Festival in 1931 was followed by not only a drastic reduction after the festival, but also increased scrutiny of new works from within the BBC's central administration.[14] This was due in part to shifts in programming policies in the 1930s, as the BBC's administration argued for a greater emphasis to be placed on programme popularity and accessibility.[15] Doctor elaborates: 'although the central administrators still pursued their horizon-expanding policy, they now believed that popular reaction had to be addressed to some extent. Cultural and artistic merit were still taken into account, but they were no longer the sole or even the primary considerations in music programme building.'[16] In what was likely a response to the administration's concerns, Wright outlined definitions of 'contemporary' and 'experimental' in the Music Department's proposal for its Contemporary Concerts for the 1931–2 season:

> Our recent policy for concerts of Contemporary Music has been to concentrate on those masters who have been accepted as having advanced the scope and art of musical composition. We have, as a general rule, neither included those composers who are writing music to-day which, from its type, might have been written thirty of [*sic*] forty years ago, nor the experimental work of those young pioneers who, while attempting to find new paths, have not yet found an ultimately satisfactory form of expression. [...]
>
> The music suggested for this year does not include 'experimental' works or (for the most part) works by composers who have not established an important

12 Kenneth Wright to Elizabeth Maconchy, 14 April 1932, BBC WAC EM1.

13 Owen Mase to Elizabeth Maconchy, 17 June 1931, BBC WAC EM1.

14 Plans for the 1931–2 season were initially criticised by Eckersley in September, who wrote to Boult, 'I think it unlikely in the present circumstances that such a series will be sanctioned, and I should like to discuss the matter with you or Mase before anything further is done.' Though it is unclear as to whether Eckersley may have been referencing financial concerns owing to the economic depression, Doctor notes, 'it may be significant that a short time later they [the BBC's central administration] questioned for the first time the BBC's commitment to contemporary music dissemination.' See Doctor, *The BBC and Ultra-Modern Music*, 220–2.

15 Doctor, *The BBC and Ultra-Modern Music*, 292–4. Until 1938, the BBC measured programme popularity by box office sales.

16 Doctor, *The BBC and Ultra-Modern Music*, 196.

> position in Contemporary Music. They are, in fact, programmes of 'consolidation', and all the works at present in mind have passed into the repertoire stage, at least on the Continent and America, and in some cases this country also.[17]

Though it is unclear as to whether any of Maconchy's works had been under consideration for inclusion, the BBC's official stance on contemporary music signalled a shift from the experimental works that had dominated much of the contemporary programmes in the late 1920s to a much more conservative approach that dominated programming in the 1930s as the BBC's idea of 'the best for the most' became increasingly scrutinised as entertainment was deemed more important than education.

At the end of April, Maconchy's doctor declared that she was well enough to leave Brighton.[18] Though she had hoped to be able to return to London, her doctor advised against it, as he believed that it would be more beneficial for her to spend at least a year or two in the country. Maconchy and her husband subsequently settled in the village of Seal Chart, Kent, renting a cottage called Chart Corner, where she spent most of her time living in an open-sided hut, as fresh air and rest was considered to be one of the standard courses of treatment for tuberculosis at the time.[19]

In May, Maconchy received promising news from Wright as the BBC intended to include her Piano Concerto in an upcoming Regional Programme broadcast of orchestral music on 7 July. Wright asked Maconchy if there was a soloist that would be available to play the work at such short notice.[20] Maconchy mentioned Schulhoff, who had premièred the work in Prague and would be in London later in the year; however, Wright stated that the BBC was not interested in employing Schulhoff for an additional solo date beyond what they

17 Kenneth Wright to Roger Eckersley, memo, 'Contemporary Concerts, 1931/2. Summary', BBC WAC R27/67 Music – General/Contemporary Concerts, 1929–36. Also quoted in Doctor, *The BBC and Ultra-Modern Music*, 221. Wright's proposal for the 1931–2 season consisted of individual programmes devoted to Schönberg, Kodály, Delius, and Honegger, as well as programmes devoted to English, Russian, German, and Hungarian works. With regards to the English programme, Wright states that works would be included 'provided sufficient works can be found not already catered for by another series such as Symphony Concerts. There will definitely be Lambert's Pianoforte Concerto, and probably a new String Quartet by Ireland. It should be remembered that there are many outlets for new English works, catering for all styles and types of work.'

18 Elizabeth Maconchy to Grace Williams, 11 March 1932.

19 The hut was placed on a turntable, which enabled it to be rotated to avoid harsh winds. Although Maconchy did spend time indoors during the winter, she and LeFanu continued to sleep outside in the hut, which was fitted with two beds as well as a piano. See Dunlop, 16.

20 Wright wrote to Maconchy, 'Who knows your concerto, and would be willing and able to play it during July? We should like to find a place for it then, if the pianist you mention is on our books and available.' Kenneth Wright to Elizabeth Maconchy, 13 May 1932, BBC WAC EM1.

Figure 5. William LeFanu and Maconchy at Chart Corner, 1935 (reproduced by permission of the Maconchy Estate).

had already contracted.[21] As Gwendo Paul, who played the work at the RCM in 1928, lived in Australia, Maconchy suggested pianist Kathleen Long, who graciously agreed to learn the work at short notice.[22]

Maconchy travelled to London in mid-June to rehearse the work on two pianos with Long shortly before the broadcast. After the rehearsal, Maconchy wrote to Williams, 'she is going to play it frightfully well – much better than Schulhoff'.[23] As the BBC planned for only one short rehearsal with Stanford Robinson, who would be conducting the BBC Orchestra, the lack of rehearsal time, compounded by the use of a conductor who was far more comfortable with choirs as opposed to orchestras, resulted in a less than favourable performance. Nevertheless, the performance garnered Maconchy at least one new fan, as Long recounted in a letter to Maconchy that Rebecca Clarke was an admirer of the work.[24]

21 Kenneth Wright to Elizabeth Maconchy, 19 May 1932, BBC WAC EM1.

22 Kathleen Long (1896–1968) studied at the RCM from 1910 to 1916, and was hired to teach piano at the College by Allen in 1920. She was highly regarded for her interpretations of Holst and Bridge. See Diana McVeagh, 'Long, Kathleen', *Grove Music Online*, 2001, https://doi.org/10.1093/gmo/9781561592630.article.16947 [accessed 5 September 2010].

23 Elizabeth Maconchy to Grace Williams, 23 June 1932.

24 Kathleen Long to Elizabeth Maconchy, 8 July 1932, private collection.

As Maconchy's health improved, she was able to devote more of her time and limited energy to composing. By June, she was busy with work on *Two Motets for Double Chorus*, which consisted of settings of John Donne's *A Hymn to Christ* and *A Hymn to God the Father*. Maconchy also began work on an overture for a projected opera that she decided to turn into a stand-alone piece titled *Comedy Overture*,[25] and was asked by Gwen Raverat to write music for a ballet intended for a children's school based upon Hans Christian Andersen's fairy tale *The Red Shoes*.[26] Though Maconchy's health seriously declined in August, she nevertheless managed to compose an oboe quintet in an astounding six weeks.[27]

In September, Vaughan Williams wrote to Stanford Robinson to inquire if he would be willing to look over Maconchy's *Two Motets for Double Chorus*.[28] In his letter, Vaughan Williams remarked, 'I think them [the motets] very remarkable, but very hard – indeed I believe that only your Wireless Singers c^{d} do them full justice.'[29] Robinson told Vaughan Williams that he would try them out with the Wireless Singers, and Maconchy quickly copied all the parts, which she sent to Robinson on 30 October.[30]

Though none of Maconchy's recent works received performances in 1932, her Sonata for Violin and Piano (1927) was included in a Macnaghten-Lemare concert at the Ballet Club Theatre on 18 October. The reviews of Maconchy's sonata were mixed. While Hugh Evelyn Wortham remarked in the *Daily Telegraph*

25 The overture was taken from an opera Maconchy had begun 1931 titled *The Willow Plate*. Based upon 'The Story of Wong T'sin and the Willow Plate Embellishment' in the orientalist novel *Kai Lung's Golden Hours* (1922) by Ernest Bramah, Maconchy's opera was never completed.

26 Gwen Raverat (1885–1957) was an artist known for her wood engravings and her autobiography *Period Piece* (1952). Related to the Darwin family, she knew Vaughan Williams particularly well and collaborated with him on the ballet *Job*. See Reynolds Stone and James Hamilton, 'Raverat, Gwendolen Mary (1885–1957)', *Oxford Dictionary of National Biography*, 2004, https://doi.org/10.1093/ref:odnb/35685 [accessed 6 September 2020].

27 In her handwritten list of works held at SHC, Maconchy notes under Quintet for Oboe and Strings, 'the slow mvt was taken from my variations for orchestra, written when a student, so that I could complete the 5^{tet} and enter it for the D.T. [the *Daily Telegraph*] prize, as I got ill for a second time while writing it'. Maconchy's husband, William LeFanu, wrote in a letter to Williams in August of 1932 that Maconchy 'had another attack of haemorrhage and she has been flat on her back for a week'. Quoted in Mathias, *Lutyens, Maconchy, Williams and Twentieth-Century British Music*, 51–2.

28 Stanford Robinson (1904–84) was an English conductor. He studied at the RCM and joined the BBC as the Chorus Master for the Wireless Singers in 1924. Arthur Jacobs, 'Robinson, Stanford', *Grove Music Online*, 2002, https://doi.org/10.1093/gmo/9781561592630.article.O007148 [accessed 6 September 2020].

29 Ralph Vaughan Williams to Stanford Robinson, 26 September 1932, BBC WAC EM1.

30 Elizabeth Maconchy to Stanford Robinson, 11 October 1932 and 30 October 1932, BBC WAC EM1.

that 'the slighter movements impressed one most',[31] the critic at the *Observer* denounced the work for its ultra-modern tendencies: 'one asks oneself whether it is not time to drop the pose that music has nothing to do with emotion? Ought we not at the end to be able to say, How lovely! and not have to think, How clever! Can't we leave chess or mathematics, or whatever it is, to the Continent?'[32] Christian Darnton's review in the *Music Lover* offered a more balanced assessment of the work: 'Elizabeth Maconchy's five-year-old violin and piano sonata was not as raw as one might expect from a composer who is still so young. Not many people of her age can look back so far with so little cause for bashfulness.'[33]

If 1932 had been marred by setbacks, 1933 proved to be far more successful. Although health issues required a return to Brighton, Maconchy's Quintet for Oboe and Strings (1932) was awarded third prize in the *Daily Telegraph* Chamber Music Competition, with first prize awarded to Edric Cundell (1893–1961) for his string quartet, and second prize to Cecil Armstrong Gibbs (1889–1960), also for a string quartet.[34] Created specifically for the encouragement of chamber music by British composers, the competition, which was judged by Hugh Allen, Henry Wood, Adrian Boult, and Arthur Bliss, received nearly 500 entries.[35]

Between 11 and 15 March, the competition was discussed ad infinitum in the *Daily Telegraph*. On the 13th, an article on the competition declared that the vast number of entries had been no less than 'a revelation to them [the adjudicators] of the extent to which the composition of chamber music is practised to-day in Great Britain'.[36] The importance of encouraging British music was reinforced by remarks made by Wood, who was quoted as stating,

> I want particularly to say that, in the opinion of the world's greatest musicians, we have to-day in Great Britain a body of young men and women who are really writing fine, original stuff.
>
> … I wish when celebrated Continental chamber music combinations visit our shores they would make a point of performing English chamber music from time to time. It seems a great shame to me that the Léner, the Busch, and other great Continental chamber music combinations entirely neglect so much

[31] H.E.W. [H.E. Wortham], 'Macnaghten String Quartet', *Daily Telegraph*, 19 October 1932.

[32] 'The Ballet Club Theatre', *Observer*, 23 October 1932. Maconchy remarked in a letter to Williams that she was not entirely satisfied with the work, and that its performance had left her feeling quite disappointed. Elizabeth Maconchy to Grace Williams, 22 October 1932.

[33] C.D. [Christian Darnton], 'Young England', *Music Lover*, 29 October 1932.

[34] Victor Hely-Hutchinson and Benjamin Britten received honourable mentions. 'Chamber Music – The Prize Winners', *Daily Telegraph*, 13 March 1933.

[35] The reason for the high number of submissions was likely due to the fact that the competition did not place a limit on the number of compositions a composer could submit. Elizabeth Maconchy to Grace Williams, 13 March 1933.

[36] 'Chamber Music Competition: Prize-Winners' Careers', *Daily Telegraph*, 14 March 1933.

> splendid chamber music which our British composers have written during the last twenty years.[37]

The winning works were broadcast over the BBC in a chamber music concert on 13 May, played by the Griller Quartet with oboist Helen Gaskell (1906–2002), with a recording to be issued by HMV shortly thereafter.[38]

In advance of the broadcast, an article by Richard Capell appeared in the 5 May edition of *Radio Times* to discuss the three works in relation to current trends in British music. Of Maconchy, Capell wrote the following,

> If these three works can be taken as at all representative, what trend do they indicate? One of the three definitely belongs to a certain school – the 'New English' school, whose masters are Dr. Vaughan Williams and Mr. Gustav Holst. This is Miss Maconchy's quintet. It is always wounding to a composer to suggest affiliations and sources. But what, when the meanings of describing music are so limited, is a critic to do? If only composers would be so kind as to regard such suggestions as an attempt at definition and not as a reproachful hint of plagiarism!
>
> 'Holstian' must be applied to the new oboe quintet, not as a reproach (far from it!), but simply as a way of indicating in one word a certain sturdiness, a certain economy of statement, an open-air feeling, expressiveness without sentimentality, and animation without feverishness.
>
> The feeling in this music is singularly fresh, the form unconventional but satisfying. …
>
> Miss Maconchy's musical landscape is not of southern character. It has something of the bright bleakness of a northern March. The New English school likes harmonies of certain tartness and disdains luxuriant detail.[39]

When the *Daily Telegraph* interviewed Maconchy in March, she kept her remarks short and succinct: 'There is nothing in particular that I can say about it. I wrote it specially for the competition. Ill-health rather interfered with its progress – and it may be due to this fact that its prevailing mood is one of quiet.'[40] Arranged in three movements, the first movement opens with a descending three-note motif that consists of A, G-sharp, and F stated boldly by the oboe that expands to form theme 1 (Example 4.1). This motif permeates the entire movement and in bar 9, a contrasting theme is introduced by the first violin (Example 4.2). Though this contrasting second theme is in a Hungarian major mode (Forte 7-31), when combined with the opening motif, it becomes clear that Maconchy is using an octatonic pitch collection. Theme 2 is then followed by the introduction of a third theme in bar 18. The texture of the part writing is predominately homophonic, with the movement structured around the exchange of thematic material between the oboe and strings.

[37] 'Chamber Music: Judges' Verdict', *Daily Telegraph*, 13 March 1933.

[38] The Griller Quartet consisted of Sydney Griller (1st violin), Jack O'Brien (2nd violin), Philip Burton (viola), and Colin Hampton (cello).

[39] Richard Capell, 'Prize-winning Works to be Broadcast', *Radio Times* (5 May 1933): 272.

[40] 'Chamber Music Competition: Prize-Winners' Careers', *Daily Telegraph*, 14 March 1933.

Example 4.1. Maconchy, Quintet for Oboe and Strings, mvt. I, opening. Copyright © Chester Music Ltd. International Copyright Secured. All Rights Reserved. Reproduced by permission of Hal Leonard Europe Ltd.

Example 4.2. Maconchy, Quintet for Oboe and Strings, mvt. I, bars 9–14. Copyright © Chester Music Ltd. International Copyright Secured. All Rights Reserved. Reproduced by permission of Hal Leonard Europe Ltd.

For the second movement, Maconchy used material from one of her student works, *Theme and Variations* (1928). It begins with a tritone figure, whose unsettling presence casts a shadow over the movement and is only momentarily interrupted by the strings with melodic phrasing highly reminiscent of Vaughan Williams. The third movement offers a contrast to the ominous character of the preceding movement. It begins with a light-hearted melody in the oboe supported by an oscillating whole-tone figure in the strings that quickly expands as Maconchy re-introduces themes from the preceding movements.

Though the *Daily Telegraph* competition was intended to improve the climate for contemporary British chamber music, the broadcast of the winning works only seemed to reinforce the negative stereotype of chamber music as an elitist genre that was difficult, if not downright impossible, for the public to comprehend.[41] In spite of the predominately negative reviews of the broadcast, Maconchy's quintet was widely considered to be the best of the three works. One critic who took this position was Arthur Henry Fox Strangways, who argued in his rather scathing review in the *Observer*,

> Most people when they go to concerts can bring away with them some sort of memory of what they heard; but except for a foolish little hautboy phrase of three notes – foolish, that is, in isolation – in Miss Maconchie's [*sic*] quintet, my mind is a complete blank. That is, of course, my own original sin, and it is lucky I was not one of the judges in the competition for which this and two quartets (by Armstrong Gibbs and Edric Cundell) were sent in, for I should have given this the first prize, as leaving at least some impression, whereas the others, it appears, left none. The impression was unlovely, not ugly; if one did not have it one would not miss it: but it was positive, not negative.[42]

Fox Strangways concluded his review with a backhanded compliment to the BBC 'for responding so readily to a request made to them lately to show kindness to the young English composer. … If this policy is maintained, and if the musical *intelligentsia* of London will make that possible by taking and showing a greater interest, we may expect to see progress'.[43] The critic in the *Times* came to a similar conclusion, arguing that the competition's elevation of technical skill above artistry was entirely misguided.[44]

While dismissive of certain aspects of Maconchy's work, the critic in the *Sunday Times* nevertheless offered some slight praise: 'Miss Maconchy's quintet was, in its unaffected and pensive way, the most poetic. … Miss Maconchy's

[41] The conflation of chamber music as an elitist art form was reinforced by the BBC, which used the term 'chamber music' synonymously with 'contemporary music'. A letter from a listener appearing in the *Radio Times* on 4 March 1932 aptly captures the prevailing public perception of chamber music: 'It has been in my mind for some time past to write to you on the subject of the almost universal condemnation of Chamber Music, which puzzles musicians and bewilders your musical director. From time to time I have arguments about it with people who took no interest in music and knew nothing about it until they obtained wireless sets, and I ask them whether they like *Andante Cantabile* by Tchaikovsky, the Beethoven setting of *The Lost Chord*, and one or two other well-known things, and always receive a surprised answer in the affirmative. When I tell them that these are examples of Chamber Music I am scorned, and informed that Chamber Music is that awful noise like cats squealing that they hear on the wireless, labelled "Chamber Music" in the programme. Now the fact is that the programme compilers are to blame for this; they reserve the description of "Chamber Music" for the music of modern "advanced" composers and very rarely apply it to the Chamber Music of the classical or more orthodox composers whose compositions are almost always described simply as trios, quartets, or quintets'. F.J. Hargreaves, 'Listeners' Letters: Chamber Music', *Radio Times* 34 (4 March 1932): 578. Also quoted in Paul Kildea, *Selling Britten: Music and the Market Place* (Oxford: Oxford University Press, 2002), 53; and Doctor, *The BBC and Ultra-Modern Music*, 122.

[42] A.H. Fox Strangways, 'Modern Works', *Observer*, 21 May 1933.

[43] Ibid.

[44] 'B.B.C. Chamber Music', *Times*, 15 May 1933.

little work – so seriously simple and unforced – struck one as music that will make many friends. A certain Vaughan-Williamsian flavour is undeniable.'[45] The comparisons to Vaughan Williams bothered Maconchy as she revealed in a letter to Williams the day of the announcement of the results: 'I'm sick of being told I'm immature though, (and Vaughan Williamsian: they didn't know I was his pupil this time – is it very obvious?)'[46] In his review published in the *Music Lover*, Darnton, who questioned the validity of the competition as an adequate assessment of British musical trends, nevertheless praised Maconchy's quintet, even though he did not find it to be her best work:

> I was tempted, while listening to the music on this evening, to think that the competition has little value except to show where the three judges approximately find themselves able to meet on common ground. Necessarily the main points of agreement will be on the least striking no-man's-land of mediocrity. ... Miss Maconchy's quintet had so many good ideas in it that I am astonished that it got a prize at all. It is not her best work. I suspect her of having watered down her style and her thoughts for the occasion.[47]

In June, Maconchy's Oboe Quintet was included in a concert arranged by the SWM. The reviews, though brief, were on the whole more positive, as the critic at the *Morning Post* noted that the work 'improves on further acquaintance'.[48] The critic in the *Observer* offered further compliments, remarking, 'The three movements are informed with really musical thought, and the whole work is vigorous and definite.'[49] Writing in the *Daily Telegraph*, Capell was far less generous and damning with faint praise by characterising the quintet as a 'beautiful little work, so sincere and unaffected in its quiet, idyllic way'.[50]

On 1 July, Maconchy held a private concert and party at her home, presumably to celebrate the success of her quintet and its commercial recording. The Macnaghten Quartet played a short programme featuring two Fantasias by Purcell and Haydn's String Quartet op. 76, No. 4, in addition to Maconchy's quintet with oboist Sylvia Spencer (1909–78). For the occasion, Maconchy had a blue dress made and was joined by her sisters as well as Williams and Gow, who devoured the delectable asparagus sandwiches and meringues she had made for the occasion.[51]

The release of HMV's recording of Maconchy's quintet along with the quartets by Cundell and Armstrong Gibbs in the summer yielded similar opinions to those expressed after the initial broadcast. The critic in the popular evening paper the *Star* cautioned readers that Maconchy's work was 'not for the man in the street. ... But chamber music enthusiasts will appreciate Helen Gaskell

45 '"Daily Telegraph" Chamber Music', *Sunday Times*, 14 May 1933.

46 Elizabeth Maconchy to Grace Williams, 13 March 1933.

47 C.D. [Christian Darnton], 'So this is England', *Music Lover*, 20 May 1933.

48 'Society of Women Musicians', *Morning Post*, 19 June 1933.

49 'Yesterday's Concerts', *Observer*, 18 June 1933.

50 R.C. [Richard Capell], 'Women Musicians', *Daily Telegraph*, 19 June 1933.

51 Elizabeth Maconchy to Grace Williams, 15 June 1933; and Grace Williams to Elizabeth Maconchy, [after 1 July] 1933.

and the Griller String Quartet in this interesting work.'[52] Blom contended in his review in the *Birmingham Post* that Maconchy's quintet was 'the most daring and also the most poetical of the three works, and therefore perhaps the most disconcerting. If imagination were a jury's foremost qualification, it would have gained the first prize; its unconventional technique, though perfectly adequate to its purposes, was doubtless against it.'[53] The most scornful – and overtly sexist – review came from Constant Lambert, who quipped in the *New Statesman*, 'It is a pity that Miss Maconchy is so determined not to allow feminine charm to come into the picture.'[54]

Throughout all of the excitement of the *Daily Telegraph* competition, Maconchy continued to balance negotiations with the BBC with concentrated work on her *Comedy Overture*, a string quartet, and a ballet titled *Great Agrippa, or the Inky Boys*. At the end of February 1933, Maconchy submitted *The Land* to the BBC in the hope that it might be considered for a broadcast. She received an encouraging response in June stating that Boult wished to include the work in a programme in the near future.[55] After recovering from a mild haemorrhage in September, Maconchy wrote to Robinson to follow up on the status of her *Two Motets for Double Chorus*.[56] In his reply, Robinson explained that though he had rehearsed the motets with the Wireless Singers, he felt that they required a larger number of singers and informed the Music Director that the works were better suited for the larger Wireless Chorus.[57] Robinson promised to follow up on the matter. After further discussion, the BBC decided to return the motets to Maconchy, stating that they could not find a place for them in the upcoming season, but that she should consider resubmitting them at a later date.[58]

On 6 November, Maconchy's newly composed string quartet was premièred by the Macnaghten Quartet in the opening concert of the Macnaghten-Lemare

[52] 'Chamber Music', *Star*, 19 September 1933.

[53] E.B. [Eric Blom], 'Three Prize Chamber Works', *Birmingham Post*, 11 August 1933.

[54] Constant Lambert, 'The HMV Connoisseur's List', *New Statesman*, 7 April 1934.

[55] Arthur Wynn to Elizabeth Maconchy, 30 June 1933, BBC WAC EM1. Wynn worked in the BBC's booking department in the early 1930s. See Doctor, *The BBC and Ultra-Modern Music*, 230.

[56] Elizabeth Maconchy to Stanford Robinson, 30 September 1933, BBC WAC EM1. Maconchy mentions the haemorrhage, which occurred shortly after she returned from a trip to Ireland, in an undated letter to Williams. Based on the context of the letter, the haemorrhage likely occurred sometime in early-to-mid September. Elizabeth Maconchy to Grace Williams, [before 17 October 1933].

[57] Stanford Robinson to Elizabeth Maconchy, 3 October 1933, BBC WAC EM1.

[58] In his letter to Maconchy, Mase states, 'It sometimes happens that when works are sent to individuals on the staff, changes in organisation here may mean delay. It is always better to submit works simply to the B.B.C., when they will receive the correct handling automatically.' Owen Mase to Elizabeth Maconchy, 6 October 1933, BBC WAC EM1.

Example 4.3. Maconchy, String Quartet No. 1, mvt. I, opening.
Published by Alfred Lengnick & Co., a division of Universal Music Publishing Group.
Reproduced by permission of Hal Leonard Europe BV (Italy).

Concerts' third season.[59] Maconchy succinctly described the quartet's contrasting movements as 'extrovert, direct and rhythmical'.[60] The quartet certainly exhibits many characteristics of Maconchy's musical language: the use of short themes, rhythmic motifs, and the frequent oscillation of major and minor intervals.[61] Within the first fourteen bars of the first movement, Maconchy

59 In addition to Maconchy's quartet, the following works were included in the programme: William Shield's Quartet for Flute and Strings, op. 3, No. 2, Helen Perkin's Four Preludes for Piano, Grace Williams's Sonatina for Flute and Piano, and Haydn's String Quartet in B-flat Major, op. 76, No. 4. In 1932, the lineup of the Macnaghten Quartet consisted of, in addition to Macnaghten, Elise Desprez (2nd violin), Beryl Scawen-Blunt (viola), and Mary Goodchild (cello). In 1934 cellist Olive Richards replaced Goodchild.

60 Elizabeth Maconchy, 'Elizabeth Maconchy On Writing String Quartets', liner notes included with Unicorn-Kanchana DKP, CD 1989.

61 Macnaghten, 'Elizabeth Maconchy', 299–300.

reveals the primary motific and thematic material that forms the foundation of its structure, as the accented rhythm in bars 1–4, and its shortened variation in bars 12–14, remain almost constant throughout, along with the continual pull towards the resolution of the descending semitone (Example 4.3).

The musical form of the first movement loosely falls in an ABA'B'A" pattern. In bar 28, Maconchy introduces a contrasting theme in the viola. After the introduction of this second theme, the first theme is repeated, which leads directly into the contrasting B section of the movement that sounds as if it is a presage of passages in Vaughan Williams's Fourth Symphony, which was completed two years later (Example 4.4).

The second movement is a lively scherzo, built around a short theme (Example 4.5). As with the first movement, rhythm plays a pivotal role and remains a persistent driving force throughout the movement. In the opening bars, Maconchy once again articulates the primary motific material of the movement with an oscillating semitone, with major and minor thirds forming the basic melodic and harmonic structure of the movement.

The third movement offers a sharp contrast to the extroverted character of the second, as it is built around the repetition and expansion of a principal melodic theme from the third movement of her Symphony, which Maconchy varies with some minor alterations. Just as in the first movement, the descending minor third plays a prominent motific role (Example 4.6). Of the energetic finale, Presto, Maconchy described it as 'in very high spirits, in this perhaps recalling Haydn. Its theme has lots of unexpected twists and turns: it can develop into *fortissimo* repeated chords, or appear as a light-hearted tune, *pianissimo*' (Example 4.7).[62]

Maconchy's quartet received glowing reviews in the press. In the *Music Lover*, Darnton offered enthusiastic praise:

> The main work of the evening was really outstanding: Elizabeth Maconchy's new string quartet. It struck me once again that Miss Maconchy is a kind of English Bartók; Béla Bantock, as it were. There is that same devotion to the augmented fourth, that *diabolus in musica*, for which she would assuredly have been incinerated had she lived six or seven centuries ago. The music itself is full of vigour, soundly and clearly constructed, and possessing a kind of burning originality which for me is one of the essentials of first-class music. This is definitely a work which should bring the composer into prominence.[63]

In agreement with Darnton, the critic in the *Times* proclaimed: 'Elizabeth Maconchy has already achieved the enviable position in which she can be sure that anything she may say will be listened to with attention, and in her new string quartet ... she gives further warrant for that interest in her music.'[64] Maconchy's quartet was also performed by the Macnaghten Quartet on 7 November in a chamber music concert at the Grotrian Hall, and again on the 14th in Oxford in a concert

[62] Ibid.

[63] C.D. [Christian Darnton], 'A Really Outstanding Work', *Music Lover*, 11 November 1933.

[64] 'Works of Women Composers', *Times*, 7 November 1933.

Example 4.4. Maconchy, String Quartet No. 1, mvt. I, rehearsal number 4. Published by Alfred Lengnick & Co., a division of Universal Music Publishing Group. Reproduced by permission of Hal Leonard Europe BV (Italy).

Example 4.5. Maconchy, String Quartet No. 1, mvt. II, opening.
Published by Alfred Lengnick & Co., a division of Universal Music Publishing Group.
Reproduced by permission of Hal Leonard Europe BV (Italy).

Example 4.6. Maconchy, String Quartet No. 1, mvt. III, opening.
Published by Alfred Lengnick & Co., a division of Universal Music Publishing Group.
Reproduced by permission of Hal Leonard Europe BV (Italy).

Example 4.7. Maconchy, String Quartet No. 1, mvt. IV, opening.
Published by Alfred Lengnick & Co., a division of Universal Music Publishing Group.
Reproduced by permission of Hal Leonard Europe BV (Italy).

organised by the Oxford University Musical Club and Union. The Grotrian Hall performance received highly favourable reviews in the *Daily Telegraph*, the *Music Lover*, and the *Monthly Musical Record*.[65] The performance did, however, receive a negative review from Lambert in the *Sunday Referee*:

> Miss Elizabeth Maconchy, whose quartet was played by the Macnaghten quartet at Tuesday's Grotrian Hall Chamber Concert, has little of Arthur Bliss's fluency and none of his amiability, but her work is energetic and invigorating. The influence of Béla Bartók is a little too apparent, particularly in the first and last movements, and the construction of the first movement is rudimentary. But the rhythmic energy of the work and its evident sincerity console us for certain technical weaknesses, which no doubt will soon be overcome.[66]

65 See C.D.G., 'Grotrian Chamber Concert', *Daily Telegraph*, 8 November 1933; and C.D. [Christian Darnton], 'A New Star: The Grotrian Tuesday Concert', *Music Lover*, 11 November 1933.

66 Constant Lambert, 'Musical Matters', *Sunday Referee*, 12 November 1933.

On 11 December, Maconchy's *Two Motets for Double Chorus* received its first performance at a Macnaghten-Lemare concert. Though the prospect of having the motets premièred at a Macnaghten-Lemare concert had been discussed in 1932, Macnaghten initially advised against it, as she thought that Lemare's choir would be unable to handle the challenging work.[67] Macnaghten was likely referring to the high tessitura in 'A Hymn to God the Father'. Unfortunately, Macnaghten's earlier concerns were fully realised in both the rehearsals and performance as Lemare's choir struggled unsuccessfully to remain in tune. Of the rehearsals and performance, Maconchy recounted in a letter to Williams,

> The physical and mental strain involved in waiting for the next ♭A, ♮A or ♭B in the sopranos ought to cure me of writing a part like that again! – but I like lots of high notes – or at least a high texture in choral writing – it seems to me one can get a sort of suspended-in-mid air feeling – (less 'of the earth' than choral writing in the middle & low registers –).[68]

In the *Musical Times*, Howes quipped, 'in Miss Maconchy's "Hymn to God the Father" her imaginative purpose was sometimes discernable, but it is not much good [for] composers writing works that only archangels can sing in tune'.[69] The review in the *Times* was equally dismissive: 'Miss Maconchy disregarded the *tessitura* of the voices as outrageously as Beethoven. Granted that what we heard was not always what the composers had written, the impression was inescapable that they had not really conceived their works in terms of voices at all.'[70] Capell's review in the *Daily Telegraph*, however, was surprisingly sympathetic: 'Donne's tensity had, it seemed, urged the composer to put a taxing strain upon the singers, and the result last night was an imperfect rendering, which, however, did not altogether obscure some uncommonly purposeful part-writing.'[71]

In January 1934, Maconchy's health declined once more and she was forced to return to Brighton, where she remained until March. Unwilling to let her health get in the way of her work, she kept herself occupied with work on an oratorio titled *Deborah*, based upon the biblical prophet, as well as revisions to a work for small chorus and chamber orchestra titled *The Leaden Echo and the Golden Echo* (1930–1), based upon Gerard Manley Hopkins's poem of the same

[67] Elizabeth Maconchy to Grace Williams, 23 June 1932. Lemare decided to begin rehearsing the motets on 17 October 1933. As the copyist hired to do the parts decided to quit after completing one copy, Williams, Britten, Gow, and Eleanor Bevan Ramsbotham helped Maconchy to copy the remaining parts needed for Lemare's choir. Elizabeth Maconchy to Grace Williams, [before 17 October 1933]; and Elizabeth Maconchy to Grace Williams, 17 October 1933.

[68] Elizabeth Maconchy to Grace Williams, [after 11 December 1933].

[69] F.H. [Frank Howes], 'London Concerts: Macnaghten-Lemare Concerts', *Musical Times* 75/1091 (January 1934): 75.

[70] 'Macnaghten-Lemare Concert', *Times*, 14 December 1933.

[71] R.C. [Richard Capell], 'Young Composer's Concert', *Daily Telegraph*, 12 December 1933.

title. She submitted this score to the BBC in late February.[72] Though a slight disappointment arrived when she received word that her String Quartet No. 1, which had been forwarded to the international jury for consideration for the upcoming ISCM Festival, had been rejected, she nevertheless had more than enough to keep her busy, as she copied parts in preparation for the première of her *Comedy Overture* on 7 March by Sir Dan Godfrey (1868–1939) and the Bournemouth Municipal Orchestra.

At the beginning of March, Maconchy travelled to Bournemouth to attend both the rehearsal and performance of her *Comedy Overture*. Constructed around three short animated themes developed contrapuntally, the overture exudes both wit and charm. The rehearsal and performance, which was also broadcast, proved disheartening as Maconchy's work proved too challenging for the orchestra – which was also woefully under-rehearsed – and its irascible conductor, as Maconchy recounted in a letter to Williams:

> the orchestra (as you had gathered on the wireless) really is very bad now – I believe it used to be better – and Dan Godfrey was in the middle of having a desperate row with them, and everything was at sixes & sevens, and everyone on the worst possible terms with each other. He just found fault & railed at them, and didn't attempt to get the best out of them. He was in an incredibly 'rattled' state all the time – and just kept saying 'I'm totally out of sympathy with your work – I don't like it' – and then 'what can one do with this damned orchestra', 'I've no time, no time – –'[.][73]

Despite an inadequate performance, the condescending critic in the *Manchester Guardian* nevertheless managed to find some nice things to say about it:

> This overture is a rough, raw-boned affair containing, however, a fair amount of material that is imaginative and even impressive in its own stark fashion. The style is mainly contrapuntal, and Miss Maconchy crashes through discords in the light-hearted manner befitting an adherent of the Hindemith school. When she has gathered experience she will find that assertions of individuality are not necessarily convincing because they are uttered as abruptly as possible.[74]

On 20 March, Maconchy's String Quartet No. 1 was included in 'A Light Classical Concert' broadcast,[75] and on 1 April, Boult conducted *The Land* in a BBC Regional Programme.[76] Just prior to the broadcasts, Maconchy had received a

[72] The work was rejected by the BBC in May. Owen Mase to Elizabeth Maconchy, 17 May 1934, BBC WAC EM1.

[73] Elizabeth Maconchy to Grace Williams, 19 March 1934.

[74] G.A.H., 'Yesterday's Broadcast Music', *Manchester Guardian*, 8 March 1934.

[75] The work was performed by the Macnaghten Quartet.

[76] The reason for the long delay in scheduling a broadcast for *The Land* was discussed in a memo Wynn sent to Herbage on 10 January 1934, to which Herbage responded on 11 January: 'I had a note early last Autumn to include the above work [*The Land*] in a Studio Concert conducted by Dr. Boult. At that time we were engaged in building programmes during the Promenade Season when the Studio Orchestra is, of course, insufficient to perform this piece, and since this Dr. Boult has undertaken practically

letter from Edward Godfrey Brown (1874–1955), the Director of Music for the BBC's Northern Ireland station in Belfast, asking if Maconchy would send some of her scores, as they were interested in devoting an entire forty-five-minute programme to her orchestral works. After further discussions, Maconchy sent the score and parts of her Piano Concerto, *The Land*, and her *Comedy Overture* to Godfrey Brown at the beginning of April. Though the broadcast was originally slated for the summer, Godfrey Brown sent a letter to Maconchy on 31 May stating that the concert was to be postponed until the autumn owing to changes in summer programming, which would contain much more light music.[77]

In July, Godfrey Brown conducted Maconchy's Suite for Chamber Orchestra with the Belfast Wireless Symphony Orchestra, which was broadcast over the Belfast station. After not having heard anything further regarding the concert, Maconchy sent a letter to Godfrey Brown at the beginning of September. He responded by stating that the concert was to be postponed indefinitely.[78] This was devastating news for Maconchy, as the six months she had reserved the works for the Belfast station prevented her from being able to send her orchestral works to other interested parties for consideration for the autumn and winter season, such as the New Chamber Orchestra in New York, which had expressed a strong interest in her Piano Concerto.[79]

Deeply frustrated, Maconchy explained her situation in a letter she sent to Boult inquiring if there might be any slight chance for the BBC to consider one of her orchestral works.[80] Though Maconchy's letter was well intentioned, Boult subsequently had the matter investigated and Godfrey Brown responded with a scathing letter to Maconchy in which he placed the blame squarely on her, arguing that he never suggested a performance of her Piano Concerto, despite evidence to the contrary. The most damning portion was the letter's conclusion:

> the main reason for my writing to you was my being under the impression you were a composer of much needed Irish music, but instead I found there was nothing Irish about your work. Nevertheless, on examination of the scores, I became interested, and looked forward to finding an occasion to perform some

no Studio Concerts except in the Sunday Orchestral series. It was, as a matter of fact, hoped that we would be able to include it in a Sunday Orchestral Concert, but a suitable opportunity did not occur. Unless, therefore, Dr. Boult would like to have it given as early as possible, even if by another conductor, it will probably have to wait until after the Symphony Concerts are finished when Dr. Boult will presumably again be conducting Studio Concerts.' A broadcast date was then subsequently arranged for 1 April 1934. Julian Herbage to Arthur Wynn, memo, 'The Land – Elizabeth Maconchy', 11 January 1934, BBC WAC EM1.

77 Elizabeth Maconchy to Adrian Boult, 21 September 1934; and Edward Godfrey Brown to Elizabeth Maconchy, 26 September 1934, BBC WAC EM1.

78 Ibid.

79 Ibid. The New Chamber Orchestra was conducted by Bernard Herrmann (1911–75). Though there is no correspondence between Maconchy and Herrmann, Maconchy did in fact send her Suite for Chamber Orchestra, which was subsequently performed.

80 Ibid.

of them. Had you waited a little longer, it was our intention, as I have said before, to give a programme of your compositions, and as proof of my interest, it must be remembered that I took very considerable pains to give on July 10th a performance in public of your Chamber Suite.

> All things considered, I feel it is a pity you should have written to me as you have done on September 21st, and to have troubled Dr. Boult. To the latter I am sending a copy of this letter.[81]

In a memo attached to the letter he sent to Boult, Godfrey Brown wrote, 'Instead of being disgruntled, we cannot help thinking that the lady is really already in our debt, and had she held her tongue – or rather pen – might have had more satisfaction.'[82]

Mase attempted to be diplomatic in handling the matter for Boult, and in a letter to Maconchy on 28 September, he wrote,

> Dr. Boult has passed to me your letter of 21st September. We have looked into the matter as far as possible and we are so sorry that this misunderstanding with Belfast has arisen. These necessary changes in intended arrangements are very trying for everyone and it is one of the drawbacks of our work that they do occur.
>
> As you say, it is rather late now, but if you would send the Overture which you especially hoped to get performed to me, I will place it before our people here and see if it be anyhow possible to perform it in a London broadcast before the end of the season. I am sure you will not interpret this as a promise, but only as a hope that we may be able to do something about it.
>
> May I say in conclusion that I am quite sure Mr. Godfrey Brown did not intend in any way to be discourteous. Occasionally these little frictions ahd [*sic*] cross-purposes arise quite unintentionally on either side.
>
> If you care to fall in with my suggestion to send the Overture to me, perhaps you would do so as soon as possible.[83]

Maconchy immediately sent Mase her *Comedy Overture*, and on 1 October, Mase forwarded the score to Aylmer Buesst along with a memo stating,

> The attached Comedy Overture by Elizabeth Maconchy has been sent in at my request owing to an unfortunate mix-up that she has had with Belfast concerning it. You will see by my letters that I have not committed us in any way, but so that no bad feeling should be left, it would be a happy thing if we could find a place to do it at a studio concert during this winter – it is very short.[84]

The following day, Buesst responded, 'Will you please bear this in mind; I think we can safely perform it.'[85] Shortly thereafter, the work was added to an orchestral concert slated for 28 December.[86]

81 Edward Godfrey Brown to Elizabeth Maconchy, 26 September 1934, BBC WAC EM1.

82 Edward Godfrey Brown to Mrs Beckett, 26 September 1934, BBC WAC EM1.

83 Owen Mase to Elizabeth Maconchy, 28 September 1934, BBC WAC EM1.

84 Music Executive [Owen Mase] to A.M.D. [Assistant Music Director, Aylmer Buesst], memo, 'Comedy Overture – Elizabeth Maconchy', 1 October 1934, BBC WAC EM1.

85 Ibid.

86 The BBC included Maconchy's *Comedy Overture* in an orchestral concert on 28 December 1934 with the BBC Orchestra, conducted by Vaughan Williams. The

In October, the Macnaghten Quartet played Maconchy's quartet in a concert produced by the Music Society at St John's Institute, Westminster. Titled 'A Programme of Ancient and Contemporary English Music', the programme also featured Purcell's Sonata in C Major, No. 7, short works for harpsichord by John Bull, Martin Peerson, and William Byrd, a group of songs by Warlock, as well as *Four English Lyrics* (1934) and Sonata for Two Violins in A Major (1930) by Ernest John Moeran (1894–1950). The concert title certainly encouraged comparisons to be made, as Bonavia noted in his review in the *Daily Telegraph*: 'Elizabeth Maconchy's string quartet breaks away abruptly not only from the old English, but also from the nineteenth century Continental tradition. It is an essay in the futuristic idiom of modern Germany and, as such, quite successful.'[87] Other critics, however, were far less kind. In the *Musical Times*, Scott denounced the work as:

> a disturbing human document vitalised with the energy of despair and expressed with a nervous, forceful technique. It left an indescribable impression of tragedy – perhaps because no solution was offered for the tremendous questions raised. Beethoven and Wagner never rested till they had carried their tragedies upward to the height at which recompense is found.[88]

Evans's review in the *Liverpool Post and Mercury* was equally harsh, as he described the quartet as 'vigorously modern ... full of ideas, but so pugnacious in spirit that one involuntarily thought of Kipling's remark concerning the female of the species'.[89]

On 4 February 1935, Maconchy's *Great Agrippa, or the Inky Boys* was premièred, without choreography, at a Macnaghten-Lemare concert that also included Orlando Gibbons's Pavan and Galliard, Byrd's *The Leaves be Greene: A 'Browning' for Strings*, Lutyens's *The Dying of Tanneguy du Bois* (1934), Williams's Suite for Chamber Orchestra (1932), and Buxtehude's Passacaglia, arranged by

programme also included Grace Williams's *Two Psalms for Soprano and Chamber Orchestra*, R.O. Morris's Concertino, Robin Milford's *Prelude on St. Columba* and *May in the Greenwood*, as well as Vaughan Williams's *Five Mystical Songs*. The programme was reviewed by J.A. Westrup in the *Daily Telegraph*, who remarked that Maconchy's work 'shows the influence of Vaughan Williams, but nothing like his forcefulness or originality. The composer tends to overwork a few rather gawky tunes. The orchestration as far as one could tell over the wireless, showed signs of inexperience.' J.A.W. [Jack Allan Westrup], 'Concert of British Music: Two Women Composers', *Daily Telegraph*, 29 December 1934.

87 F.B. [Ferruccio Bonavia], 'New English Music', *Daily Telegraph*, 24 October 1934.

88 M.M.S. [Marion Scott], 'Chamber Music of the Month', *Musical Times* 75/1102 (December 1934): 1129.

89 E.E. [Edwin Evans], 'Novelties in Music', *Liverpool Post and Mercury*, 24 October 1934. Evans is referencing Kipling's 1911 anti-suffragist poem 'The Female of the Species'. For further discussion of Kipling's views, see Kaori Nagai, 'Kipling and Gender', in Howard J. Booth (ed.), *The Cambridge Companion to Rudyard Kipling* (Cambridge: Cambridge University Press, 2011), 66–79.

Lutyens. Based upon Heinrich Hoffman's 'Die Geschichte von den schwarzen Buben' from *Der Struwwelpeter* (1845), *Great Agrippa* is a cautionary children's tale in which three boys are punished by Agrippa – St Nicholas in the original version – for harassing a black child. Outraged by the boys' behaviour, Agrippa decides to teach them a lesson by dipping them in his inkwell. Maconchy arranged the short ballet, which was intended to last a brief ten to eleven minutes, for five dancers and fourteen instruments and percussion. The concert performance of Maconchy's ballet left the critics divided. Scott found the work impressive, writing in her review for the *Musical Times*, 'Miss Maconchy has certainly got the black and white non-humanism of "Struwwelpeter" into her music, and its style is so different from her earlier compositions that it heightens respect for the versatility of her invention.'[90] While the critic in the *Times* referred to the music as 'both witty and cheerful',[91] Westrup was more critical in his review in the *Daily Telegraph*, noting that although the music was 'pert and lively', it was also inconsistent, as he further added, 'She seems at times, however, to have mistaken emphasis for vigour, and the thematic material is rather thin, a weakness which the ingenious scoring did not quite conceal.'[92]

Another critic of the work was Vaughan Williams, who wrote in a letter to Maconchy,

> I can't help feeling that in Agrippa – there are certain stravynskyesque [*sic*] clichés which are not really you & are not worthy of you – they rather stood out & prevented my listening properly to the tunes – but I dare say a 2^{d} time the good w^{d} come out & the framing fall into its proper background – but still I do feel that you are capable of so much finer *thought* than that Russian Monkey-brain & that you injure your real self by condescending to use any of his monkey-tricks.
> – But everyone else (even the Times) seemed to have liked it. So you must forgive the old & ancient uncle for being stupid.[93]

While Vaughan Williams does not elaborate upon what exactly he found to be 'stravynskyesque', he was likely referring to the percussive and repetitive rhythm that permeates much of the score. In a letter to Maconchy, Williams offered greater insight into their erstwhile teacher's criticisms, writing,

> Now Uncle Ralph is a dear, we all know, but he's got a great bee in his bonnet about one thing – he always turns his deaf ear to works which are brilliantly effective. Think of what he said about 'Sacre'! – & even worse things about 'Wozzeck'
> I know they are far removed from his own particular genre & perhaps it is only natural that they mean little to him. He is rhythmically so far removed from them. – & I think perhaps he is rhythmically very far removed from Agrippa!! that is probably what upset him. He couldn't really have heard it as music or he wouldn't have said he so much preferred the Overture because musically I

90 M.M.S. [Marion Scott], 'London Concerts: Macnaghten-Lemare Concerts', *Musical Times* 76/1105 (March 1935): 261.

91 'Macnaghten-Lemare Concert', *Times*, 8 February 1935.

92 J.A.W. [Jack Allan Westrup], 'Women Composers: Elizabeth Maconchy's New Work', *Daily Telegraph*, 5 February 1935.

93 Ralph Vaughan Williams to Elizabeth Maconchy, February 1935, VWL 530.

> find the Overture & Agrippa have a lot in common. I feel Agrippa scores over the Overture inasmuch as there is so much more invention & inspiration in the orchestration.
>
> ...You musn't bother your head any more, my girl, about writing safe scores. It doesn't become you. Besides it isn't necessary: your difficult things always come off best.[94]

Though attention was often paid to the prominent role of women in the Macnaghten-Lemare Concerts, several of the reviews of this particular concert were more derogatory in tone than usual.[95] McNaught, who titled his review in the *Evening News* 'The Mind of a Woman Composer: Three Concert Studies', was a work of blatant objectification:

> Miss Iris Lemare's orchestral concert at the Ballet Club Theatre last night was an interesting study of the young female mind of to-day.
>
> This organ, when it takes up musical composition, works in mysterious ways. No lip-stick, silk stocking, or saucily-titled hat adorns the music evolved from its recesses.
>
> All is grim, intense, and cerebral. Sibelius himself is not more bleak and stark. [...]
>
> The problem taken on by Miss Elizabeth Maconchy ... was half solved by humour, even though the humour was knotty.
>
> ... Her music seemed to deal less with the characters of the book than with their complexes.[96]

Never one to be outdone, Lambert's review in the *Sunday Referee*, which appeared on 10 February, gave McNaught a run for his money. Titled 'Women Composers are so forceful', Lambert's 'review' offered an unsubtle exposition vividly expressing his contempt for women artists:

> Why is it that women artists are always so determined to be forceful? In the art of the novel, it is true, a certain womanliness is cultivated and even flaunted. There the 'feminine instinct' and the 'quiet touch' are allowed full play, and the authoresses, to quote Wyndham Lewis, 'peep' at their characters.
>
> But in the visual and audible arts this is not so. Give a woman a chunk of granite or a few trombones and she immediately proceeds to out-Epstein Epstein and out-Holbrooke Holbrooke. [...]
>
> Miss Elizabeth Maconchy's 'Great Agrippa,' a short ballet based on 'Shock-Headed Peter,' at least succeeded in what it set out to do. ... [I]t is very well scored, and was given an effective performance under Miss Iris Lemare, with Adolph Hallis at the piano.
>
> Miss Maconchy has in her chamber music shown considerable talent and it is a pity that in this work she should revert to the conventionally spiky and short-winded manner of post-War ballet music.

94 Grace Williams to Elizabeth Maconchy, [after 11 February 1935].

95 See Sophie Fuller, '"Putting the BBC and T. Beecham to Shame"'.

96 W.McN. [William McNaught], 'The Mind of A Woman Composer: Three Concert Studies', *Evening News*, 5 February 1935.

> This grotesque style, though usually attributed to Stravinsky, really owes more to Bartok. Unfortunately, Bartok's followers imitate only the superficial asperities of his style which have nothing to do with his essential austerity.[97]

As Fuller has suggested, the heavy criticism that this concert received in the press was likely due to the fact that all of the new compositions were by women, which only occurred twice in the history of the Macnaghten-Lemare Concerts.[98] Though it was far from unusual for London audiences to attend concerts with women orchestras, conductors, and composers, the number of women involved in the Macnaghten-Lemare series garnered considerable attention in the press from the start, with Cecil Gray declaring the second Macnaghten-Lemare concert on 14 December 1931 'a decidedly feminist affair'.[99] Though neither Lutyens, Macnaghten, Lemare, nor Maconchy thought that they were engaging in anything overtly feminist (after all, only 42 percent of the new works performed were by women), the label 'woman composer', was a title that many, including Maconchy, would try to distance themselves from.[100]

While Maconchy's gender was frequently pointed out in reviews in her early career, it was often construed as praise, with Maconchy's success situated as evidence to bolster the claim that women had achieved equality with men. In a discussion of Dame Ethel Smyth and opera in Britain, Lambert quipped in 1933, 'That a composer like Elizabeth Maconchy gets quite as many performances as any male composer of her generation points, I think, to the fact that the undoubted neglect of Dame Ethel Smyth's work was due not to any sex prejudice but to the disadvantages of being an English operatic composer at the beginning of this century.'[101] As Maconchy began to feature more prominently in concerts and broadcasts, however, attacks based on her gender grew more frequent, and while the sexist vitriol espoused by Lambert and McNaught was far from new, the shift of critics such as Evans – who had previously avoided using Maconchy's gender to disparage her music – began to do so more freely, as exemplified by his reference to Kipling.

In late February, Maconchy travelled to Edinburgh, as Sir Donald Tovey had included *The Land* in one of the Reid Symphony's concerts on the 28th. Although Tovey was also interested in her Symphony, financial constraints prevented him from tackling the work.[102] Nevertheless, Tovey devoted a substantial amount of time to rehearsing *The Land* with the orchestra and his thoughts on the work are described in his eloquent and insightful programme notes, in which he declared, 'Miss Maconchy, like Beethoven, achieves *Ausdruck*

[97] Constant Lambert, 'Women composers are so forceful', *Sunday Referee*, 10 February 1935.

[98] See Fuller, '"Putting the BBC and T. Beecham to Shame"', 400. The concert series ran from 1931–7, and was later resumed in the 1950s.

[99] Cited in ibid., 397.

[100] Ibid., 400–1; Maconchy, 'A Composer Speaks', 29.

[101] Constant Lambert, 'Operatic Extracts', *Sunday Referee*, 24 December 1933.

[102] Donald Tovey to Elizabeth Maconchy, 1 January 1935, private collection.

der Empfindung.'[103] In addition to *The Land*, the Reid Symphony Orchestra's programme included Beethoven's Fifth Symphony, Brahms's Variations on a Theme of Haydn, and Schumann's *Manfred* Overture.

Once again, *The Land* garnered positive comment from the musical press. While attention continued to be drawn to Maconchy's gender, the reviews were far from disparaging in tone. Though the commentator in the *Scotsman* began by rehashing the tiresome woman composer question, this critic's comments on *The Land* were nevertheless laudatory:

> Why, apart from song-writers, there should be so few women composers, when the sex has achieved such distinction in other fields of musical effort, is a subject which is rich in potentialities of no doubt rather inconclusive discussion. It is only very rarely, however, that the name of a woman composer appears in a concert programme. … [In *The Land*] Miss Maconchy has attacked the problem of registering these impressions [of Sackville-West's poem] in orchestral tone with freshness and obvious sincerity. The stark quality of a snow-bound winter day, the animation of bright, blowy spring weather, the slower movement of a summer day, and the animation of the time of harvest are all made out for the listener provided with the necessary clues. Sir Donald Tovey's renderings of the movements were rewarded with applause which brought the composer to the platform to bow her acknowledgements.[104]

The perceptive critic at the *Edinburgh Evening News* not only praised Maconchy's work, but also hinted, albeit subtly, at the inherent disadvantages she faced in a world that was still far from accepting women on equal terms with men: 'It is rare to have the opportunity to hear a work by a woman composer, and on this score alone Miss Maconchy's music would find acceptance, but her gifts are of such a magnitude as to compel admiration apart from any considerations other than those that determine a good composer.'[105]

March proved to be busier than February, as Maconchy's string quartet was performed by the Macnaghten Quartet at the Aeolian Hall on the 5th in a programme consisting of Haydn's String Quartet in B-flat Major, op. 76, No. 4, two fantasias by Purcell, and Brahms's String Quartet in A Minor, op. 51, No. 2. In the *Musical Times*, Scott quipped, '[Maconchy's string quartet] has so lately been discussed in these columns that it suffices to say it strongly impressed its hearers at this concert and that the Macnaghten people have a special talent for the interpretation of British music.'[106] The *Times* was slightly less enthusiastic, with the anonymous critic remarking,

> Elizabeth Maconchy's Quartet was given a place of honour between Purcell and Brahms. She is still in the stage of conscious modernism oppressed by the duty of seeking discord and ensuing it. Possibly Purcell was in the same stage when he wrote the opening of his Fantasia in C minor and insisted over-much on F sharps

103 Tovey, '*The Land*', in *The Classics of Music*, 132.

104 'Reid Concerts: Miss Elizabeth Maconchy', *Scotsman*, 1 March 1935.

105 'Reid Orchestra', *Edinburgh Evening News*, 1 March 1935.

106 M.M.S. [Marion Scott], 'Chamber Music of the Month', *Musical Times* 76/1106 (April 1935): 359.

> against F naturals and the like. She may outgrow it as well as he. Her ideas are definite if crude, and sometimes when the harmonic obsession becomes ameliorated she can produce moments of unaffected beauty. The work was interesting for itself and for what may come of it.[107]

McNaught was the most critical yet again, as he used Maconchy's work to go off on another diatribe against women composers in a review titled, 'A Woman Composer "Goes Modern": Grim String Quartet at Aeolian Hall':

> It has been remarked before that the young women who take up musical composition in the modern vein are more downright and unflinching about it than the men. It is not really so, but one notices it the more, coming from them.
>
> A typical case is Miss Elizabeth Maconchy's string quartet of two years ago [...].
>
> There are definite outstanding ideas, largely sardonic and rhythmic, to which the trenchant language gives a point. ...The [Purcell] Fantasias are, in other ways, admirable music, and peculiarly satisfying to the ears of to-day. Whether people will be saying the same of Miss Maconchy's music 250 years hence no man can tell.[108]

Ten days later, Maconchy's *Two Motets for Double Chorus* was broadcast over the BBC in a programme that included Warlock's *Three Carols* and van Dieren's *Sinfonia per Orchestra, Soloisti, e Coro*, op. 6. The celebrated choral conductor Leslie Woodgate (1900–61) conducted the BBC Wireless Chorus in this performance of Maconchy's motets. Aware of the work's high level of difficulty, Woodgate had asked Maconchy for the parts several months ahead of time so that he could begin working on them with the Chorus.[109] Woodgate's investment in Maconchy's work was reflected in the glowing reviews it received in the press. The critic in *Musical Opinion* remarked, 'By far the most interesting music came from Elizabeth Maconchy. ...This essay in choral writing shows real ability.'[110] The broadcast even impressed Westrup, who wrote in the *Daily Telegraph*, 'The style seemed a little heavy and cumbrous, but the firm grasp of choral technique and the ability to say something worth while in traditional tonality made these works a significant achievement.'[111]

While the debate about modern music was persistent throughout the interwar years, the deaths of Elgar, Holst, and Delius fuelled tremendous anxiety about the future of British music and the place of modernism within it. As Arnold Whittall has argued in 'British Music Thirty Years Ago' (1964), citing the *Musical Times* in 1934:

> [1934] might therefore be fairly described as a year of transition – between generations, if not between musical styles. Transitional was not a word in much favour with the critics of the time, however. ...There is an evident doubt as to the direction which British music is taking; doubt as to the direction it should take.

107 'Recitals of the Week: Macnaghten Quartet', *Times*, 8 March 1935.

108 W.McN. [William McNaught], 'A Woman Composer "Goes Modern": Grim String Quartet at Aeolian Hall', *Evening News*, 6 March 1935.

109 Elizabeth Maconchy to P. Philips, 2 January 1935, BBC WAC EM1.

110 N.V.D., 'B.B.C. Concert of Contemporary Music', *Musical Opinion*, April 1935, clipping in Maconchy's first scrapbook, SHC.

111 J.A.W. [Jack Allan Westrup], 'A Chinese Symphony', *Daily Telegraph*, 16 March 1935.

> The most positive point arises from the feeling that the only *honest* musical language for a British composer is tonal romanticism. The romantic era represented the apotheosis of tonality: the one cannot be abandoned without the other, and to abandon both would not merely be revolutionary – it would be anti-musical.[112]

According to Whittall, several patterns clearly emerge within the press during the period: any work that was perceived to be anti-emotional and too intellectual was to be viewed with suspicion. If a composition veered too far in the other direction, displaying tendencies deemed too energetic, it was also met with suspicion, as Whittall states: 'Even if you experiment, the assumption is, you will only succeed if you ignore the unsteady, precipitate Europeans, the anti-romantics and atonalists.'[113]

Viewed within this context, Westrup could thus praise the inventiveness of Maconchy's *Two Motets for Double Chorus* because the works stayed within the safe limits of tonality. Similar reasoning can be applied to the reception of Maconchy's Quintet for Oboe and Strings. Though the work was criticised for being too intellectual, its lyricism – a characteristic perceived to be inherently English – enabled some critics to offer praise and overlook some of the more suspiciously modern elements of the quintet. As for Maconchy's string quartet, some critics, such as Scott, condemned the work for its lack of emotion, a characteristic that again veered too close to the territory of continental modernism.

At the beginning of 1935, Maconchy was informed that her *Prelude, Interlude and Fugue for Two Violins* (1934) had been selected for the upcoming ISCM Festival in Karlsbad in September.[114] The other British works selected were an overture by Lennox Berkeley (1903–89) and *Dialectic* for string quartet by Alan Bush (1900–95). Two months before the start of the festival, the city council of Karlsbad announced that financial difficulties meant that they would no longer be able to host the festival. This was a complete shock to the ISCM, and especially its Czech delegates, who learned of the city council's decision only when it appeared in the press. Financial concerns, however, were merely an excuse to cover a much more insidious agenda, as the cancellation conveniently coincided with the shift in political power after the Sudeten German Party's success in the May parliamentary elections.[115] Initially, it was unclear as to whether the festival would take place at all. After much debate, it was subsequently relocated to Prague with some minor programme alterations.[116]

112 Arnold Whittall, 'British Music Thirty Years Ago', *Musical Times* 105/1453 (March 1964): 186.

113 Ibid.

114 On 24 June, the BBC included Maconchy's *Prelude, Interlude and Fugue for Two Violins* in a broadcast of works written for two violins that also included Moeran's Sonata for Two Violins and *Andantino* from Honegger's Sonatina for Two Violins, performed by André Mangeot and Macnaghten.

115 Anne C. Shreffler, 'The International Society for Contemporary Music and Its Political Context (Prague, 1935)', in Jessica C.E. Gienow-Hecht (ed.), *Music and International History in the Twentieth Century* (New York: Berghahn, 2015), 62–5.

116 Ibid. As Shreffler discusses, the relocation of the festival was highly politicised. When Karlsbad fell through, the Czech delegates tried to relocate the festival to Prague. After negotiations in Prague failed on 6 August, the Soviet Union, via Hanns Eisler, who was

Maconchy travelled to Prague for the festival, where she was warmly greeted by many of her old friends. She also met with Jirák and showed him a new work she had completed titled *Divertissement for Twelve Instruments* (1935).[117] Maconchy's *Prelude, Interlude and Fugue* was played by André Mangeot (1883–1970) and Orrea Pernel (1906–93) at the festival's second chamber concert, that included a string quartet by Sándor Veress, Raymond Chevreuille's String Quartet No. 4, Webern's *Concerto for Nine Instruments*, op. 24, Sándor Jemnitz's Sonata for harp, op. 34, Vladimir Vogel's Chaconne and Etude-Toccata for piano, and Alexander Moyzes's Wind Quintet, op. 17.

Prelude, Interlude and Fugue is a work exhibiting extreme economy: the programme organisers knew what they were doing when they put it in the same concert with the Webern Concerto. The correspondent for the *Times* wrote that the work was 'received with something like an ovation',[118] with Bush describing the work in the *Musical Times* as 'brilliantly written for the medium'.[119] The work also impressed the local critics, with glowing reviews appearing in *Venkov*, *Pragger Presse*, and *Nárdoní Osvobození*.

Shortly after Maconchy returned to Britain, she was prominently featured in the fashionable Czech ladies magazine *Eva*,[120] and on 18 October, her *Divertissement for Twelve Instruments* was included in a Czech radio broadcast of English music, conducted by Czech composer and conductor Otakar Jeremiáš (1892–1962).[121] The impact that the ISCM Festival had on increasing Maconchy's reputation abroad was significant, and in the years that followed, the popularity of her music increased steadily in both Prague and Kraków.

---

employed at the Comintern's International Music Office in Moscow, offered to host the festival in November, promising to cover the cost of all travel and lodging expenses for the festival's delegates. E.J. Dent – the ISCM's president – was quick to decline the offer, citing the fact that the Soviet Union did not have a national section. The threat of having the festival moved to the Soviet Union ended up encouraging the negotiations to resume, as Shreffler writes: 'A representative of no less than the prime minister called a meeting of the heads of all the relevant ministries and artistic organizations, at which it was decided to hold the ISCM festival in Prague after all. The political pressures on the Czech government were clear. To allow the festival to be snatched up by the USSR after being rejected by the Sudeten Germans of Karlsbad would look too much like fleeing into the arms of Moscow' (65). Owing to the lack of adequate rehearsals, the third orchestral concert, which included Berkeley's *Overture*, had to be cancelled. Alan Bush, 'The I.S.C.M. Festival at Prague', *Musical Times* 76/1112 (October 1935): 940.

117 Elizabeth Maconchy to Kenneth Wright, 27 February 1936, BBC WAC EM1.

118 'The Prague Festival', *Times*, 14 September 1935.

119 Alan Bush, 'The I.S.C.M. Festival at Prague', *Musical Times* 75/1112 (October 1935): 941.

120 Maconchy was featured in the 15 September 1935 issue of *Eva*.

121 Clipping from *World Radio* in Maconchy's second scrapbook, SHC. In a letter to Wright, Maconchy noted that Jeremiáš took the work far too slow. Elizabeth Maconchy to Kenneth Wright, 27 February 1936, BBC WAC EM1.

5

A Growing Reputation, 1936–9

As a result of Maconchy's successful debut at the ISCM Festival, her music began to feature more prominently both at home and abroad. On 20 January 1936, Pártos Ödön (1907–77) and Salgó Sándor (1909–2007) performed her *Prelude, Interlude, and Fugue* in Budapest.[1] A mere seven days later, André Mangeot and Beatrice Huckell (1913–98) performed the work at a Lemare concert.[2] This British performance left the critics divided. While the progressive Michel Dimitri Calvocoressi praised Maconchy for her skilful writing in *Musical Opinion*, the critic in the *Observer* found the work to be monotonous.[3] Lambert offered his typically misogynist opinion that the work embodied an 'uncompromising and anti-sensual attitude towards musical texture'.[4] The critic in the *Times* arrived at a similar conclusion: 'If she could overcome her dutiful devotion to harshness Miss Maconchy might write something worth having.'[5] McNaught, on the other hand, showed remarkable restraint, declaring that the instrumental works in the programme simply 'belonged to the department of modern research, experiment, and labour towards new artistic planes, and could not be sympathetically listened to or reviewed except by one of the same conviction'.[6]

In the late 1930s Maconchy's fraught relationship with the BBC continued, with occasional improvements that were often followed by more setbacks. Though a broadcast of her Quintet for Oboe and Strings was scheduled for 27 January, it was abruptly cancelled on the 24th owing to the recent death

1 Salgó Sándor was a Hungarian Jewish composer, violinist, and conductor who emigrated to the United States in 1939, and served on the music faculty at Stanford from 1949 to 1974. See Robert P. Commanday, 'In Memoriam Sandor Salgo', *San Francisco Classical Voice*: http://www.sfcv.org/arts_revs/sandor_tribute_1_23_07.php. Pártos Ödön was also a Hungarian Jewish composer and violinist, who studied with Kodály at the Budapest Conservatory. In 1938, he moved to Palestine. William Y. Elias, 'Partos, Oedoen', *Grove Music Online*, 2001, https://doi.org/10.1093/gmo/9781561592630.article.20985 [accessed 6 September 2020].

2 Mangeot and Huckell gave several performances of *Prelude, Interlude and Fugue* during the year, including one in Paris in May.

3 M.-D. Calvocoressi, *Musical Opinion*, March 1936, clipping in Maconchy's second scrapbook; 'Lemare Concert', *Observer*, 2 February 1936.

4 Constant Lambert, 'Musical Matters', *Sunday Referee*, 2 February 1936.

5 'Lemare Concert', *Times*, 31 January 1936.

6 W.McN. [William McNaught], 'Lemare Concerts', *Musical Times* 77/1117 (March 1936): 265.

of His Majesty George V, who had died four days earlier. Shortly thereafter, the broadcast was rescheduled for 23 March.[7] On 13 February, Maconchy was informed that a broadcast had finally been arranged for her Piano Concerto on 20 March with Harriet Cohen (1895–1967) as soloist and Boult conducting.[8] A broadcast of another work followed shortly after, with Lemare conducting *Great Agrippa, or the Inky Boys* on 15 April in a programme that also included Vaughan Williams's Overture to *The Wasps*, Darnton's Concerto for Viola and String Orchestra, and Jacob's *Passacaglia on a well-known theme*.[9]

While Maconchy was on holiday in Switzerland in April, she received a letter from the BBC, stating that Paul Helsinger, the principal oboist of the Düsseldorf Orchestra, had written to inquire about her quintet. Helsinger asked if Maconchy would be willing to loan the manuscript to him so that he could copy it. Maconchy agreed to have the manuscript sent to Helsinger, who performed the work in Düsseldorf later that year.[10]

Toward the end of August, Maconchy received a letter from Wright regarding the status of her *Divertissement for Twelve Instruments* (1935), which she had submitted to the BBC in February:

> I am sorry that we have kept your 'Divertissement for twelve instruments' so long. The reason was that there seemed some likelihood that we might be able to include it in our Contemporary Season 1936–7, but I am afraid we now feel that there will not be room for it, and I think, therefore, that you ought to have the score back without further delay. I need scarcely assure you that if and when you have other manuscripts for our consideration we shall be only too happy to receive them.[11]

Initially, the work had received a positive assessment from composer Edmund Rubbra (1901–86), who was employed as a reader by the BBC. Rubbra, who was a tough critic of other composers' music, declared:

> Excellently controlled & well-moulded music. But the question arises to the value of the underlying ideas – personally I think the interest is more intellectual than emotional, using intellectual in the sense of a mathematical ordering of agreed upon groups of notes, such as the clash of minor & major in the 1st movement.
>
> This could be seen again I think.[12]

[7] Wright sent a telegraph to Maconchy that read: 'Much regret chamber concert next Monday cancelled owing special national orchestral and choral programmes.' Kenneth Wright to Elizabeth Maconchy, undated, BBC WAC EM1.

[8] Maurice Johnstone to Elizabeth Maconchy, 13 Feburary 1936, BBC WAC EM1. The primary reason for the long delay in arranging a broadcast for the Piano Concerto was Cohen's health, as she had been ill and required surgery. Cohen expressed an interest in Maconchy's Piano Concerto in 1933 and the idea of approaching the Hallé Orchestra was raised; however, nothing proceeded further. See Ralph Vaughan Williams to Elizabeth Maconchy, [23 September 1933], VWL 1097.

[9] 'Wednesday National Programme', *Radio Times*, 10 April 1936.

[10] St George Philips to Elizabeth Maconchy, 6 April 1936; and Elizabeth Maconchy to St George Phillips, 13 April 1936, BBC WAC EM1.

[11] Kenneth Wright to Elizabeth Maconchy, 28 August 1936, BBC WAC EM1.

[12] Report of Maconchy's *Divertissement*, c. 21 July 1936, BBC WAC EM1.

B.J. Dale remarked, 'I, too, feel that the composer is so preoccupied with theories that she has little time to be interesting. In view of her reputation, a Contemporary programme would appear to be indicated for this work – if anything at all.'[13] Waddington simply added 'agreed'.[14] While these remarks suggest that the majority of the panel was in favour of giving the work a hearing, Bliss's condemnation of the work ultimately sealed its fate.[15]

Though the rejection of her *Divertissement* was a disappointment, it was not long before she had another person interested in the work. Shortly after the broadcast of her Oboe Quintet in March, Maconchy received a letter from Franciszek Nierychło (1905–77), an oboe player and the directing secretary of the Kraków Chamber Music Society, inquiring if she might be able to send him a copy of the score.[16] After several months of correspondence – all conducted in fractured German – Nierychło broached the topic of arranging an entire concert of her chamber works in Kraków. At his request, Maconchy sent copies of several of her chamber works, including the recently rejected *Divertissement*, which Nierychło was very eager to have performed.[17]

The performance of Maconchy's Piano Concerto at the Proms in September elicited a typically mixed reaction from critics. While Howes praised the work, remarking that, in spite of its age, the work 'seemed nevertheless to have survival value, partly because the technical problem of the place of the piano in the ensemble had been so cleverly solved',[18] the critic in the *Observer* was far less generous:

> on Wednesday there was a large assembly of composers to hear Elizabeth Maconchy's Concerto for Pianoforte and Chamber Orchestra. […]
>
> Miss Maconchy's concerto … had not the advantage of so persuasive a soloist, and we were left to perceive clearly its lack of great and sweeping thoughts, and to feel that there was nothing distinctively human in it. The slow movement was delicate; the rest, just sprightly. There are works by Miss Maconchy in

[13] Ibid.

[14] Ibid.

[15] Ibid. Bliss wrote, 'I do not find sufficient musical interest to warrant performance – the first movement allegro scherzando is really very feeble.'

[16] Owing to his reported involvement in the Third Silesian Uprising, Nierychło was arrested and later sent to Auschwitz in 1940. In addition to working as a Kapo in the prisoners' kitchen, he conducted the Auschwitz I orchestra. Nierychło was a highly controversial figure, with his cruelty noted in the testimonies of those who worked under him in the kitchen. In May 1944, he was released from Auschwitz after he signed the Volksliste. Following the war, he was arrested and sentenced to twelve years' imprisonment. See Jacek Lachendro, 'The Orchestras in KL Auschwitz', *Auschwitz Studies* 27 (2015): 5–174.

[17] Though Nierychło planned to arrange the concert for the autumn of 1936, it was later pushed back to February 1937. Franciszek Nierychło to Elizabeth Maconchy, 17 October 1936, SHC.

[18] F.H. [Frank Howes], 'The Promenade Concerts', *Musical Times* 77/1124 (October 1936): 937.

which she flouts her modernity with more aggression than here; the concerto is empty, not unpleasant.[19]

In December, Maconchy travelled to Edinburgh, as Tovey had programmed her Piano Concerto in a Reid Symphony Orchestra concert. This was a slightly different arrangement than the one Tovey initially had in mind, having written earlier in the year of his desire to play the work himself. Tovey's gout may have prevented this arrangement from coming to fruition, and they later settled on Cohen as the soloist.[20] Maconchy enjoyed working with Tovey immensely and considered her visits with him to be among some of the highlights of her early career. She recalled Tovey as being 'steeped in music', and perceived a similarity between him and one of her other mentors: '[Tovey was] dedicated wholly to music – like Holst.'[21] On one occasion, the two even spent an afternoon playing a Mozart concerto on two pianos.[22] Though Tovey was encouraging, he could also be highly critical, as exemplified in a letter he sent Maconchy while he was considering her Piano Concerto for the December concert in which he criticised her treatment of the piano:

> As compared with the orchestral work we did last year, I have the impression that your notions of the pianoforte are inhibiting your imagination. Your treatment of the instrument oscillates like Rachmaninoff's between the chopsticks notion implied in the word "Hammerklavier" and an excessively lean and ascetic economy of notes in not very sustained melody accompanied by thin arpeggios. I don't for a moment suppose that you really believe in the chopsticks theory. I tried to expose its fallacy once for all in the Ass. Bored edition of the Beethoven sonatas, but certain Stuffed Owls of the higher sort ruled out my illustration as undignified. The chopsticks theory of the pianoforte asserts that the instrument should continually display the nature of a hammer hitting a string. … The accident that the strings of the pianoforte are set in motion by the impact of a hammer is as relevant to the sound of it as the fact that plum-pudding is boiled in a cloth; and the chopsticks theory of pianoforte style amounts to the inference that the proper treatment of a plum-pudding is to throw away the pudding and do your best to digest the cloth.[23]

In addition to Maconchy's Concerto, the Reid Symphony Orchestra concert also included Bax's *Saga Fragment*, Schumann's Overture, Scherzo, and Finale, op. 52, Mendelssohn's *Hebrides* Overture, and Haydn's Second Symphony. The performance of Maconchy's Concerto in Edinburgh made a far better impression on the critics than the Proms performance, with the critic in the *Evening Dispatch* praising it highly:

19 'Promenade Concerts', *Observer*, 6 September 1936.

20 Donald Tovey to Elizabeth Maconchy, 29 February 1936, private collection.

21 Elizabeth Maconchy, draft of talk titled 'To the Classic Club at Chelmsford', 17 February 1954, SHC.

22 Ibid.

23 Donald Tovey to Elizabeth Maconchy, 29 February 1936, private collection. Also quoted in Doctor, 'Intersecting Circles: The Early Careers of Elizabeth Maconchy, Elisabeth Lutyens, and Grace Williams', 99.

> Miss Maconchy's work is definitely modern in spirit, and although its atonal tendencies preclude it from coming under the category of having immediate appeal, one feels that after a second and third hearing its attractive qualities would become increasingly apparent. There is considerable skill in the treatment of both piano and orchestra, particularly in the graceful slow movement and animated finale.[24]

The critic in the *Edinburgh Evening News* noted 'the pleasure derivable from this complex composition depends upon a sympathy with advanced tendencies in musical art'. Both commentators nevertheless noted that the work received a warm reception from the audience.[25]

At the beginning of 1937, Maconchy was informed that her Second String Quartet had been selected for the ISCM Festival in Paris in June. Prior to the festival, the work was premièred by the Brosa Quartet at a Lemare concert on 1 February in a programme that included van Dieren's String Quartet op. 15, No. 3, and Mozart's Quartet in C Minor.[26] Whereas Maconchy's First Quartet was constructed as four self-contained movements with each having their own distinctive thematic material, in her Second Quartet, Maconchy sought to connect each movement through a series of short motifs: oscillating major and minor seconds, and the alternation of whole tones and semitones to construct a minor third. The first movement begins with a drone in the cello that is followed by the entrance of the viola, which oscillates between C and D, before expanding in bar 2 (Example 5.1) as the melody unfolds gradually over the course of the movement.

The second movement begins with the same motific material as the first. Set to a much more lively rhythm, the time signature alternates back and forth between 5/8 and 4/8 every other bar (Example 5.2). Maconchy repeats this concise opening theme, gradually building the dynamic energy as she combines it with the previously introduced motifs. The second movement leads directly into the third, which features a melody in the viola built upon minor thirds that is repeatedly interrupted by the agitated entrance of the violin and cello.

This back and forth exchange of motifs grows more persistent until it finally builds to a climax and suddenly dies down to reveal a lush, romantic melody in the violin (Example 5.3) that vividly recalls Vaughan Williams's *Riders to the Sea* (Example 5.4). The violin and cello then revert to their previous agitated exchange, with the lush melody resurfacing at the end of the movement.

[24] 'Miss Elizabeth Maconchy's Piano Concerto', *Evening Dispatch*, 4 December 1936.

[25] 'Reid Orchestra: Complex Examples of Modern Composition', *Edinburgh Evening News*, 4 December 1936.

[26] The Brosa Quartet (1925–39) comprised Spanish violinist Antonio Brosa (1st violin), Norman Chapple (2nd violin), Leonard Rubens (viola), and Livio Mannucci (cello). Mozart's Quartet in C Minor was a last-minute replacement for Britten's Suite for Violin and Piano, op. 6, which was originally included in the programme and later withdrawn 'on account of a bereavement'. See Fuller '"Putting the BBC and T Beecham to shame"', 414.

Example 5.1. Maconchy, String Quartet No. 2, mvt. I, opening.
Published by Alfred Lengnick & Co., a division of Universal Music Publishing Group.
Reproduced by permission of Hal Leonard Europe BV (Italy).

Example 5.2. Maconchy, String Quartet No. 2, mvt. II, opening.
Published by Alfred Lengnick & Co., a division of Universal Music Publishing Group.
Reproduced by permission of Hal Leonard Europe BV (Italy).

Maconchy's allusion to Vaughan Williams's highly octatonic work suggests that her emerging musical style, with its frequent emphasis on alternating whole tones and semitones, owes much to Vaughan Williams's influence.[27]

The fourth movement is a high-spirited development of rhythmic and melodic material that Maconchy described as a 'cross-play' of counterpoint.[28] This interplay continues to grow, and as the counterpoint becomes less dense, the fourth movement's connection to the primary motific material stated at the beginning of the first movement is fully revealed as it concludes with reiterations of the principal motifs.

[27] See Walter Clark, 'Vaughan Williams and the "night side of nature": Octatonicism in *Riders to the Sea*', in Byron Adams and Robin Wells (eds), *Vaughan Williams Essays* (Aldershot: Ashgate, 2003), 55–71.

[28] Maconchy, 'Elizabeth Maconchy On Writing String Quartets'.

Example 5.3. Maconchy, String Quartet No. 2, mvt. III, bars 33–7.
Published by Alfred Lengnick & Co., a division of Universal Music Publishing Group.
Reproduced by permission of Hal Leonard Europe BV (Italy).

Maconchy's Second Quartet was universally hailed in the press. In the *Musical Times*, Scott wrote:

> The advance shown upon her first quartet is great. … [T]his new quartet is emotionally as interesting yet is music before and above all else. The material is alive with imagination; it has grown by its own volition into these four movements. … I do not know anything quite like it elsewhere, and it moved me very much.[29]

The critic in the *Times* likewise offered praise, asserting that the work would be 'likely to enhance her reputation'.[30] Westrup, writing for the *Daily Telegraph*, declared:

> Hitherto Miss Maconchy's work, for all its cleverness and dexterity, has given the impression of a lack of certain direction. She has since tried more than one style without expressing a confident individuality. Now, in this work, she has found

[29] M.M.S. [Marion Scott], 'Lemare Concerts', *Musical Times* 78/1129 (March 1937): 266.
[30] 'Recitals of the Week: Lemare Concert', *Times*, 5 February 1937.

Example 5.4. Vaughan Williams, *Riders to the Sea*, text adapted from J M Synge (1871–1909), 'They are all gone now', three bars after rehearsal number 42. © Oxford University Press 1936, 1972. Reproduced by permission. All rights reserved.

herself. The ideas are taut and passionate, the technique supple and effective, and the whole work is bound together by a vivid coherence of thought and emotion.

The idiom is not 'modern' in the accepted sense. Indeed, if we are to look for influences the 19th century Russians come to mind most readily. But Miss Maconchy is not fettered by any obvious convention. She has taken the stuff of music and made her own idiom from it.[31]

The quartet even managed to earn high praise from McNaught:

At the Mercury Theatre last night a small and expert audience consisting largely of composers, conductors, musical performers and critics listened to the second of Miss Iris Lemare's present series of concerts.

[31] J.A.W. [Jack Allan Westrup], 'Notable New Work: Elizabeth Maconchy's Second Quartet', *Daily Telegraph*, 2 February 1937.

> To Miss Elizabeth Maconchy, whose String Quartet No. 2 was given its first performance, this was better than a crowded Queen's Hall, for her music is written for the nucleus of the inner circle.
>
> Her Quartet is grim-visaged music, dark with the determination to search out the truth from the bottom of the well, whatever the colour of the water.
>
> It is not a pretty process, but it is done in first-class style. Miss Maconchy has a musical brain of a high order, and can organise her ideas with outstanding skill. Few works in modernism so clearly convey their meaning and their design.[32]

At the following Lemare concert on 22 February, Maconchy's *Divertissement for Twelve Instruments*, conducted by Lemare, was included in a programme that also featured Vaughan Williams's *Two Hymn Preludes for Small Orchestra*, Rawsthorne's Concerto for Clarinet and String Orchestra, Stanley Bate's *Two Preludes for Chamber Orchestra*, Grace Williams's *Elegy for Strings*, and Handel's Overture to *Giustino*. Sadly, the 22 February Lemare concert was also the series' last until it was revived in 1950.[33] Cast in two movements, Maconchy's *Divertissement* is both lively and inventive, with the playful exchange between instruments in the Allegro scherzando section of the second movement reflecting Maconchy's comedic flair.

The reviews of Maconchy's *Divertissement* were less favourable than those for her quartet, with a principal criticism being that it lacked the quartet's solid cohesion. Though Lambert surprisingly acknowledged the work as 'full of interesting musical material', he further noted, 'Where it failed, to my mind, was in the adaptation of the material to the difficult medium of twelve solo instruments. The first movement seemed to call for a large modern orchestra, whereas the last movement suggested a piano piece. However, it is well worth hearing again.'[34] Westrup's critique was unenthusiastic. While acknowledging that the score evinced 'personality', he added that 'Much of the writing was uncouth'.[35]

February was also an important month for Maconchy's reputation abroad, as Nierychło succeeded in arranging an entire concert of her chamber works in Kraków that was also broadcast. This concert featured her Toccata for Piano, String Quartet No. 1, Quintet for Oboe and Strings, and *Divertissement for Twelve Instruments*. The concert and broadcast ended up being such a great success that Nierychło subsequently made plans to repeat the concert in Warsaw in the autumn with the addition of her Piano Concerto.[36]

In June, Maconchy and her husband travelled to France ahead of the ISCM Festival, spending a fortnight in Touraine before travelling to Paris. Piano

[32] W.McN. [William McNaught], 'An Audience of Critics', *Evening News*, 2 February 1937.

[33] Macnaghten, 'The Story of the Macnaghten Concerts', *Musical Times* 100/1399 (September 1959): 461.

[34] Constant Lambert, 'Musical Matters', *Sunday Referee*, 28 February 1937.

[35] J.A.W. [Jack Allan Westrup], 'New English Music', *Daily Telegraph*, 23 February 1937.

[36] Nierychło offered to cover all travel expenses for Maconchy to attend the concert; however, it is unclear as to whether or not she ended up attending. In a letter to Wright on 26 August, Maconchy mentions that Nierychło had mentioned that he wanted to include another orchestral work for the concert. Elizabeth Maconchy to Kenneth Wright, 26 August 1937, BBC WAC EM1.

works by Miloje Milojević, Luigi Dallapiccola, and Paul Dukas were played alongside Maconchy's quartet in the sixth concert of the festival.[37] Performed by the Brosa Quartet, the work was well received by the audience, with the critic of the *Chesterian* noting that the work was 'well built and perfectly balanced'.[38] In *Musical Opinion*, Lockspeiser found the work to be 'a skilled, serious piece of writing, devoid of pedantry, and a credit to her training with Professor Kitson at the R.C.M.'[39]

In July, Maconchy's Second String Quartet was included in a BBC broadcast of chamber music, performed by the Brosa Quartet, and in October, the work was played yet again by the Brosa Quartet at an LCMC concert.[40] Of the latter, Westrup remarked, 'This work not only shows a high degree of musical science in its development of a single significant gem of thought, but also conveys the impression of personal adventure. It is precisely because Miss Maconchy has put so much of herself into the music that it succeeds in retaining attention when [the] performance is over.'[41]

In 1937, Maconchy took a sudden interest in composing for viola, completing three works in the span of a year.[42] She completed the first work, Concerto for Viola and Orchestra, in the spring and sent it off to the BBC in June. In July, Wright wrote to Maconchy to let her know that the programmers for the BBC were seriously considering placing the work in a Contemporary Concert on 18 March, conducted by Lambert, with violist Bernard Shore as soloist.[43]

37 The works performed on 26 June were *Musica per tre pianoforti* by Italian twelve-tone composer Luigi Dallapiccola (1904–75), *Variations, Interlude and Finale on a Theme by Rameau* by the recently deceased French composer Paul Dukas (1865–1935), and *Grimaces Rythmiques* by Miloje Milojević (1884–1946), who was a leading Serbian composer who wrote in smaller forms. For a full listing of works played at the festival, see Irving Schwerké, 'The I.S.C.M. Festival', *Musical Times* 78/1133 (July 1937): 650–1.

38 Renée de Saussine, 'International Society for Contemporary Music', *Chesterian* (September/October 1937): 20.

39 Edward Lockspeiser, 'The I.S.C.M. Festival in Paris', *Musical Opinion*, August 1937, clipping in Maconchy's second scrapbook, SHC.

40 J.A.W. [Jack Allan Westrup], 'Contemporary Music', *Daily Telegraph*, 6 October 1937.

41 Ibid.

42 The reason for this sudden inspiration is unclear. None of the works bear any dedication, and based on Maconchy's correspondence with Boult and Wright, there is no indication that her concerto was composed with a specific violist in mind. Among Maconchy's personal papers, however, there is a draft of a letter addressed to the Czech violist Ladislav Černý (1891–1975) dated 21 September 1937, that suggests Maconchy had intended to send the work to him; however, it is unknown as to whether the letter was ever sent.

43 Kenneth Wright to Elizabeth Maconchy, 2 July 1937, BBC WAC EM1. Maconchy initially discussed the concerto with Boult and in a letter dated 2 July 1937, Maconchy notes that Boult had suggested to have violist Lionel Tertis (1876–1975) take a look at it; however, Tertis later retired. In a letter to Maconchy on 2 July confirming the BBC's intention to broadcast the work, Wright mentioned Scottish violist William Primrose (1904–82), who was unfortunately unavailable, as he was under contract with the NBC Symphony Orchestra. Shore was confirmed as the soloist on 6 July, as Wright detailed

In the autumn, other performances arose on Maconchy's horizon, encouraging her greatly. Several of Maconchy's songs received performances with soprano Norah Scott Turner, including Maconchy's setting of Keats's *The Thrush* (1934), Bridges's *I made another song* (c. 1937), Meredith's *The Arab* (1935), and Brontë's *Sleep brings no joy to me* (1937), in a recital at the Grotrian Hall on 12 October.[44] In the *Sunday Times*, Foss described the works as 'clever', which was hardly a compliment, further noting that they 'shared with their predecessors certain harmonic mannerisms, notably a tendency to oscillate upon the major and minor thirds of a chord'.[45] Capell, who often dismissed Maconchy's music for its abrasiveness, criticised her songs for not being harsh enough, contending in his review that her music was 'less impulsive than the lines of her several poets'.[46] He did, however, conclude his discussion of Maconchy's songs with the acknowledgment that *I made another song* embodied 'an excellent musical design'.[47] Further praise came from the critic in the *Times* who declared 'A group of songs by Elizabeth Maconchy, standing between Purcell and Schubert, held their own successfully.'[48]

On 3 December, *The Land* was broadcast by the BBC with Lemare conducting the BBC Orchestra.[49] Maconchy was ultimately disappointed with the performance. This was due in part to issues with not only the microphone, but also Maconchy's growing dissatisfaction with the work itself, as she detailed in a letter to Williams,

> I don't know what to think about The Land, really: I think perhaps the first piece just is rather long & dreary – the performance could have been more sensitive, but I don't think it was only that: also I think the addition of accents would perhaps give it more punch – but even that wouldn't really make much difference. … The performance of the 2nd one wasn't very good … actually I quite like no. 2. I think it's the best one – & can sound all right. I've never thought much of 3 & 4, & always think 4 only half comes off – 3 does come off, more or less, I think, but isn't very interesting.
>
> Well, well, – sometimes I think all my music is a bit dry & dull.[50]

---

in a letter to Maconchy: 'Referring to our conversation this morning, we agree to Mr. Bernard Shore as soloist to the first performance of your Viola Concerto under Constant Lambert's direction in a public Contemporary Concert to be given in the Concert Hall on March 18th 1938.'

44 The great collaborative pianist Gerald Moore accompanied Scott Turner on this occasion.

45 H.F. [Hubert Foss], 'Recitals of the Week', *Sunday Times*, 17 October 1937.

46 R.C. [Richard Capell], 'Miss Maconchy's New Songs', *Daily Telegraph*, 12 October 1937.

47 Ibid.

48 'Recitals of the Week', *Times*, 15 October 1937. Further performances of Maconchy's songs took place on 17 November, with Lutyens's then husband, Ian Glennie, performing *The Thrush* and *The Arab* in a recital at the Grotrian Hall, and on 10 December, Scott Turner gave a further performance of Maconchy's songs at an SWM concert.

49 The other works on the programme included Mozart's Three German Dances (K. 605), Rawsthorne's Clarinet Concerto, and Falla's Three Dances from *The Three-Cornered Hat*.

50 Elizabeth Maconchy to Grace Williams, 2 January 1938.

In spite of Maconchy's reservations about *The Land*, the autumn also led to some encouraging developments regarding another early work, as she began corresponding with oboist Josef Marx (1913–78) who had expressed an interest in her Quintet for Oboe and Strings. Marx had been introduced to the work by Gaskell, whom he had met two years prior when he spent a summer studying with the renowned oboist Léon Goossens (1897–1988). Though born in Berlin, Marx was living in New York and although he was unable to make any promise of performance, he nevertheless expressed a committed interest in promoting her chamber works.[51]

On 1 January 1938, Maconchy had some encouraging news to celebrate as Oxford University Press began handling *The Land*, the Concerto for Viola and Orchestra, the Suite for Chamber Orchestra, the Concerto for Piano and Chamber Orchestra, *Great Agrippa, or the Inky Boys*, and the *Divertissement for Twelve Instruments*.[52] Though they were added to the Hire Library, OUP did not have any of them typeset, which had the effect of restricting their performance both at home and abroad. Nevertheless, it managed to free up some of Maconchy's time as she no longer had to handle negotiations and the frequent lending of scores herself.

Though the broadcast of her Viola Concerto had been slated for March, the BBC's programme planners decided to move the work to a Contemporary Concert on 4 February conducted by Maconchy's critical nemesis Constant Lambert, with the up-and-coming Bernard Shore as the viola soloist. While the BBC had assured Maconchy in August that Shore would be playing the work, she was deeply dismayed to discover in late December that Shore had been completely unaware of this and was only told of the upcoming performance in December. As Maconchy recounted in a letter to Williams, '[Shore] was in an awful fuss about it & has made me change all the difficult bits'.[53] As with many of Maconchy's works from this period, it is structured around a series of pithy motifs, and the opening of the first movement, with its emphasis on a three-note descending pattern that persists throughout the work, is simply ravishing.

Despite having to alter the score to accommodate Shore, the work received a highly favourable review in the *Daily Telegraph*, with the often censorious Capell declaring, 'It is probably the composer's most effective utterance so far.'[54] The critic of the *Musical Times*, however, thought otherwise:

[51] Josef Marx to Elizabeth Maconchy, 7 December 1937, private collection.

[52] G.O. May [OUP Music Department] to Elizabeth Maconchy, 14 December 1937, SHC. Maconchy appears to have initially considered approaching Boosey & Hawkes in October 1936 to see if they would be interested in publishing her Piano Concerto, String Quartet, and *Prelude, Interlude and Fugue*. While a draft of this letter exists among Maconchy's papers, it is unclear as to whether or not it was ever sent. Elizabeth Maconchy to Leslie Boosey, 10 October 1936, SHC.

[53] Elizabeth Maconchy to Grace Williams, 2 January 1938.

[54] R.C. [Richard Capell], 'New Russian and English Music', *Daily Telegraph*, 5 February 1938.

> Miss Maconchy's Viola Concerto (Bernard Shore) was, after a promising opening, a disappointment. The balance between soloist and orchestra was clumsily contrived, and indeed the only occasional satisfactory patches were in the *tuttis*. There was a certain theatrical striving in the music which seemed forced and unnatural. Above all, Miss Maconchy must rid herself of the habit of taking a short chromatic figure … and teasing it to death throughout every movement. The consequent monotony, coupled with lack of any repose, becomes irritating.[55]

While Edwin Evans's review of the concerto in the March-April issue of the *Chesterian* sounded some notes of praise, he was also critical of Maconchy's determination to adopt 'masculine' tendencies: 'Miss Maconchy's star is certainly in the ascendant, and the Viola Concerto is one of her best achievements. In all her music, however, one feels conscious of a dread of being thought feminine which results in a rather forbidding earnestness. Still, that is one of the works that will be heard again with interest.'[56]

Four days later, Maconchy's scena *How Samson bore away the Gates of Gaza* (1937) was featured at an LCMC concert devoted to songs by young British composers. On the day of the concert, the *Star* featured an article titled, 'These Names May Be Famous – a generation hence: Britain's young composers are on parade to-night', in which Arnold Gyde proceeded to rank some of the composers featured in the concert that evening. 'Pride of place goes to a girl', is the condescending manner in which he declared Maconchy as the finest composer on the list. Maconchy was followed by Britten, Berkeley, Lutyens, Moeran, Leigh, and Rawsthorne.[57] Gyde's prediction was confirmed by reviews in the press, with Evans declaring in the *Daily Mail*, 'The outstanding piece was Elizabeth Maconchy's setting of Vachell [*recte* Vachel] Lindsay's "How Samson bore away the gates of Gaza," which should at once be orchestrated.'[58]

On 15 February, Maconchy's Sonata for Viola and Piano (1937–8) was premièred by violist Frederick Riddle (1912–95) and pianist Adolph Hallis (1896–1987) as part of Hallis's chamber music concert series at the Wigmore Hall. The sonata exudes an energy that is positively electric. The first movement, in which the themes are centred on the interval of a major third, also

[55] F., 'B.B.C. Contemporary Concert', *Musical Times* 79/1141 (March 1938): 223.

[56] Edwin Evans, 'London Letter', *Chesterian* 19/138 (March-April 1938): 228. Evans wrote a similar review for the *Liverpool Daily Post*: 'Elizabeth Maconchy … is the most interesting of the women composers who now abound in our midst, but like most of them she seems to have a terrible fear of being thought feminine in an old-fashioned sense. She would rather be ugly. There are plenty of ideas in the work, if only she could be induced to express them a little more graciously. But, after all, if she were different she would not be herself, and anyway her individualism is sane and healthy.' E.E. [Edwin Evans], 'Contemporary Music Concert: Woman Composer's Viola Concerto', *Liverpool Daily Post*, 5 September 1938.

[57] Arnold Gyde, 'These Names May Be Famous', *Star*, 8 February 1938.

[58] Edwin Evans, 'Concert of 29 Songs', *Daily Mail*, 9 February 1938. The American poet Vachel Lindsay (1879–1931) is remembered today for his appalling poems in 'Negro dialect' as well as for one poem, 'Abraham Lincoln Walks at Midnight'. During the 1920s, Lindsay enjoyed considerable fame in Anglophone countries.

exhibits an assured balance between the piano and viola – an element that many critics felt the Viola Concerto had lacked.

In the *Musical Times*, Scott praised Maconchy's writing for the skilful interplay that she achieved between the two instruments.[59] Ernest Newman, on the other hand, found the work to be brief yet monotonous, which he complained about at length in the *Sunday Times*; however, he conceded 'there is an undoubted talent in this young lady, the further developments of which we shall watch with interest'.[60] The most scathing review appeared in the *Times*:

> We came to the new work chiefly to discover whether that strident style which Elizabeth Maconchy's admirers call 'austere' shows any signs of amelioration. The importance of ugliness is very well in a young student, but the programme told us that the composer is now past 30. It is time that all that earnest insistence on strong rhythms and harsh harmonies should begin to expand into a beauty of its own.[61]

On 3 March, Maconchy travelled to Switzerland for a holiday. She brought along her score of *How Samson bore away the Gates of Gaza*, which she planned to orchestrate. Maconchy was also contemplating a short trip to Vienna where the German conductor Hermann Scherchen (1891–1966) planned to conduct her Suite for Chamber Orchestra.[62] As soon as she heard that the Nazis had marched into Austria, she withdrew her work from the concert in a principled protest of the invasion.[63]

After five weeks in Switzerland, Maconchy travelled to Ireland where her Piano Concerto was to be included in a concert of contemporary music by Irish composers Hamilton Harty (1879–1941), Moeran, and Fred May (1911–85), as well as Ina Boyle (1889–1967). Maconchy had been long acquainted with Boyle, who had also been a private pupil of Vaughan Williams. The two would often meet whenever Boyle was in England, with Maconchy making visits to Boyle's home in Enniskerry, County Wicklow, on her trips to Ireland.[64] Maconchy's concerto was conducted by the Irish composer and conductor Aloys Fleischmann (1910–92), with pianist Charles Lynch (1906–84) as soloist. The concert was heavily promoted in the Irish press and it was the first public performance of Maconchy's music in Dublin. The general consensus of the Irish critics was that the work was a bit hard to comprehend. Philip Dore remarked in his review

[59] M.M.S. [Marion Scott], 'British Sonatas at Recitals', *Musical Times* 79/1141 (March 1938): 224.

[60] Ernest Newman, 'St. Peter's Toe', *Sunday Times*, 20 February 1938.

[61] 'Hallis Chamber Concert', *Times*, 16 February 1938.

[62] Elizabeth Maconchy to Kenneth Wright, 2 March 1938, BBC WAC EM1.

[63] Elizabeth Maconchy to Kenneth Wright, 13 March 1938, BBC WAC EM1. The concert was cancelled shortly thereafter. See Kenneth Wright to Elizabeth Maconchy, 15 March 1938, BBC WAC EM1. On 27 June, Scherchen rescheduled the concert and broadcast, which was moved to Lausanne. Shortly thereafter, Scherchen wrote to Maconchy to inquire if she could send some of her more recent works for him to consider.

[64] For further information on Boyle, see Ita Beausang and Séamas de Barra, *Ina Boyle (1889–1967): A Composer's Life* (Cork: Cork University Press, 2018).

Figure 6. Maconchy with her sister Sheila in Switzerland, 1938 (reproduced by permission of the Maconchy Estate).

for the *Dublin Evening Mail*, 'Elizabeth Maconchy's concerto for pianoforte and chamber orchestra is a hard technical nut. ...This concerto is big music, and, if Miss Maconchy will permit me to say so, essentially masculine.'[65]

Following the concert in Ireland, Maconchy returned to Kent where she set to work on her orchestration of *How Samson bore away the Gates of Gaza*, as well as a song cycle titled *The Garland*.[66] During these busy months, Maconchy also completed her Third String Quartet. In May, she was invited to take part in a two-day congress at Queen Mary Hall devoted solely to the topic of contemporary music. Titled 'Music and Life – 1938', the two-day affair was sponsored by the LCMC and intended as an educational prelude to the upcoming ISCM Festival, which was to be held in London that summer. Michael Tippett contributed an entertaining report of the congress in the July-August 1938 issue of the *Monthly Musical Record*:

> The definitions proposed in answer to the question 'What is contemporary music?' were negative. One speaker suggested that contemporary music was music not built on the tonal or key system and its forms. Another suggested

[65] Philip Dore, 'Dublin Radio Concert', *Dublin Evening Mail*, 26 April 1938.

[66] Maconchy wrote *The Garland* for Sophie Wyss who showed it to Wright sometime in the late summer. Elizabeth Maconchy to Kenneth Wright, 11 September 1938, BBC WAC EM1.

that contemporary art was divorced from the instinctive and sterile, as 'straight' music from jazz, studio painting from the poster, and so on. The first definition provoked a question too late to be discussed ...The Congress constantly came up against the question of music's and the composer's relation to the so-called 'spirit of the age'. Dr. Malcolm Sargent frankly expressed an escapist view – he did not want to hear the 'spirit of the age' in music but the solace and comfort of another world. On the whole the Congress rejected this view, though at the same time it endorsed the Unknown Listener's complaint of the 'misery music' which the uncultivated public like himself is fobbed off with as the music of liberation and joy.[67]

Though the aims of the organisers were well intentioned, reports in the press suggested that heated debates broke out in some of the sessions, as a correspondent for the *Times* reported:

Opinion was divided whether it [contemporary music] should be defined technically by the dethronement of tonality, as was proposed by Mr. Alan Bush, or whether it was a question not so much of method as of spirit. Professor Wellesz urged that the word 'modern' should be used for technical innovations and 'contemporary' kept for works produced by modern social conditions. Mr. Lennox Berkeley defined it as 'representative of the age in which we live' and Miss Harriet Cohen made the good point that a big thing like the 12-tone system would hardly come into existence without some social necessity behind it.

Miss Elizabeth Maconchy, who came out bravely on the side of pure reason, explained modernism in purely musical terms of counterpoint: modern music is logical, contrapuntal, a kind of impassioned dialogue. Until Mr. Humphrey Searle mentioned it the word 'evolution' had not been used in the discussion, and in a subsequent paper on Hindemith's system of harmony Mr. Franz Reizenstein flung the idea back in his face. ... Definite conclusions were not to be expected, but the ground was cleared and order discovered in the welter of modern tendencies. The great defect in current ideas, as reflected by this congress, is its disregard of evolution. The greatest philosophical discovery of the nineteenth century is no doubt out of fashion, though there was no disposition to deny the organic character of works of art; perhaps revolutions, rather than evolution are preferred in music as in life in 1938.[68]

On 4 October, Maconchy's String Quartet No. 3 was premièred by the New Hungarian Quartet at an LCMC concert that also featured string quartets by Henk Badings (1907–87), Sándor Veress (1907–92), and Arthur Honegger (1892–1955).[69] Cast in one movement, Maconchy's Third String Quartet is cyclic

[67] Michael Tippett, 'Music and Life – 1938', *Monthly Musical Record* 68/798 (July-August 1938): 175–7.

[68] 'Music and Life Congress', *Times*, 30 May 1938.

[69] The New Hungarian Quartet consisted of Zoltan Székely (1st violin), Alexandre Moskowsky (2nd violin), Dénes Koromzay (viola), and Vilmos Palotai (cello). Székely (1903–2001) was one of Bartók's closest friends and champions. Maconchy's introduction to the New Hungarian Quartet was likely facilitated by Alan Bush, as Maconchy had written to Bush on 23 March 1936, 'I should particularly like to show my quartet [String Quartet No. 2] to the New Hungarian quartet when they are

in the manner in which ideas recur and are transformed throughout. The opening theme is built upon oscillating minor seconds and their inversion, which is enlivened by frequent changes in metre.[70] This fluctuation between major and minor, which has occurred in most of the scores under discussion in this chapter, comprised what Anne Macnaghten refers to as 'an unmistakable "finger-print"' of Maconchy's style, and most certainly derives from her use of octatonic pitch collections.[71] In the Third Quartet, Maconchy exploits this ambiguity between major and minor by harmonically supporting the melody by alternating between a C major chord and an E-flat minor chord, clearly outlining an octatonic collection (Example 5.5). This alternating pattern is a clear allusion to the entrance of the strings in the first movement of Vaughan Williams's *Flos campi*, a score in which there are long passages saturated by octatonic pitch collections.

The Lento section leads directly into the lively presto section, which is characterised by its pattern of falling sevenths. Maconchy continues to develop and expand the initial motifs, which is followed by the andante section where she expands upon the initial melody introduced at the beginning of the quartet. This procedure leads directly into a return of the rhythmic intensity of the presto. A sustained diminuendo gradually calms the frenetic activity: the music ebbs downwards to the final coda, bringing the quartet back to where it initially began.

Williams was especially impressed with this quartet, as she wrote to Maconchy: 'This is just to say that a second hearing confirmed my impression that Quartet no. 3 is one of your best works if not the best. Apart from its being the real stuff of music, & making a lovely sound, it is your most mature work (Dorrie [Gow] agrees with me, too) & is really first-rate quartet writing.'[72] Despite Williams's praise, it was a score whose creation Maconchy felt had been rushed, as she later recalled: 'I wrote it much more quickly than any of the others. … It is the quartet I like least. It does not seem to progress as the others do (I hope): but to come back to where it started without enough sense of achievement.'[73]

Despite Maconchy's reservations, the work was highly praised by several critics. McNaught even declared, 'The most interesting work was the single-movement quartet by Elizabeth Maconchy, whom international modernism

here – and I was going to ask you if you would introduce me to them – but now, alas! I shan't be here. I am going abroad on Wednesday till the end of April. Would it be bothering you too much to ask if you would show it to them? I feel a little diffident of asking you to do this – but I do love their playing so much, and would awfully like them to see my quartet if it's possible.' Elizabeth Maconchy to Alan Bush, 23 March 1936, MS Mus 452, vol. 127, Alan Bush correspondence, 1922–36, BL.

[70] Maconchy, 'Elizabeth Maconchy On Writing String Quartets'.

[71] Macnaghten, 'Elizabeth Maconchy', 299.

[72] Quoted in Mathias, *Lutyens, Maconchy, Williams and Twentieth-Century British Music*, 99–100.

[73] Elizabeth Maconchy, draft of lecture titled 'Talk on String Quartets', 1959, SHC.

Example 5.5. Maconchy, String Quartet No. 3, opening.
Published by Alfred Lengnick & Co., a division of Universal Music Publishing Group.
Reproduced by permission of Hal Leonard Europe BV (Italy).

hails as one of its leading lights. It is a characteristic one-idea composition, worked out with determination, notable skill, and complete independence of any model.'[74] The review in the *Musical Times* was virtually an encomium:

> Of the four new string quartets performed at Cowdray Hall on October 4, Miss Elizabeth Maconchy's alone filled us with any desire for a second hearing. … like much of Miss Maconchy's music, it does not escape the charge of monotony, because of her habit of taking the germ of an idea and persistently teasing it – in this case the germ was no more than a falling semitone. But this is so characteristic of her methods that we accept it, and willingly admit that the work is logical, and not without a passionate drive. Moreover – and this is a new departure for Miss Maconchy – it has euphony. It is slighter than her previous quartets, but more immediately likeable.[75]

Though Maconchy's Third Quartet was a resounding success, toward the end of 1938, she began to encounter more difficulties in securing broadcasts over the BBC. After she completed the orchestration of *How Samson bore away the Gates of Gaza*, she sent it to the BBC on 5 September. As Wright was on holiday when Maconchy submitted the score, she checked with his secretary, Miss Evans, to ensure that the work had been received and properly forwarded to the reading committee. In her response to Maconchy, Evans evidently informed her that the work had received a positive report from the committee.[76] When Wright returned from his holiday, he sent a memo to A.C. Lewis on 6 October, to inquire about the status of the work. The contents of the memo, however, reveal that Wright had already come to a decision without having heard the work:

> Is there any likelihood that we can use this work this season? If not, I think we should return it to the composer, as she may have other ideas for it. We are already doing her String Quartet, and 'The Garland' cycle she wrote for Sophie Wyss is being produced in the Hallis Concerts; and there does not appear to be room in our Contemporaries for a further work by Miss Maconchy this year.[77]

On 7 October, one of the readers, composer Herbert Murrill (1909–52), responded,

> I heard this at the recent concert of modern British songs given by the C.M.C. It struck me then as a dull and arid bit of work, with a crabbed and edgy vocal line and the usual rhythmic and harmonic distortions. The orchestration seems to me to add little interest to what was always, in my opinion, a poor work. I would not recommend its inclusion in our programmes.[78]

74 W.McN. [William McNaught], 'Brilliant Playing: Hungarians' Three Quartets New to England', *Evening News*, 5 October 1938.

75 F., 'Contemporary Music Centre', *Musical Times* 79/1149 (November 1938): 858.

76 This is detailed in Elizabeth Maconchy to Kenneth Wright, 14 October 1938, BBC WAC EM1.

77 Kenneth Wright to Herbert Murrill, 6 October 1938, BBC WAC EM1.

78 Herbert Murrill to Kenneth Wright, 7 October 1938, BBC WAC EM1.

Although Murrill's assessment contradicted the many stellar reviews that the arrangement of *Samson* for piano and voice had received in February, it nevertheless gave Wright a plausible excuse to return the score, as he wrote the following in a letter to Maconchy on 13 October:

> I am afraid I must after all be disappointing about 'How Samson bore away the Gates of Gaza', which I am sending back to you by registered post. It was heard by us at the recent C.M.C. Concert, and the score has been reconsidered by our advisers and programme builders. Although they had quite liked what they saw at a first glance of the score, their considered opinion after the performance was not so favourable. I think therefore it is better for us not to keep the score.[79]

Maconchy was understandably upset by this complete reversal of the earlier report she had received from Miss Evans over the telephone, and she questioned Wright directly in a letter on 14 October.[80] In an attempt to cover up his complicity in the matter, Wright wrote the following to Maconchy on the 18th: 'The misunderstanding is as to when "Samson" was heard at the C.M.C. concert. I had gathered it was recently. In view of what you say I will discuss it further, and let you know what the chances are.'[81] The following day, Wright sent a lengthier letter to apologise and promised that the BBC would include the work if an opening became available. He did conclude his letter with some good news, however, remarking, 'In the meantime I am asked to say also that we hope to include a repetition of the Viola Concerto some time during the season, as it is a pity for it only to have one hearing.'[82]

In early 1939, Maconchy's career continued to garner interest abroad. In an article about British music in *Schweizerische Musikzeitung*, Scherchen included Maconchy among the six composers of the younger generation he discussed: 'Elizabeth Maconchy, has developed a thoroughly personal craftsmanship, drawing upon impressionist tone-formations, dance-rhythms, and polyphonic

79 Kenneth Wright to Elizabeth Maconchy, 13 October 1938, BBC WAC EM1.

80 Maconchy's letter reads, in part, 'I'm very disappointed about "Samson", but also rather mystified – because you say: "It was heard by us at a recent C.M.C. concert, & the score has been reconsidered by our advisers and program builders". … – But there hasn't been a performance. – Directly after I had finished the score a few weeks ago I sent it straight up to you. … The only time Samson has been sung was when Sophie Wyss sang it with piano at the C.M.C. concert last February, and it was on the strength of its success then that I decided to score it for orchestra (Edwin Evans and a number of other people urged me to score it at once.) So that I am puzzled … but can you elucidate?' Elizabeth Maconchy to Kenneth Wright, 14 October, 1938, BBC WAC EM1.

81 Kenneth Wright to Elizabeth Maconchy, 18 October 1938, BBC WAC EM1.

82 Wright states, 'I was in a muddle in that I thought the C.M.C. had followed the original reading of your score. What happened was that only recently was there a coming together of the readers and two people who had heard the piano version at the C.M.C. Concert. In view of the confusion, to which I seem to have contributed considerably, it has been agreed that if and when we can find a suitable place for "Samson" in a studio concert with or without Miss Lemare we will include it, of course inviting Sophie to sing it.' Kenneth Wright to Elizabeth Maconchy, 19 October 1938, BBC WAC EM1.

methods. Her melody is easily recognizable, and unexpected folk-tune-like turns impart charm to it.'[83] In Paris, the Blech Quartet played Maconchy's Second Quartet at the beginning of the year, and in March, Calvocoressi delivered a broadcast on Paris P.T.T. on contemporary British composers, featuring Maconchy, Finzi, Darnton, Dolmetsch, and Rawsthorne.[84]

During this period, Maconchy was also busy with some politically charged choral works. In 1938, she was asked by Alan Bush if she would be willing to compose a short work for female chorus set to a text by Sylvia Townsend Warner titled *The Mothers* after John Ireland had rejected the offer.[85] Intended for a choral contest organised by the London Co-operative Education Committee, Maconchy warmly agreed to make a simple arrangement for SSAA to the overtly political text.[86] Unfortunately, the work was later declined owing to personnel changes on the Co-operative Education Committee.[87] Maconchy also contributed a piece of music titled *The People Advance*, set to text by the British communist poet Randall Swingler (1909–67), for a pageant that was performed at the Festival of Music for the People on 1 April 1939 at the Royal Albert Hall.[88] Another work Maconchy wrote for the Workers' Music Association (WMA) was *The Ribbon in her Hair*, set to text by the Irish playwright and socialist Seán O'Casey (1880–1964), which was published by the WMA in 1939.

Maconchy's involvement with the WMA, which was founded by Bush in 1936, raises intriguing questions regarding Maconchy's political activities during this period. While poor health earlier in the decade prevented her from being as politically active as she would have liked, with what little time and energy she did have, she managed to raise funds to support the Republican cause at the beginning of the Spanish Civil War, and later contributed her music to a fundraising concert arranged by the Hammersmith Borough Labour Party and Trades Council to raise funds for an ambulance to be sent to Spain.[89] Unlike Bush, she was never a member of the communist party. Interestingly,

[83] 'Scherchen on British Music', *Musical Times* 80/1153 (March 1939): 186. The other young British composers Scherchen discussed were Lutyens, Rawsthorne, Darnton, Berkeley, and Britten.

[84] 'Musical Notes from Abroad', *Musical Times* 80/1152 (February 1939): 146.

[85] In a letter to Ireland dated 6 September 1938, Bush wrote, 'The subject of the poem which I discussed with the committee should be, we feel, a Mother's Song against war. We want something which is strong and in no sense vague in its terms but we want to avoid anything in the nature of a passive pacifism.' Quoted in Rachel O'Higgins, *The Correspondence of Alan Bush and John Ireland* (Aldershot: Ashgate, 2006), 82.

[86] See O'Higgins, 83.

[87] The work was never performed. Alan Bush to Elizabeth Maconchy, letter, nd. [1939], MS Mus. 454, Alan Bush Collection, misc. correspondence vol. 129: 1939, BL.

[88] The pageant comprised music by Maconchy, Vaughan Williams, Arnold Cooke (1906–2005), Lutyens, Rubbra, Erik Chisholm (1904–65), Darnton, Frederic Austin (1872–1952), Norman Demuth (1898–1968), Rawsthorne, and Bush.

[89] See LeFanu, 'Elizabeth Maconchy DBE (1907–1994)'. The fundraising concert, titled 'Ambulance for Spain', included a movement from Maconchy's String Quartet No. 1, played by the Macnaghten Quartet.

Maconchy and LeFanu did, however, name one of their cats after Karl Marx. Marx was one of two cats the couple had while they lived at Chart Corner with their other cat, Gussie, named after Holst. Not long after they got Gussie, Marx became pregnant and was subsequently renamed Markie.[90] Though Maconchy's politics often aligned with socialist causes, and she was active in The Left Book Club, she was never known to be a member of any official socialist party.[91] As Maconchy and LeFanu later burned many of their personal papers in the 1940s, further details pertaining to their political activities during this period remain largely unknown.[92]

In addition to her composing, Maconchy was also attempting to help her friends in Prague. In January 1939, one of the Löwenbachs' daughters, Vera (1914–92), came to stay with Maconchy as Jan and Vilma sought to make their way to Britain via Switzerland as they struggled to obtain visas.[93] Known by her nickname, Mima, she spent a couple of weeks at Chart Corner before settling with a friend in London while she waited for her parents. Fortunately, Jan and Vilma were able to secure their visas at the beginning of April, travelling to England, where they stayed a few months before travelling on to Cuba with Mima in the autumn, eventually settling in New York.[94]

On 14 February, Maconchy's *The Garland* (1938), a song cycle set to Anacreontic poems translated by Maconchy's husband, William LeFanu, was premièred by the work's dedicatee, soprano Sophie Wyss (1897–1983) at a Hallis chamber music concert.[95] Though the work elicited a mixed response from critics, Newman found some merit in the songs, especially 'No end to Love', which he discussed in the *Sunday Times*:

> The humour of these trifles from the Greek Anacreontea … is the thinnest of butter on the driest of old crusts, but even so it is not difficult to imagine more musical point being given to it than Miss Maconchy has achieved. It shows some courage, by the way, on the part of a modern composer to write a 'Catalogue' song of twenty loves in Athens, two thousand in Lesbos; [*sic*] Ionia, Caria, and Rhodes, a few thousand more in Crete, Parthia, India, and elsewhere, and all the rest of it. The competition in this field from friend Leporello would discourage most people.[96]

90 Elizabeth Maconchy to Sheila Maconchy, 19 February 1939.

91 Nicola LeFanu, interview by author. The Left Book Club was founded in 1936 by publisher Victor Gollancz (1893–1967), British Labour politician Stafford Cripps (1889–1952), and John Strachey (1901–63), a writer and also a British Labour politician. The organisation was a book of the month club devoted to 'help in the struggle for world peace and a better social and economic order, and against fascism'. See John Lewis, *The Left Book Club: An Historical Record* (London: Victor Gollancz, 1970); and Paul Laity (ed.), *The Left Book Club Anthology* (London: Victor Gollancz, 2001).

92 Nicola LeFanu, interview by author.

93 Elizabeth Maconchy to Sheila Maconchy, 3 January 1939, private collection.

94 Vera (Mima) Löwenbach to Elizabeth Maconchy, 5 November 1940, private collection.

95 Wyss was well-known for her championing of contemporary works and also premièred Britten's song cycle *Les Illuminations*.

96 Ernest Newman, 'This Week's Music', *Sunday Times*, 19 February 1939.

In the *Musical Times*, Scott remarked, 'Miss Maconchy has set them [the verses] to a free line of music for the voice that is neither melody nor declamation, but comprises both … There is nothing emotional or sham-antique in her method, yet it somehow conveys a sense of strangeness, and of things remote – Elizabeth Maconchy being at heart a poet.'[97]

Wyss was eager to include the song cycle in a broadcast, and was planning to meet with Wright in the spring to discuss it with him. In a letter sent to Wright on 25 March, Maconchy observes unhappily that the BBC was growing increasingly hesitant about programming her newer works:

> I heard from Sophie saying that she was going to see you in a few days, and would talk to you about my 'Garland' Song Cycle, which I wrote for her, and she had I think suggested for a broadcast, but which she says 'they do not seem keen to do'.
>
> I am a bit distressed about this. I remember when I came with Sophie to see you in the autumn and we talked about 'The Garland' & 'Samson' your saying 'it isn't a question of whether we do what Betty Maconchy writes, but when & where we do it'! – which I thought was very nice of you – and nice to hear!
>
> But then I was rather upset by the odd affair about Samson (of course I kept this private, and didn't tell Sophie about it) – also because you wrote in the autumn to let me know that another performance of my Viola Concerto was to be fixed for this season – and I haven't heard anything further about a date for it or Samson. And now 'The Garland' seems to be meeting with difficulty. – So please forgive me for a good grumble and for coming to you with it.–
>
> I have one nice piece of news in this gloomy world, which is that I am having a baby – (not till the autumn.) We are very pleased about it so I shan't be coming to London so much for a bit, but am looking forward to a quiet summer here, and getting lots of work done. I'm just finishing the sketch of a thing for piano & orchestra, and now must start scoring it – & I've just begun what may be another quartet.[98]

Aside from her pregnancy, Maconchy had other good news in the spring, as Hinrichsen decided to publish Maconchy's Third String Quartet as well as a work for piano titled *Impromptu*,[99] which was announced in the *Musical Times* in May of 1939:

> Miss Elizabeth Maconchy has decided that in order to make her work known to a wider circle of music-lovers it will be to her advantage to work in close collaboration with a publisher. She has therefore appointed Mr. Max Hinrichsen as her business representative, and (with the exception of some of her earlier orchestral works) all her compositions will now be handled, either in MS. or in printed form, by Hinrichsen Edition Ltd.[100]

[97] M.M.S. [Marion Scott], 'Adolph Hallis Chamber Music Concert', *Musical Times* 80/1153 (March 1939): 224.

[98] Elizabeth Maconchy to Kenneth Wright, 25 March 1939, BBC WAC EM1.

[99] Originally titled Fantasia on One Note, Maconchy composed the work in 1938 and dedicated it to Harriet Cohen.

[100] 'Notes and News', *Musical Times* 80/1155 (May 1939): 375.

On 11 August, Maconchy submitted a newly composed set of brief works for viola titled *Five Pieces for Viola* to the BBC. Koromzay, the violist of the New Hungarian Quartet, was especially interested in playing the work, and Maconchy suggested that if the BBC wished to place it in a programme, Koromzay would be the ideal choice. Though the BBC indicated their interest in broadcasting the pieces, as the month progressed – and with Britain being drawn inexorably into another world war – on the 29th Wright wrote to Maconchy:

> We have been interested to see them, and would like to do them, but assuming international events allow us to go our normal way in the last quarter of this year our programme planning has now to be on a much more rigid system day by day and week by week. … There might be a chance in May 1940, but of course it is too far ahead yet to say.[101]

Then, on 1 September 1939, the Nazis invaded Poland; war against Germany was declared soon after; and, along with every other British subject, Elizabeth Maconchy's life was disrupted irrevocably.

[101] Kenneth Wright to Elizabeth Maconchy, 29 August 1939, BBC WAC EM1.

6

Darker Days Ahead, 1939–45

Maconchy spent the initial months of the war in Ireland, living with her aunt in Dublin along with her elder sister, Maureen, who had also travelled to Ireland with her young son, Richard. On 24 October, Maconchy gave birth to her daughter, Elizabeth Anna. As there was already another Anna in the household in the form of her aunt's dog, the new arrival was given the moniker 'baby Anna' and the dog was bestowed the title of 'real Anna'.[1] While Maconchy was relieved that her abundance of caution ensured that she was able to give birth safely without the threat of air raids, she nevertheless lamented having to leave her husband behind in England.[2]

Maconchy remained primarily in Ireland through March. Though she had her hands full with a new baby, she was also busy with a new project: a collaboration with the Irish Ballet Club on a ballet titled *Puck Fair*. During her time in Ireland, Maconchy was also invited by the Dublin Music Society to present a talk on modern music, which she delivered in March. Titled 'What is modern music?', Maconchy structured her talk as an exploration of underlying ideologies and schools of thought, from nationalism to Gebrauchsmusik, quarter-tone music, popular music, atonality, and twelve-tone music. Eloquent, succinct, and easily accessible, Maconchy's talk, which included musical examples illustrated by Charles Lynch, was written with the intent of inspiring dialogue and encouraging the audience to form their own conclusions as opposed to accepting her own.[3] It also offers the first detailed record of Maconchy's own thoughts about her musical process, namely the importance of counterpoint as a means of harmonic development, as well as the underlying principle of 'impassioned argument':

> for me a musical argument must always be an impassioned one: music cannot be written by the cold light of reason alone. I do not believe it possible to write good

[1] Dunlop, 16.

[2] Elizabeth Maconchy to Grace Williams, 26 October 1939. While Maconchy remained primarily in Ireland through March, based on details provided in two articles appearing in the *Dublin Evening Mail* in 1940, she made at least one trip back to England prior to her permanent return in the spring. See 'Fashion And Gossip In Dublin To-day', *Dublin Evening Mail*, 5 February 1940; and 'Fashion And Gossip In Dublin To-day', *Dublin Evening Mail*, 18 March 1940.

[3] Elizabeth Maconchy, draft of talk titled 'What is Modern Music?', SHC. While dated 1940, the draft also includes alterations that were made for a subsequent talk delivered to the Witham Gramophone Society on 13 October 1950.

> music without a high degree of what I shall call 'intellectual passion' – where the mind is in a state of great intellectual and emotional excitement, and is yet at the same time intensely concentrated & controlled.
>
> This impassioned argument, this sensitive and moving musical logic, is for me true music.[4]

In the spring, Maconchy returned to England via a blacked-out plane to Liverpool, followed by a train to Kent.[5] LeFanu, who was unable to serve in the military owing to problems with gastric ulcers, continued to commute to London for his job as a librarian for the Royal College of Surgeons.[6] With war activity increasing in the summer, Anna was sent to stay with cousins in Devonshire along with a nurse to ensure her safety.[7] Though Maconchy did not feel as though the war made it impossible for her to work, her time was nevertheless limited as she found herself busy attending lectures on first aid and gardening.[8] Likely inspired by the 'Dig for Victory' campaign, which was launched by the Ministry of Agriculture at the beginning of the war to encourage the British to take up gardening as a means to cope with food rationing, Maconchy was doing her part in the effort, as she recounted in a letter to Williams: 'I've felt it my duty to make a lot of jam & so on, & work hard at growing my vegetables & am even keeping a few hens! I quite enjoy all this housewifery, but it does take time.'[9] Despite frequent air-raid warnings with a bomber crashing a mere two miles from their home in Kent, by mid-August, war activity had yet to come any closer. Desirous to keep her family together, and encouraged by the relatively calm atmosphere, Maconchy wrote to Williams on 17 August, 'We are thinking of having Anna home again – because the feeling that whatever happens it is better to be all together is getting stronger.'[10] Anna subsequently returned to Kent later that month. The relative calm, however, was soon to end as the Battle of Britain wore on, with the heaviest air assaults taking place in September, during which Maconchy sought shelter with her daughter in a cupboard under the stairs of their cottage.[11]

In spite of wartime conditions, the spring and summer proved to be productive. In July she completed a song for the WMA titled *The Winkle Woman*. Arranged for mezzo-soprano and piano set to text by Sigerson Clifford, the

4 Ibid.

5 Dunlop, 16.

6 During the war, LeFanu helped with the supply of periodicals to Army and Military hospitals. Locally, he also served as an air raid warden and was a member of the Home Guard. Formed in May 1940 to defend against a potential invasion and occupation, the Home Guard largely comprised individuals who were deemed ineligible for military service. For further details, see Penny Summerfield and Corinna Peniston-Bird, *Contesting Home Defence: Men, Women and the Home Guard in the Second World War* (Manchester: Manchester University Press, 2007).

7 Elizabeth Maconchy to Grace Williams, 17 August 1940.

8 Elizabeth Maconchy to Sheila Maconchy, 4 September 1940, private collection.

9 Elizabeth Maconchy to Grace Williams, 17 August 1940.

10 Ibid.

11 Dunlop, 16.

Figure 7. Maconchy and her daughter Anna, 1939 (reproduced by permission of the Maconchy Estate).

work was recorded the following year. In the early 1940s, Maconchy also took some time to explore twelve-tone technique. Though she was never a disciple of the method, ultimately finding it too restrictive, she nevertheless found the experience to be rewarding.[12] Maconchy was also able to make substantial progress on *Puck Fair* and had plans to resume work on her Fourth String Quartet, which she had begun shortly before the war. Yet much had changed in the world, and as Maconchy soon discovered, shifting priorities and ideological visions created an environment in which securing performances and broadcasts would become an ever-increasing uphill battle.

With the Second World War, changes to musical life were inevitable as all concert life in London came to a precipitous halt.[13] As the BBC was reduced to a single airwave, this necessitated dramatic changes in programming. Initially, the BBC focused exclusively on popular genres, with the theatre organ dominating a significant number of musical broadcasts in the initial weeks of the war. The press was quick to attack the BBC's low-brow programming, as the *Birmingham Post* quipped on 11 September, 'When we shall be hearing of people over half Europe suffering want, we shall not be satisfied with "Tea for

[12] Elizabeth Maconchy, draft of talk for Goodmayes Gramophone and Music Society, 31 January 1963, SHC.

[13] 'Notes of the Day', *Monthly Musical Record* 69/810 (October 1939): 223.

Two" and similar fare.'[14] On 18 October, Vaughan Williams, who was incensed by the BBC's early wartime programming, wrote the following in a letter to the BBC's Director-General:

> It appears to me that one of the things we are fighting for is a free as opposed to a regimented culture. In that case we must prove that we have a culture worth fighting for.
>
> I believe that in times of stress such as these when peoples' purpose & determination need special encouragement that only the best & most vital art is of any use – Anything else is enervating & discouraging and I believe that the 'ordinary man' will respond to the stimulus in a way which in normal times he possibly would not do.
>
> It has, I think, been a great pain to many people to find that in the early days of the war it was apparently the opinion of your programme makers that the English people when their hearts & minds were strung up to great endeavour only wanted to listen to the loathsome noises of the so-called cinema 'organ'. Later on I admit the programmes began to get better, but to judge from this weeks 'Radio Times' things have taken a turn for the worse again & the so-called 'serious' programmes are filled with second-rate material which nobody wants.
>
> In times like these when so many people are looking for comfort & encouragement from music, among them those who have probably never attended to music before, surely we ought to give them something that will *grip*. I believe that really great music, especially if it is familiar will grip everybody. … Are we not missing a great opportunity which may never recur?[15]

In response to growing criticism, the BBC outlined a new policy for music programmes in November:

> Our primary aim is still the presentation of the best music of all categories, planned in a comprehensive scheme and performed under the best possible conditions. We consider that the B.B.C. has a responsibility towards the musical profession as a whole (concert organisations, solo artists, composers, etc.) and that every opportunity should be taken to make B.B.C. programmes as representative as possible of British music-making, though our criterion in assisting outside musical activity should always be value to broadcast programmes; any question of subsidy being completely subordinate.
>
> The recent modifying influences in our policy have been as follows:
>
> 1. The absence of an alternative programme has made it necessary for every concert to appeal to an infinitely wider audience. This cannot be achieved by any compromise or half-hearted method. The best of every type of music must be presented in the manner most acceptable even to the purist. The widening of appeal must come through the shortening of programmes where artistically possible, and the rigorous ruling-out of the mediocre both as regards music and performance.[16]

14 Quoted in Nicholas Kenyon, *The BBC Symphony Orchestra* (London: British Broadcast Corporation, 1981), 157.

15 Quoted in Doctor, '"Working for her own Salvation"', 198.

16 Music Policy, 17 November 1939, BBC WAC R27/245/1/Music General/Music Policy, File 1a, 1930–43.

While the BBC maintained that they were still committed to offering music of the highest standard to the public, works deemed too modernist were all but absent from wartime programming.[17] Although the language of the BBC's music policies in 1939 did not state that modernist works would be banned outright, their revised policy, which was drafted over the course of 1941 and 1942, was far more explicit in articulating their newly populist and nationalist aims:

> Statement of Policy
>
> 1. (a) The BBC exists to further the cause of music through broadcasting, i.e. through the transmission of programmes of music or about music. It follows that musical programmes that don't make good broadcasting ... are intrinsically a hindrance. This is an important principle which often conflicts with non-broadcasting musical activities and considerations.
>
> (b) The BBC believes that the recognition of the above principle, and adherence to it in practice, will prove to be in the best interests of music as a whole (as an art and as a profession outside the BBC), even when at times loyalty to the requirements of broadcasting seems to conflict with non-broadcasting musical and professional considerations. Just as a strong national idiom in music is likely to produce better music than the aping of Beethoven, so a strong broadcasting policy in music is likely in the long run to operate in favour of the interests it may seem to be temporarily opposing.
>
> (c) Music is an international 'language', which through the medium of broadcasting is heard and understood all over the world. This impact involves immediate competitive and prestige considerations of great consequence to broadcasting, with ultimate implications in the sphere of international goodwill of the very highest importance.
>
> (d) In spite of this recognition of the international factor, the BBC regards it as a matter of first importance to develop a strong nationalism in British music as a means of exorcising the long-standing national sense of inferiority in music and ridding music of its status as a foreign art, in selfconscious [*sic*] pursuit of which this country is content as a matter of course to take a second place.[18]

These policy changes, combined with Maconchy's reputation as a determinedly modernist composer, greatly affected the marketability of her music.[19] On 20 December 1939, the score of Maconchy's *How Samson bore away the Gates of Gaza* was returned to the Welsh tenor Parry Jones (1891–1963), with

[17] At the beginning of the war, the BBC also stopped accepting new compositions from British composers. After the establishment of the Music Department's new policy, however, they resumed their activities in late November. S.P. Waddington to RST, 24 November 1939, BBC WAC R27/249/1/Music General/Music Programme/Advisory Panel, File 2, 1936–40.

[18] First draft of BBC Music Policy, 16 December 1941, BBC WAC R27/245/1/Music General/Music Policy, File 1a, 1930–43.

[19] See Doctor, 'Intersecting Circles', 105.

the BBC writing in an enclosed letter, 'owing to our single programme-working, we can see no likelihood of it being used in broadcast concerts'.[20] On 29 March 1940, Maconchy's publisher, Max Hinrichsen, wrote to Julian Herbage to inquire about a performance of the work, which had been promised much earlier by Wright. In utter disregard to previous discussions of the work, which had already gone through a panel of readers, Herbage suggested Hinrichsen submit the score once again.[21] Hinrichsen did so, and it was read once again by the BBC's readers. On 29 October 1940, he received what amounted to the same reason given for the BBC's decision to return the score in December 1939: 'we very much regret that, under existing conditions, there is no likelihood of our being able to include a work of this nature in any of our programmes'.[22]

Despite the BBC's restrictive programming policies, Maconchy nevertheless had a couple of promising performances on the horizon in September 1940. The first was the inclusion of her Third String Quartet in a National Gallery concert on 4 September. Begun by pianist Myra Hess (1890–1965) in October 1939 as a means to sustain musical life and offer a respite to the public in the face of increasing uncertainties at a time when few other musical outlets were available, the National Gallery Concerts took place at lunchtime every weekday through the spring of 1946. Drawing large crowds and long queues with approximately 750,000 people attending the concerts over the course of the series' span, the concerts continued even as air raid sirens blared.[23] Though Maconchy's Third Quartet was scheduled to be played by the Blech Quartet, shortly before the concert, the quartet's violist, Douglas Thomson, was called up for service in the RAF. While the Hirsch String Quartet stepped in to take the Blech Quartet's place, the short notice led to a slight change in the programme with Maconchy's work omitted.

Later that month, a work she had recently completed titled *Dialogue for Piano and Orchestra* was set to be premièred at a Proms concert on the 26th with pianist Clifford Curzon (1907–82). After the 1939 Proms ended mid-season, the fate of the series was uncertain.[24] When Wood's negotiations with the BBC came to no avail for the 1940 season, he subsequently arranged for the Proms to take place under the auspices of the Royal Philharmonic Society.[25] At a rehearsal in mid-August with the London Symphony Orchestra, Maconchy found the level of disorganisation alarming as she recounted in a letter to Williams:

20 Music Librarian (for Music Executive) to Parry Jones, 20 December 1939, BBC WAC EM2.

21 Julian Herbage to Max Hinrichsen, 5 April 1940, BBC WAC EM2.

22 LD (for Music Executive) to Max Hinrichsen, 29 October 1940, BBC WAC EM2.

23 See https://www.nationalgallery.org.uk/about-us/history/the-myra-hess-concerts [accessed 4 April 2019].

24 David Cox, *The Henry Wood Proms* (London: BBC 1980), 109–11.

25 For details regarding the complexities of the situation and animosities between Wood and the BBC, see Cox, 109–16; and Arthur Jacobs, *Henry J. Wood: Maker of the Proms* (London: Methuen, 1994), 343–51.

> We had a run-through rehearsal last week – most unexpected, & I had a job getting the parts ready in time. It also came as a surprise at very short notice for Clifford Curzon. But he is excellent – most intelligent, & extremely nice & easy to work with. I did it with him twice last week with 2 pianos. The orchestra read it very very badly – it is scored much more for wind than strings, & the wind seemed pretty weak. I longed to conduct, too – as Henry is so awful about tempi etc – altogether it was rather agonizing – : & it is so hard to tell exactly what is bad playing & what bad scoring at a quick first run-through like that. However it has enabled me to alter the balance in various places – smallish things, & that's useful.[26]

As the bombings intensified with the onset of the Blitz, the 1940 Proms season concluded early once again, with the final concert taking place on 7 September, thus indefinitely postponing the work's première.[27]

A personal tragedy arrived the following month when Maconchy received word of her mother's death in Switzerland on 8 November after a short illness. Of this devastating news Maconchy wrote to Williams:

> We could not get out & be with her, as it's impossible to go to Switzerland now & felt terribly cut off & helpless. Sheila is alone there now of course – but seems pretty well, better than she has been for some time, I think. It was a great shock to us, & I feel terribly sad that she never saw Anna.[28]

In late 1940, Maconchy began work on a setting of *Dies Irae* for contralto, chorus, and orchestra, in memory of her mother. Although 1940 ended on a sombre note, life nevertheless went on at Chart Corner. While Maconchy felt tremendously isolated – a sentiment that she felt was not limited to her, but rather the circumstances of the war – she benefitted greatly from the assistance of a nanny, which enabled her to work on her compositions, even if she had to balance her writing between feeds.[29] In late January 1941, Maconchy began work on two songs for Sophie Wyss set to text by the Anglo-Irish poet Sheila Wingfield (1906–92), with whom Maconchy and LeFanu were personally acquainted, and on 9 February her ballet *Puck Fair* was set to be premièred by the Irish Ballet Club in Dublin.[30]

The Irish Ballet Club was founded in 1939 by dancer and choreographer Cepta Cullen (1914–92), the Club's director, and poet and theatre director Frederick Robert Higgins (1896–1941), who served as its president. From the outset, the Club aimed to further the development of ballet in Ireland through the establishment of a national ballet company.[31] The Irish Ballet Club was not the first organisation in Ireland to take on such an ambitious task: in 1927, W.B. Yeats,

[26] Elizabeth Maconchy to Grace Williams, 17 August 1940.
[27] Ibid.
[28] Elizabeth Maconchy to Grace Williams, 10 January 1941.
[29] Ibid.
[30] Maconchy's setting of Wingfield's *The Disillusion* was later featured in a broadcast on 7 January 1942. A broadcast of Maconchy's setting of Wingfield's *Sailor's Song of the Two Balconies* took place on 15 February 1942.
[31] Victoria O'Brien, *A History of Irish Ballet from 1927 to 1963* (Bern: Peter Lang, 2011), 75.

along with choreographer and former Ballet Russes dancer Ninette de Valois (1898–2001), had attempted something similar through the creation of the Abbey Theatre School of Ballet. Both Cullen and Higgins had direct ties to the Abbey School and its creators: Higgins was a friend of Yeats and also served as a member of the Abbey Theatre's board and Cullen had trained under de Valois.[32]

The lofty aims of the Irish Ballet Club were perhaps best encapsulated in a speech Higgins delivered at the conclusion of the club's first performance. Drenched in nationalist rhetoric, excerpts of Higgins's speech appeared in the *Irish Times*: '"We must have a native ballet in Ireland", he declared. "We must contribute our racial qualities in pictorial art, in music and in dance, to the modern stage, and by doing that we contribute an important addition to the development of ballet in the Europe of to-day."'[33] To create a decidedly Irish national ballet, the Club focused on the utilisation of Irish talent from the dancers to the musicians, choreographers, designers, and composers.[34]

Exact details pertaining to how Maconchy became involved with *Puck Fair* are somewhat unclear. According to an article in the *Dublin Evening Mail*, she attended a performance by the Irish Ballet Club in December 1939, after which she went backstage and spoke with members of the Club's committee which led to further discussions with Cullen and Higgins.[35] Art critic James White, who was involved with the Irish Ballet Club at the time, has stated, however, that Maconchy's enlistment in the project came at the bequest of artist Mainie Jellett (1897–1944), who designed the décor and costumes.[36] Known for her abstract paintings, Jellett was a pioneering figure in modern art circles in Ireland. As the Poë and Jellett families ran in the same Dublin social circles, with the Jelletts attending Maconchy and LeFanu's wedding, Maconchy and Mainie were presumably acquainted with one another.

The short ballet, which was intended to last twenty-five minutes, is based upon the traditional Irish fair that takes place in Kerry. The scenario for the ballet was written by Higgins and arranged in five scenes, beginning on the first evening of the fair where a male goat – the literal translation of the title of the fair, Aonach an Phoic, is Fair of the He-Goat, with the goat often referred to as 'King Puck' – is placed in a cage upon a wooden pedestal. Set in the middle of the fair in front of decorated shops and drinking tables, the plot revolves around the daughter of a farmer, Lovable Girl, who falls in love with the Fiery Tinker.[37] When the Lovable Girl's mother discovers her daughter dancing with

32 O'Brien, 76–80. After de Valois's resignation from the Abbey School in 1933, Cullen, along with another former pupil, Muriel Kelly, took over the direction of the school. As O'Brien notes, the Irish Ballet Club's structure was also likely influenced by Marie Rambert's Ballet Club, which had been influential in developing a British school of ballet.

33 'Native Ballet Needed', *Irish Times*, 15 March 1939. Also quoted in O'Brien, 78.

34 O'Brien, 78–80.

35 'Fashion And Gossip In Dublin To-day', *Dublin Evening Mail*, 5 February 1940.

36 O'Brien, 91.

37 *Puck Fair* scenario, SHC. 'Tinker' is a derogatory term for a traveller.

the Fiery Tinker, she is outraged and attempts to take back her daughter but is thwarted by the Fiery Tinker. Then the Black-coated Gentleman, a priest, arrives and the Lovable Girl runs away, with both her mother and the priest in pursuit. The priest later returns with the Civic Guards who intend to arrest the Fiery Tinker; however, their attempts come to no avail. The Lovable Girl then returns to the stage. Seeing her lover in distress, she rejoins him as a crowd of travellers thwart the Civic Guards. The final scene opens with a solemn procession of the farmers and the Lovable Girl's mother, followed by the re-entry of the travellers and the Lovable Girl, who, having beaten the Civic Guards, rejoice as they eat all the food left by the farmers on the tables before finally stealing the fair's prized ceremonial goat.[38]

Over the course of the ballet's creation, Maconchy corresponded regularly with Jellett who kept her abreast of news regarding the production. Owing to the limited financial capabilities of the Irish Ballet Club, Maconchy composed the work for two pianos. Early in the project's development, Jellett expressed grave concerns regarding the quality of the Ballet Club's pianists.[39] Fortunately, plans were subsequently arranged for Charles Lynch, who had worked extensively with Marie Rambert's ballet company in London prior to the war, to play the first piano part, with one of the Club's other pianists, Miles Rumbold, who had been studying with Lynch, taking on the second part.[40] Although there were initial doubts about the future of *Puck Fair* after the unexpected death of Higgins on 6 January 1941, arrangements were subsequently made for the work to be performed on 9 February.[41]

In her score, Maconchy made a concerted effort to avoid the use of folk tunes as it was a practice that made her uneasy.[42] Though the whereabouts of Maconchy's original score for two pianos is unknown, later versions of the ballet reveal the work as both vivacious and light-hearted, with one of the most admired sections being the moment the lovers meet, brilliantly captured by Maconchy with a lush, rapturous melody. Though Maconchy was unable to attend the performance, which took place at the Gaiety Theatre, both Jellett and Boyle kept her informed of details of the rehearsals and performance. In spite of some concerns regarding the relative inexperience of the dancers, the sold-out performance came off surprisingly well, with Jellett crediting Lynch's playing as crucial to its success.[43]

[38] Ibid.

[39] Mainie Jellett to Elizabeth Maconchy, 23 April 1940, private collection.

[40] Mainie Jellett to Elizabeth Maconchy, 25 January 1941, private collection. Lynch, who was a pacifist, returned to Ireland during the war. Though Jellett had brought up Lynch as a possibility in her letter to Maconchy on 3 May 1940, it was not until January 1941 that his involvement was officially confirmed.

[41] Mainie Jellett to Elizabeth Maconchy, 16 January 1941, private collection.

[42] Elizabeth Maconchy, draft of talk for Radio Éireann broadcast, 20 September 1959, SHC.

[43] Mainie Jellett to Elizabeth Maconchy, 10 February 1941, private collection.

According to the *Irish Times*, at the conclusion of the performance, Irish poet Donagh MacDonagh (1912–68) spoke a few words to the audience: 'Perhaps for the first time, he said, they had in Ireland upon the stage all the arts gathered together.'[44] The significance of the ballet's Irish subject matter as ushering in a new era in Irish ballet was a central theme in many of the reviews. Overall the reviews were glowing, with the many critics remarking upon the marked improvement of the dancers.[45] In the *Irish Press*, the critic quipped, 'I do not know if Elizabeth Maconchy's music was intended for the pianos rather than an orchestra, but certainly her composition, interpreted on the pianos, was better adapted to the general atmosphere of the ballet than is usually the case when piano replaces orchestra.'[46] The critic at the *Leader*, however, found the music a bit too modern for their liking:

> Its musical setting rings somewhat strangely modern on a first hearing, for when one's small mind is over busied in receiving impressions through the eye it is more than likely the aural receptions will weaken as the others gain strength through beauty of movement, of colour and of design. A second presentation is therefore called for. We do not for a moment wish to imply that the musicianship of the composer is wanting even in the most remote sense or that its interpretation by two such pianists as Charles Lynch and Miles Rumbold is at fault. Quite the contrary is the simple truth, for the choreography that delighted our eye received its inspiration and its perfection from the very music that felt strange to our duller ear.[47]

Puck Fair was performed again later in the year in a memorial concert to honour Higgins on 1 June, after which nearly two years elapsed until the work was performed once again by the Irish Ballet Club on 6 March 1943.[48] Despite the legacy of *Puck Fair* as a seminal work in the history of Irish ballet, the Irish Ballet Club's optimistic vision would ultimately be short-lived, with the organisation's last known performance taking place in June 1943.[49]

44 'Colourful Irish Ballet', *Irish Times*, 10 February 1941.

45 Both Jellett and Ina Boyle, who attended some of the rehearsals, made comments in letters to Maconchy about the quality of the dancing being a concern; however, both noted that as a whole, the dancers had improved tremendously and dedicated an extensive amount of time to rehearsing *Puck Fair*, running through it three times in the final dress rehearsal. Ina Boyle to Elizabeth Maconchy, 9 February 1941, private collection. Both the reviewers in the *Irish Times* and the *Irish Independent* remarked upon the improved quality of the Club's dancing. See 'Colourful Irish Ballet', *Irish Times*, 10 February 1941; and D.S., 'Ballet Club's Programme', *Irish Independent*, 10 February 1941.

46 '"Puck Fair" Produced By Ballet Club', *Irish Press*, 10 February 1941.

47 C. Sharp, 'Puck Fair in Ballet', *Leader*, 22 February 1941.

48 The 1943 production featured an orchestral version of the ballet. As Maconchy was unable to take on the task of orchestrating it herself, the arrangement was done by Boyle. Elizabeth Maconchy to Sheila Maconchy, 21 April 1942, private collection.

49 O'Brien, 96, 107.

Though Maconchy had initially hoped to attend the première of *Puck Fair*, any attempt was likely thwarted by her impending move to Downton Castle near Ludlow, Shropshire in March 1941. This move was prompted by concerns regarding the safety of the Royal College of Surgeons's library collection. At the beginning of the war, the Royal College of Surgeons began the process of evacuating portions of its collection, with roughly 30,000 items eventually sent to Downton Castle where Maconchy and her family remained through early 1945.[50] Maconchy had her doubts about the move, writing to Williams, 'I must admit I am a little appalled at the idea of starting wartime house-keeping in a castle.'[51] Draughty and lacking electricity and gas, conditions were far from ideal in the eighteenth-century Gothic-revival castle. Away from the constant threat of bombings, however, Maconchy found life in the countryside to be a pleasant change of pace and quickly adapted to life at the sprawling estate with the aid of her nanny, a maid, and Anna who, though barely able to walk on her own, had developed a particular fondness for dusting and polishing as Maconchy devoted much of her time to working in the garden, making jams, and tending to several chickens.[52] Of these years living at Downton, Anna recalled,

> Betty told me stories at bedtime or my father read to me, and later on Betty gave me lessons. Once a week she drove to Ludlow to buy food. On one occasion, probably in 1944, she arranged to meet Benjamin Britten there and I remember the teashop and enjoyed watching the fish in the aquarium while they talked. [...] My mother made picnics in the summer and taught me to swim in the Teme. She packed the sandwiches in blue sugar bags and my father made paper boats after tea. One very cold winter we 'tobogganed' down the slopes below the castle terrace, using teatrays which got rather bent! My parents occasionally enjoyed long walks but were usually too busy.[53]

Though Maconchy found that her obligations left her little time to compose, she was nevertheless able to continue making progress on *Dies Irae*. In October, Maconchy travelled to London, meeting with her publisher as well as Anthony Bernard. She also found time to attend a performance of *The Sleeping Beauty* by the Sadler's Wells Ballet and met with Lambert and de Valois to see if they might be interested in mounting a production of *Puck Fair*. Maconchy played through the score and although both Lambert and de Valois appeared to like the work, they felt that it would be unsuitable owing to the number of male dancers it required.[54] Maconchy also paid a visit to Vaughan Williams, who she found to be a shell of his former self, as she detailed in letter to Williams,

50 Susan Isaac, 'Evacuating the Library in World War II', *Royal College of Surgeons Library Blog*, 12 May 2017, https://www.rcseng.ac.uk/library-and-publications/library/blog/evacuating-the-library-in-world-war-ii/ [accessed 27 May 2019].

51 Elizabeth Maconchy to Grace Williams, 10 January 1941.

52 Dunlop, 17; and Elizabeth Maconchy to Sheila Maconchy, [1941], private collection.

53 Ibid.

54 Elizabeth Maconchy to Sheila Maconchy, 16 October 1941, private collection.

> I went down to Dorking to see Uncle Ralph while I was up, & was rather shocked to find how much older & almost 'fallen away' he looked. He spends his time on committees, fire-watching, digging potatoes etc – I remonstrated but he said he felt he must 'do what he could to help' & then any time he had got left he felt he could use for his own work. I'm sure he's wrong, but if he has made up his mind there is no changing it. He talked away cheerfully a lot of the time, but I thought he was restless & not himself.[55]

Maconchy showed Vaughan Williams her *Dies Irae*, and though she found his comments helpful, she remained dissatisfied with the work. Maconchy subsequently sent a copy of the score to Williams, who offered constructive criticism as per usual. Although Williams thought highly of several sections of the work, neither Williams nor Vaughan Williams were able to sway Maconchy's confidence in it, as she remarked to Williams: 'I have found it very hard to see it dispassionately & sometimes think it good, sometimes bad.'[56] Though Maconchy continued to work on the score, she remained deeply dissatisfied, eventually withdrawing the work.

Later in the autumn, Maconchy resumed work on her Fourth String Quartet, which she completed in January 1942. She also began work on a piece for cello and piano that she would eventually title *Divertimento*.[57] Though her works continued to garner a handful of performances and broadcasts, this was a discouraging period for Maconchy as she grew increasingly frustrated with the challenges she faced in securing performances, as she remarked in a letter to Williams: 'It certainly is pretty difficult to get any performances now. I don't expect ever to get any B.B.C. performances as Julian Herbage (who loathes me) apparently controls the programmes now & K.A.W. [Kenneth A. Wright] does Overseas music.'[58]

Maconchy's frustrations with the BBC were soon to escalate in early January when records that Maconchy had previously loaned them of her Second String Quartet, played by the Brosa Quartet, were returned to her via the post completely broken, in spite of her explicit request that they refrain from posting them back owing to their fragility.[59] To make amends, the BBC offered to include Maconchy's

[55] Elizabeth Maconchy to Grace Williams, 27 October 1941.

[56] Elizabeth Maconchy to Grace Williams, 6 January 1942.

[57] Elizabeth Maconchy to Grace Williams, 20 November 1941. Maconchy had originally intended the work for viola and chamber orchestra.

[58] Elizabeth Maconchy to Grace Williams, 27 October 1941.

[59] Elizabeth Maconchy to Grace Williams, 6 January 1941. Maconchy writes, 'I'd lent them for extracts to be used in a series of broadcasts (for America) by a man called Edward Lockspeiser – & specially asked them to keep the records till I could get someone to call for them.' Though Maconchy stated that she had sent a letter outlining her request, according to BBC internal memos, they were unable to locate any such letter. Nevertheless, memos reveal that Maconchy had in fact verbally requested that she be asked to retrieve the records; however, her request was interpreted as not appearing 'emphatic', and a decision was made to return them by post, which was the routine manner in which the BBC returned such items. Miss Legge to A.O.M.D.,

quartet in a broadcast, during which another recording could be made. As the Brosa Quartet had disbanded in 1939, the BBC proposed using a quartet composed of members of the BBC's Salon Orchestra. Maconchy agreed to the BBC's proposition and the work was subsequently broadcast and recorded from the BBC's Bedford Station on the afternoon of 10 April over the Home Service.[60]

In the spring and early summer, Maconchy was busy with work on a new symphony as well as alterations to the parts of her *Dialogue*, which Wood had decided to include in the 1942 Proms season, which was once again under the auspices of the BBC.[61] At the end of June, Maconchy travelled to London for a rehearsal of *Dialogue*. She was thrilled to have Curzon as the soloist again and the two ran through the work on two pianos at Curzon's home in Highgate.[62] The following day she attended a rehearsal of the work with the orchestra at the Royal Albert Hall. Of the rehearsal, Maconchy recounted in a letter to her sister, Sheila,

> It went very well for a first run-through, & I was pleased. I felt it was well worth while having made the alterations in the score & there isn't anything I want to change now. It ought to come off quite well, I think. The conductor [Basil Cameron] … was friendly & pleasant & took trouble & was competent – (not brilliant.) Apparently he is often difficult & touchy, so it was lucky.[63]

Maconchy returned to London on 13 July, rehearsing with Curzon once again on two pianos at his home. The following day, she attended another rehearsal at the Royal Albert Hall. Unlike the encouraging first run-through, the rehearsal on the 14th proved far more disconcerting:

> we waited & waited – there was a lot to get through in the rehearsal & Basil Cameron got fussed & behind time, & finally at ¼ to 1 when the orchestra were exhausted we had about 10 minutes rehearsal – the orchestra simply broke down then & we had to stop! [I]t was far worse than when they had read it at the preliminary rehearsal a fortnight before. Mr Cameron said he'd do it the next morning instead – but Curzon had to practice & said he couldn't come, so I had to play the solo-piano part![64]

memo, 14 January 1942, BBC WAC EM2. In an acknowledgement of the BBC's culpability in the matter, Bliss remarked in an internal memo, 'The attached memo from Miss Legge to me explains itself. We obviously owe this composer a new set of records.' Arthur Bliss to D.D.M. Bedford, memo, 15 January 1942, BBC WAC EM2.

60 The Quartet was composed of Jean Pougnet (1st violin), Tom Jenkins (2nd violin), Frederick Riddle (viola), and Anthony Pini (cello). Negotiations regarding the arrangements for the broadcast and recording are detailed in Maconchy's BBC file between 15 January and 15 April 1942 in BBC WAC EM2.

61 Elizabeth Maconchy to Julian Herbage, 3 February 1942, BBC WAC EM2.

62 Elizabeth Maconchy to Sheila Maconchy, 8 July 1942, private collection. Of Curzon, Maconchy remarked, 'he is an excellent pianist – & most suggestible to what one wants: in fact he plays it exactly as I want it.'

63 Ibid. Also see Maconchy's letter to Williams from 29 June 1942.

64 Elizabeth Maconchy to Sheila Maconchy, 24 July 1942, private collection.

Fortunately, the rehearsal the next morning went better than the previous day's and by the final rehearsal on the morning of the 16th the work finally began to come together.

As its title implies, *Dialogue* is structured more as a conversation as opposed to a conventional concerto. Nevertheless, it is the piano that takes the lead, with the work's four relatively short movements characteristic of Maconchy's idiomatic development of thematic material, with the interval of a minor third playing a pivotal role in the first movement. For the performance, Maconchy was not in the audience, but rather on the stage, turning pages for Curzon. On the whole, Maconchy felt satisfied with the performance, with reception of the work largely mixed in the press, as usual.[65]

Following the Proms, Maconchy turned her attention to a short piece she had been asked to write as part of a broadcast in honour of Vaughan Williams to take place on his seventieth birthday on 12 October.[66] Titled *Variations on a Well-known Theme*, Maconchy's succinct four-and-a-half-minute orchestral work was played alongside other equally brief works composed especially for the occasion by Alan Bush, Patrick Hadley, Gordon Jacob, Constant Lambert, Robin Milford, and Edmund Rubbra. When she was initially approached by Arthur Bliss about contributing a work, she was fired with several ideas, as she detailed in a letter to Sheila:

> The others (except Constant Lambert) are all a bit 'village pump' – so I must at all costs avoid that. It's awfully hard to know what to write. Something very modern, very brilliant – and at the same time good music, & characteristic of me is what's wanted but I feel quite incapable of producing it. However, I must have a shot at something, & I feel it's very nice to have been asked. The trouble is that my serious music is inclined to be gloomy, which isn't very suitable ... If I can't produce anything else I might try a set of variations on 'for he's a jolly good fellow' – treated in as modern a way as possible – with the theme only hinted at in the earlier variations & only appearing in full at the very end.[67]

Maconchy ultimately decided to go with the latter theme of 'For He's a Jolly Good Fellow'. Maconchy travelled to London for the concert and broadcast. Aside from Maconchy, Bush, Rubbra, and Finzi were the only other contributors in attendance. Following the concert, Maconchy had dinner with Bush at a Chinese restaurant. Though Vaughan Williams was not in attendance for the concert, he listened to the broadcast at home. The following day he wrote to Maconchy, 'I thought the joke came off very well.'[68]

Working on the short piece for Vaughan Williams appears to have renewed Maconchy's own interest in the genre as she decided to tackle a theme and variations on a larger scale, as she wrote to Sheila in the late summer: 'I'd been wanting for some time to write something for string orchestra – in fact I'd

[65] Ibid.

[66] Maconchy was approached about this in May by Bliss. Arthur Bliss to Elizabeth Maconchy, 15 May 1942, private collection.

[67] Elizabeth Maconchy to Sheila Maconchy, 19 May 1942, private collection.

[68] Ralph Vaughan Williams to Maconchy, 13 October 1942, VWL 1702.

written most of one movement for it: now I think I'll make it a set of Variations, using some of the material out of the movement I'd already written.'[69] Maconchy subsequently finished her *Theme and Variations for String Orchestra* in January 1943. Although she had hoped that the work would be suitable for the Proms, Wood was uninterested. Hinrichsen subsequently submitted it to the BBC's reading committee.[70]

Though Maconchy continued to find her time for composing limited, in January 1943 she was busy working on a setting of *By the Waters of Babylon* for women's chorus and orchestra, which was inspired by another composer's setting she disliked, as she detailed in a letter to Sheila: 'I've vaguely wanted to do it for years – it is so lovely: – & there is such a bad setting of it in William Walton's "Belshazzar's Feast" that it has always made me want to do it better!'[71] Other works that occupied her time during the year included an orchestral suite arrangement of her ballet *Puck Fair*, a new violin sonata, which she completed the following year, and a setting of a poem on the subject of Stalingrad by Jacqueline Morris, a fifteen-year old student at Hengoed Girls' School in Wales. Titled *The Voice of the City* and arranged for female chorus and piano, the work, which was intended for use in schools, was published later in the year by the WMA.[72]

While opportunities for performances and broadcasts remained precarious, some doors were opened for Maconchy when Norman Fraser, who worked for the BBC's Latin American Service, took it upon himself to include some of her works in broadcasts.[73] On 9 April, the BBC did a run-through of Maconchy's Fourth String Quartet, ahead of its scheduled broadcast over the Latin American Service on 19/20 April.[74] Of the works the Blech Quartet played at the

[69] Elizabeth Maconchy to Sheila Maconchy, 27 August 1942, private collection.

[70] Elizabeth Maconchy to Grace Williams, 14 March 1943. *Theme and Variations for String Orchestra* was read by Jacob, Ireland, and Benjamin Dale and received negative evaluations. BBC WAC R27/603 Music General/Music Reports, 1928–54, March–April 1943.

[71] Elizabeth Maconchy to Sheila Maconchy, 12 January 1943, private collection.

[72] Elizabeth Maconchy to Grace Williams, 28 May 1943. Another work Maconchy wrote for the WMA aimed for children was *The Shark and the Whale* (1942).

[73] Elizabeth Maconchy to Grace Williams, 14 March 1943. Fraser arranged for overnight broadcasts on the BBC Latin American Service on 16/17 December 1942 of Maconchy's Viola Sonata, performed by violist Lena Wood and pianist Tom Bromley, which was repeated on 5/6 March 1943. The first movement (Serenade) from Maconchy's *Divertimento for Cello and Piano*, which was played by Sela Trau (cello) and John Willis (piano), was broadcast on 10/11 March 1943. Maconchy's *Samson* was also featured in a broadcast of songs performed by Wyss that was relayed on 19/20 July 1941.

[74] Based on correspondence between Maconchy and the BBC, the purpose of the play-through on 9 April was to determine whether or not the work would be suitable for a future broadcast and was unrelated to the broadcast already scheduled to take place on 19 April on the Latin American Service. Maconchy initially sent the

run-through, Maconchy's earned the most favourable, yet far from glowing, evaluation from Wright, who noted that the quartet was '[e]asily the best work of the afternoon. Well made and up to a point effective, but I cannot feel in sympathy with such unsmiling music. It is always hard and soulless like a calculating machine. Mr. Vowles has the timings of this work.'[75] Bliss subsequently decided to pass Maconchy's quartet so that it could be considered for a future broadcast.

On 30 April, the Blech Quartet gave the first concert performance of the work at the Wigmore Hall, and on 6 June the work was broadcast again, this time over the BBC's European Service. In String Quartet No. 4, Maconchy takes her use of interrelated motific themes to new heights as all four movements derive almost entirely from the opening central motif in the cello (Examples 6.1–6.4). In the first movement, Allegro, the cello's motif is a persistent driving force with the metre alternating between 5/4 and 3/4. The cello is then joined by the viola, followed by the violins, who expand upon the principal motif by means of inversion and retrograde motion. A brief respite from the cello's repetitive strain arrives in the guise of a lush lento appassionato before a forceful return of the chromatic dominance of the central motif. (Despite the chromatic motif, the work is, in fact, largely diatonic.)

The second movement is a spirited scherzo that seamlessly grows out of the conclusion to the first movement. The third movement begins in the violins with a theme once again derived from the work's central motif. The movement is arch-like in shape with Maconchy heightening the emotional tension of her richly lyrical contrapuntal lines through her characteristic play between major and minor intervals. The third movement leads directly into the energetic fourth movement, which features a fleeting reference to String Quartet No. 3 expertly woven into the fabric of the work. Though the concert performance of the work was not widely covered by the press, a brief review appeared in the *Times*: 'Elizabeth Maconchy's fourth quartet … broke no new ground in her own line of thought. … The new quartet successfully repeats on a new text the method which had already yielded interesting and distinctive music.'[76]

On 3 July, Maconchy received a broadcast of *Great Agrippa* in a Home Service programme of works by British women composers. Performed by the BBC Scottish Orchestra in Glasgow and conducted by Guy Warrack, the programme also featured the overture to Smyth's *The Boatswain's Mate*, Williams's *Fantasia on Welsh Nursery Tunes*, and Phyllis Tate's *Valse lointaine*.

score of her Fourth String Quartet to the BBC on 19 May 1942. On 8 July, she was informed that the BBC was interested in a play-through of the work at a later date.

[75] Kenneth Wright to D.D.M., 19 April 1943, BBC WAC EM2. The Blech Quartet also played works by G.H. Bryce, F. Chagrin, Frederick May (String Quartet in C Minor), and Ian Parrott in the run-through. Harry Vowles was the Music Department's Senior Administrative Assistant.

[76] 'Music in London', *Times*, 7 May 1943.

Example 6.1. Maconchy, String Quartet No. 4, mvt. I, opening.
Published by Alfred Lengnick & Co., a division of Universal Music Publishing Group.
Reproduced by permission of Hal Leonard Europe BV (Italy).

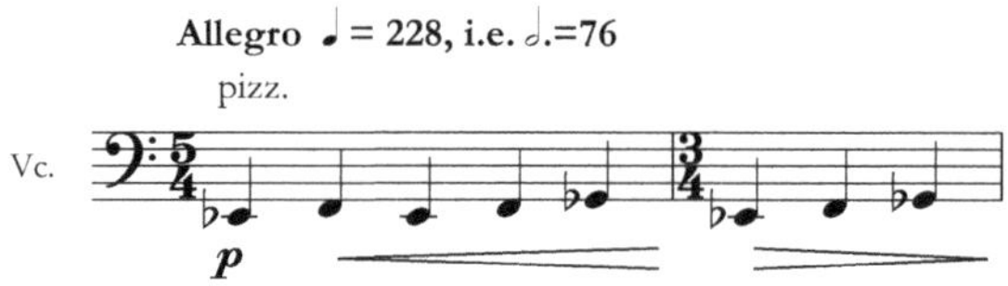

Example 6.2. Maconchy, String Quartet No. 4, mvt. II, opening.
Published by Alfred Lengnick & Co., a division of Universal Music Publishing Group.
Reproduced by permission of Hal Leonard Europe BV (Italy).

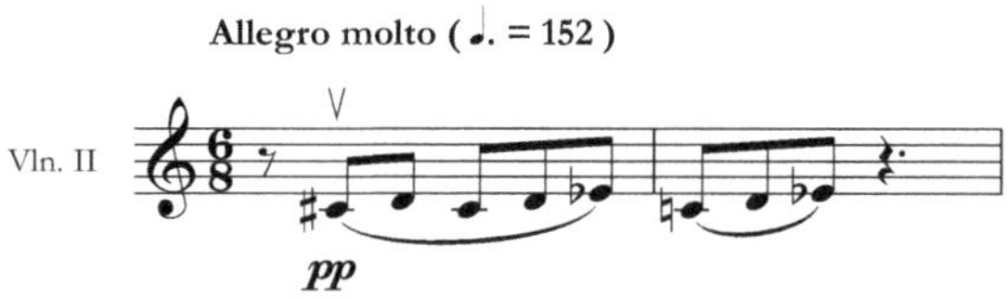

Example 6.3. Maconchy, String Quartet No. 4, mvt. III, opening.
Published by Alfred Lengnick & Co., a division of Universal Music Publishing Group.
Reproduced by permission of Hal Leonard Europe BV (Italy).

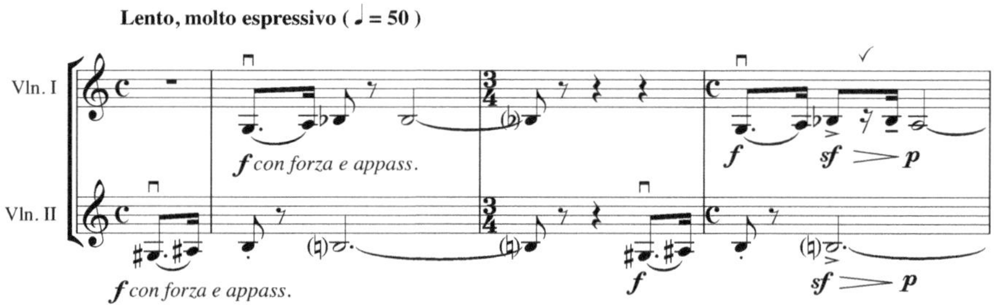

Example 6.4. Maconchy, String Quartet No. 4, mvt. IV, opening.
Published by Alfred Lengnick & Co., a division of Universal Music Publishing Group.
Reproduced by permission of Hal Leonard Europe BV (Italy).

The broadcast left Maconchy deeply dissatisfied, as she revealed in a letter to Williams:

> I thought poor Agrippa sounded too awful – all the tempi too slow & some very bad omissions indeed – in at least 3 places no tune. ... Quite a lot of the time I didn't recognise the music at all. ... The only thing I liked was that it sometimes made quite a nice kind of sound – but sounded much too much the same all the time. ... However, it's not worth bothering about, as it's not a good work, I fear – & doesn't stand up to concert performance.[77]

While this brief renewal of interest in her music at the BBC seemed promising, in August, she was dealt another blow when the BBC returned her *Dialogue for Piano and Orchestra*. Although the BBC noted that they would include the work in a programme if an opportunity became available, any likelihood of a future opportunity was dismal, as Vowles wrote in his letter accompanying Maconchy's score: 'It is with regret, however, that I must say we cannot hold out any hope of this happening in the near future, as we have a long list of new works to place in programmes, and very little opportunity of suitably placing them under wartime broadcasting conditions.'[78] A note attached to a copy of the letter sent to Lennox Berkeley, who worked at the BBC during the war, however, suggested otherwise: 'D.M. [Director of Music] does not want any priority given to this.'[79]

By September, Maconchy's feelings of despondency were growing stronger. Frustrated with Hinrichsen, she wanted to end her connection with the publisher, writing to Williams, 'I'm trying to make a clean break ... he's dithering & trying to avoid the issue & I don't know yet if he'll let me off. I can't stand his hopeless muddles etc any longer. He's done me much more harm than good.'[80] Beyond issues with her publisher, delays in broadcasts surely took their toll as well as feelings of isolation, as she continued in her letter: 'I get depressed about my work pretty often – & feel that I'm drying up. Or is it lack of stimulus, – lack of time – hearing no music – & will it come back? [B]ut sometimes I feel it's lack of new ideas with advancing age, which is depressing.'[81]

77 Elizabeth Maconchy to Grace Williams, 6 July 1943.

78 Harry Vowles to Elizabeth Maconchy, 12 August 1943, BBC WAC EM2.

79 Ibid. Maconchy initially submitted *Dialogue* to the BBC in November 1941. When Wood inquired about including the work in the 1942 Proms season, it was on condition that the Proms would be guaranteed the first performance. Maconchy subsequently wrote to the BBC on 3 February 1942 to request that the work be considered for a BBC broadcast sometime after the Proms. Two days later, a rather scathing evaluation of the work was written by Murrill. Herbert Murrill to A.D.M., 5 February 1942, BBC WAC EM2.

80 Elizabeth Maconchy to Grace Williams, 6 September 1943. Unfortunately, there is no surviving correspondence to indicate more specific information regarding Maconchy's frustrations with Hinrichsen, though she had previously noted that she found his methods unorthodox.

81 Ibid.

Unbeknownst to Maconchy, Williams, who received an increasing number of performances during the war, had already begun to lobby on Maconchy's behalf. Shortly after a broadcast of one of her works, Williams wrote to the BBC Symphony Orchestra's assistant conductor, Clarence Raybould (1886–1972), on 14 January 1943:

> Have you ever conducted anything of Elizabeth Maconchy's? I didn't think you have. I mention it simply because you are one of the few conductors interested in new works & for ages I've been wanting to write to someone at the B.B.C. about her. You know that she had a fine reputation until about a year before the war. Since then she has had nothing broadcast – except some chamber works – & those of us who know her work, & swear by her, feel we'd do anything to bring her works back into the programmes. I know she is misunderstood by some people – one hears her described as cerebral & un-lyrical, which is rubbish. For those of us who really know her stuff, there is more sense of beauty in her little finger than there is in lots & lots of contemporary composers put together. [...]
>
> What a pity that she wasn't born a Welshwoman instead of an Irishwoman – because then she'd be played every month![82]

Raybould replied:

> It was nice of you to take up the cudgels on behalf of Elizabeth Maconchy, but I am afraid that your remarks have fallen on rather stony ground in my case, as I have yet to see anything of this charming musician which appeals to me. However, I am quite prepared to believe that the defect is in myself and if I have the opportunity I shall be quite ready to do my best on her behalf. I am sure you would much rather that I be quite honest with you on this subject, although, of course, I should naturally prefer you should not convey these remarks to the lady herself.[83]

Unwilling to take no for an answer, Williams sent Raybould another letter on 31 January to try to persuade him once again.[84] As nothing came of her letters to Raybould, Williams decided to write to Kenneth Wright, who was often more sympathetic towards Maconchy's music. On 30 December 1943, Williams wrote the following:

> A word about Betty ... For the last few months her letters have shown that she is terribly depressed about composing. She has never shown any signs of losing heart before – but now she does sound very down-hearted and writes things like 'I think that perhaps I am finished as a composer' which isn't a bit like her, but hardly to be wondered at when you consider how consistent the neglect of her music has been ever since the war began. A composer just can't carry on indefinitely without contact with players and performances. You know what I think about her things and I know I'm right and others will hear them with my ears some day – but don't let it be too late.[85]

[82] Grace Williams to Clarence Raybould, 14 January 1943, BBC WAC EM2.

[83] Clarence Raybould to Grace Williams, 27 January 1943, BBC WAC EM2.

[84] Grace Williams to Clarence Raybould, 31 January 1943, BBC WAC EM2.

[85] Quoted in Mathias, *Lutyens, Maconchy, Williams and Twentieth-Century British Music*, 105–6.

Williams was not the only individual to lobby for Maconchy, as Vaughan Williams was also trying to secure performances for her. However, as he detailed in a letter to Williams, Maconchy's idiom made her case a challenge to plead:

> As regards Betty I don't know what to do – she's known at the BBC & to H.J.W. & has a publisher to push her.
>
> – I think we must recognize that her kind of music does not make a sensation like say Britten – she is Wordsworth to his Byron & therefore cannot expect to take the world by storm but be deeply loved by a few.
>
> But if there is anything you think I could do, do suggest it – I'm not very good at pushing, as you know.[86]

In November 1943, Vaughan Williams wrote to Boult to suggest a performance of *The Land*. Boult responded that he would take Vaughan Williams's suggestion under consideration.[87] Then, on 23 December, Vaughan Williams made his own attempt to persuade Raybould:

> The admirers of Elizabeth Maconchy (among whom I number myself) want very much to hear some of her music again. It is a long [time] since any orchestral work of hers was broadcast – So many people were struck by the 'Land' & the pfte concerto – but they are works one wants to hear more than once or twice. I can't believe that if she had pushed (or been pushed) as many young composers are she would have been a 'household word' by now.[88]

The responses from the BBC were far from encouraging, as Vaughan Williams wrote to Maconchy on 18 February 1944:

> Now about you – I do feel it very bad that you do not get your stuff done – Have you anything new you could send in to the proms? If so let me know at once … I have tried to persuade [the] B.B.C. to do the Land again – but as usual, they hedged.
>
> I fear we must confess that you are not popular – I know though theoretically that is a very noble aspiration practically, it is galling.
>
> But dearest Betty, you are still young – I was about 30 before I ever heard even a song of mine done in public – so your time may come – so push on and one day perhaps the key will turn in the lock.[89]

On 25 February, Vaughan Williams wrote to Wood to inquire if he might consider an orchestral suite consisting of arrangements of six dances from

[86] Ralph Vaughan Williams to Grace Williams, 2 November [1940s], VWL 3886.

[87] Adrian Boult to Ralph Vaughan Williams, 5 November 1943, BBC WAC EM2. Boult states, 'I will send it [*The Land*] up to London and hope it will find its way in in time.' A couple of weeks later, Herbage sent a memo to Berkeley, stating the following: 'Sir Adrian Boult has passed me a letter he has received from Dr. Vaughan Williams suggesting the inclusion of the above work [*The Land*] in a future orchestral concert. … While this is in no way a commitment, I think we should bear the work in mind for a broadcast in the near future.' Julian Herbage to Lennox Berkeley, 19 November 1943, BBC WAC EM2.

[88] Ralph Vaughan Williams to Clarence Raybould, [23 December 1943], VWL 1825.

[89] Ralph Vaughan Williams to Elizabeth Maconchy, 18 February [1944], VWL 1866.

Maconchy's ballet *Puck Fair* for the 1944 Proms season. Vaughan Williams wrote to Wood:

> You will hate me for worrying you – but I have just heard that another ex-pupil Elizabeth Maconchy has sent in a work for the Proms 'Puck Fair'. I do not know the work, but from what I do know of her I think it ought to be worth consideration.
>
> Could you please find time to glance at it & see if it is likely to suit you?
>
> Do not answer this please.[90]

Wood subsequently noted 'Already seen & included' on the letter and the work was scheduled for a performance by the BBC Orchestra conducted by Boult on 5 August.

Though the forthcoming Proms performance was encouraging, Maconchy nevertheless continued to find herself struggling. Aside from finishing her Violin Sonata, she only composed two completely new works in 1944: a work for chorus and piano titled *Pioneers of Rochdale* and a work for men's chorus titled *A Song of Freedom*, both written for the WMA. On 1 June, her *Impromptu* and piano suite, *A Country Town*, was played by Eric Hope in a recital at the Wigmore Hall. The latter event marked the first public performance of the work, which Maconchy had completed in 1939. A few days later on 5 June, the women's section of the WMA Singers included *The Voice of the City* as one of their selections for the London Musical Competition Festival. The choir earned second prize, with their performance generating a tremendous amount of interest in the work.

In July, Maconchy travelled to Bedford for a preliminary rehearsal of her suite arrangement of *Puck Fair*, which was held on the 2nd. Though the Proms season had come to a halt once again only a few days prior, plans were subsequently made for Maconchy's suite to be broadcast in a General Forces Programme that took place on 5 August, the same date of the originally planned Proms concert. The broadcast of the suite, which was arranged in six short movements, opens with 'The Goat', followed by 'The Priest', 'The Lovers', 'The Policemen', and 'The Tinkers'. Reviews of the broadcast were mixed. Williams, who knew the score quite well, remarked in a letter to Maconchy that 'it was quite good as first performances of new works go in this country nowadays. – but having listened with a very alert ear, I couldn't help feeling that the music deserved a much more understanding & human performance.'[91] In spite of the disappointing broadcast, the work garnered interest in Ireland, with a studio performance taking place in mid-December. This second hearing proved more encouraging, as Maconchy wrote to Williams: 'I heard it here – reception not very good – but good enough to tell that it was a surprisingly good performance, – mood & feeling right & tempi excellent, which pleased me a lot.'[92] The work was played once again on 11 February 1945 in a Radio Éireann symphony concert broadcast.

[90] Ralph Vaughan Williams to Henry Wood, 25 February [1944], VWL 1867.

[91] Grace Williams to Elizabeth Maconchy, 6 August 1944.

[92] Elizabeth Maconchy to Grace Williams, 20 December 1944.

Though Maconchy and her husband envisioned returning to Kent after the war, a few days prior to the BBC's broadcast of *Puck Fair*, Maconchy received word that their rented cottage at Chart Corner had been destroyed by a flying bomb that landed in the garden on the afternoon of 1 August.[93] Desirous to stay close to family, they eventually settled on a home in Essex near Maconchy's sister, Maureen, and LeFanu's sister, Lucie, which they purchased via auction in September 1944.[94] At the beginning of 1945, Maconchy and her family packed up their remaining belongings at Downton Castle and moved into a more modest home, Wickham Lodge, in the village of Wickham Bishops.[95]

With the end of the war in sight, some musical organisations, such as the LCMC, began to resurrect their concert series, offering faint hope, however short-lived, to composers such as Maconchy. On 3 May, the LCMC programmed Maconchy's new Violin Sonata in a concert that took place at the Cowdray Hall alongside new works by Berkeley, Lutyens, and Priaulx Rainier. The reviews of the sonata, which was played by Maria Lidka (violin) and Anthony Hopkins (piano) proved disappointing, however, as the work was criticised for its 'astringent quality'.[96] A few days later, the same programme was featured in a Gerald Cooper concert on the 8th at the Wigmore Hall.[97] As the concert coincided with VE Day, the audience at the Wigmore Hall was small, but the work garnered a slightly more favourable, but still critical review from Lionel Cranfield in the *New Statesman*, who found the work 'competent' but ultimately lacking in melodic expression.[98] In spite of the harsh criticism of the sonata, Maconchy had been cheered by the rehearsals, even if she had some misgivings about the work and the musical world at large:

> It was so nice hearing good players rehearse one's stuff again – I greatly enjoyed the rehearsals – but don't now feel, after two performances, absolutely satisfied with the work. I just can't quite make up my mind about it. In a way I feel it's good – or is it second-rate? – – I feel more than ever about the world of music and music critics – 'plus ça change plus c'est la meme chose' – & hate them all.[99]

93 Yona Swain to Elizabeth Maconchy, 1 August 1944, SHC.

94 Elizabeth Maconchy to Grace Williams, 26 September 1944.

95 Maconchy described the home as having 'a very nice friendly feeling – a mixture of dates, with a pretty Georgian face looking down the garden – good sunny rooms and a nice feeling of space. It faces south & west – & the garden is full of good things – lovely fruit & shrubs & roses etc.' Elizabeth Maconchy to Grace Williams, 26 September 1944.

96 'New Chamber Music', *Times*, 4 May 1945. Another harsh review appeared in the *Daily Mail*. See Ralph Hill, '3 New English Works', *Daily Mail*, 4 May 1945.

97 The Gerald Cooper Concerts series was started by Gerald Cooper (1892–1947) in the 1920s and was devoted to chamber music. The series ceased for a time when Cooper's interests turned to financing theatrical endeavours; however, he later resumed his chamber music concerts in 1942. 'Gerald Melbourne Cooper', *Musical Times* 88/1258 (December 1947): 399.

98 Lionel Cranfield, 'New Chamber Music', *New Statesman*, 19 May 1945.

99 Elizabeth Maconchy to Grace Williams, 12 May 1945.

7

Balancing Motherhood and a Career, 1946–50

The year 1946 began promisingly with the première of Maconchy's *Theme and Variations for String Orchestra* (1942–3), which was featured in a Radio Éireann symphony concert broadcast on 13 January.[1] In May, the American-born organist Virginie Zinke-Bianchini included one of Maconchy's works in a concert held at her home in Paris on the 18th, providing a boost for Maconchy's career in Europe after the war. October saw a performance of *The Voice of the City* in a studio recital arranged by the Committee for the Promotion of New Music (CPNM), and on 27 November, Maconchy's Viola Sonata was included in a BBC Midlands Home Service broadcast.[2] Maconchy's isolation from London briefly seemed poised to come to an end when she and her husband began searching for homes in Hampstead and Highgate. For whatever reason, they abandoned this idea in favour of remaining in Essex.[3] Maconchy celebrated when she learned that she was pregnant with her second child, Nicola, who was born on 28 April 1947. Despite all this good news, she was dissatisfied with her own works during this period as she detailed in a letter to Williams in March 1946:

[1] The broadcast concert, which featured the Radio Éireann Orchestra, conducted by Michael Bowles, was held at the Capitol Theatre in Dublin. The programme also featured Sibelius's *Finlandia* and two works by Beethoven: Piano Concerto No. 4 in G Major, op. 58, and Symphony No. 1 in C Major, op. 21.

[2] The CPNM was formed in 1943 by composer Francis Chagrin to promote works by young and less established composers. During the war, the CPNM's activities were subsidised by the Council for the Encouragement of the Arts. In 1952, the organisation became known as the Society for the Promotion of New Music (SPNM). See Hugh Wood, 'SPNM 20', *Musical Times* 104/1448 (October 1963): 708–10.

[3] *MLCT*, 102–5. The decision to begin searching for homes in London was motivated in part by a desire to improve the commute for LeFanu as Maconchy detailed in a letter to Williams: 'The trains have got worse instead of better – & Billy has no life at either end – & it really isn't good enough for him. I think it would in the end make him ill again too. I really never can get up to hear any music either – or not often: so we think it's the best thing to do, though I can't help being very sorry. I love this, & it's splendid for Anna.' Elizabeth Maconchy to Grace Williams, 2 February 1946. Although the exact date and reasoning for their abandonment of a move to London is unclear, it does coincide with Maconchy's second pregnancy, suggesting that this may have been a mitigating factor.

> I decided last week that I would scrap my Symphony. It was after hearing the Bartok – although I don't think the Bartok a completely satisfactory work at all – yet I feel it was alive and original & full of vitality – & that mine was still-born & dull. – However, I've now had new ideas about it … so I'll give it one more chance, – though I'll probably be right to scrap it in the end.[4]

While one can point to a multitude of factors that posed challenges for Maconchy during this period, such as her reputation as a 'modernist' composer, her continued isolation from London, as well as the inherent challenges of balancing motherhood and a career, there were also broader shifts in the post-war music scene that made re-establishing her expanding pre-war reputation a daunting, if not insurmountable, task. Much had changed within the music profession during the war, and despite any appearances to the contrary, there was a great deal of continuity from the late 1930s that spilled into the ways in which decisions were made in the initial post-war years. Although the incorporation of the Arts Council in 1946 ushered in a new era of state-sponsored support of the arts, and greater opportunities for new music broadcasts became available with the launch of the BBC's Third Programme, their structure had much in common with their wartime predecessors. The Arts Council was, after all, an outgrowth of the CEMA with its principal players remaining largely in the same roles. At the BBC, it was the composers who had forged deeper connections with the organisation during the war who were able to transition more seamlessly into the BBC's post-war programming. Even with greater governmental support many smaller organisations, such as the LCMC and CPNM, found themselves facing new challenges in the post-war years as fees for halls and musicians greatly outpaced subsidies provided by the Arts Council, thus greatly hampering their ability to promote the works of composers such as Maconchy, who often faced obstacles within the BBC.[5]

Some of the most significant obstacles Maconchy encountered in securing performances of her work in the early post-war years were due to errors made by the BBC and her previous publisher, Hinrichsen. These missteps resulted in significant delays of broadcasts. One such example is the delay of presenting her *Theme and Variations for String Orchestra*, which the Boyd Neel Orchestra wished to include in a Third Programme broadcast on 13 October 1946. A couple of weeks before the broadcast, Maconchy was informed by the Boyd Neel Orchestra's

4 Elizabeth Maconchy to Grace Williams, 12 March 1946.

5 According to the CPNM's annual report to the Arts Council in 1946, the organisation struggled to find halls to rent at reasonable rates. Combined with increases in Musicians' Union rates, the total cost for the CPNM's Experimental Rehearsals was double what it had been in previous years. 'Report to the Arts Council of Great Britain on the Activities of the Committee for the Promotion of New Music in 1946', Committee for the Promotion of New Music, ACGB/50/174, V&A Theatre and Performance Archives. Also see Nicholas Kenyon, *The BBC Symphony Orchestra: The first fifty years* (London: BBC, 1981), 208–9.

secretary that the BBC had objected to the work's inclusion.[6] As the BBC was unwilling to let the Boyd Neel Orchestra include the work without approval from its reading panel, Maconchy had to wait until late November to receive word regarding the work's fate. Fortunately for her, the work was approved and the Boyd Neel Orchestra was able to include it in a Third Programme Chamber Orchestral Concert that took place on 9 February 1947.

While Maconchy was relieved that the obstacle placed in her path by the BBC had been eventually removed in the case of the *Theme and Variations*, sadly, the same could not be said for her *Dialogue for Piano and Orchestra*. Shortly after Maconchy received the positive news about her *Theme and Variations*, she wrote to Vowles to inquire about the status of *Dialogue*, which had been approved by the reading panel in August 1943. Though she had been told that the work would 'be included in a programme as soon as opportunity occurs', Vowles had stated at the time that wartime conditions made the future possibility of a broadcast uncertain.[7] With the addition of the Third Programme, Maconchy hoped that this would lead to a long-awaited broadcast: 'Now that conditions have improved, (and the Third programme has started in addition) I hope you will soon be able to include the "Dialogue" in a programme?'[8] Vowles suggested Maconchy send the score to the BBC for reconsideration so that they could 're-assess things in the light of present-day experience, but please do not read into this any hope of programme placing'.[9] This reversal of position was surely a blow to Maconchy and she would have to wait until 1955 for the BBC to broadcast the work.

Further problems illustrating the chaotic and disorganised environment at the BBC during this period can be gleaned from internal correspondence regarding a broadcast of Maconchy's Fourth String Quartet which took place on the Third Programme on 20 January 1947.[10] In advance of the broadcast, the BBC announced that the concert would mark the first performance of the work. When Maconchy became aware of the BBC's error – the work had already received two broadcasts during the war – she telephoned the BBC's Marylebone office. This information, however, was not passed on and when Maconchy broached the matter again at a rehearsal, it was too late to correct the programmes or alert the press. In dealing with this matter, internal memos reveal that none of the BBC's staff were aware of the previous broadcasts. Blame was even levelled at Maconchy for not informing them, despite the fact that none of her correspondence indicated that the 20 January broadcast would be the work's first performance.[11] In spite of the confusion, the broadcast went well and Maconchy received encouraging letters from Williams and Vaughan

6 Elizabeth Maconchy to Robert Collett, 2 October 1946, BBC WAC EM2.

7 Harry Vowles to Elizabeth Maconchy, 12 August 1943, BBC WAC EM2.

8 Elizabeth Maconchy to Harry Vowles, 5 December 1946, BBC WAC EM2.

9 Harry Vowles to Elizabeth Maconchy, 12 December 1946, BBC WAC EM2.

10 Maconchy's Fourth String Quartet was played by the Philharmonia Quartet.

11 See W.W. Thompson to DM [Kenneth Wright], 21 January 1947, and Lowe's memo dated 22 January 1947, BBC WAC EM2.

Williams, with the latter offering some much-needed words of encouragement: 'don't talk any more nonsense about giving up composing – but go on from strength to strength.'[12]

Early in 1947 Maconchy completed a work that she had begun in 1946 titled *Sonnet Sequence*. With an ensemble consisting of soprano and nine instruments, and set to poetry by Kenneth Gee (1908–86), the work was written at the request of Gerald Cooper. This score explores the analogous relationship between aging and the changing of the seasons, beginning with old age and winter and ending with summer and youth.[13] The work was premièred on 29 April – the day after Maconchy gave birth to her second daughter, Nicola, appropriately enough – in a Gerald Cooper concert held at the Wigmore Hall with soprano Joan Cross and featuring members of the Kathleen Merritt Orchestra, conducted by Merritt. Programmed alongside works by Purcell, Bach, and Mozart, *Sonnet Sequence* was played both before the intermission and once again after. The sparsely attended concert received the typically mixed reviews to which Maconchy had become accustomed.[14] While the critic in the *News Chronicle* found the work 'competent and vigorous' they nevertheless noted that it 'at times suffers from opposing styles.'[15] The critic in the *Times*, however, viewed the work more favourably, noting 'there was little word-painting, but the deep feeling of the poem was translated into lyrical music of great power. This lyricism is a new note in Miss Maconchy's music; the concision, pungency, and sincerity are familiar characteristics.'[16] While lyricism could hardly be perceived as a new feature of Maconchy's music, the critic's emphasis on this characteristic highlights the frequent stereotypes that followed Maconchy, portraying her music as inaccessible and cold. The decision to play the work twice in the programme, however, worked in Maconchy's favour as the critic for the *Western Morning News* remarked that 'The second performance was the better as one heard more of the vocalist and as a musical picture of the sonnets the work was expressive.'[17]

On 3 June, Maconchy's Concertino for Clarinet and String Orchestra was premièred at the 1947 ISCM Festival, which was held in Copenhagen.[18] Completed in 1945, the work was written for the distinguished clarinettist Frederick

[12] Ralph Vaughan Williams to Elizabeth Maconchy, 23 January [1947], VWL 2148.

[13] For further discussion of the work see Mathias, *Lutyens, Maconchy, Williams and Twentieth-Century British Music*, 109–10.

[14] New works were usually played twice at Gerald Cooper Concerts. According to music critic George Dannatt, there were approximately fifty people in the audience at the Wigmore Hall. George Dannatt, 'Concerts in London', *Penguin Music Magazine* 4 (1947): 87.

[15] G.D. [George Dannatt], 'New music and a new London play', *News Chronicle*, 30 April 1947.

[16] 'Two New Works for Strings', *Times*, 30 April 1947.

[17] 'Gerald Cooper Concert', *Western Morning News*, 1 May 1947.

[18] The other works listed on the programme included *Serenade for Pianoforte and Twelve Instruments* (David van de Woesteyne), *Duao Fugao novem compositae sonis quatuor sine nomine vocibus* (Adone Zecchi), *Spoon River Anthology* for soloists, chorus, and

Thurston (1901–53). Arranged in three movements, it exemplifies Maconchy's characteristic economy and use of interrelated motific themes. As with many of Maconchy's scores from this period, its technical demands are exacting, with intricate figuration and scales requiring a virtuosic soloist.[19] Though Maconchy was unable to attend the festival herself, she received an encouraging telegram from the ISCM's president at the time, Edward Clark, telling her that the work was a tremendous success.[20] Others, however, were more circumspect in their assessment. Although Thurston served as an outstanding soloist, the same could not be said of the orchestra, as composer Humphrey Searle (1915–82) lamented in the *Monthly Musical Record* that while the work 'appeared to be well written and effective ... it suffered from a poor performance by the orchestra.'[21]

In spite of the lacklustre performance, the work appeared to have made an impact on Searle, who at the time was also working as a programme producer at the BBC. Eager to include Maconchy in the *Contemporary British Composers* series of studio recitals, he broached the topic in a letter to her on 3 September and plans were subsequently arranged to broadcast her Fourth String Quartet and *How Samson bore away the Gates of Gaza* on 7 October.[22] Although both Maconchy and Searle had requested the Philharmonic Quartet for the broadcast, for reasons unclear, the work was instead performed by the Zorian String Quartet.[23] Maconchy travelled to London for the broadcast and despite her initial fears regarding the young quartet's inexperience with her music, she was pleased with their playing and found them engaging and professional.[24] *How Samson bore away the Gates of Gaza* was performed by Wyss, accompanied by pianist Josephine Lee. The performance ultimately left Maconchy dissatisfied, as she detailed in a letter to Williams: 'I've never yet felt satisfied with Samson – I like it when I play it & yet (so far) it has never seemed to be successful in performance, to me.'[25] Despite her concerns, the broadcast elicited ambiguous praise from W.R. Anderson, who wrote in the *Musical Times*, 'Elizabeth Maconchy is one of the most consistent of contemporaries. I rank that quality high,

orchestra (Gino Negri), *Préludes joyeux* (Camille Schmit), *Sonetto di Michelangelo* (Fartein Valen), and Concerto for String Orchestra (Hilding Rosenberg).

19 In a letter to Williams, Maconchy remarked that Thurston had initially said that the work was 'much too difficult'. Elizabeth Maconchy to Grace Williams, 2 February 1946. Also see Mathias, *Lutyens, Maconchy, Williams and Twentieth-Century British Music*, 107–8.

20 Edward Clark to Elizabeth Maconchy, 5 June 1947, private collection.

21 H.S. [Humphrey Searle], 'The Copenhagen I.S.C.M. Festival', *Monthly Musical Record* 77/888 (July-August 1947): 158.

22 Humphrey Searle to Elizabeth Maconchy, 3 September 1947; and Elizabeth Maconchy to Humphrey Searle, 5 September 1947, BBC WAC EM2. For a brief overview of the series, see Carpenter, 55.

23 Ibid.

24 The Zorian String Quartet (1942–9) comprised Olive Zorian (1st violin), Marjorie Lavers (2nd violin), Winifred Copperwheat (viola), and Norina Seminor (cello).

25 Elizabeth Maconchy to Grace Williams, 12 October 1947.

even if I often don't get much from the music.'[26] Another broadcast followed shortly thereafter, with Maconchy's Concertino for Clarinet and String Orchestra featured in a Third Programme broadcast on 2 November with Thurston and the London Chamber Orchestra, conducted by Anthony Bernard.

As Maconchy adjusted to life with a second child, she was fortunate once again to have the aid of a nanny, thus enabling her to devote more time to composition. Parenting, however, still took priority, with knitting, dressmaking, and cooking taking up a great deal of her time. Despite her bustling home life, Maconchy still managed to carve out time for other creative outlets, writing a short story about a haunted harpsichord for Anna, quite fittingly titled *The Harpsichord*.[27] As for finding time to listen to music, the family occasionally had dinner in their drawing room so that they could listen to the Third Programme on their radiogram.[28]

By October 1947, Maconchy had finally reached a breakthrough with her symphony; however, she remained doubtful of its merits, writing to Williams, 'I THINK I have got the music of the Symphony finished at last. Unless I decide to scrap it in the next day or two I will send you the piano-score of the whole thing. You will condemn it if necessary, won't you? I really can't judge it at all.'[29] Maconchy's initial fears were soon assuaged by an encouraging response from Williams who declared the work 'a magnum opus', further adding that 'We need a work like this very badly.'[30] Maconchy evidently took Williams's words to heart and began scoring the work in late 1947. Working primarily in the evenings between 9 and 11 pm, when the children were asleep, Maconchy sought out the advice of Williams and Vaughan Williams in 1948; both composers offered some much-needed encouragement.[31]

[26] W.R. Anderson, 'Round about Radio', *Musical Times* 88/1257 (November 1947): 357.

[27] On a whim, Maconchy entered *The Harpsichord* in a ghost story competition in the spring of 1975 under her married name. The competition was organised by publisher John Cape and the *Times* and judged by actor Christopher Lee, and novelists Kingsley Amis and Patricia Highsmith. The competition reportedly received several thousand entries. In late 1975, her story was announced as one of the top thirteen entries and was published in *The Times Anthology of Ghost Stories* at the end of the year. J.C. Trewin, 'Spectres for our times', *Times*, 8 December 1975.

[28] Anna Dunlop, interview by author; and email from Nicola LeFanu to author.

[29] Elizabeth Maconchy to Grace Williams, 12 October 1947.

[30] Grace Williams to Elizabeth Maconchy, 5 December 1947.

[31] Elizabeth Maconchy to Grace Williams, 5–10 February 1948; and Elizabeth Maconchy to Grace Williams, 16 February 1949. The first known visit Maconchy made to Dorking in 1948 took place on 25 May, as Adeline Vaughan Williams remarked in a letter sent to Cordelia Curle: 'Today Betty McConchy [*sic*] (Lefanu) is coming with her new Symph – so R will have an exacting after[noon] but he is very fond of her so she is welcome.' Adeline Vaughan Williams to Cordelia Curle, October 1948, VWL 4683. The next known trip took place on 11 September, as detailed in a letter that Boyle sent to Maconchy. Ina Boyle to Elizabeth Maconchy, 12 September 1948, private collection.

During the summer of 1948, Maconchy travelled to Dublin hoping for a brief respite. The journey took an unhappy turn, however, when Anna was diagnosed with appendicitis and Nicola, who had been staying with family in England, fell ill as well, to the point of requiring hospitalisation at Great Ormond Street Hospital in London.[32] Despite the high level of stress these maladies surely induced, Maconchy was nevertheless able to complete her Fifth String Quartet in what must have been a determined concentration of focus and energy. A grant from the George Butterworth Music Fund to the amount of £50, which was received in November, offered some much-needed financial assistance as she completed scoring her symphony; this was especially valuable in defraying the expenses of having the parts copied.[33]

In spite of the support from Williams and Vaughan Williams, Maconchy continued to be beset by doubt. After a Third Programme broadcast of her Fourth String Quartet, which was played by the Blech Quartet on 25 January 1949, Maconchy wrote to Williams:

> I think you are right in what you say – & suggested in the summer – that I too often 'control my themes instead of letting them control me'. It's my worst weakness, I believe. It may be an inherent weakness – i.e. a lack of sufficient powers of invention, not a sufficient flow of musical ideas – making too little musical material go to [*sic*] far by dint of intellectual effort. If this is so – as I fear is very probable! – nothing can be done about it, my music will die a speedy & natural death – which is the natural & proper thing. It might possibly (as I hope) be a symptom of the way I have to work – I mean having to break off (– for days, & often weeks or even months) just when one feels underway with a movement & one's material has taken a hold of one's imagination. One has to start again in cold blood & consciously take hold of the material again – & though all may go ahead again after a bit, one doesn't get into the same musical-emotional condition. Also, I lack the stimulus of performances & of hearing other music – of just having orchestral sound in the flesh. Of course too much of this may be nearly as bad as too little – but there must be some musical stimulus: you know the way something suddenly sets one's musical imagination alight. … If these practical conditions of work account, or partly account for the condition, they may improve (I'm always hoping for that!) though perhaps not till the children are nearly grown-up, & then I'll be too old. (One is very unlikely to improve with age like Uncle Ralph – in fact I feel at times getting a bit worn out already!)[34]

Although reassuring recognition was soon to follow with String Quartet No. 5, which was awarded the inaugural Edwin Evans Memorial Prize in 1949, Maconchy suffered bouts of uncertainty about the work's merits. She confided

[32] LeFanu, 'Elizabeth Maconchy DBE (1907–1994)'.

[33] Dorothea Croft to Elizabeth Maconchy, 23 November 1948, private collection. The George Butterworth Fund was established in memory of the composer, who died in the Battle of the Somme in 1916. The Fund's activities were broadly defined, with an emphasis on helping composers. According to Croft, the grant was awarded on the recommendation of Vaughan Williams.

[34] Elizabeth Maconchy to Grace Williams, 16 February 1949.

to Williams, 'I don't know yet if it's any good – but I think perhaps there's rather more freedom than in the 4th.'[35]

Maconchy's Fifth String Quartet was premièred by the Hurwitz Quartet on 5 April 1949 at an LCMC concert held at the RBA Galleries.[36] The work concluded the first half of the concert, which was broadcast over the Third Programme. Maconchy was formally presented with the Edwin Evans Memorial Prize by Edward J. Dent on behalf of Mrs Edwin Evans during the interval. For all the composer's scruples, her Fifth String Quartet is a strong and vital score that merited this prize. The first movement opens with an expressive four-part canon in which she lays out the thematic ideas that pervade the entire work (Example 7.1). As the opening bars illustrate, Maconchy's emphasis on alternating semitones and whole tones implies an octatonicism that permeates the character of this quartet. The brief canon leads into a spirited allegro molto section in which Maconchy expands the alternating semitone and whole-tone motif with its inversion in the form of descending minor ninths and falling major and minor sevenths, which is underpinned by reiterations of an oscillating semitone figure that is a variation of the opening motif. A brief three-bar lento reintroduces the opening thematic material in the first violin, which is followed by another allegro molto section that further expands upon the melodic and rhythmic ideas expressed at the opening, followed by a concluding lento section.

The second movement is a lively scherzo structured upon a variation of the opening motif, ornamented by grace notes (Example 7.2), offering a playful variation upon the motific material laid out in the opening of the first movement. The third movement, Lento expressivo, beautifully encapsulates Maconchy's ability to weave brief motific ideas and gestures into a tapestry of rich contrapuntal lyricism. The movement opens with falling major sevenths in the second violin, viola, and cello. In bar 3, the first violin enters and gradually expands upon this falling major seventh motif, which then flows into an expressive melody that vividly recalls the same passage of Vaughan Williams's *Riders to the Sea* that Maconchy had previously referenced in the third movement of her Second String Quartet. The fourth movement features a compelling and energetic syncopated variation of the oscillating semitone pattern, which creates a sense of forward momentum as the movement progresses through a series of metre changes and a section of pizzicato that brings a brief respite from the intensity of the music, after which the momentum picks up as thematic material from the opening is reintroduced, concluding the work.

[35] Ibid. The Edwin Evans Memorial Prize was established by Evans's widow and administered by the LCMC. The competition, which sought to recognise a chamber work of outstanding merit, was restricted to composers born in Great Britain or the Dominions and included a monetary prize to the amount of £25. See 'London Contemporary Music Centre', *Musical Times* 89/1266 (August 1948): 236.

[36] The members of the Hurwitz Quartet (1946–51) at the time of the première consisted of Emanuel Hurwitz and Jorgen Laulund (violins), Kenneth Essex (viola), and Terence Weil (cello).

Example 7.1. Maconchy, String Quartet No. 5, mvt. I, opening.
Published by Alfred Lengnick & Co., a division of Universal Music Publishing Group.
Reproduced by permission of Hal Leonard Europe BV (Italy).

Example 7.2. Maconchy, String Quartet No. 5, mvt. II, opening.
Published by Alfred Lengnick & Co., a division of Universal Music Publishing Group.
Reproduced by permission of Hal Leonard Europe BV (Italy).

While the audience greeted the quartet with enthusiastic approbation – one could distinctly make out the voice of a male audience member shouting encore[37] – Maconchy remained unsure about its merits, as she wrote in a letter to Williams,

> I haven't quite made up my mind about it yet. I only heard one rehearsal – chaotic – then the performance which was much better than I'd expected – but I think it can actually sound a good bit better all through: & I believe it will after a bit, as the 4th has – each performance has seemed to get nearer to one's original 'conception' – even though played by a different quartet each time.[38]

[37] Grace Williams to Elizabeth Maconchy, 5 April 1949.

[38] Elizabeth Maconchy to Grace Williams, 24 April 1949.

Maconchy subsequently set about revising the score, which was published by Lengnick the following year.[39]

By and large, performances of Maconchy's music were few and far between in 1949.[40] Though her time to compose remained limited, she nevertheless found time to complete a new composition for soprano and string quartet based upon another of Gee's poems, titled *A Winter's Tale*, as well as create a piece for piano and orchestra that she titled Concertino for Piano and String Orchestra. While Maconchy found working on her new concertino deeply enjoyable, she was characteristically sceptical of its value, writing to Williams on 11 November,

> I really can't tell yet if it's any good. … I seem to find it much harder to make up my mind about my own music – and also, I think, other people's – than I used to: and also to decide with certainty about the ordinary things of life: is it just increasing old age? & partly perhaps because one gets too tolerant & sees all sides of the question too easily?[41]

Acutely aware of his former pupil's struggles, Vaughan Williams lobbied tirelessly on her behalf. On 19 October 1949, he wrote to Steuart Wilson, the BBC's Head of Music[42]:

> I have been lately seeing a new Symphony by Elizabeth Maconchy which I admire very much.
>
> I feel I ought not perhaps to approach you personally on matters like this but I do not quite know how to get to the centre of things without you. Do you think there is a chance that the B.B.C. would give it a performance? I ask this because, if not, I must make moves to try and get it done elsewhere; but naturally I would rather the B.B.C. did it.[43]

Discouraged by the BBC's lack of interest, Vaughan Williams began to formulate a plan of his own with an idea of organising a concert the following year:

> I hope next May to be able to help in organising a concert of new or unknown orchestral works, and I should like, if possible, to put your Symphony in.

39 Ibid. Lengnick published Maconchy's String Quartet No. 4 in 1949.

40 Following the première of String Quartet No. 5, the next known performance of one of Maconchy's works took place on 7 June 1949 with the Blech Quartet playing String Quartet No. 4 at the Barber Institute at Birmingham University. On 4 October, cellist Sela Trau and pianist Hubert Greenslade played the first movement, 'Serenade', from *Divertimento for Cello and Piano* (1941–3) at a CPNM concert at the salle Érard. The following month, *A Country Town* (1939) was featured in a BBC Children's Hour broadcast on 25 November, played by Eric Hope.

41 Elizabeth Maconchy to Grace Williams, 11 November 1949.

42 Steuart Wilson began serving in the position of Head of Music at the BBC in 1948, replacing Kenneth Wright who had been serving as the interim Director of Music following the untimely death of Victor Hely-Hutchinson in 1947. The job title 'Head of Music' replaced Hely-Hutchinson's title of 'Director of Music'. See Humphrey Carpenter, *The Envy of the World: Fifty Years of the BBC Third Programme and Radio 3* (London: Weidenfeld and Nicolson, 1996), 81.

43 Ralph Vaughan Williams to Wilson, 19 October 1949, BBC WAC EM2.

> Could you let me know whether you would like it done under these circumstances. [...]
>
> Also have you any particular ideas as to a conductor? At present one idea is Clarence Raybould and the other is Constant Lambert. But I must explain that all is very vague yet and I do not know whether it will come off. We have not even found a place yet.[44]

While Vaughan Williams's plan did not come to fruition – the BBC was, after all, fighting its own battles as the Third Programme faced mounting criticism for its low audience figures and the 'highbrow' and 'intellectual' nature of its content, leading to internal fights over budgets and increasing caution in programme planning[45] – opportunity later arose when a conflict over the rights to the first performance of Peter Racine Fricker's Symphony No. 1 led to its withdrawal from an LCMC programme, with Maconchy's work selected to replace it.[46]

Although 1949 was largely marred by discouragement spurred by a lack of performances, it also marked a year in which Maconchy's reputation among her peers became more firmly entrenched in the fabric of British musical life. In addition to joining the Composers' Guild of Great Britain, she also began serving on the LCMC's Executive Committee, which enabled her to become more active on the contemporary music scene, even if her ability to travel to London to attend meetings and concerts remained limited owing to family commitments.[47] Further acknowledgement of her accomplishments as a composer arrived later in the year when Maconchy began corresponding with Eric Blom regarding an entry on her for the fifth edition of *Grove's Dictionary of Music and Musicians*.[48]

By the end of 1949, Maconchy began to advocate for herself for her music with greater resolve, offering the following proposal to John Lowe for a Third Programme broadcast:

> I want to make a very bold suggestion & hope you will forgive my doing so. Would you consider doing my five String Quartets – as a series – on the Third Programme? I was prompted to the idea by getting out my 1st Quartet (written in 1933) & finding to my surprise how much I liked it! It hasn't been played for about 14 years.
>
> I believe the Quartets have some reputation as serious music. ... They are too difficult for any but the better (and busier) quartets to tackle – & they feel they haven't the time to undertake numerous rehearsals without a definite 'date' to work for.

44 Ralph Vaughan Williams to Elizabeth Maconchy, 30 November 1949, VWL 3056.

45 See Carpenter, 76–82.

46 Elizabeth Maconchy to Grace Williams, 19 January 1950.

47 In 1949 the Composers' Guild had asked if Maconchy would be willing to join the Executive Committee, which she declined owing to other commitments. See Elizabeth Maconchy to Grace Williams, 11 November 1949.

48 Eric Blom to Elizabeth Maconchy, 15 October 1949, private collection. The fifth edition of *Grove* was edited by Blom, and Maconchy's entry was written by Frank Howes.

> The Brosa's & Pougnet's quartet (who both played my 2nd Quartet) have both disbanded – so has the Philharmonia (with Henry Holst), who played the 4th. The Blech's – who played the 3rd & 4th, have changed their personnel more than once. Even the Hurwitz changed their 2nd violin just after giving the 1st performance of my new 5th Quartet in April – & in consequence it hasn't had a second performance yet!
>
> I hope you do not mind my putting forward this suggestion. If you would like to see the Quartets I will send them to you.[49]

The internal discussions that Maconchy's proposal elicited among BBC personnel provide an enlightening look into the mixed reaction to Maconchy's music as well as the complicated politics within the Music Department in the late 1940s. In a note to Lowe, Herbert Murrill, who was then serving as Assistant Head of Music, quipped, 'I think her name should appear, but I can't quite feel that she merits a Maconchy Festival! Bartók in series – yes – but E.M. hardly comes into this class. I suggest either choosing two quartets for suitable offering, or fixing upon a single one, repeating it once or even twice over a period.'[50] Lowe, who was more sympathetic to Maconchy, wrote to Murrill,

> We're doing this with Tippett's Quartets, – not as an announced series, but placing them within a quarter. I wasn't thinking of doing the same with Britten, for he seems least successful, so far, as a 4tet composer. On the whole, I feel not unattracted by the Maconchy idea, supposing we can get quartets to learn them. What do you think, if we spread them out about one a fortnight?[51]

Plans were subsequently arranged for the BBC to broadcast her Fourth and Fifth String Quartets in April, demonstrating that Maconchy's self-advocacy in this instance bore fruit.

Maconchy's quartets received the largest percentage of performances during the 1950 season. The first took place on 26 January with the MacGibbon String Quartet playing String Quartet No. 5 at a University of Bristol chamber concert. Ahead of the concert, Maconchy travelled to London to hear the MacGibbon Quartet rehearse the work. Although the quartet did not rank at the same level as the Hurwitz Quartet or the Blech Quartet, Maconchy nevertheless found them promising.[52] The performance yielded positive reviews in the press, with the critic in the *Western Daily Press* referring to Maconchy as 'one of the foremost British women composers of the day', further remarking that the quartet evinced 'genuine inspiration and fervour, and not merely another product of arid experiment'.[53] The score received two further performances early in the same year by the Macnaghten Quartet on 21 February at the Cowdray Hall in London and at a Medway Music Society concert in Chatham that took place the following day.

49 Elizabeth Maconchy to John Lowe, 11 December 1949, BBC WAC EM2.

50 Herbert Murrill to John Lowe, undated, BBC WAC EM2.

51 John Lowe to Herbert Murrill, 13 December 1949, BBC WAC EM2.

52 Elizabeth Maconchy to Grace Williams, 19 January 1950. The MacGibbon String Quartet was formed in 1936 by violinist Margot MacGibbon and featured Ruth Fourmy (violin), Muriel Tookey (viola), and Lilly Phillips (cello).

53 L.R.B., 'Chamber Concert', *Western Daily Press*, 27 January 1950.

In February, Maconchy purchased a new piano – a small grand Bösendorfer – which was a marked upgrade from her Ibach upright.[54] After a brief trip to Cardiff to see Williams at the end of March, Maconchy returned home in advance of the Third Programme broadcasts of her String Quartet No. 4 on 5 April, played by the Blech Quartet, followed by the String Quartet No. 5 on 15 April, played by the Hurwitz Quartet. While Maconchy's music generally garnered scant attention in the press in the post-war years – a situation that was due in part to the significant reduction of space allotted to music coverage in newspapers[55] – the forthcoming two broadcasts elicited a snide, backhanded compliment from Harold Rutland, who quipped in the 31 March issue of *Radio Times*, 'unlike certain women composers, [Maconchy] does not attempt to conceal the date of her birth!'[56] Rutland's patent misogyny was laid bare in the following week's issue, which featured an extended discussion on the topic of women composers:

> The appearance of five women composers in the programmes this week emboldens me (and it needs a little courage!) to suggest a few reasons why women have not, so far, won much success in this sphere. [...]
>
> At the risk of being torn to pieces by angry Amazons, I would suggest that most women have quite enough to do, to keep the world going, without their being expected to indulge in fantasies, or the concentrated thought and feeling that brings these fantasies to fruition as works of art. Statistics, moreover, prove, I believe, that the characters and capacities of women keep to a happier mean than do those of men, whose range is far greater, from sheer idiocy to the heights of genius.
>
> Nevertheless, in spite of all this, and much more that might be said, there is no doubt that women composers are now making their presence felt. Chaminade, Maud Valerie White, and their like, belong to a former age: Phyllis Tate, Elisabeth Lutyens, Elizabeth Maconchy, and many others, are ornaments of our contemporary world, following with distinction the path blazed by Dame Ethel [Smyth].[57]

Incensed by Rutland's sexist vitriol, Williams wrote to Maconchy to express her outrage while also elaborating upon a rarely discussed topic regarding women composers and the demographics of their supporters:

> I wonder how you have reacted to Harold Rutland, feminologist, in next week's R.T. It would serve him right if not a single angry amazon swooped down on him – but instead a host of <u>men</u> who happen to care about our music.
>
> But it's too much to hope for. And yet – I rather think men outnumber women in the few fans we have. – a curious thought – but I have found that my <u>women</u> supporters have nearly all come from the profession – whereas quite a few of the men are laymen – Oh dear I'm becoming Ruthlandish! & had better stop this speculation.[58]

[54] An invoice lists the date of purchase as 22 February 1950 with Maconchy paying £220 for the piano.

[55] Frank Howes, *The English Musical Renaissance* (New York: Stein and Day, 1966), 353.

[56] Harold Rutland, 'Music for Holy Week', *Radio Times* 106/1381 (31 March 1950): 7.

[57] Rutland, 'Music for Easter Week', *Radio Times* 107/1382 (7 April 1950): 11.

[58] Grace Williams to Elizabeth Maconchy, 6 April 1950.

Although a response to Williams's remarks about Rutland and the gender disparity among her supporters does not appear in Maconchy's subsequent letters, Williams's words nevertheless highlight the often complicated and fraught relationship between gender and equality, challenging the conventional wisdom of women supporting other women as the primary means by which progress could be achieved.

Ahead of the broadcast of her symphony on 27 April, Maconchy travelled to London for rehearsals of the work with Adrian Boult and the BBC Symphony Orchestra that took place on the 25th, 26th, and the afternoon of the 27th.[59] For the rehearsal on the 27th, Maconchy brought along her husband as well as Williams, who had travelled from Wales to support her friend and colleague. The broadcast concert, which was held in co-operation with the LCMC, took place at 8:30pm in the BBC's Maida Vale Studio 1 with a small invited audience in attendance.[60]

Maconchy's Symphony, which is dedicated to Vaughan Williams, features her habitual procedure of employing a series of small motifs as the foundation for thematic development. Though each of the four movements – Allegro moderato, Lento moderato, Allegro scherzando, and Allegro molto – are self-contained, all are predicated on thematic material Maconchy introduces in the brass and strings at the beginning of the first movement.

Reviews of the broadcast concert were mixed. In the *Musical Times*, Colin Mason declared that '[m]any among Miss Maconchy's juniors and contemporaries might, and it is to be hoped *will*, benefit by her realization that the forties demand different music from the thirties, and that the fifties are not even the forties'.[61] Martin Cooper, writing in the *Daily Telegraph*, argued that the work 'suggested violence rather than strength'.[62] In the *Times*, Howes criticised the work on the grounds it was too tightly bound and lacking in dramatic contrast.[63]

While Maconchy received a number of supportive and congratulatory letters from her friends, Vaughan Williams was reserved in his assessment of the broadcast, writing in a brief letter, 'I thought the Symphony was fine. I will write more when I can collect my thoughts about it.'[64] A couple of weeks later, Vaughan Williams followed up on his previous letter, suggesting 'perhaps it is a little too

[59] Prior to the rehearsals in April, Maconchy also travelled to the BBC's Maida Vale Studios on 16 March to go over the score with Boult on a Steinway grand in one of the studio's rehearsal rooms. C. Beckett to Elizabeth Maconchy, 8 March 1950, BBC WAC EM2.

[60] Maconchy's Symphony was featured first in the programme and was followed by Christian Darnton's Concertino for Piano and String Orchestra and Mátyás Seiber's cantata *Ulysses*.

[61] C.M. [Colin Mason], 'London Contemporary Music Centre', *Musical Times* 91/1288 (June 1950): 235.

[62] Martin Cooper, 'Ulysses', *Daily Telegraph*, 28 April 1950.

[63] 'Contemporary Music Centre', *Times*, 29 April 1950. Maconchy mentions that it was Howes who wrote the review in her letter to Williams on 7 May 1950.

[64] Ralph Vaughan Williams to Elizabeth Maconchy, 3 May 1950, VWL 1991.

hectic all the way through'.[65] Dissatisfied with the work, Maconchy subsequently revised the beginning of the slow movement. Although the symphony was available on hire by Lengnick, Maconchy later decided to have the work withdrawn.

In the spring the family expanded once again when Anna's cat, Smoky, had a litter of kittens. As a present for her third birthday, Nicola was given one of the kittens, who was named Tinkle.[66] During this time, Maconchy continued to be busy with work on her String Quartet No. 6 which she had begun at the end of 1949, as well as an arrangement of *A Country Town* for string quartet.[67] She also revisited her score of *Puck Fair*, arranging two of the dances, 'Lovers' Meeting' and 'Tinker's Curse', for chamber orchestra. In orchestrating the work, which was originally scored for two pianos, Maconchy turned to Williams, who offered the following sage advice:

> Now – your scores – I love the Romance & Tinker's C. ought to be very effective but is a devil to score as the intervals don't lie well on strings – it wd. actually sound fine on two pianos – but it will score if you take a deal of trouble over it [...]
>
> I've given some suggestions ... & what about getting a score of say, Dukas' Apprent sorcier? I feel in a way presumptuous for hacking your score about in this way – but – well all the time you've been writing chamber music I've been doing orchestration – especially for these small orchestras. I wdn't say we were quits because I cdn't write a bar of a quartet whereas you can score – but just need to get into practice again – & it will soon become creative in itself.[68]

In another letter, Williams offered further suggestions, writing that Maconchy should make the two excerpts 'as orchestrally effective as possible – spotlight the tunes in such a way that even nitwitted critics will hear them & say "What lovely music"'.[69] This encouragement, however, did not alleviate Maconchy's own dissatisfaction with her orchestration skills as she lamented to Williams,

> I suffer very much from never having had any working experience of any orchestra – & I'm fumbling & un-sure in consequence. (I don't think really though I have a 'feeling' for it. I write my orchestral music from the wrong end – as it were – as abstract music, instead of hearing it in the first place as pure orchestral sound –. And then I set to and score it very clumsily (– not unlike Uncle Ralph's method! But his music somehow carries the day). You've got a real imaginative command of it all – and I can't tell you how grateful I am for all your advice & the time & trouble you've taken. If these pieces come off it will be entirely due to you![70]

After completing *Two Dances from Puck Fair*, Maconchy submitted the score to Mansel Thomas (1909–86), who conducted the work in a BBC Welsh Orchestra

[65] Ralph Vaughan Williams to Elizabeth Maconchy, 17 May 1950, VWL 1994.

[66] Email from Nicola LeFanu to author.

[67] The arrangement of *A Country Town* was made at the request of Anne Macnaghten, who wanted to include the work in the Macnaghten Quartet's concerts for schoolchildren. Elizabeth Maconchy to Grace Williams, 2 July 1950.

[68] Grace Williams to Elizabeth Maconchy, June 1950.

[69] Grace Williams to Elizabeth Maconchy, 12 May 1950.

[70] Elizabeth Maconchy to Grace Williams, 2 July 1950.

broadcast on 30 September 1950. Clearly taking Williams's advice to 'spotlight the tunes', this engaging score demonstrates greater clarity in allowing the primary thematic material to shine forth: the orchestration is at once rich and colourful. The *Two Dances* received another broadcast on 14 December as part of a BBC Light Programme, played by the BBC Midland Light Orchestra, conducted by Gilbert Vinter.

Though the increasing number of broadcasts Maconchy received in 1950 might have given the appearance of an improving relationship with the BBC, this was far from the complex reality. In early April, Maconchy wrote to Lowe to inquire about *A Winter's Tale*, which he had expressed an interest in placing in a Third Programme broadcast.[71] As Lowe was busy with travel at the time, he responded that upon his return in a few weeks he would take a look over the score, which Maconchy had sent along with her letter.[72] In the meantime, Merritt wrote to the BBC to inquire if they would consider allowing her to include Maconchy's *Sonnet Sequence* and new Concertino for Piano and String Orchestra in an upcoming programme in the autumn.[73] On the advice of Vowles, Merritt submitted Maconchy's new work to the BBC in April, with Maconchy later submitting *Sonnet Sequence* as well as her Violin Sonata in July.[74]

As it turned out, *A Winter's Tale* was subject to a panel reading – in this instance, it was decided that the work would be read by an internal panel. Lowe therefore tentatively placed the work in a Third Programme broadcast on 25 August.[75] While correspondence reveals that the BBC's internal readers were not in favour of the piece – a decision was made on 12 July to remove it from the 25 August Third Programme broadcast – the BBC had already listed the work in their Third Programme leaflet of upcoming broadcasts for August. It wasn't until 5 September that a final decision about the work was made by Leonard Isaacs, who had recently been appointed to the position of Third Programme Music Organiser, succeeding Lowe.[76] In his assessment of the work Isaacs wrote,

> I have read through this score, and cannot feel that it is a work which we should go out of our way to produce. It is unrelievedly gloomy, and the words are far better without music, as all the reports suggest. I think it reveals a state of mind of the composer's part, and does not convey anything to the listener as a piece of organic music.[77]

Despite having already condemned the work, Isaacs prevaricated on the subject in a letter to Maconchy on 12 October, writing, 'I am also very sorry that you

[71] Elizabeth Maconchy to John Lowe, 8 April 1950, BBC WAC EM2.

[72] John Lowe to Elizabeth Maconchy, 11 April 1950, BBC WAC EM2.

[73] Kathleen Merritt to Harry Vowles, 23 April 1950, BBC WAC EM2.

[74] Kathleen Merritt to Harry Vowles, 25 April 1950, BBC WAC EM2.

[75] John Lowe to A.H.M. [Herbert Murrill], 14 June 1950, BBC WAC EM2.

[76] Lowe left his position with the Third Programme in 1950 to become Head of Midland Region Music.

[77] Leonard Isaacs, '"A Winter's Tale" – Elizabeth Maconchy', memo, 5 September 1950, BBC WAC EM2.

put too much faith in the Third Programme leaflet, which is a compendium of pious hopes. … I will see what can be done about the "Winter's Tale".'[78] Though Isaacs made a half-hearted attempt to placate Maconchy by informing her that her new Concertino for Piano and String Orchestra had been approved, the decision arrived too late for the work to be placed in the autumn broadcast as Merritt had requested.

On 1 November, the BBC sent out a letter formally rejecting *A Winter's Tale*. Maconchy was bitterly disappointed. As she detailed in a letter to Isaacs: 'This comes as a surprise as well as a disappointment, as Mr John Lowe had told me definitely he wanted to do it on the Third: (and it has also been publicised in the Third Programme leaflet, as you know!).'[79] Further bad news arrived later in the month when Maconchy received word that both her Violin Sonata and *Sonnet Sequence* had been rejected as well.[80] As the BBC had no written agreement for *A Winter's Tale*, Isaacs wrote to Maconchy on 24 November, 'I do not feel able to fight its battle, in view of the subsequent decision to return it to you, as I have to admit that I do not myself find it particularly suited to "unseen" performance.'[81] Maconchy, who was understandably frustrated, responded on 29 November:

> Thank you for your letter, which, as you rightly supposed, I did not receive with pleasure.
>
> No, I never had a 'written promise' to perform 'A Winter's Tale' on the 3rd Programme. But, as I wrote you already, John Lowe told me that whether or no [*sic*] it was played at one of the L.C.M.C. Concerts last season 'we should like to do it on the 3rd Programme'.
>
> He was at that time a member of the L.C.M.C. Executive committee. – (Had it been in one of the L.C.M.C. programmes it would have been broadcast by the 3rd Programme.) The work, which had been chosen by the LCMC reading committee, was not in fact played at one of their concerts, as it was later decided to do my Symphony during the season. I therefore supposed Mr Lowe would wish to do it on the 3rd Programme, as he had told me. And presumably the matter must have gone forward, – otherwise why should 'A Winter's Tale' have been put down for performance, and published in the B.B.C. leaflet of 3rd Programme plans, for the week of August 20th to August 26?
>
> I had not sent anything up to the B.B.C. Panel for some time, but I roused myself this year to send up four works (three of which had performers wanting to play them) – and three of the four have been turned down. – as I heard a few days ago that my Violin Sonata & Sonnet Sequence have suffered this fate as well as 'A Winter's Tale'. – I have never before had anything I have sent up rejected by the Advisory Panel, and this is profoundly discouraging, to say the least.
>
> A composer of serious modern chamber music has an uphill road to travel, as you know: and there is no inducement to players to learn a difficult work, requiring much rehearsal & sacrifice of time if the work is debarred for ever [*sic*] from performance by the B.B.C.!

[78] Leonard Isaacs to Elizabeth Maconchy, 12 October 1950, BBC WAC EM2.
[79] Elizabeth Maconchy to Leonard Isaacs, 3 November 1950, BBC WAC EM2.
[80] Harry Vowles to Elizabeth Maconchy, 16 November 1950, BBC WAC EM2.
[81] Leonard Isaacs to Elizabeth Maconchy, 24 November 1950, BBC WAC EM2.

> You suggested that I should write to Herbert Murrill – : there is nothing I should like less than an altercation by letter, but this is a serious matter for me, and so discouraging, that if you think it would be a good thing, I will write.[82]

Isaacs forwarded Maconchy's letter to Murrill, who was now serving as Head of Music following Wilson's firing. On 20 December, Murrill wrote to Maconchy,

> I have read the correspondence that has passed between you and Mr. Isaacs with very considerable sympathy. As you rightly say, a composer of serious modern chamber music has an uphill road to travel, but will you now try to look at the matter from our point of view. We have a certain time available in our programmes for music and a certain proportion of this for contemporary music. There is far more of this than we can possibly include and some selective process has to be devised. The fairest way of making our selection is, I think, the one we have adopted, that is, to appoint a Reading Panel of three distinguished musicians unconnected with the Corporation, who are asked to make recommendations to us on the material submitted. They are not bothered with our practical problems and are asked to judge on the artistic merit of the work.
>
> This Panel is an advisory body and we are not bound to accept their advice, but in fact, of course, the more often we disregard it the less useful and impersonal does the process become. In fact, therefore, we attach great weight to the opinions of the Reading Panel and generally follow its recommendation. Even so, there is a long list of works waiting for performance in our programmes and I fear there must be many disappointments.
>
> In your own case I am glad to see that during 1950 we have broadcast your String Quartet No. 5 and your Symphony, so that at least your music has been heard in our programmes. Lack of encouragement I fear has been the composer's traditional lot, and you would probably agree with me that no worthwhile composer stops working because he cannot find positive encouragement from the world at large. At the same time, if you can devise a fairer system than we have in our Reading Panel, I will be glad to know of it![83]

The frequent changes of regime at the BBC with advocates such as Searle leaving the organisation in 1948, and the promotion of both Isaacs and Murrill in 1950 – both individuals who, moreover, made their antipathy towards Maconchy's music abundantly clear in internal BBC documents – initiated a series of setbacks for Maconchy. She was far from alone in voicing her frustrations with the BBC's panel system, its inconsistences, and its prejudices, which, according to Searle, had 'no definite ruling as to which composers' works have to go before the panel and which not', and ultimately left composers such as Maconchy with little recourse if they failed to have an advocate within the system.[84]

[82] Elizabeth Maconchy to Leonard Isaacs, 29 November 1950, BBC WAC EM2.

[83] Herbert Murrill to Elizabeth Maconchy, 20 December 1950, BBC WAC EM2.

[84] Quoted in Carpenter, 99. As Carpenter illustrates, the delays for approved works were significant: in October 1950, there were roughly ninety orchestral works that had been approved by a panel of readers awaiting broadcasts. See Carpenter, 100.

8

Glimmers of Hope, 1951–5

Though Maconchy's relationship with the BBC remained strained throughout 1951, the organisation did at least remain true to its word in regards to her Concertino for Piano and String Orchestra, which was included in a Third Programme broadcast on 21 February 1951. The work, which is cast in three movements, was played by the Kathleen Merritt Orchestra conducted by Merritt, with Margaret Kitchin (1914–2008) as the featured soloist. The broadcast elicited an encouraging letter from Vaughan Williams, who wrote to Maconchy on 28 February: 'Your work came as a great relief. It had vitality and purpose. I won't say more after just a first hearing without seeing the score. You are getting performed at last, I am so glad.'[1] Another performance of the work took place later in the year on 2 October at the Wigmore Hall featuring the London Chamber Orchestra conducted by Anthony Bernard, with Kathleen Cooper as soloist. This latter performance earned highly favourable notices in the press, with the critic in the *Times* lauding the slow movement for 'its smouldering romanticism'.[2]

In the spring, Maconchy's String Quartet No. 6, which she had completed the previous year, was premièred by the Martin String Quartet at an LCMC concert held at the RBA Galleries on 22 May.[3] This concert was part of the London Season of the Arts, coinciding with the Festival of Britain, commemorating the centenary of the Royal Exhibition. True to Maconchy's musical idiom, each movement is constructed around a series of motifs expressed at the outset. As the first few measures of the first movement, Passacaglia, illustrate, ascending leaps, followed by two consecutive falling thirds and its inversional equivalent, play a pivotal role, serving as the basis for melodic and harmonic development (Example 8.1). As the movement progresses, Maconchy varies the primary theme and motifs contained within it by means of rhythmic variation and melodic expansion and contraction. The primary theme, however, never loses its dominance, and remains a persistent driving force throughout.[4]

In the vivacious second movement, Allegro scherzando, the opening material in the first violin yields all the clues to the motific material used in the movement, such as its opening flourish and descending octave leaps. An

1 Ralph Vaughan Williams to Elizabeth Maconchy, 28 February 1951, VWL 2199.

2 'Wigmore Hall', *Times*, 4 October 1951.

3 The Martin String Quartet featured David Martin (1st violin), Marjorie Lavers (2nd violin), Eileen Grainger (viola), and Bernard Richards (cello).

4 Maconchy, 'Elizabeth Maconchy On Writing String Quartets'.

Example 8.1. Maconchy, String Quartet No. 6, mvt. I, opening.
Published by Alfred Lengnick & Co., a division of Universal Music Publishing Group.
Reproduced by permission of Hal Leonard Europe BV (Italy).

extensive pizzicato section in 5/8, which is also connected to the opening material, offers a playful and enlivened contrast, which is then followed by a return to the original tempo and opening motifs. As the music continues to grow and builds to a climax, motific variations of the opening material return, concluding the movement.

While the Sixth String Quartet features complex rhythms and intricate contrapuntal weaving of thematic material, such as in the lively pizzicato section of the second movement, in contrast to her earlier quartets, there is a greater degree of homophonic texture which Maconchy uses to create thematic contrasts. This is exemplified in the third movement, Lento espressivo, which begins with the movement's predominant theme in the viola, which is then supported by 6/4 chords in the violins. The cello then takes up the theme, which is then developed further by the viola and first violin, anchored by ostinatos and pedal points, which are momentarily interrupted by pithy sections of contrapuntal development.

In the energetic and fast-paced fourth movement, Allegro molto, con brio, Maconchy weaves together thematic and motific material from the preceding movements which she further alters by means of rhythmic and melodic counterpoint. As the intensity of the movement builds, Maconchy reintroduces an altered version of the opening of the first movement, which concludes the work. Reviews of the work were largely favourable, with Blom noting in the *Observer* that the quartet was 'the product of a distinguished specialist, with everything, it seemed, dictated by a fastidious feeling for the medium rather than deliberately contrived for it'.[5]

By and large, performances of Maconchy's works nevertheless remained few and far between for the duration of 1951. Aside from the two performances of her Concertino for Piano and String Orchestra and the première of her Sixth String Quartet, Maconchy's works appear to have garnered only a handful of notable performances and broadcasts, which included a performance of *Impromptu* played by Kathleen Cooper in a recital at the Wigmore Hall on 21

[5] Eric Blom, 'New Works', *Observer*, 10 June 1951.

April and a broadcast of the same work by Eric Hope on 10 June on the BBC's Home Service, as well as a performance of *Theme and Variations for String Orchestra* on 27 June by the Riddick String Orchestra, conducted by Kathleen Riddick (1907–73), at an SWM concert held at Queen Mary Hall that was also part of the London Season of the Arts.

During the year, Maconchy remained busy with several new projects, including an orchestral work titled *Nocturne*. In contrast to the frustrations she endured throughout much of the 1940s, the early-to-mid 1950s would prove to be more encouraging, with high-profile performances leading to greater public recognition. Though attention was often fleeting and domestic responsibilities continued to take priority over her career, she was also beginning to take on more speaking engagements, enabling her to connect with wider audiences comprising both the public and her colleagues.

At the beginning of 1952, Maconchy's String Quartet No. 6 was taken up by the MacGibbon Quartet, who played the work on 3 February at an Oxford Ladies' Music Society concert, followed by an LCMC concert on 8 February at the Institute of Contemporary Arts (ICA) in London. For both concerts, Maconchy gave an introductory talk, which she delivered from memory. Surviving drafts of these talks offer a unique glimpse into Maconchy's own thoughts about the art of composition, particularly her notion of music as an impassioned argument, as she elaborated in her talk for 3 February:

> Writing music, like all forms of creative art, is the impassioned pursuit of an idea.
>
> The great thing is for the composer to keep his head & not allow anything to distract him from the pursuit of this central idea.
>
> The temptations to stop by the way and to be side-tracked by felicities of sound and colour are ever-present.
>
> But in my view, & above all in writing a String Quartet, when one is dealing with the very bones of music, with none of the endless variety of colour of the orchestra, or the extra-musical expressiveness of the human voice – everything extraneous to the pursuit of the central idea must be excluded – – scrapped.
>
> The music is propelled by the force of its own inner logic, and by virtue of this logic every new idea derives from the original premise, & throws new light on the whole.
>
> By musical logic I do not mean a cold, dispassionate statement. To me, the best music is a sort of impassioned argument, and I personally can find no satisfaction in the coldly calculated musical discourse. […]
>
> The rigid self-discipline which the composer must impose on himself must always be directed to the fullest expression of the under-lying emotion – never to its exclusion.
>
> This passionately intellectual and intellectually passionate discourse is what I seek, however inadequately, to express in music.[6]

[6] Elizabeth Maconchy, draft of talk titled 'String Quartet No. 6', 3 February 1952, SHC.

For the 8 February concert, whose audience predominately consisted of other composers who frequented the ICA and LCMC concerts, Maconchy tailored her talk to address the practical problems facing the modern composer:

> Wondering what I should say about my String Quartets this evening set me thinking about the whole business of writing music. Why does one write at all? – [I]t is admittedly the most technically difficult of the creative arts, & requires long training: so long indeed that the learning process goes on for the whole of the composer's working life – & when he feels that he is at last master of his art – he dies of old age.
>
> It is arduous & exacting work – with plenty of spade-work to do. No-one in his senses could suppose that he will become rich as a composer – it is hard enough for a composer of serious music, as such, to earn his living at all.
>
> Fame – then, & public esteem? [B]ut for the public to esteem his work, they must first hear it. And here again the composer is at a disadvantage as compared to [a] painter or writer, because he is at an extra remove from his public. He is wholly dependent on the performer to present his work – & it is not always presented as he would wish.
>
> If he is breaking new ground – and he will be; if he is any good – his music will at first be beyond the reach of the average player, and the best players are the busiest and are not always willing, or able, to spend time on unfamiliar work when their public prefers the familiar. Again – economic reasons make it almost impossible for new works to have adequate rehearsal.
>
> One could go on like this almost indefinitely...[7]

In contrast to the attention some of her previous string quartets garnered, these performances received scant notice in the press. This may have come as a consolation for Maconchy, as she had been disappointed by the MacGibbon Quartet's playing at the ICA concert.[8] Vaughan Williams, who attended the ICA concert, however, offered words of encouragement in spite of the disappointing performance.[9] In a mark of progress in Maconchy's relationship with the BBC, the work received 'unanimous commendation from the Reading Panel', which led to its inclusion on a BBC Third Programme broadcast on 13 March.[10]

The month of February also included the première of Maconchy's *Duo: Theme and Variations for Violin and Violoncello* (1951). Featuring eight variations based upon a richly lyrical theme, the work was premièred by its

[7] Elizabeth Maconchy, draft of talk titled 'String Quartet No. 6 at I.C.A. London', 8 February 1952, SHC.

[8] In a letter to Williams, Maconchy remarks that the MacGibbon Quartet played the work twice at the ICA concert – once prior to the intermission, and again afterwards – and that in both instances, the playing was not quite up to the standard of the concert in Oxford on 3 February. Elizabeth Maconchy to Grace Williams, 19 February 1952.

[9] Ibid.

[10] Maconchy initially submitted the score to the BBC on 18 July 1951. According to the BBC's records, a final decision in favour of the work was made in mid-December. Although the broadcast was with the MacGibbon Quartet, Isaacs had initially considered engaging the Martin String Quartet. S.A.A. to Leonard Isaacs, 11 December 1951, BBC WAC EM3.

dedicatees – Macnaghten and her husband, Arnold Ashby – on the 12th at the Mercury Theatre. This concert was part of a new series of concerts Macnaghten had started in 1950, which became known as the Macnaghten New Music Group. Funded in part by the CPNM, Maconchy, Lemare, Lutyens, Williams, Patrick Hadley, and Alan Rawsthorne served as members of the Macnaghten New Music Group's concerts committee, with Vaughan Williams serving as the group's President.[11] Maconchy's *Duo: Theme and Variations* was composed especially for the concert, which also featured works by James Butt (1929–2003), Bartók, Philip Cannon (1929–2016), Roger Ellison, Stephen Dodgson (1924–2013), and a selection of folk songs arranged by Moeran, Hopkins, and Britten. Maconchy's *Duo* was warmly received, with the *Times* critic declaring that, of the programme's works, Maconchy's left '[t]he strongest impression'.[12]

The early months of 1952 were a highly productive period for Maconchy as she began work on her Symphony for Double String Orchestra, which she completed the following year. While working on this new symphony, Maconchy accidently began a new piece for bassoon that turned into her Concertino for Bassoon and String Orchestra. This new work was completed in August and dedicated to bassoonist Gwydion Brooke (1912–2005).[13] During this period, Maconchy also wrote a number of educational pieces and began work on another orchestral work, *Proud Thames*, which she completed in January 1953.

On 5 April 1952, Maconchy's *Six Settings of Poems by W.B. Yeats* (1951) was premièred by the Northgatean Singers at a concert held at Christchurch School in Ipswich. Maconchy travelled to the concert with Sophie Wyss, who served as the soprano soloist, along with LeFanu and Anna, who was now attending St Mary's Calne, a boarding school in Wiltshire.[14] The work, which Maconchy had written at the request of the Northgatean Singers' conductor, Peter Burges, is arranged for soprano solo, harp, horns, clarinet, and women's voices. Although the work received only one full rehearsal, Wyss gave a superb performance. Sadly, the same could not be said of the ensemble.[15] Nevertheless, the work received glowing praise from Cecil Armstrong Gibbs, who wrote in a letter to Maconchy,

> I had a preconceived idea of you as 'difficulty modern' & therefore I came prepared to dislike your work. I was in fact enthralled & excited by it. … [T]hree qualities in it struck me most forcibly – its vitality, its sincerity & a certain quality of 'wild' beauty that I found deeply moving.[16]

[11] Ernest Chapman, 'The Macnaghten Concerts', *Composer* 57 (Spring 1976): 15.

[12] 'Macnaghten Concerts', *Times*, 13 February 1952.

[13] Elizabeth Maconchy to Grace Williams, 19 February 1952. In a subsequent letter to Grace Williams, Maconchy states that while she had completed one movement of her Symphony for Double String Orchestra, her desire to work on the piece for bassoon and strings resulted in the completion of two movements. Elizabeth Maconchy to Grace Williams, 19 April 1952.

[14] Anna began attending St Mary's Calne in 1951.

[15] Elizabeth Maconchy to Grace Williams, 19 April 1952.

[16] Cecil Armstrong Gibbs to Elizabeth Maconchy, 7 April 1952, private collection.

Shortly after the performance, Wyss sent the score to the BBC. The high regard for the work by Armstrong Gibbs, which Maconchy mentioned in a subsequent letter to Isaacs, piqued his interest, as he wrote in an internal memo, 'I am interested that a "reactionary" like Armstrong Gibbs should have been "excited and enthralled" by her Yeats settings, and I shall read the score with interest.'[17] While approval of the work was communicated to Wyss on 20 January 1953, the tone of the letter did not indicate any sense of urgency to place it in a programme. A broadcast did not materialise until two years later when it was featured in a Third Programme broadcast on 18 January 1955.[18]

In the spring of 1952, Maconchy had some pleasant news to celebrate when her *Nocturne* (1950–1) was selected for inclusion in a BBC Orchestral Concert held in co-operation with the LCMC. As Maconchy found herself with little time to copy parts, Lengnick agreed to cover the costs in exchange for keeping the entirety of the hire and performance fees for the première.[19] The broadcast concert, which was held at the BBC's Studio 1 at Maida Vale, took place on 13 May. In addition to *Nocturne*, which was the first work played after the intermission, the concert also featured Bate's Sinfonietta No. 2, Goffredo Petrassi's Second Concertino, Bernard Stevens's Cello Concerto, and John Joubert's Symphonic Study in B Minor.[20]

Nocturne takes its inspiration from the 1817 version of Samuel Taylor Coleridge's poem *The Rime of the Ancient Mariner*, with the following gloss from part four of the poem inscribed with her score:

> [T]he journeying Moon and the stars
> still sojourn, yet still move onwards;
> and everywhere the blue sky belongs
> to them, and is their appointed rest
> and their native country and their
> own natural home, which they enter
> unannounced, as Lords that are
> certainly expected, and yet there is
> a silent joy at their arrival.[21]

The work opens with the strings playing an A in unison with the harp and clarinets oscillating back and forth from B-flat to A, creating sweeping lines that vividly evoke the movement of the sea. The flutes then enter with an arpeggiated theme, which is briefly adopted by the oboes before being taken up by the bassoons and bass clarinet. A short theme is then introduced in the horns as the woodwind and strings take turns with the opening theme. With their alternating half and whole steps, the five notes that characterise much of

17 Leonard Isaacs to A/H.M., 26 May 1952, BBC WAC EM3.

18 Frank Wade to Sophie Wyss, 20 January 1953, BBC WAC EM3.

19 Elizabeth Maconchy to Grace Williams, 19 April 1952.

20 Only the second half of the concert, which featured Maconchy's *Nocturne* and the works by Stevens and Joubert, was broadcast.

21 MS of *Nocturne*, SHC.

the material at the beginning of the work – A, B-flat, C, C-sharp, E – clearly imply octatonicism.

The work received unanimous commendation in the press. In the *Spectator*, Martin Cooper hailed the work as 'finely and poetically felt music, which gave the impression of vastness without clamour, of majestic motion and eternal stillness'.[22] Dyneley Hussey, writing for the *Listener*, found the work to be the best on the programme.[23] In the *Times*, the anonymous critic described the work as 'richly embroidered', further noting that it 'succeeded in combining heart and head in just the right proportion'.[24] Praise came not only from critics, but her friends as well, as Williams wrote to Maconchy, 'Nocturne is most lovely – & quite your best score – everything translucent & perfect for the words. You must do more programme works.'[25]

In June, Maconchy's Violin Sonata received a performance at an SPNM studio recital. Other performances that took place in England during the year included a broadcast of her Third String Quartet by the Hungarian String Quartet on 24 November, who also included the work in their US tour. On 2 December, Macnaghten and Ashby played *Duo: Theme and Variations* in an SPNM studio recital. Shortly thereafter on the 11th, Ashby and pianist Ernest Lush played *Divertimento for Cello and Piano* in a Home Service broadcast, marking the first performance of the work in its entirety.

Beyond performances in England, the autumn of 1952 also marked a triumphant return of Maconchy's music to Ireland, with several broadcasts of her works taking place in October. This included Radio Éireann broadcasts of *Nocturne* and *Two Dances from Puck Fair* on the 7th, featuring the Radio Éireann Symphony Orchestra, conducted by Milan Horvat (1919–2014); the Concertino for Piano and String Orchestra, which was again conducted by Horvat with Anthony Hughes (1928–2007) serving as the soloist on the 17th; as well as a concert performance of *Nocturne* at the Seapoint Ballroom in Galway on the 21st, which was recorded for a future broadcast.[26] On the 30th, a broadcast of *Six Settings of Poems by W.B. Yeats* was conducted by Hans Waldemar Rosen (1904–94) with Wyss serving as soloist. According to Boyle, who was in the audience at the Phoenix Hall for the broadcast, along with a handful of others including Maconchy's former teacher, John Larchet, the musicians performed the work well, with Wyss once again delivering a solid performance.[27] Further

[22] Martin Cooper, 'Contemporary Arts – Music', *Spectator*, 16 May 1952.

[23] Dyneley Hussey, 'Critic on the Hearth', *Listener* (22 May 1952): 847.

[24] 'London Contemporary Music Centre', *Times*, 14 May 1952.

[25] Grace Williams to Elizabeth Maconchy, 14 May 1952.

[26] The recording was later used for a Radio Éireann broadcast on 3 February 1953.

[27] Phoenix Hall was the radio studio that Radio Éireann used for their orchestral broadcasts. There were generally two orchestral broadcast concerts each week at the hall, with Tuesdays featuring new works and more traditional repertoire placed in programmes on Fridays. See Hugh Oram, 'An Irishman's Diary', *Irish Times*, 9 September 2006. Based on the context of a surviving letter Boyle sent to Maconchy, it appears that Maconchy attended a rehearsal of *Six Settings of Poems by W.B. Yeats*,

performances of Maconchy's music in Ireland took place the following year with the Cork Ballet Group reviving their 1948 staging of *Puck Fair* on 19 April 1953.[28]

On 10 February 1953, Maconchy delivered a paper for an LCMC's Composer's Concourse. Titled 'Composing and Its Problems', Maconchy's talk delved into topics ranging from practical and psychological difficulties facing composers as they grapple with their work, as well as the inherent challenges posed by motherhood. Beyond discussing hardships, the paper also offers further insight into Maconchy's own thoughts about compositional processes:

> The Problems are many & intimately known to most of us here. Much could be said about the obvious problems –: the practical difficulties of the composer – how to earn his bread in such a way as to leave himself time & energy for composition. We all know it is the most exacting job in the world, needing the composer's whole mind & undivided concentration if he is to do anything worthwhile – yet almost every composer must spend much of his time … with work, musical or otherwise which has no value to him as a composer. – If he is a woman, there is the added problem of rearing children, which is the most time-taking & wearing job of all.
>
> This practical aspect is too boring to discuss – we know it all already. But it is the basic problem that is there at the back of all the composer's other problems, all the time: – how to get enough time for his work. Composers are not likely to forget it, because as a rule they don't get the chance, but musicologists & others interested in the composer should bear it in mind.
>
> The real internal problems of the composer are much more interesting: but they are difficult to formulate, because he is in the process of working them out in music, not in words. It is comparatively easy to look back at a musical problem once it has been solved & to analyse it & see how it has been done, point to interesting parallels & so on & so on.
>
> But while the composer is still grappling with the problem it is in a fluid state, & to formulate it in words is to hamstring it, by trying to pin down what is still too intangible & inconclusive & is not yet ready to be pinned down. This premature dragging to earth & discussion in words of problems that are being worked out purely in terms of music & whose solution is still in the making, can only hamper the composer, it seems to me, by distracting him from his real job of solving his problem in terms of music. And since this solving of problems is always going on – is a continuous process, & is in fact the forward-looking composer's job, it follows that the discussion of his current work in words is unsatisfactory, even among composers of like mind who speak, or at any rate understand, the same musical language.

---

but was not present in Ireland at the time it was broadcast. Ina Boyle to Elizabeth Maconchy, 31 October 1952, private collection.

[28] For this performance, Maconchy revised the orchestration, which had originally been done by Boyle. The Cork Ballet Group performed the work again on 19 April in Killarney. Additional plans were made for performances in Limerick and Dublin; however, they ultimately fell through. Aloys Fleischmann to Elizabeth Maconchy, 13 May 1953, private collection.

> One might add that such discussion is totally unprofitable. But that may not be quite true, because discussion among highly intelligent people on their own subject can be highly stimulating. It is unlikely, I think, to solve any problems, but it is quite likely to suggest some new ones & to send us away with a fresh germ or maggot in our brain which does something to us, rather like yeast – it is hard to say how or why. [...]
>
> A composer's work, like all creative work, goes on inside his own head, oblivious of what is going on outside & the more he can confine himself to his own thought & follow it where it leads him, the more likely he is to get somewhere.
>
> But although his best work must, in my view be done in mental isolation, it requires from time to time, some stimulus from outside, some fertilising factor, or it ceases to be creative, & the composer finds he is working in a spiral, ever narrowing inwards. (In the end I suppose the composer himself will be the only person who will consent to listen to his music.) [...]
>
> The nature of the stimulus to the composer, seems to vary very widely & to be arbitrary and individual in operation. He may get a kick from the contemplation of a work of art – even from a piece of contemporary music – or as likely from some totally irrelevant experience.
>
> What this stimulus does, I suppose is go to excite the composer's creative imagination that he is thrown into a state of mind in which he is more likely to hit upon a good idea. (The idea may come spontaneously or only after laborious trial & error & monumental scrapings.)[29]

Maconchy's talk was to be among some of the few remaining activities of the LCMC as plans were finalised that month for the organisation's amalgamation with the ICA. Although Maconchy was approached by the ICA to join a newly formed committee to guide the direction of the organisation's musical activities, she ultimately declined the invitation.[30]

The late winter and early spring of 1953 yielded further performances of Maconchy's music, with the Concertino for Piano and String Orchestra featured in a Third Programme broadcast on 27 February with Merritt conducting her orchestra and Margaret Good serving as soloist. In March, Macnaghten and Ashby gave another performance of *Duo: Theme and Variations* at a Macnaghten New Music Group concert on the 9th that was held at the Arts Council's Great Drawing Room. A couple of weeks later, on the 24th, Maconchy's Concertino for Bassoon and String Orchestra was premièred by the Goldsbrough Orchestra conducted by Edric Cundell, with the work's dedicatee, Brooke, in a BBC broadcast that was held in co-operation with the LCMC.[31]

29 Elizabeth Maconchy, draft of talk titled 'Composing and its Problems', 1953, SHC.

30 Herbert Read to Elizabeth Maconchy, 26 February 1953, private collection. Other composers approached included Alan Rawsthorne, Arnold Cooke, and Peter Racine Fricker. As Maconchy was travelling to London for Composers' Guild meetings during this time, which required a great deal of planning to coordinate child care, this may have been a factor in her decision to decline the ICA's invitation.

31 According to the date on the manuscript, Maconchy completed the Concertino for Bassoon and String Orchestra on 8 August 1952. Based on details in her BBC file, the score appears to have been received in December 1952 and was read internally, with

In the summer of 1953, *Proud Thames* (1952–3), which Maconchy had completed in January, was announced as the winner of an overture competition held by the London County Council (LCC) to commemorate the coronation of Elizabeth II. The competition, which was adjudicated by Boult, Rubbra, and Finzi, also included an award to the amount of £150.[32] Considering that the coronation exclusively featured works by male composers, with music written by women largely absent from other concert stage celebrations, Maconchy's prize takes on a greater sense of significance, even if it is impossible to divorce it from the disparities between composers who received commissions versus composers such as Maconchy who wrote *Proud Thames* without any financial incentive. Though the gender imbalance of composers included in coronation festivities failed to garner discussion in the press, it did not go unnoticed by Boyle, who wrote in her letter of congratulations to Maconchy that she was particularly pleased that musical celebrations for the Queen would not be entirely masculine.[33]

Ahead of the première of *Proud Thames* in October, Maconchy and her family spent a few weeks in Ireland in August. In addition to visiting family, it was also their last holiday at Ballymorris, a house that LeFanu had inherited from his uncle, Victor LeFanu, which they had decided to sell. These two weeks were filled with activities, including a trip to the Dublin Zoo on the 17 August, followed by a visit with Boyle on the 18th.[34] Back in England, Maconchy and LeFanu were also busy with selling Wickham Lodge as they prepared for their move to a larger home.

Proud Thames was premièred on 14 October in a BBC Symphony concert at the Royal Festival Hall, conducted by Malcolm Sargent. Like *Two Dances from Puck Fair* and *Nocturne*, *Proud Thames* demonstrates Maconchy's scoring for large forces at its finest. As its title suggests, *Proud Thames* was inspired by its namesake, the River Thames. In the overture, Maconchy wanted to evoke 'the changing moods of the river', further suggesting 'its growth from small beginnings to a great river of sound: from its source in the green countryside, to London, where the full-tide of the life of the Capital centres on its River'.[35] The work opens with a motto theme in the trumpet (Example 8.2), which is then followed by the entrance of the flutes and clarinets with an ascending arpeggio theme, supported by pizzicato in the strings, which is meant to evoke the trickle along of the river's stream (Example 8.3). The entrance of the

---

the work being approved in January 1953. Frank Wade to Leonard Isaacs, 16 January 1953, BBC WAC EM3.

[32] 'Prize for Coronation Overture', *Times*, 29 July 1953.

[33] Ina Boyle to Elizabeth Maconchy, 30 July 1953, private collection. The coronation took place on 2 June. Notably, Pathé's documentary of the coronation, *Elizabeth is Queen*, was scored by Doreen Carwithen (1922-2003).

[34] According to Maconchy's appointment diary, they travelled to Ireland on 11 August and returned to England on the 27th.

[35] A detailed programme note written by Maconchy is included as an attachment in a memo in her BBC file. [Miss] Wood to Rutland, 8 September 1953, BBC WAC EM3.

Figure 8. The première of *Proud Thames* (reproduced by permission of the Maconchy Estate).

trombones, anchored by a pedal note in the bass trombone, adds an additional layer of support as this theme is meant to conjure the 'hidden power below the surface' as the strings and woodwind continue to embody the trickling stream of the river. As intensity begins to build gradually, the work falls into a brief lull with triads in the trombones as the violins and harp play soaring glissandi in the background as the flutes introduce a new theme which is then extended and further developed in the woodwind, horns, and trumpets. With a return of the trombones' theme, the intensity begins to increase as the woodwind and horns continue to develop the new theme introduced by the flutes as the motto theme is incorporated and inverted, creating a rich and climactic interweaving of thematic material that comes to an abrupt halt, with the brass and timpani playing an inversion of the motto theme, followed by a 'flaming brass chord' that brings the work to its triumphant conclusion.[36]

Aside from Maconchy's work, the programme also featured the overture to Berlioz's *Benvenuto Cellini*, Sibelius's Symphony No. 4, Wagner's *Fünf Gedichte von Mathilde Wesendonck*, which was performed by Kristen Flagstad in her farewell appearance, as well as Ravel's *La Valse*. For the concert, Maconchy

[36] The formal title of the work, *Proud Thames*, was suggested by LeFanu. Elizabeth Maconchy to Grace Williams, 27 July 1953.

Example 8.2. Maconchy, *Proud Thames*, trumpet opening.
Published by Alfred Lengnick & Co., a division of Universal Music Publishing Group. Reproduced by permission of Hal Leonard Europe BV (Italy).

Example 8.3. Maconchy, *Proud Thames*, bars 2–8.
Published by Alfred Lengnick & Co., a division of Universal Music Publishing Group. Reproduced by permission of Hal Leonard Europe BV (Italy).

was seated in the hall's ceremonial box, and in addition to her husband and daughter Anna, many close friends and mentors such as Williams and Vaughan Williams were in attendance, with those unable to attend in person tuning into the broadcast of this momentous occasion. Following the conclusion of *Proud Thames*, Maconchy was formally awarded the coronation prize by the LCC's chairman, Sir Arthur Middleton.

The critical reception of *Proud Thames* was almost unanimously favourable. Although the *Times* critic complained that the work was 'too short', they added that this was 'a fault as commendable as it is rare'.[37] Writing in the *Daily Telegraph*, Capell offered considerable praise, declaring that '[i]t is rare for the outcome of a competition to be as successful as Miss Maconchy's new overture'.[38] In the *Observer*, Blom likewise extolled the work's virtues, while also making a similar observation as the critic in the *Times* in regards to its brevity: 'The work is short to the point of abruptness, but this was felt to be a fault only because the music is so vital, shapely, tellingly orchestrated and individual that one wants it to develop at greater length. More could be said in its favour if there were space enough.'[39]

On the day of the première, Maconchy also had encouraging news when Richard Howgill, then the BBC's Controller of Music, 'went out of his way to be friendly … & muttered about my not having to bother about the Panel'.[40] Unsure as to the veracity of Howgill's remarks, which suggested that her music was now 'panel-free', Maconchy turned to her publisher Bernard de Nevers to confirm her status with the BBC. De Nevers had in fact already written to the BBC on 9 October to inquire about the matter, with Howgill responding a few days later with 'the works of Miss Maconchy can certainly be regarded as panel free'.[41]

In the days following the première of *Proud Thames*, Maconchy received a number of congratulatory letters from her friends. She also had the opportunity to further catch up with Williams, and on the 17th Maconchy travelled to London along with Nicola to hear Williams's *Merry Minstrel*, which was featured in an Ernest Read Children's Concert at the Royal Festival Hall. The remainder of the year was busy with preparing for the family's move. As per usual, Christmas Day was spent at her sister's farm, and on the 30th Maconchy had a special treat in store for her daughters with a trip to London to see a production of Humperdinck's opera *Hansel and Gretel* at Sadler's Wells. Then, on 6 January 1954, Maconchy and her family officially moved into a larger home, Shottesbrook, located in Boreham, Essex.

[37] 'B.B.C. Concert', *Times*, 15 October 1953.

[38] R.C. [Richard Capell], 'First and Last Performances', *Daily Telegraph*, 15 October 1953.

[39] Eric Blom, 'Fin de Siècle,' *Observer*, 18 October 1953.

[40] Elizabeth Maconchy to Grace Williams, 18 October 1953.

[41] See Bernard de Nevers to Richard Howgill, 9 October 1953; and Richard Howgill to Bernard de Nevers, 12 October 1953, BBC WAC EM3. In August 1953, Howgill announced in a letter published in *Musical Opinion* that the BBC was expanding the 'panel-free' list to include a number of established composers. See Carpenter, 147–8.

On 17 February, Maconchy delivered a talk to The Classic Club in Chelmsford. Like her talks from the previous year, she was frank with her audience about the harsh financial realities of the professional musical world. Of her early, critically successful works, she wrote the following in the draft of her talk:

> These performances did not bring in 1d … [the] heavy cost of copying parts: later P.R.S. fees, later still a publisher: but at no time can a composer of serious music count on living on his work. Holst made £50 a year – had to teach – . More openings now (films) – but always something apart from his real work. … A woman – with a family to look after – comes to much the same thing.[42]

In addition to settling into her new home, Maconchy's time was occupied with a commission from Radio Éireann for a full orchestral arrangement of a work she had completed the previous year, *Suite on Irish Airs*. Based upon airs in the Petrie and Feis Ceoil Collections, Maconchy re-scored the work between January and March.[43] The work was premièred later in the year on 2 July in a Radio Éireann Symphony Orchestra programme, conducted by Horvat. Of her reservations about the incorporation of folksongs, Maconchy stated the following in a later interview:

> Almost every composer in every country seems to have been setting folksongs since the revival of interest in national traditional music at the beginning of the century. And I sometimes wish they hadn't. At the end of a folksong suite I often feel that all the ingenuity of treatment and brilliance of orchestration are misplaced, and that I would rather hear the tunes themselves, unadorned. Even the arrangements made with real scholarship and good taste are not always very satisfactory – they seem to embalm the tune, instead of giving it new life.
>
> I feel that the only justification for using a folksong is to be so deeply and inwardly moved by it that for the time being it becomes part of one's musical thought. It is only through this saturation, that the tune itself and the music with which one surrounds it will be all of a piece, and one will not do violence to the other.
>
> Adopting a folk-tune is like adopting a child – to be successful you must cherish it and treat it as your own.[44]

Suite on Irish Airs was not the only Irish-themed work Maconchy had been working on in the 1950s: in 1952, she wrote a work for violin and orchestra titled *Toombeola*, after the village in Connemara. The Hungarian-born violinist François D'Albert (1918–99) had initially hoped to play the work with the Radio Éireann Symphony Orchestra in the spring of 1952. Owing to prior engagements, the orchestra was unavailable. Although there were initial hopes that the work could be placed in a programme at a future date, no further records concerning the work can be traced and Maconchy later withdrew the score. In August 1954 Maconchy wrote an arrangement of the Irish lullaby *Shoheen Sho* with an English translation by LeFanu at the request of Elizabeth Poston for

42 Maconchy, 'To the Classic Club at Chelmsford'.

43 The first version of *Suite on Irish Airs* was arranged for small orchestra and completed in November 1953.

44 Maconchy, draft of talk for Radio Éireann broadcast.

a programme of folk songs that was broadcast on 20 September on the Home Service.[45] Beyond the influx of performances in Ireland and the broadcast of *Shoheen Sho*, Maconchy was also busy with work on a number of compositions, including an educational arrangement of Hungarian folk songs for clarinet and piano, a work for Eugene Cruft (1887–1976) titled *Four Improvisations for Solo Double-Bass*, as well as her Seventh String Quartet, which she completed the following year.

In 1954, several of Maconchy's orchestral works received high profile performances and broadcasts. This began with a broadcast on 1 March of *Proud Thames* on the Home Service with the BBC Northern Orchestra, conducted by John Hopkins (1927–2013). In the summer, the Concertino for Bassoon and String Orchestra was included in a Proms concert held on 30 July, marking the work's first concert performance. For this performance, the work was played by the BBC Symphony Orchestra, conducted by Sargent and featuring Brooke as soloist. In contrast to the previous year's broadcast, the work's inclusion at the Proms garnered a great deal of discussion in the press, including some highly favourable reviews. Featured alongside Beethoven's overture to *Egmont*, Concerto No. 3 in C minor for Pianoforte and Orchestra, and Symphony No. 2 in D, and Dvořák's Symphonic Variations, Eric Blom wrote the following in his review in the *Observer*:

> only a very absurd person intent on providing a new type for a Thackerayan Book of Snobs would pretend that the new work for bassoon and strings, heard for the first time at a public concert on July 30, could stand up beside the three Beethoven items that preceded it with any pretence at the same kind of permanence. Not even the composer herself, Elizabeth Maconchy, who, in fact, modestly calls it a Concertino. Nevertheless, one can take Beethoven for granted and write with pleasure about a small work of such distinction and charm. … Everything is heard, nothing is put in to stuff up the texture, and the result is a delicate, aristocratic little work of art.[46]

Even the critic in the *Times* couldn't help but admire the work, even if they had some disdain for Maconchy's penchant for major and minor thirds:

> Miss Maconchy is probably tired of reading that her music is accomplished; yet from this work, too, that is the dominant impression. The texture of the music is always effective and interesting, the ideas always cogently and comprehensively elaborated, for although hers is expressive music it bears the imprint of a good mind. When she produces a new work we are apt to expect a theme featuring the false relation, in her case mixed thirds, major and minor; it is no surprise to hear these intervals in the opening theme of her bassoon concerto, though it made one wonder when she will shake a really new tune from her inventive sleeve.
>
> Nevertheless, when the music gets under way the most fastidious listener must forget to quibble in his admiration of the enthralling ideas and sounds adumbrated by the now familiar tags. The other, more impressive feature of this

[45] The work was performed by soprano Eva Mitchell and pianist Clifton Helliwell.

[46] Eric Blom, 'Promenade Novelties', *Observer*, 8 August 1954.

> bassoon concerto is that it dispenses with what Tovey called the Great Bassoon Joke; it is the lyricism of the instrument that is exposed, and with Mr. Gwydion Brooke to play the solo – the concerto is dedicated to him – even the bubbling humour of the finale is made to sound melodious.[47]

The Proms performance also elicited two articles drawing attention to the fact that beyond her career as a composer, Maconchy was also juggling her job as a mother, with the *Evening News* running a short article titled 'Music Mother' on the day of the concert.[48] Closer to home, the *Essex Weekly News* published an article titled 'She's a Housewife, Mother – and Composer' which featured a photo of Maconchy seated at her piano, surrounded by her family.

The article went on to describe Maconchy as

> [a] Boreham housewife – with an Irish heritage – is snapping her fingers at what has, for years, given women disparity in the arts.
>
> For she can cook and she can sew and do all that women and a mother of two can find to do about a house – and yet go ahead and carve herself a place in contemporary British music. The 'wearing' ties of domesticity, she is resolved, are not to be a barrier to a musical career.
>
> Forty-seven-year-old Elizabeth Maconchy … and Mrs. William Le Fanu … mother of two schoolgirls, are one and the same people.
>
> But on Friday evening she went as Elizabeth Maconchy to the Albert Hall to hear the first public performance of her concertino for bassoon and strings. […]
>
> As housewife and mother of two youngsters (Anna, 15, and Nicola, 7) Mrs. Le Fanu becomes Elizabeth Maconchy in snatches between washing, cooking and mending. She composes at her piano and writes scores 'whenever I can manage'.[49]

While both article titles are certainly sensationalist in their framing, they nevertheless reveal the continuing challenges of Maconchy's working environment. After the Proms performance, a few other notable performances included another performance of *Duo* in an SPNM studio recital on 7 September, as well as a performance of String Quartet No. 4 at a Macnaghten New Music Group concert on 1 November.[50] Later in November, *Proud Thames* received its first performance in Birmingham when it was featured in a City of Birmingham Symphony Orchestra concert, conducted by Harold Gray (1903–91), on the 18th.

On 30 November, Maconchy's Symphony for Double String Orchestra (1952–3) was premièred at an ICA concert held in cooperation with the BBC. For the broadcast concert, Maconchy's work was played by the Royal Philharmonic, conducted by Walter Goehr (1903–60).[51] Whether the work can truly

47 'A New Bassoon Concerto', *Times*, 2 August 1954.

48 Music Mother', *Evening News*, 30 July 1954.

49 'She's a Housewife, Mother – and Composer', *Essex Weekly News*, 6 August 1954.

50 *Duo: Theme and Variations* was played by Macnaghten and Ashby. String Quartet No. 4 was played by the Macnaghten Quartet.

51 The other works featured in the concert were Reginald Smith Brindle's *Cantata da Requiem* for soprano, baritone, chorus, and orchestra, Fartein Valen's Violin Concerto,

Figure 9. Maconchy seated at her Bösendorfer piano surrounded by family, 1954 (reproduced by permission of the Maconchy Estate).

qualify as a symphony is debatable as it features extensive sections for solo violin. In later years, Maconchy clarified her thoughts on the subject:

> I have called this work a Symphony on account of its weight and serious content, and to some extent its form, though the string writing is consistently contrapuntal – (comparable perhaps to a Brandenburg Concerto) and so does not conform to the conventional idea of a Symphony, which is harmonically, rather than contrapuntally, organised. But I felt it to be a Symphony when I was writing it, and I still do.[52]

In contrast to many of Maconchy's works during this period – particularly her quartets – the Symphony for Double String Orchestra is unique in that only two movements, the first and fourth, bear any direct relation. The first movement, Allegro molto, opens with a declarative motif, which is then followed by a brief two-bar introduction of thematic material before a return to the opening motif (Example 8.4). The solo violin is then introduced, with both orchestras

op. 37, and Roger Sessions's Symphony No. 2. Maconchy's Symphony for Double String Orchestra was first on the programme.

[52] Elizabeth Maconchy, 'Symphony for Double String Orchestra', liner notes included with Lyrita SRCD.288, CD 2007. Also see Mathias, *Lutyens, Maconchy, Williams and Twentieth-Century British Music*, 116–9.

Example 8.4. Maconchy, Symphony for Double String Orchestra, mvt. I, opening. Published by Alfred Lengnick & Co., a division of Universal Music Publishing Group. Reproduced by permission of Hal Leonard Europe BV (Italy).

interjecting with lively dialogue. Maconchy then introduces a contrasting section of pizzicato which she described as 'a kind of second subject',[53] which is followed by a more lyrical turn by the first orchestra, which is soon followed by the second orchestra as the movement builds to a climax. The solo violin then returns as the opening motif is restated and previous thematic material reappears in various guises.

The second movement begins with a slow theme in violas featuring octave leaps oscillating back and forth. The violas are then joined by the violins, with the solo violin expanding upon the violas' opening theme, transforming it into a richly lyrical melody underlined by a pedal note in the basses, which then leads to a scalar ascending pattern that increases in frequency as the violins, violas, and finally cellos begin to follow suit, combining this pattern with the opening theme in the violas as tension builds. The re-entry of the solo violin with an extended passage offers a brief respite. The tension then begins to build once again, gradually increasing in intensity until it finally reaches a climax, which is followed by a return of the opening thematic material of the oscillating octaves as the solo violin plays an expressive melody. The orchestra then begins a slower pattern of scalar ascent as the solo violin continues to soar above, bringing the movement to a close.

The third movement, Scherzo, offers a vivid contrast to the preceding movement, with the first and second orchestras engaged in lively debate. While antiphonal treatment of the orchestras is used throughout the symphony, it is most dominant in the third movement. The fourth movement, Passacaglia, begins with a motif that hearkens back to the opening of the first movement (Example 8.5). The cellos in the first orchestra then enter with a melodic theme, followed by the violins and violas, underpinned by a pedal note in the bass of the second orchestra and reiterations of the opening motif which then grows into a contrasting theme. After various strings take their turns expanding upon the theme initiated in the cello, a lengthy allegro section follows with the introduction of a new rhythmic theme that turns into a fugue. A return to the opening theme brings a brief respite, before an ensuing lento section that concludes with a return of the movement's opening motif.

Ahead of the broadcast, Maconchy travelled to London for a rehearsal, which sadly, did not go as planned. The orchestra struggled significantly with the first movement's 7/8 time signature, and as a consequence, they ended up having to spend nearly the entirety of the allotted rehearsal time on that movement. The broadcast proved equally disastrous when, after the third movement, the announcer told listeners that the work had concluded.[54] Unsurprisingly, the broadcast received a lukewarm review from the critic in the *Times*.

While the broadcast left Maconchy feeling deeply discouraged, personnel changes at the BBC that year, with Isaacs moving to the Home Service and Peter Crossley-Holland replacing him as Third Programme Music Organiser, led to a

[53] Ibid.

[54] Elizabeth Maconchy to Peter Crossley-Holland, 20 June 1955, BBC WAC EM3.

Example 8.5. Maconchy, Symphony for Double String Orchestra, mvt. IV, opening. Published by Alfred Lengnick & Co., a division of Universal Music Publishing Group. Reproduced by permission of Hal Leonard Europe BV (Italy).

period of improved relations.[55] As BBC correspondence reveals, Crossley-Holland took a keen interest in Maconchy's music, which led to more broadcasts of her works. On 18 January 1955, Maconchy's *Six Settings of Poems by W.B. Yeats* was featured in a Third Programme broadcast; then, in February, Maconchy's quartets were featured in a series of weekly broadcasts that ran from 15 to 22 March on the Third Programme.[56] Ahead of the series, Williams delivered a talk on Maconchy's music that was broadcast on 13 February. Although these broadcasts elicited a marked boost of interest in Maconchy's music and many congratulatory letters, self-criticism remained an ever-present issue. Shortly after the conclusion of the series, during which time Maconchy had been working on her Seventh String Quartet, she wrote to Williams:

> I think my finales are my worst mvts. on the whole. No. 1 is all right on its small scale – I loathe [the] last mvt. of No. 2. – no 3 hasn't got one. No 4 finale is the best, I think – No. 5 too difficult to bring off for a finale, I think – this is the first time it has come off. No. 6 the last mvt. is the weakest & I don't much like it.[57]

Following the broadcasts, Maconchy began corresponding with Richard Howgill, the BBC's Controller of Music, about her Seventh String Quartet. The work, which was nearing completion, was written with the Hungarian String Quartet in mind and it was initially suggested that the work could be placed in the Thursday Concerts on the Home Service later in the year.[58]

Maconchy also spent a great deal of time thinking about the broadcast of her Symphony for Double String Orchestra the previous year, and in June 1955, she wrote the following to Crossley-Holland:

[55] Peter Crossley-Holland (1916–2001) was a composer and ethnomusicologist. Prior to becoming Third Programme Music Organiser – a post Crossley-Holland held from 1954 to 1960 – he had served as Home Service Music Organiser from 1950 to 1954. After leaving the Third Programme, Isaacs took up Crossley-Holland's post as Home Service Music Organiser from 1954 to 1960. See Kenyon, 440.

[56] Maconchy's quartets were played by the following: String Quartet No. 1, Allegri Quartet (15 February); String Quartet No. 2, Martin Quartet (24 February); String Quartet No. 3, MacGibbon Quartet (2 March); String Quartet No. 4, New London Quartet (7 March); String Quartet No. 5, Aeolian Quartet (14 March); String Quartet No. 6, MacGibbon Quartet (22 March). While Maconchy had initially broached the topic of a series of broadcasts some years prior, in this instance it appears to have been Crossley-Holland who managed to put the series into action. Peter Crossley-Holland to Elizabeth Maconchy, 26 October 1954, BBC WAC EM3. The Allegri String Quartet was founded in 1953 and comprised Eli Goren (1st violin), James Barton (2nd violin), Patrick Ireland (viola), and William Pleeth (cello). At the time of the recordings, the line-up of the Aeolian String Quartet (1944–81) consisted of Sydney Humphreys (1st violin), Trevor Williams (2nd violin), Watson Forbes (viola), and John Moore (cello). The New London Quartet comprised Erich Gruenberg (1st violin), Lionel Bentley (2nd violin), Keith Cummings (viola), and Douglas Cameron (cello).

[57] Elizabeth Maconchy to Grace Williams, 29 March 1955.

[58] Richard Howgill to Elizabeth Maconchy, 28 March 1955, BBC WAC EM3. Also see Jennifer Doctor, 'Maconchy's String Quartet No. 7 and the BBC', *Musical Objects* 1 (1995): 5–8.

> I was of course very much disturbed by this, and thought of scrapping this movement altogether, feeling that it was not admissible to have a movement which stole so much rehearsal time from the rest of the work and still sounded so tentative at performance. But after going very carefully over the score & thinking a lot about it, I decided that I ought, in fairness to the work, so to speak, to let it have another performance before taking this drastic step. … I felt very disheartened by the performance, and I was glad when Bernard de Nevers told me you'd said you liked the work in spite of all this & said 'We must do it again'. I indeed hope this may be possible?
>
> I fear I have written rather a rigmarole about it – but I feel myself that this String Symphony is one of the best things I have done, and I naturally want very badly to hear it sound as I believe it can & should sound![59]

Sympathetic to Maconchy's letter, Crossley-Holland wrote back, 'I agree that this did have rather a rough passage. … It may be possible to arrange another performance early in the New Year.'[60]

Beyond performances and broadcasts, Maconchy was busy with a host of other activities in the early months of 1955. In December 1954, she was elected to the council of the Composers' Guild, which led to more trips to London for meetings the following year, and on 1 February 1955, she gave a brief talk at one of the SPNM's studio recitals. Though the winter and spring of 1955 were also marred by managing colds and flus, Maconchy also finished a new arrangement of *Suite on Irish Airs* for the King Edward VI Grammar School in Chelmsford. This arrangement was featured in an Anglo-German concert on 13 April with a combined orchestra made up of students in Chelmsford-area schools and visiting students from Germany. Maconchy attended the concert, receiving a standing ovation and a bouquet of flowers.[61]

The following day, Maconchy flew to Ireland along with Anna, where they spent a week with Boyle along with the Macnaghten Quartet. During their visit, Boyle hosted a small gathering at her home for the Composers' Group of the Music Association of Ireland.[62] On 20 April, Maconchy's music was featured in a Radio Éireann broadcast, which included the Macnaghten Quartet playing String Quartet No. 4. Following what was undoubtedly a busy and exciting week of activity, Maconchy and Anna returned to England on the 22nd. On 14 May, Williams came to visit Maconchy, staying over until the following day. Then, on the 16th, Maconchy travelled to London to have supper with Vaughan Williams and attend a Macnaghten New Music Group concert. The work that concluded the concert that evening was a series of variations based on Alfred Scott-Gatty's 'Where's my little basket gone?', titled *Diabelleries*. This work was a collaborative effort, with Vaughan Williams selecting Scott-Gatty's tune and Bush, Howard Ferguson, Finzi, Jacob, Lutyens, Maconchy, Rawsthorne, and

59 Elizabeth Maconchy to Peter Crossley-Holland, 20 June 1955, BBC WAC EM3.

60 Peter Crossley-Holland to Elizabeth Maconchy, 3 August 1955, BBC WAC EM3.

61 'Anglo-German Concert', *Essex Weekly News*, 15 April 1955; I.M. 'Music and Memorials', *Irish Independent*, 30 April 1955.

62 Dunlop, 19; 'Composers Meet at Enniskerry', *Evening Herald*, 20 April 1955.

Williams all contributing a variation. It was also a fitting tribute to mark what, at the time, was thought to be the final Macnaghten New Music Group concert as they continued to struggle with finances. Fortunately, this final concert was not to be the last, as the Macnaghten New Music Group continued their series through 1957.[63]

In June, the *Musical Times* featured an in-depth profile of Maconchy written by Macnaghten.[64] Given that the last time Maconchy's music had generated an entire article was in 1938, this was indeed a promising development and indicative of a career that seemed to be, once again, on the ascent. Maconchy was also occupied with a number of new works during this period, including more educational pieces, such as *Three Pieces for Clarinet*, which she wrote for her eldest daughter, Anna, who had been studying clarinet at St Mary's, as well as four part songs for the school, which were completed in 1956. In addition to work on her Concerto for Oboe, Bassoon, and String Orchestra, and a Suite for Oboe and String Orchestra, Maconchy also completed her Seventh String Quartet, as well as a work titled Movement for Viola and Piano in 1955.[65] The latter work was written for violist Margaret Major, who premièred the work along with pianist Dorothy Manley at a Macnaghten New Music Group concert on 21 November.

Notably, the autumn also featured two broadcasts of Maconchy's orchestral works: on 10 October, *Theme and Variations for String Orchestra* was featured in a Third Programme broadcast, played by the Riddick String Orchestra, conducted by Riddick, then, on 8 November, a much older work, *Dialogue for Piano and Orchestra*, received its long-awaited first broadcast in a Third Programme concert of choral and orchestral works, with pianist Robin Wood (1924–2004) and the Royal Philharmonic Orchestra, conducted by Maurice Miles (1908–85). The broadcast of *Dialogue* elicited a number of enthusiastic letters, with Vaughan Williams writing to Maconchy, 'Your piece is first rate, why have I never heard it, or even of it, before?'[66] Vaughan Williams had of course undoubtedly heard about the work, but the long lapse between its first performance – from the cancelled Prom in 1940, to its first performance in 1942, its initial approval from the BBC's panel during the war, followed by disputes after the war when Maconchy was asked to submit the work again – could have understandably led to a lapse in memory. Vaughan Williams was not the only one to write to Maconchy: she also received a letter from Gordon Jacob, who wrote shortly after the broadcast: 'It is so rare to get enjoyment & satisfaction from contemporary music that I feel I must write a line to say that I got both from your "Dialogue" the other day. … In Utopia such a piece would get many performances & would become popular in the best sense of the word.'[67]

[63] Chapman, 15–16.

[64] See Macnaghten, 'Elizabeth Maconchy'.

[65] The Suite for Oboe and String Orchestra (1955–6) was written for Finzi's Newbury String Players.

[66] Ralph Vaughan Williams to Elizabeth Maconchy, 10 November 1955, VWL 3218.

[67] Gordon Jacob to Elizabeth Maconchy, 11 November 1955, private collection.

9

A Musical Block and an Operatic Solution, 1956–9

On the surface, the year 1956 seemed both successful and highly productive. In addition to completing her Concerto for Oboe, Bassoon, and String Orchestra (1955–6) as well as a series of part songs for St Mary's School, Maconchy also arranged *A Country Town* for small orchestra for the school, composed a new work titled String Trio, and wrote two new songs for voice and piano.[1] Although domestic responsibilities continued to take priority over her career, as indicated by her appointment diary, she was nevertheless able to make an increasing number of trips to London to attend concerts and Composers' Guild meetings.

Though performances outside the UK and Ireland continued to remain rare, on 7 November, the Quintet for Oboe and Strings (1933) was featured in a broadcast in Denmark. The mastermind behind the broadcast was violist Richard Dahl Eriksen, who had played in the orchestra for the performance of Maconchy's Concertino for Clarinet and String Orchestra at the ISCM Festival in Copenhagen. This trajectory of events demonstrates just how vital a role the ISCM Festivals played in promoting the works of composers such as Maconchy to international audiences.

Maconchy's improved relationship with the BBC also led to a number of broadcasts in 1956. Of these, the majority were on the Third Programme and restricted to small-scale works. Although there were plans for another broadcast of the Symphony for Double String Orchestra in March, the programme was unfortunately cancelled and Maconchy had to wait another year before it was included in a Third Programme broadcast on 10 March 1957. Some of her works, however, were featured in much more desirable slots on the Home Service, with a broadcast of the String Quartet No. 5 on 15 March, and *Proud Thames* taking place on 26 November.[2]

While it was surely a relief for Maconchy to have her music featured more frequently in broadcasts, she continued to find herself dissatisfied with the quality of performances. With musicians often asked to learn her works at short

[1] *The Exequy* and *Come Away, Death*.

[2] The broadcast of String Quartet No. 5 was featured in the Home Service's Thursday Concerts and was played by the Aeolian Quartet. The broadcast of *Proud Thames* featured the BBC Scottish Orchestra, conducted by Stanford Robinson. Two of Maconchy's educational piano works, *Nodding*, and *The Sewing Machine*, were played by Jean Mackie in a Home Service broadcast on 24 November.

notice, combined with an inadequate number of rehearsals, dismal outcomes could hardly be surprising.[3] For a broadcast of *Duo: Theme and Variations* with violinist Jan Sedivka (1917–2009) and cellist Sela Trau that took place on 1 March, Maconchy lamented in a letter to Williams, 'it wasn't a good performance – they had to get it up much too quickly (that was the B.B.C.'s fault) – so un-necessary, because they are good players & nice people & wanted to do it well, & enthusiastic – but they barely knew it – (thank goodness I had one rehearsal with them, the day before).'[4]

For the 15 March broadcast of String Quartet No. 5 with the Aeolian Quartet, Maconchy travelled to London to rehearse the work with the group ahead of the broadcast that evening. Although the group was familiar with the work and Maconchy was satisfied overall with the broadcast, in a letter to Williams, she remarked, 'one must be grateful for a performance that isn't actually bad – – & as things go, this was good: but how one does long for a really good one!'[5] Maconchy was not the only one to express these sentiments as Scott Goddard perceptively wrote in the *Musical Times*:

> Elizabeth Maconchy's fifth string quartet appeared in a Home Service Thursday concert in mid-March, giving a welcome opportunity to renew acquaintance with the work of a highly intelligent and perceptive writer of chamber music. … Her mind, one of the most interesting among the mature composers working in this country at present, has come to express itself with increasing ease. Not that the understanding of that mind is a simple matter; its involutions are curious, as one was forcibly reminded when listening to this recent broadcast … Small wonder, therefore, that there was a feeling of strain about the performance; listening may be exciting but manifestly performance is exacting. With all due respect to these players (the Aeolian Quartet), I still have to hear this and the other Maconchy string quartets played without apparent nervous tension and the resultant instability. I cannot feel that I have yet heard a Maconchy string quartet in perfect perspective.[6]

While the inherent level of difficulty of some of Maconchy's compositions presented a challenge for performers and conductors, more often than not, adequate preparation and rehearsal with the right musicians led to favourable outcomes. One such example is the rescheduled Third Programme broadcast of the Symphony for Double String Orchestra on 14 March 1957, which featured the London Symphony Orchestra, conducted by Maurice Miles. The work, which received an ample amount of rehearsal time, resulted in a performance that left Maconchy 'immensely cheered at hearing it sound just as I wanted it

[3] In a letter to Maurice Johnstone, Head of Music Programmes, Maconchy remarked, 'My chamber music is not very easy, and this explains, I think, why performances have never been very frequent and sometimes, unfortunately, not rehearsed quite adequately enough to give a really convincing performance'. Elizabeth Maconchy to Maurice Johnstone, 27 July 1959, BBC WAC EM4.

[4] Elizabeth Maconchy to Grace Williams, 15 March 1956.

[5] Ibid.

[6] Scott Goddard, 'Radio Notes', *Musical Times* 97/1359 (May 1956): 258.

to and felt that the work had justified itself to me'.[7] Maconchy was not the only one to find the work impressive, as both Vaughan Williams and Bliss expressed similar sentiments.[8] This validation arrived at a particularly important moment for Maconchy who was once again doubting the quality of her work. Following the broadcast, Williams wrote to Maconchy, 'You are right to feel dejected at lack of performances – & wrong, too, because the all important thing is that you have composed all these truly original & fine works & there must come a time (I'm sure it will come suddenly) when they will be recognized for what they are worth.'[9]

The spring and early summer of 1957 yielded two further Third Programme broadcasts with the première of Maconchy's String Trio (1956) on 22 May, followed by another broadcast of *Dialogue for Piano and Orchestra* on 27 June. The broadcast of the String Trio left Maconchy deeply disheartened:

> I've had such a revulsion against almost everything I've written. I'd decided before hearing it that the Trio wasn't much good – then when I heard it I almost came to like it – but I've gone back to the other opinion now! I don't think I shall write any more serious chamber music – nobody wants to play the large quantity I've written anyway! And what one goes through in writing it nearly kills one: & then if one doesn't like it oneself even in the end – well, it's surely better not to do it.[10]

Reflecting back on this period of her career in 1966, Maconchy remarked, 'I felt I had got a bit stuck: that I had been writing in the same sort of forms for too long, and I wanted to do something quite different. So I made a break away from chamber-music and abstract music in general, and wrote my 3 one-act operas.'[11]

This was, of course, hardly Maconchy's first exploration of the genre, as she had experimented with opera projects during her studies at the RCM with *The Knight's Tale*, followed a few years later by her incomplete *The Willow Plate*. Many years then passed before Maconchy seriously began to contemplate tackling another opera project, as she detailed in a letter to Williams in 1949 that both she and LeFanu had 'an itch to write an opera – but feel we haven't the skill

7 Elizabeth Maconchy to Peter Crossley-Holland, 13 March 1957, BBC WAC EM3. Bliss attended the rehearsal on 10 March which presumably also included a rehearsal of his *Music for Strings*, which was also featured in the programme. Vaughan Williams attended the rehearsal that took place on 11 March.

8 Ibid.

9 Grace Williams to Elizabeth Maconchy, 10 March 1957.

10 Elizabeth Maconchy to Grace Williams, 23 May 1957.

11 Elizabeth Maconchy, draft of talk for BBC programme titled 'Conversation between Anne Macnaghten and Elizabeth Maconchy', 4 May 1966, SHC.

& experience – real practical experience one needs'.[12] Several years then passed before Maconchy began the first of her three one-act operas, *The Sofa*, in 1956.[13]

Based upon Claude Prosper Jolyot de Crébillon's libidinous satirical pastiche of the *Arabian Nights*, *Le Sopha, conte moral* (1762), the racy subject matter of *The Sofa* was a stark departure from the generally more serious themes that had inspired much of Maconchy's musical output. Indeed, the thematic contrast was so profound that even Williams questioned whether the libertine novel Maconchy had selected was a proper fit.[14] Determined to stretch her artistic prowess, Maconchy went ahead with the project, working with Vaughan Williams's second wife, the poet Ursula Vaughan Williams (1911–2007), who contributed the libretto.

Over the course of the project, Maconchy made many trips to London to work on the opera at the Vaughan Williams' residence at 10 Hanover Terrace. Ralph Vaughan Williams appears to have played at least a modest role, critiquing the music as well as contributing to the libretto. As Maconchy later remarked, 'he particularly liked the frivolous music'.[15] By 1956, Ursula Vaughan Williams had already developed some skill in writing librettos, primarily working with her husband. Although Maconchy found Ursula amenable to work with, she was concerned that the work might be too 'vieux jeu', elaborating in a letter to Williams: 'it is impossible to get her to write the kind of thing I really want. She has a nice flair for light verse & is most inclined to be co-operative – but there are too many words – not always telling & to the point – or good to sing – or in the [*sic*] enough variety of mood & so on. I think the only thing is to do a libretto oneself.'[16] For her next one-act opera project, *The Three Strangers* (1957–8), Maconchy did just that, adapting Thomas Hardy's *The Three Wayfarers* to create her own libretto.

A potential contributing factor to Maconchy's general sense of disillusionment during this period may have been the BBC's continued delays of the broadcast of String Quartet No. 7. Although there had been initial talks to have the Hungarian Quartet première the work in a Home Service broadcast in the autumn

[12] Elizabeth Maconchy to Grace Williams, 24 April 1949. The impetus behind this 'itch' was likely the Arts Council's opera competition which had been announced that year.

[13] Around the time that Maconchy was contemplating *The Sofa*, she was also considering an opera based upon Pedro Calderón de la Barca's play *Life is a Dream* (*La vida es sueño*, 1635) with a libretto translated and adapted by LeFanu. Undated drafts of the libretto and a surviving pencil draft of the score for the first act suggest that Maconchy and LeFanu dedicated a substantial amount of time to this project. Their reasons for abandoning it are unclear.

[14] Grace Williams to Elizabeth Maconchy, 10 March 1957. Although Ursula Vaughan Williams claimed that the idea to use Crébillon's novel had come from LeFanu, in a letter to Williams, Maconchy states that the idea was her own. See Ursula Vaughan Williams, *Paradise Remembered* (London: Albion Music Ltd, 2002), 188; and Elizabeth Maconchy to Grace Williams, 30 May 1957.

[15] Skiba, 9.

[16] Elizabeth Maconchy to Grace Williams, 30 May 1957.

of 1956, the quartet unfortunately had to postpone their trip to England, with their next visit initially projected to take place in the spring of 1957.[17] Shortly after Maconchy wrote to Howgill to update him about the Hungarian Quartet's schedule in February 1956, Isaacs wrote in a memo to Howgill, 'I wonder really if Maconchy No 7 isn't a bit tough going for Home Service. I would certainly take your decision on the point & book the Hungarian Quartet for a Thursday Concert in Spring '57 if you though it was the right thing to do.'[18] Shortly thereafter, Howgill asked Maconchy to send the score to the BBC so that they could look it over, writing in his letter to her, 'This is not a question of merit but you have suggested it for a Thursday concert and it may be rather tough for that particular programme.'[19]

Maconchy subsequently sent the score to the BBC. A few days later, Isaacs wrote the following in a memo to Howgill:

> I don't think it will be harder to listen to than Seiber No 3, & possibly less difficult than Bartok 5 (which it looks like in places).
>
> I'm all for first performances in H.S. where possible, & the compliment paid to it by the Hungarian Quartet may tend to offset the unfamiliarity.
>
> On the face of it, it is 'Third Programme music' though! And a performance in a Thursday Concert of a contemporary work is taken usually as a demonstration that the work in question has 'arrived'. I wouldn't want to do many first performances of toughish works there, nor to single out one particular composer too often.[20]

Isaacs's position could hardly be perceived as surprising given his general distaste for Maconchy's music. Although Howgill stated in a letter to Maconchy that he would see what could be done regarding a Home Service broadcast with the Hungarian Quartet, any hopes of the work being premièred by the group were soon dashed when they informed Maconchy that they no longer had plans to travel to England in 1957.[21] Unwilling to wait an indefinite amount of time for her quartet of choice, Maconchy subsequently settled on offering the first performance to the Amadeus String Quartet.[22]

Believing the matter settled, Maconchy was in for a shock in June 1956 when she received a letter from the BBC's Music Hire department informing her that her Seventh String Quartet had been scheduled for a Third Programme broadcast with the Martin String Quartet on 6 December. Maconchy was understandably upset by this and Howgill sought to reassure her by informing her that the hire request had been incorrect and that the work was to be in a Thursday Concert on the Home Service. Although the concert had to be

[17] Elizabeth Maconchy to Richard Howgill, 22 February 1956, BBC WAC EM3.

[18] Leonard Isaacs to Richard Howgill, 29 February 1956, BBC WAC EM3.

[19] Richard Howgill to Elizabeth Maconchy, 6 March 1956, BBC WAC EM3.

[20] Leonard Isaacs to Richard Howgill, 12 March 1956, BBC WAC EM3. Also quoted in Doctor, 'Maconchy's String Quartet No. 7 and the BBC', 7.

[21] Elizabeth Maconchy to Richard Howgill, 28 June 1956, BBC WAC EM3.

[22] The Amadeus Quartet had been suggested by Howgill. Richard Howgill to Elizabeth Maconchy, 6 March 1956, BBC WAC EM3.

cancelled, Howgill suggested it be moved to the following week.[23] By August, however, plans for the broadcast were placed on hold once again.[24]

On 8 July 1957, Maconchy wrote to Isaacs to resume discussions about broadcasting her quartet. Although she had sent String Quartet No. 7 to the Amadeus Quartet, who apparently liked the work, they felt that its level of difficulty would require more rehearsals than they would be able to devote to it.[25] She then approached the Aeolian Quartet, who were eager to take it on.[26] Though Maconchy was hopeful that the work would now be able to be placed in a Home Service programme, Isaacs, sadly, did not have positive news. Citing the BBC's cuts, as he wrote to Maconchy in July: 'As you appear to be aware of the "horrible changes" you may also not be surprised to hear that I may find a good deal more difficulty than I anticipated in placing your Quartet No. 7.'[27] The work was then placed in a Third Programme broadcast to take place on 27 November, but by August, the work was postponed once again.

The delay of a broadcast on the Third Programme was undoubtedly a result of the BBC's decision to restructure its programming to address declining listener figures as the organisation faced increasing pressures to compete with the rising popularity of television. Rumours of cuts to the Third Programme, which were confirmed in early 1957, generated considerable outrage and criticism, particularly from the cultural elite. After months of drawn-out debates in the press, the BBC published their plans for their new autumn schedule at the end of August, which amounted to a reduction of the Third Programme's hours by forty percent. In response, the Sound Broadcasting Society, an organisation that had been formed earlier in the year to protest against the BBC's cuts, released a statement condemning the decision, arguing that the Third Programme 'cannot give full coverage in three hours a night', further contending that the cuts were not 'justified in terms of economy when other programmes are not similarly curtailed although their audiences are the ones that have fallen'.[28]

On 29 September 1957 – the eleventh anniversary of the Third Programme – the Sound Broadcasting Society presented a concert at the Royal Court

[23] Richard Howgill to Elizabeth Maconchy, 23 August 1956, BBC WAC EM3. For the proposed rescheduled broadcast on 13 December, it was suggested that the Aeolian Quartet be approached to play the work.

[24] In a letter Isaacs wrote to Maconchy shortly after they had discussed matters over the telephone, he states, 'This is just to confirm our telephone conversation on Friday afternnon [*sic*]. We will do nothing more about your 7th Quartet until we hear from you as to the result of your negotiations with the Amadeus Quartet.' Leonard Isaacs to Elizabeth Maconchy, 27 August 1956, BBC WAC EM3.

[25] The lack of adequate rehearsal time was due to the Amadeus Quartet's forthcoming world tour. Elizabeth Maconchy to Leonard Isaacs, 8 July 1957, BBC WAC EM3.

[26] Ibid.

[27] Leonard Isaacs to Elizabeth Maconchy, 12 July 1957, BBC WAC EM3.

[28] 'Music to Suffer Biggest Cut in Third Programme', *Times*, 27 August 1957. The Sound Broadcasting Society initially started as the Third Programme Defence Society in March 1957. They later changed their name to the Sound Broadcasting Defence Society before finally settling on the Sound Broadcasting Society.

Theatre titled 'A "Third Programme" Entertainment'. This concert, which was described in the *Times* as a mixture of both 'nostalgia' and 'protest', opened with Maconchy's String Quartet No. 1, played by the Allegri Quartet, and also featured actress Jill Balcon and poet Cecil Day-Lewis reading a series of poems, as well as Peggy Ashcroft and John Gielgud reciting sonnets by Shakespeare and scenes from Milton and Dryden.[29] The decision to include Maconchy's quartet was made by the Society's president, Vaughan Williams.[30] The programme also included a recorded address by T.S. Eliot that was played for the audience. Though the address was certainly tinged with elitism, it eloquently surmised the larger toll that cuts to the Third Programme represented in the eyes of many:

> It is the assumption that the minority audience which finds entertainment in what also gives it mental and emotional nourishment – that is, the best music, the best poetry and drama, and the words of our most powerful thinkers – that this public, because it is a minority, is less important than the majority – that this assumption should be made in high quarters is what frightens me.
>
> The assumption behind the attitude of the BBC is alarming, because when generally unquestioned and accepted, such an assumption tends to demoralise democracy, discourage excellence, and enervate the nation.[31]

The BBC's reduced Third Programme schedule started the following evening.

On 9 October Maconchy attended a Royal Philharmonic Society concert held at the Royal Festival Hall along with her husband and Anna. The concert was held in honour of Vaughan Williams's forthcoming eighty-fifth birthday on the 12th, and Maconchy and her family attended a party for Vaughan Williams held afterwards. The following day, Anna left for Oxford where she would commence her studies at St Hilda's College. On the 11th, the recently renamed Macnaghten Concerts held a concert in honour of Vaughan Williams's birthday.[32] For the occasion, Maconchy wrote a series of variations for cello based upon Vaughan Williams's ballet *Job*. Owing to the unfortunate illness of Arnold Ashby, the work had to be removed from the programme, with Maconchy's *Divertimento* taking its place.[33]

29 The Allegri Quartet also played Mozart's String Quartet in G Major, K. 387.

30 'Vice-Presidents and Others', *Manchester Guardian*, 23 September 1957. Both Maconchy and LeFanu were supporters of the Society. Maconchy had also urged the Composers' Guild to officially support the organisation. Elizabeth Maconchy to Grace Williams, 30 May 1957.

31 T.S. Eliot, 'The Spoken Word', text of the recorded address, printed in the concert programme.

32 Following increasing financial difficulties, the Macnaghten New Music Group relaunched in 1957 with a revamped committee of considerably younger individuals, which included Ernest Chapman (1914–83), Jeremy Dale Roberts (1934–2017), Christopher Finzi (1934–2019), Louis Halsey (b. 1929), and Geoffrey Winters (b. 1928). The concert held in honour of Vaughan Williams was the first in this new series. See Chapman, 'The Macnaghten Concerts', 16–17.

33 The *Divertimento* was played by Muriel Taylor (cello) and Clifton Halliwell (piano).

Shortly after Anna left for Oxford, both LeFanu and Nicola came down with the flu, greatly disrupting Maconchy's progress on *The Sofa*. The illness couldn't have come at a worse time as Maconchy needed to send a copy of the score to the New Opera Company for consideration for their upcoming season.[34] Though a production of *The Sofa* in the New Opera Company's forthcoming season did not materialise, Maconchy appears to have completed a rough score by the end of the year, later arranging a vocal score in early 1958.[35] As for a full score of the work, Maconchy decided to hold off on its completion until she had a definite agreement for a performance in order to allow her to adjust the orchestration to the particular needs and limitations of the production.[36] Though she was able to make some progress by working late at night, she ultimately ended up having to send the work unfinished.[37]

Following all of her frustrations with the delays of the broadcast of her String Quartet No. 7, Maconchy had some good news to celebrate when the work was finally rescheduled for a pre-recorded broadcast on 8 January 1958, with the Aeolian Quartet recording the work on 20 December 1957. Arranged in five movements, the String Quartet No. 7 opens with all the strings playing a series of eighth notes on C, followed by an ascending minor second and a descending major second (Example 9.1). In the first movement, one can certainly detect traces of the previous quartet, as the drone in the cello, combined with the melody played by the other strings in the meno mosso, calmo section, bears a close affinity to the passacaglia theme that dominated String Quartet No. 6 (Example 9.2).

The second movement, Scherzo, is centred around the interval of a major third, which is derived from ideas presented in the preceding movement (Example 9.3). In the third movement, Lento, richly lyrical melodies, supported by alternating sections of pizzicato feature heavily throughout. Descending major and minor thirds also play a prominent role, with the pattern of alternating major and minor intervals (Example 9.4) providing a thematic link to the first movement. In the fourth movement, Scherzo, pizzicato is back with a vengeance, dominating the entirety of the energetic movement, which features a 7/16 metre (Example 9.5). The intervallic relationship of the opening four notes of the fifth movement, F, G-flat, A-flat, and G-natural, connect the movement back to the first, further demonstrating the degree of interrelated thematic connections.

As a whole, the Seventh Quartet possesses an arch-like structure. Of this design, Maconchy openly acknowledged the firm connections between the first, third, and fifth movements, with the thematic material of the second and fourth

[34] Elizabeth Maconchy to Grace Williams, 10 November 1957.

[35] Elizabeth Maconchy to Grace Williams, 28 January 1958. In Maconchy's handwritten list of works at SHC, *The Sofa* is given the date range of 1956–7, suggesting that the opera was primarily composed during this period, aside from the vocal score with piano arrangement and full ink score.

[36] Ibid.

[37] Ibid.

Example 9.1. Maconchy, String Quartet No. 7, mvt. I, opening.
Published by Alfred Lengnick & Co., a division of Universal Music Publishing Group.
Reproduced by permission of Hal Leonard Europe BV (Italy).

Example 9.2. Maconchy, String Quartet No. 7, mvt. I, bars 16–21.
Published by Alfred Lengnick & Co., a division of Universal Music Publishing Group.
Reproduced by permission of Hal Leonard Europe BV (Italy).

Example 9.3. Maconchy, String Quartet No. 7, mvt. II, opening.
Published by Alfred Lengnick & Co., a division of Universal Music Publishing Group.
Reproduced by permission of Hal Leonard Europe BV (Italy).

Example 9.4. Maconchy, String Quartet No. 7, mvt. III, opening.
Published by Alfred Lengnick & Co., a division of Universal Music Publishing Group.
Reproduced by permission of Hal Leonard Europe BV (Italy).

Example 9.5. Maconchy, String Quartet No. 7, mvt. IV, opening.
Published by Alfred Lengnick & Co., a division of Universal Music Publishing Group.
Reproduced by permission of Hal Leonard Europe BV (Italy).

movements closely related to one another.[38] In this sense, one can certainly draw comparisons to Bartók's own use of symmetrical structures, which may have served as an inspiration.[39] The actual music, however, remains distinctive to Maconchy's own individual voice.

By all accounts, the broadcast appears to have been well received. In a highly favourable review appearing in the *Listener*, Dyneley Hussey declared, 'Miss Maconchy's concentration upon chamber-music has prevented her from gaining the high place in general public estimation that is really her due. This new quartet is yet another manifestation of her remarkable ability as a composer and her complete mastery of her chosen medium.'[40] Despite the work's positive reception, Maconchy remained unsure about the work as she detailed in a letter to Williams: 'I have had such changes & revulsions of feeling about it, for so long. On the whole after hearing it, I think I am fairly pleased with it (& after all, glad I wrote it!) but there are certain things I'm not quite sure about yet.'[41] The work received its next performance on 5 December, with the Aeolian Quartet playing the work at a Macnaghten concert.

The majority of Maconchy's time in 1958 was devoted to continued work on *The Three Strangers*. Aside from the broadcast of String Quartet No. 7 in January, only a few other performances of her works appear to have taken place during the year, with a performance of *Divertimento* taking place in March in Belfast and one of her educational works, 'Good Night' from *A Country Town*,

[38] Maconchy, 'Elizabeth Maconchy On Writing String Quartets'.

[39] See Mathias, *Lutyens, Maconchy, Williams and Twentieth-Century British Music*, 205.

[40] Dyneley Hussey, 'Music: For Five Strings and Four', *Listener* 942 (23 January 1958): 175.

[41] Elizabeth Maconchy to Grace Williams, 28 January 1958.

featured in an educational television programme in North Carolina.[42] During the summer, Norman Tucker, who was the managerial head at Sadler's Wells, expressed an interest in *The Sofa*. Although Maconchy sent a vocal score to him, sadly, no correspondence from Tucker indicating his thoughts on the work survives.[43]

Throughout 1958, Maconchy and her husband continued to be frequent visitors at the Vaughan Williams' residence. On the morning of 26 August, they were awoken by a telephone call from Ursula, notifying them that Ralph had died that morning. Although Vaughan Williams had been in fairly good health given his age of eighty-five, his sudden death was a tremendous loss for Maconchy. Following a week-long caravan trip to the Suffolk coast ahead of Nicola's first term at St Mary's in September, Maconchy attended Vaughan Williams's funeral service, which was held at Westminster Abbey on 19 September. In the years that followed, Maconchy contributed a number of written tributes to Vaughan Williams, highlighting his generosity and inspiring nature.

In the summer and autumn Maconchy was also on the hunt for a more serious subject that would be suitable for another one-act opera. Possibly sometime around the summer of 1958, Maconchy was introduced to the poet Anne Ridler (1912–2001).[44] Referencing what was likely a previous meeting, Ridler wrote to Maconchy on 23 July 1958,

> I haven't forgotten my promise to search my mind for a tragic subject for opera, but nothing that seems just right has yet occurred to me. However, I think I may as well write now to give you a couple of tentative suggestions, and perhaps you would write me a line if you had already found a subject, and did not want me to think any more.[45]

[42] According to the *Belfast Telegraph*, the performance of *Divertimento* took place on 9 March at the Performers' Club. Details of the performers, however, were not included. See Rathcol, 'Musical events which clash with Belfast Festival', *Belfast Telegraph*, 3 March 1958. The television programme featuring 'Good Night' was presented on the educational channel WUNC-TV in North Carolina on 25 November as part of the *Piano by Television* series, which focused on the North Carolina Music Educators Association's repertoire. 'Good Night' was played by Margis Jones with a discussion of the work's technical aspects by Claire Atkisson. 'WUNC Shows Piano Series', *Rocky Mountain Telegraph*, 24 November 1958.

[43] Maconchy lists the date that she sent the score as 3 September in her notebook for 1951–63, held at SHC.

[44] Anne Ridler (neé Bradby) was a close friend of LeFanu's brother-in-law and sister, John and Lucie Christie. John had been acquainted with Ridler's father, Henry Bradby, during their respective careers as headmasters. After serving as headmaster at Repton School, followed by Westminster School, Christie served as Principal of Jesus College, Oxford from 1949–67. Ridler lived in Oxford with her husband, Vivian, who was a printer and typographer for the University of Oxford and the OUP. Maconchy and LeFanu frequently visited the Christies, which is presumably how Maconchy became acquainted with Ridler. Email from Nicola LeFanu to author.

[45] Anne Ridler to Elizabeth Maconchy, 23 July 1958, SHC.

Over the next several months, Ridler offered a number of suggestions, with Italian novelist Ignazio Silone's antifascist work *Fontamara* (1933) particularly capturing her imagination. By November, Ridler had already drafted a scenario based on the work; however, it was later abandoned owing to concerns about their ability to get Silone to agree to the adaptation and its deviations from the novel.[46] In 1959, Maconchy proposed the idea of an opera exploring the concept of death through the lens of a woman struggling to accept her fate post-mortem. Over the course of the year, Ridler and Maconchy worked on refining their scenario and libretto for the opera, which they titled *The Departure*.

On 21 January 1959, *A Winter's Tale* (1949) received its much-belated Third Programme broadcast, which was pre-recorded by soprano April Cantelo (b. 1928) and the Amici String Quartet on the 19th. Although Maconchy was pleased overall, revisiting the work after so many years led her to make minor revisions to the score.[47] On 23 January, Maconchy's *Variations on a Theme from Vaughan Williams's 'Job'* received its rescheduled first performance at a Macnaghten concert. More Third Programme broadcasts followed in the spring, with a broadcast of the String Quartet No. 7 on 10 March[48] and the première of her Concerto for Oboe, Bassoon, and String Orchestra (1955–6) on 8 June in a Chamber Orchestral Concert with the Welbeck Orchestra, featuring Evelyn Rothwell (oboe), Archie Camden (bassoon), and conducted by Miles.[49]

The Concerto for Oboe, Bassoon, and String Orchestra reflects Maconchy's established musical idiom and penchant for interweaving motifs. Arranged in three contrasting movements, Maconchy described the work as more a conversation between oboe and bassoon as opposed to a double concerto, with a motif consisting of D, F, and C-sharp serving as the building blocks for much of the work.[50] The broadcast yielded predominately favourable notices in the press, with Goddard writing in the *Listener*, 'I could wish to go down to posterity as one who had the good uncommon sense to salute the gifts of Elizabeth Maconchy and in an attempt to make that journey I recall now the pleasure and stimulus I had when listening last week … to the first performance of her Concerto for oboe, bassoon, and strings.'[51] Always the perfectionist, Maconchy was unmoved by the press notices, as she wrote to Williams:

> The first movement is the trouble. It didn't go smoothly when I wrote it & I scrapped & scrapped, with the result probably that I somehow lost its natural impetus & growth. As it stands I fear it has too many changes of mood (& tempo)

[46] Anne Ridler to Elizabeth Maconchy, 12 January 1959, private collection.

[47] Elizabeth Maconchy to Grace Williams, 28 January 1959.

[48] The BBC had initially planned to broadcast the String Quartet No. 4 on 3 March with the Hirsch String Quartet; however, an accident suffered by the quartet's violist, Stephen Shingles, led to its cancellation. David Stone to Elizabeth Maconchy, 19 February 1959, BBC WAC EM4.

[49] The programme also included Ann Hamerton's *The Persian Flute*, Thomas Rajna's Suite for String Orchestra, and Berkeley's *Four Poems of St. Teresa of Avila*.

[50] Elizabeth Maconchy to Miss Wood, 18 May 1959, BBC WAC EM4.

[51] Scott Goddard, 'Ancient and Modern', *Listener* (18 June 1959): 1083.

& too much material not properly integrated. And playing it again to-day I felt that some of the material is rather second-rate – (though some of it I like.) I think when writing I felt that often I overwork my material – (getting a sort of intensity of feeling from it, by hammering away at it) & that I wanted to get away from that method a bit, & give freer rein to the imagination. But the result is not very happy![52]

In March, Maconchy completed an initial version of *The Three Strangers*, later meeting with Norman Tucker to play through the work at Sadler's Wells on 11 June. Though the New Opera Company was planning to mount a production of *The Sofa*, by the spring these plans had evidently fallen through. In the summer, the Concerto for Oboe, Bassoon, and String Orchestra had its first public performance at a Proms concert on 31 July.[53] For this first concert performance, the work was played by the London Symphony Orchestra conducted by Basil Cameron, with Rothwell and Camden serving once again as soloists. In spite of Maconchy's reservations about the work, it garnered further praise in the press, with Felix Aprahamian declaring the work in the *Sunday Times* 'one of Miss Maconchy's most successful pieces'.[54]

The summer also featured a Radio Éireann broadcast of *Dialogue* on 10 July with pianist Lawrence Glover (1931–88) and the Radio Éireann Symphony Orchestra, conducted by Miles. In September, Maconchy travelled to Dublin where she recorded a talk that was broadcast by Radio Éireann on 20 September. In this talk, Maconchy discussed her own beliefs on using folksong arrangements, as well as some of the downsides of her personal idiom: 'I have never been a popular composer: I have always been more interested in following my own musical thought and in developing a personal technique that most clearly expresses it, than in writing what is fashionable, or what other people may want to hear.'[55] The programme was aired once again on 6 October. The following month, her *Suite on Irish Airs* was featured in a concert on the 8th as part of the Autumn Proms at the Gaiety Theatre. Back in England, Maconchy remained busy, with a talk on her string quartets delivered to the Oxford University Contemporary Music Club on 20 November. A few days later on the 23rd, *Nocturne* was featured in a Thomas Beecham Concerts Society programme with the Royal Philharmonic, conducted by Beecham.

Though Maconchy had initially expressed doubts as to whether a production of *The Sofa* would materialise, against all the odds a workshop production was mounted on 13 December. The work was premièred by the New Opera Workshop as part of a double-bill with John Joubert's *In the Drought*. A subsidiary of the New Opera Company, the New Opera Workshop was formed in 1958 to

52 Elizabeth Maconchy to Grace Williams, 10 June 1959.

53 Maconchy initially tried to submit the work for consideration for the 1957 Proms season; however, she did so too late. Richard Howgill to Elizabeth Maconchy, 19 February 1957, BBC WAC EM3.

54 Felix Aprahamian, 'Prom Novelties', *Sunday Times*, 2 August 1959.

55 Maconchy, draft of talk for Radio Éireann broadcast, SHC.

serve as a suitable venue to train singers, producers, and conductors, with a particular emphasis on producing works by contemporary British composers.

While *The Sofa* is a tamer reinterpretation of Crébillon's tale, the opera retains, at its very core, the satirical spirit of the original. Maconchy's inventive score is constructed from a series of short melodic and rhythmic themes, extended and varied by chromatic alteration and inversion, with counterpoint structured through canonic reiteration of the thematic material, which is primarily predicated upon major and minor seconds and thirds. The deeply lyrical and comedic music brilliantly entwines with Ursula Vaughan Williams's suggestive libretto.[56]

The Sofa is set in the anteroom to a ballroom in 1860s Paris where Dominic, a rakish young prince, is hosting a ball. The opera opens with a jubilant, short, and succinct recurrent musical figure built upon the notes B-flat, C, D, and E-flat (motif a) in the woodwind, followed by an expansion of the figure into an extended melodic phrase built upon major and minor seconds. Seated on a sofa in the anteroom is Monique, the object of Dominic's dissolute intentions. As the woodwind continues playful exchanges of this motif back and forth, Dominic, confident in his powers to charm, prematurely declares his victory with the triumphant declaration, 'Ah, my sweet consolation!'

Unwilling to satisfy Dominic's desires immediately, Monique flirtatiously inquires as to why Dominic is in need of erotic 'consolation'. This inquiry prompts Dominic to set forth his reasons in a playfully light-hearted strophic patter-song aria set in 5/8 ('Easy come, and easy go…'), in which he recounts the unfortunate nature of his situation. The melody of Dominic's aria has a tonal centre of F-natural, and primarily consists of the alternation of both major and minor seconds and thirds, with occasional intervallic leaps of a perfect fourth and octave. The aria also constitutes the first musical allusion of the work, as the melodic line is highly reminiscent of a similar melodic phrase from the second movement of Mahler's Symphony No. 4.

Dominic's light-hearted avowal then takes on a more sombre hue as he laments a most unfortunate impediment: his Grandmother is a witch. With his cheerfulness now marred by thoughts of his Grandmother, the curiously chimerical short melodic flourish of motif a reappears in the woodwind. Desirous to claim his prize, Dominic returns to seducing Monique. He begins by complimenting 'the flutter of her wrist', which is musically echoed by a trill in the clarinet. Monique mockingly responds, imitating his melody, which effectively forms a canon.

As their playful exchange swells and grows more harmonious, motif b is introduced. Here, Maconchy alludes to another score, as the material for motif b has a distinct resemblance to the opening melody of the first movement of Prokofiev's Second Violin Concerto. As Dominic begins a short but impassioned aria, a new gesture, motif c, emerges, based on a typically octatonic alternation of whole and half steps, which quickly becomes more impassioned

[56] The ensuing discussion of *The Sofa* uses Maconchy's published score, which deviates slightly from the original.

as Dominic and Monique exchange remarks. As their duet progresses, motif b prominently re-emerges in the woodwind as motif c grows stronger and more persistent in the strings. On the cusp of coitus, the lovers' joy is abruptly interrupted, as the persistent repetition of motif b announces the brusque entrance of Dominic's Grandmother. Startled, Monique hurriedly exits the anteroom.

Furious with Dominic's philandering, which is most unseemly for a prince, the Grandmother launches into an impassioned declaration, built upon the robust rhythm that marked her dramatic entrance. Determined to teach her grandson a lesson, she casts a spell, turning him into a sofa until the act of 'love's consummation' takes place upon him, at which point the spell will be broken, and he will be able to return to his mortal form. Summoning all her enchantments, she enters into a fiery aria emblazoned with a coloratura passage that patently alludes to the famous Queen of the Night aria, 'Der Hölle Rache kocht in meinem Herzen', from Mozart's *Die Zauberflöte* (Example 9.6).

With a clap of thunder the spell is cast, followed by a stage blackout. When the lights go back up, a sofa appears, the upholstery of which resembles the clothes that Dominic was wearing before the spell. The music resumes: a short rhythmic gesture based upon oscillating minor seconds in the first and second violins. Maconchy uses this theme to make a transition into a leisurely waltz, eventually expanding the figure into a short melodic theme played by solo cello forming motif d. This in turn serves as the primary melodic material for a trio sung by the young ladies Yolande, Laura, and Lucille, who have just entered the anteroom, in which they sing of their longings for love and romance. The ladies' attention is quickly diverted by the arrival of three young men. Two of the boys inquire if Yolande and Laura would like to dance, and lead them to the ballroom, leaving Lucille alone with the remaining young gentleman, who is one of her suitors. As the suitor expresses his ardent feelings, motif c slyly returns as they both express their ardour for one another.

Convinced that the young couple will free him from his predicament at last, the voice of Dominic – that is, the voice of the sofa – sings 'So far, so good'. His hopes are quickly dashed as it becomes all too clear that the suitor's intentions are strictly honourable: he asks for Lucille's hand in marriage. Enraged, the voice of Dominic sings of his angry, bitter disappointment; this outburst is predicated upon motif c.

As Lucille and her suitor exit, Dominic's aria comes to a close. A polka then quickly fills the anteroom as a group of guests enter from the adjoining ballroom, with the young ladies singing a short, light-hearted laughing chorus. Here, both the opening of the polka and the beginning of the brief laughing chorus are reminiscent of Johann Strauss Jr.'s *Tritsch Tratsch Polka*. The chorus then enters into a series of lively canonic inquiries as to the location of their host. After the chorus contemplates the frivolous notion that Dominic had been turned into a bat, his voice is heard as he responds, 'warmer', alarming the guests, until their attention is diverted to more immediate pleasures. They then sing a 'brindisi', a drinking song in praise of champagne, which begins with the chorus doubling octaves. The drinking chorus is followed by a return

Example 9.6. Maconchy, *The Sofa*, bars 285–93.

of the polka theme, as the guests begin to filter out of the anteroom and back into the ballroom.

As the guests leave, the serially flirtatious Monique enters on the arm of a young Englishman named Edward with whom she has been previously acquainted. Edward inquires as to the nature of Monique and Dominic's friendship. To avoid answering directly, she inquires after Edward's activities of late. Edward commences a brief, rhythmic aria about his love of hunting. The shape of the melodic line in the strings, woodwind, and brass, followed by the explosive entrance of the horns, tenor drum, and bass drum, recall the scherzo of Beethoven's Ninth Symphony. Quite bored by the dashing Englishman's story of blood sport, Monique interrupts with the flirtatious remark that Edward 'enjoys the chase'. Her meaning is made plain by the ensuing canonic imitation between the two voices. A sly caricature of a fox-hunting British officer, Edward is a little slow to understand Monique's intention. Eventually, he finally comprehends Monique's insinuation and motif c again reappears. Now the two embrace passionately, the lights dim, and 'love's act' finally takes place upon the sofa.

After a streak of lightning and a roll of thunder, the lights are raised, revealing that the curse has been broken: the sofa has disappeared, and Dominic has regained his humanity. Furious at being bested in his pursuit of Monique, Dominic angrily confronts Edward, and the two hurl insults back and forth, as the flourish of motif a returns in the woodwind. Attracted by all the commotion, the guests have already re-entered the anteroom. Edward then proceeds to accuse Dominic of actually being the sofa, and Dominic responds by calling Edward a madman, and calls for his footmen to have him ejected from the hall. The curious guests follow Edward and the footmen, leaving Monique and Dominic alone.

Meanwhile, the sofa has miraculously reappeared. After Dominic locks the door, he leads Monique to the sofa, and they resume their lovemaking. After the lush harmonies of their duet lead to their declaration of 'love's delights', the music swells with a feverishly agitated reiteration of motif c, followed by a brief return of the thematic material from Dominic's bitter lament, which swiftly brings down the curtain.

A unique feature of *The Sofa* is its extensive use of allusion and outright quotation. Before writing the libretto, Ursula Vaughan Williams had been engaged in the process of revising the libretto and dialogue to her husband's comic opera *The Poisoned Kiss*. She rewrote a great deal of its stilted dialogue in pantomime rhymes.[57] In *The Sofa*, she used a similar technique, for the majority of the libretto is cast as rhyming couplets. Curiously, Ursula Vaughan Williams's libretto directly alludes to a phrase from Evelyn Sharp's libretto to *The Poisoned Kiss*, in which the character Gallanthus, having heard the sound of a cat, remarks:

> What's that? A cat?
> A bat? A rat?
> Oh, drat!
> Not that I'm anymore afraid of cats,
> Or bats, or rats,
> Than I am of gnats.[58]

This verse is virtually identical to a phrase from an ensemble in *The Sofa*, during which the guests engage in speculation about Dominic's fate in bars 725–35:

> Not a bat, or a cat, or a rat, or a toad, or a lizard, no, no!
> Not a knife, or a fork, or a bed, or a chair, or a table, no, no, not a table!

Why Ursula Vaughan Williams quoted Sharp's libretto cannot be determined, but it is possible that this action might have been suggested by *The Sofa*'s 'unofficial' librettist, Ralph Vaughan Williams.

While the widespread use of rhyming couplets in the libretto creates an atmosphere reminiscent of British pantomime and Gilbert and Sullivan, the overall narrative structure of the opera significantly diverges from both traditions. In fact, the opera's arrangement fails to fully satisfy any format common to comic opera. Its highly eroticised subject matter might place it in the same category as a racy ballad opera in general, such as *The Threepenny Opera*, but unlike a ballad opera, it contains no spoken dialogue. Perhaps the closest conventional genre appropriate to *The Sofa* is Offenbach's *opéra bouffe*, hardly a genre cultivated by British composers, even Sir Arthur Sullivan. *The Sofa* resembles Offenbach in the absurdity of the story; the proliferation of rhyming couplets (albeit in English); and musical quotations of popular, well-known works, as exemplified in Offenbach's *La belle Hélène* (1864). And at its core, *The*

[57] Ursula Vaughan Williams, *Paradise Remembered*, 188.

[58] Ralph Vaughan Williams, *The Poisoned Kiss or The Empress and the Necromancer* (Oxford: Oxford University Press, 1936), 16–17.

Sofa is a satirical parody of 1860s Parisian society and operetta of the Second Empire, the very subject of Offenbach's satirical works.

As reflected in her correspondence with Ursula Vaughan Williams, Maconchy's central ambitions for the opera reveal another aspect that conjures Offenbach: creating a gradual accelerando of farce and ebullience over the course of the dramatic action.[59] Maconchy's overriding concern regarding the opera's length was the driving force behind her decision not to provide an overture, as well as her rejection of the idea for a gambling scene with the young men engaged in a game of roulette and the sofa calling out the winning number.[60] The original libretto contained an extended drinking song, which, while not entirely cut out, was later trimmed extensively.[61]

By contrasting small ensemble numbers and frequent entries (and re-entries) of the chorus, the musical momentum hurtles forward as the arias, interspersed between lively waltzes and chorus numbers, become increasingly concise. This formal design creates the sense of a gradual accelerando as the farcical action becomes increasingly dynamic and dramatic as the opera moves rapidly toward the climactic scene of Edward and Monique on the sofa and Dominic's restoration. Maconchy achieved this sense of relentless forward motion in a similar manner as one would construct a play. In order to generate the right amount of comedic flair, she decided to take the dramatic tension a step further, emphasising the importance of increasing contrasts between characters as well as the need for highlighting the dramatic points, even if it required over-exaggeration.[62]

While Maconchy was clear concerning the effect she wanted to create, there is very little mention in her correspondence of the music she intended to parody. Two exceptions to this reticence stand out, however. In her manuscript without amendments, Maconchy wrote, near the beginning of Edward's brief aria: 'gun-shots to be delivered in the manner of Beethoven's 9th symphony'.[63] While there are no literal gun-shots, his 'shooting aria' certainly evokes a spirit reminiscent of the lively scherzo of Beethoven's Ninth Symphony. The second reference, from an undated draft of the opera's synopsis, indicates that the Grandmother's aria is to be sung 'in Queen of the Night Style'.[64] While the role of the Grandmother is written for mezzo-soprano, along the margin, Maconchy had written, 'Coloratura Aria, (Soprano) Grandmother'.[65] One can only

59 Elizabeth Maconchy to Ursula Vaughan Williams, 17 March 1957, Ursula Vaughan Williams Correspondence, MS Mus. 1714/3/4: 1937–1999, BL.

60 Indication of the cuts are made by Maconchy on the original manuscript.

61 The extended drinking song is present in the original MS. Also see Ursula Vaughan Williams, *Paradise Remembered*, 188.

62 Elizabeth Maconchy to Ursula Vaughan Williams, 3 June 1957, Ursula Vaughan Williams Correspondence, MS Mus. 1714/3/4: 1937–1999, BL.

63 This indication is made on page 245 of Maconchy's original manuscript of *The Sofa*, SHC.

64 Undated draft of the opera's synopsis, SHC.

65 Ibid.

speculate as to whether or not the idea of writing the role of the Grandmother for a soprano was ever seriously contemplated, but the resulting coloratura passage, transposed for mezzo, makes the allusion all the more amusing. As for the other allusions, in the absence of any further evidence, why Maconchy chose to mention them (if they were indeed conscious) remains unclear.

As a semi-professional production with the aim of providing training, the actual performance of *The Sofa* left much to be desired. Ursula Vaughan Williams's humorous recollections of the opera's rehearsals in her autobiography paint a vivid portrait of the hands-on approach required of a limited budget, as well as some of the early surprises that she and Maconchy encountered:

> The producer, Michael Geliot, was very young, and we had to explain the procedure at balls, for instance, that chaperones sat around the room, and did not dance (there were some extra women in the chorus for this production) and that everyone, men and women, wore gloves. We felt that we were, probably, the last survivors of an age that had gone to such festivities, but we were startled when we discovered that word had got round that we had both been at the Eve of Waterloo Ball in Brussels. As it was a workshop production I found myself much involved in helping with wardrobe problems, for the choice was limited to a collection of hireable old clothes from a sub-department of the Wardrobe of Sadler's Wells kept in a house a few doors up the road from the theatre. Michael Geliot and I blundered about in the confined spaces between dress racks, clutching lists of measurements of the cast, and later I spent a good deal of time inventing decorations for hair, based on old fashion plates. This was an amusing occupation involving combs, feathers, flowers, sequins and glue, and I eventually helped with the disguise of the all-important sofa.[66]

Echoing some of their frustrations, Maconchy wrote to Williams a couple of weeks after the production: 'I did all I could to make the New Opera boys realise they couldn't put on something that was a travesty (feeling like Ethel Smyth!) – and some pro. players were engaged – but it was all left to the last minute, & muddled in every kind of way.'[67]

The reception of the opera's single performance in the press was neither overwhelmingly bad nor bracingly good. In the *Times*, Maconchy's skill for writing for voices was praised. The anonymous critic noted that both Joubert and Maconchy's operas 'suffered from inadequate projection and inaudible words, as is almost inevitable in the circumstances of production, but both composers misjudged their orchestration. Nevertheless, each in its way had operatic virtues.'[68] The title of Donald Mitchell's review in the *Daily Telegraph* proclaimed, 'Sofa as Hero of Ironic Plot'. While he noted that the opera made 'a diverting half-hour or so', he felt that the music contained 'a strange mixture of Offenbach and Vaughan Williams'. Ultimately, he concluded that the opera

[66] Ursula Vaughan Williams, *Paradise Remembered*, 201–2.

[67] Elizabeth Maconchy to Grace Williams, 28 December 1959.

[68] 'Double Bill By New Opera Workshop', *Times*, 14 December 1959.

did not successfully capture 'the ironic flavour of the dénouement. For what is basically so erotic a subject, her music is altogether too amiable and innocent.'[69]

In the *Observer*, Edmund Tracey noted, as did several others, that the performers were not quite up to par with the material. He also found the orchestration to be a bit 'dense and fussy' in places, writing:

> The Sofa, had a distinct and agreeable personality of its own. It was, so far as I could judge from a rather inadequate performance, uneven in quality. The musical texture was sometimes dense and fussy, and there seemed to be a lack of co-ordination, as well as seriously diminished momentum, in the larger ensembles. But for the most part the musical invention was lively and apt – though if Miss Maconchy and her librettist Ursula Vaughan Williams, would prune some of the verbal jokes and trust to the music to articulate the dramatic movement, the piece would gain in swiftness and point.
>
> 'The Sofa' is unique in that it includes the only attempt I have ever seen to present the act of copulation on the public stage – and that this was achieved, both vigorously and without offence, reflects very creditably upon the ingenuity of the two ladies who, with every appearance of moral health and charm, came to bow and beam at us at the end.[70]

Harold Rosenthal was Maconchy's harshest critic; his reviews of the opera appeared in both the *Financial Times* and *Opera*. While he echoed sentiments expressed by others, noting that the diction and the singers left much to be desired, his greatest qualm was with Ursula Vaughan Williams's libretto:

> As in the case of *The Poisoned Kiss*, Ursula Vaughan Williams makes the joke go on too long: and although Miss Maconchy has written some most pleasant and singable music, one wants a later-day [*sic*] Offenbach to do this story musical justice. … The moments of attempted seduction and love's consummation left little to the imagination, and one wonders whether a public performance would have got away with them![71]

In the *Chesterian*, Scott Goddard lamented again that the diction was poor, even remarking that it deserved better performance. As for the climactic scene, he wrote, 'for a moment one's eyes hardly dare accept their own testimony. There was raucous laughter, much indiscreet giggling and one felt the shudder of the superstitious; indeed I gather that some people that night were startled out of their lives, others indeed mortally shocked.'[72]

While the opera may have been viewed by some critics as too risqué, it was far milder than many theatrical works mounted on the British stage, such as the plays of John Osborne and Joe Orton.[73] But within the context of the conservative operatic stage in England, *The Sofa*'s frank treatment of erotic

69 DCPM [Donald Charles Peter Mitchell], 'Sofa as Hero of Ironic Plot', *Daily Telegraph*,14 December 1959.

70 Edmund Tracey, 'Two New Operas,' *Observer*, 20 December 1959.

71 Harold Rosenthal, 'New Opera Workshop', *Financial Times*, 16 December 1959.

72 Scott Goddard, 'London Letter', *Chesterian* 34/201 (Winter 1960): 100.

73 For further discussion of this topic, see Anthony Aldgate and James C. Robertson, *Censorship in Theatre and Cinema* (Edinburgh: Edinburgh University Press, 2005);

subject matter was nearly unheard of. While the Lord Chamberlain had the power to censor any theatre work deemed obscene or indecent until 1968 (at which time the Theatres Act was abolished), restrictions had begun to ease after the Second World War. While homosexuality was strictly banned until 1958, displays of heterosexual amorousness were accepted. The passage of the Obscene Publications Act on 21 July 1959, proved to be further evidence of the gradual easing of censorship, enabling D.H. Lawrence's *Lady Chatterley's Lover* to be printed legally in Great Britain the following year.[74]

Early on in the creative process, both Maconchy and Ursula Vaughan Williams appear to have been aware of the balance and delicacy needed for the work to meet the requirements for licence from the Lord Chamberlain. In one of her letters to her librettist, Maconchy wrote, 'I think you have been very successful in setting the Grandmother to make her meaning quite clear, while keeping on the right side of the Censor. "Consummation" is excellent.'[75] An early synopsis of the plot likewise questions even the possibility of staging the scene during which the curse is lifted. At that point, the synopsis reads, 'After a few moments there is a sudden crash, a loud scream from the lady, – and the lights go up, revealing no sofa, the lady on the floor (if permitted by the censor) and the Prince confronting the dumbfounded and infuriated Englishman.'[76]

To prevent any accusations of 'indecency', this climactic scene was ultimately solved with a blackout. Yet even this solution did not save the production from raised eyebrows, as Nicola, who attended the première along with Anna, recounted in an excerpt from an account of the New Opera Company's history:

> I was entranced by the upholstered tenor who turned into an upholstered sofa, and even more so by Monique. In my innocence the point of the plot (the seduction) was quite lost on me: I was mystified that people were shocked by the lovely moment when Dominic ('so far so good') embraced Monique embracing Edward and her necklace went trickling downstage.[77]

While the production did not appear to create any issues with the censor, the opera's frankness was still scandalous enough for one affronted composer to walk out of the performance.[78]

Despite the high musical values evinced in *The Sofa*, circumstances beyond Maconchy's control worked against a proper evaluation of the opera. While one factor was the demanding music, another contributing factor may have been its genre, given that the operas that proved successful in Britain tended to be those with serious subject matter, with comedic opera failing to find a consistent and

---

and Anthony Aldgate, *Censorship and the Permissive Society: British Cinema and Theatre 1955–1965* (Oxford: Clarendon Press, 1995).

[74] Aldgate and Robertson, 129.

[75] Elizabeth Maconchy to Ursula Vaughan Williams, 17 March 1957, Ursula Vaughan Williams Correspondence, MS Mus. 1714/3/4: 1937–1999, BL.

[76] Undated synopsis of *The Sofa*, SHC.

[77] This excerpt is quoted in Independent Opera's programme for the 2007 production of *The Sofa* and *The Departure*.

[78] Email from Nicola LeFanu to author.

successful formula over the course of the early twentieth century.[79] Combined with Britten's dominance of the genre in England, it was often difficult for any opera composer other than him to receive a fair hearing. Deeply disheartened, Maconchy lamented to Williams, 'I fear all three of my one-acters are going to prove too difficult for University & similar opera-groups – who are the sort of people who might do them: the only alternative is Sadlers Wells [*sic*] proper, & I'm afraid they never will!'[80]

[79] Howes, *The English Musical Renaissance*, 317.
[80] Elizabeth Maconchy to Grace Williams, 28 December 1959.

10

Administrative Diversions, 1959–66

The Sofa was not the only significant event towards the end of 1959 to which Maconchy's name would be linked in the press: after serving for a year as Chairman-elect of the Composers' Guild, Maconchy ascended to the role of Chairman at the conclusion of the Guild's Annual General Meeting held on 5 December. As the first woman to be elected to the position, the significance of the appointment generated ample coverage in the press, with notices appearing in the *Times*, the *Birmingham Post*, the *Star*, and *Essex Weekly News*, in addition to an interview with David Jones for the BBC's day-time television programme *Mainly for Women*, which aired on 2 December.[1] This feat, however, could have arrived a few years earlier: in January 1956, Guy Warrack approached Maconchy about serving as Chairman the following year. In his letter, Warrack cited a complaint that had been received at the Composers' Guild's Annual General Meeting in December 1955 that women were inadequately represented.[2] Maconchy ultimately decided to decline the invitation, with the heavy workload that the job entailed, combined with having Nicola still at home presumably a contributing factor.

With Composers' Guild matters taking up a sizable amount of Maconchy's time in 1960, it should come as no surprise that she found herself with little time to compose. Nevertheless, she continued to make strides on *The Departure* and also began work on a carol cantata titled *Christmas Morning*, which she completed the following year. Though performances of her music remained scarce for the duration of 1960, Maconchy's fortunes would soon change as her work with the Composers' Guild dramatically elevated her visibility and public profile, thus leading to an increasing number of performances and commissions in the ensuing years.[3] In 1960 alone, she received a commission from the City of Birmingham Symphony Orchestra (CBSO) for an orchestral work to be

1 Elizabeth Maconchy to Grace Williams, 1 December 1959.

2 Guy Warrack to Elizabeth Maconchy, 4 January 1956, private collection.

3 At least six performances are known to have taken place in 1960: on 18 April the Concertino for Bassoon and String Orchestra was played by Brooke and the Kathleen Merritt Orchestra at the Wigmore Hall; on 6 May *A Winter's Tale* was performed by Cantelo and the Amici Quartet in Birmingham; on 16 October the Macnaghten Quartet played *A Country Town* at an Oxford Ladies' Musical Society concert; on 12 November the Concerto for Oboe, Bassoon, and String Orchestra was featured in a concert by the Astra Chamber Orchestral Society in Melbourne, Australia; and on 23 November a performance of *The Voice of the City* took place in the USSR.

included in their 1961–2 season, as well as an invitation from William Glock to write a work for the BBC's Thursday Invitation Concerts.[4]

The 1960s was not without its challenges, however, as changes in musical fashions marked by the rising popularity of serialism and electronic music spurred heated debate and fears of marginalisation among composers whose works were lumped into the broad category of 'tonal' music. As Maconchy would discover, her music, which had once faced so much visceral criticism in the press for its 'modernist' and 'cerebral' tendencies, was now increasingly perceived as practically tame, with the Manchester School of composers, among other serial composers, dominating the new music scene.[5]

As part of her duties as Chairman, Maconchy made trips to both Canada and the USSR as a representative of the Composers' Guild. Maconchy set off for Canada in early August 1960, arriving in Toronto on Saturday 8 August for the International Conference of Composers, which was held in Stratford, Ontario from 7 to 18 August. The conference was largely organised and arranged by Canadian composer Louis Applebaum (1918–2000), who had established the Stratford Music Festival in 1955 as an offshoot of the Stratford Festival, well known for its Shakespeare productions. Inspired by an exchange scheme between the Stratford Festival and the Soviet Union, Applebaum set about arranging the conference with the aim of bolstering Canada's visibility on the international music stage. With support from the Stratford Festival, the Canadian League of Composers, and the Canada Council, over fifty delegates from over twenty countries descended upon the Festival's theatre office where the eight-day conference took place.[6]

Maconchy was put up in a private house with several of the other delegates, including two participants from the USSR: Otar Taktakishvili (1924–89) and Vassily Kukharski. Mornings were filled with panel sessions both 'good and indifferent' covering a broad range of topics ranging from tonality, serialism, and electronic music, as well as approaches to opera and theatrical music, contemporary training of composers, and the composers' relationship to the public. In addition to Maconchy, Guy Warrack and Iain Hamilton (1922–2000) were the other two composer delegates from Great Britain. Following lunch,

4 The commission from the CBSO, which totalled £100, was made possible by the financial support of the Fenney Trust. The BBC's invitation did not include any remuneration.

5 For a discussion of the rise of serialism and the Manchester Group, see Philip Rupprecht, *British Musical Modernism: The Manchester Group and their Contemporaries* (Cambridge: Cambridge University Press, 2015).

6 Louis Applebaum, 'Foreword', in John Beckwith and Udo Kasemets (eds), *The Modern Composer and His World* (Toronto: University of Toronto Press, 1961), vi–ix. Some of the other composers who took part included István Anhalt, Violet Archer, Luciano Berio, Cesar Bresgen, Aurelio de la Vega, Václav Dobiáš, Henri Dutilleux, Ignacio Fernández Esperon, Roy Harris, Ernest Krenek, Karl Schiske, Josef Tal, Vladimir Ussachevsky, and Edgard Varèse.

Figure 10. Maconchy representing the Composers' Guild at the International Conference of Composers in Stratford, Ontario, 1960 (reproduced by permission of the Maconchy Estate).

which was held at the Stratford Country Club, afternoons were filled with additional sessions, concerts, and some of the Festival's plays: *Romeo and Juliet*, *A Midsummer Night's Dream,* and *King John*.[7]

Over the course of the conference, Maconchy participated in two discussions with other composers for the CBC. There was also a trip to Niagara Falls that included some of the participants being televised as they listened to and discussed the sound of the Falls.[8] For the final panel session held on Saturday 13 August, which reflected upon the conference as a whole, Maconchy served as a discussant. Typical of Maconchy's style, her remarks are discerning, perceptive, and to the point:

> One of the most interesting things about this uniquely interesting Conference has been its diversity [...]

[7] Elizabeth Maconchy to Grace Williams, 29 August 1960.

[8] Ibid.

> We have heard a great deal that is interesting and stimulating among the works played and in the Panel sessions. I have only regretted that there has not been more time for questions and discussion after the reading of the papers ... I would only like now, very briefly, to suggest one or two points that I should very much like to hear answered.
>
> Little has been said about the future direction which serial music is likely to take. Total serialism, may be the right way in the view of some composers – but others feel that this strait-jacket is restricting to the point of immobility ... Will the strait-jacket burst at the seams? [A]nd in what direction?
>
> One of the most frequent criticisms of the serial technique is that it must, anyway to some extent, inhibit spontaneity. And it seems that many composers now feel the need of a greater degree of spontaneity in their work: and so the performer is given freedom of choice as to the order in which he will play certain sections of a work – for instance, – or in some cases he is instructed to extemporise.
>
> But why does the composer wish to surrender to the performer the spontaneity which is surely the composer's own birthright?
>
> I only suggest these questions in the hope that there may still be time to talk about these or other points concerned with the actual process of composition.[9]

A couple of weeks after her return to England, Maconchy reflected in a letter to Williams:

> There was quite a lot of electronic music & also of talk about it – & I was glad of the chance to hear it as one has heard so little here. But I found it depressing on the whole: I think no-one has gone near creating a work of art in it yet & only the two Italians, Berio (who was there) & Maderna, seem to me to have begun to get any sort of form or discipline into it ...
>
> I feel that the heart has gone out of writing tonal music – & yet I'm sure strict 12-tone technique isn't the answer to the music of the future. I think perhaps it has done something in sweeping away tonality, or rather the accepted use of it: but what it has put in its place seems to me to be totally inadequate.[10]

At the beginning of November Maconchy was busy with preparations for her upcoming ten-day trip to the Soviet Union. Similar to the exchange that had prompted the International Conference of Composers, this trip was part of a broader scheme of exchanges aimed at easing tensions through cultural diplomacy during the Cold War. This particular trip had been proposed by the Union of Soviet Composers, with Maconchy and Alan Bush representing the Guild.

Maconchy and Bush left for Moscow on the 16th. Upon their arrival they were greeted by composer Dmitry Kabalevsky (1904–87). Their first evening included a party hosted by Kabalevsky as well as a performance of Prokofiev's

[9] Elizabeth Maconchy, draft of talk titled 'For Final Panel Session of Stratford Conference', 13 August 1960, SHC. Maconchy's remarks, with some editorial changes, were included in *The Modern Composer and His World*, 157–8. For Maconchy's review of the book, see Elizabeth Maconchy, 'Book Review – The Modern Composer and His World', *Composer* 10 (Winter 1962): 4–5.

[10] Elizabeth Maconchy to Grace Williams, 29 August 1960.

opera *War and Peace*. The trip was filled with concerts of Russian music, with each day featuring a trip to an opera, ballet, or concert hall. Though the majority of their visit was spent in Moscow, Maconchy and Bush also spent two days in Leningrad where they visited the Hermitage Museum and attended performances at the Mariinsky Theatre of Borodin's opera *Prince Igor* and Prokofiev's ballet *The Tale of the Stone Flower*.[11]

The 23rd featured a concert in honour of Maconchy and Bush, which was broadcast on Radio Moscow. This concert featured Maconchy's *The Voice of the City* as well as a work for baritone and chorus by Bush. Both Maconchy and Bush had prepared a brief talk which they delivered at the concert. In Maconchy's report to the Guild, she remarked that the inclusion of her work along with Bush's came as a complete surprise. Unbeknownst to Maconchy, Bush had sent the score to musicologists Sergey Aksiuk and Grigorii Shneerson in October, writing in an enclosed letter to Shneerson that he wanted the matter to remain strictly confidential: '[Maconchy] is such a modest person that she would be very angry with me. On the other hand, she is such an honest person that she would think that I had acted dishonestly in putting this work of hers forward.'[12] Following the broadcast concert, Maconchy was invited to give a lengthier talk about British contemporary music. With half a day's notice, Maconchy prepared a twenty-five-minute talk for a programme that also included thirty-five minutes of musical illustrations, which was broadcast by Radio Moscow on 5 January 1961.[13]

Beyond concerts and a banquet on their last night in Moscow, the trip was filled with meetings with the Union of Soviet Composers in both Moscow and Leningrad. Maconchy and Bush also presented twenty-seven scores by British composers to the Union, playing recordings of several of the works.[14] Though there were some disagreements between Maconchy and Bush regarding which recordings would be played, they did, however agree on including Williams's *Penillion*.[15] With explicit permission obtained from publishers prior to the trip, they were allowed to gift some of the scores and commercial recordings to the Union of Soviet Composers. Owing to the Soviet Union's noncompliance with international copyright conventions, Maconchy and Bush were concerned that the differing approach to copyright there would prove to be a hindrance to furthering the promotion of British music. To discuss this matter further,

[11] These details are included in Maconchy's list of activities for the trip held at SHC.

[12] Quoted in Louise Wiggins, '"Story of a friendship": Alan Bush, Grigorii Shneerson and cultural diplomacy before and during the Cold War', *Russian Journal of Communication* 8/3 (2016): 264.

[13] Elizabeth Maconchy, draft of article titled 'Exchange visit with the Union of Soviet Composers', 30 November 1960, SHC.

[14] Ibid. According to Maconchy, recordings of roughly seven or eight of the works were played.

[15] Elizabeth Maconchy to Grace Williams, 27 November 1960. Although most of the recordings played were limited to brief excerpts, Williams's work was played in its entirety.

Maconchy and Bush met with the head of the Ministry of Culture's copyright department along with the department's legal advisor on the final morning of their visit. During their meeting, several potential solutions to the issue were discussed, including developing a bilateral agreement.[16] Later that day, Maconchy and Bush were escorted to the airport by Kabalevsky and Tikhon Khrennikov (1913–2007), armed with the many gifts they had received over the course of their short visit. The abundance was so great that some had to be shipped.[17]

With scarcely any time to devote to her own music throughout 1960, Maconchy was fortunate to receive extensions for her work for the BBC's Thursday Invitation Concerts: *Reflections for Oboe, Clarinet, Viola, and Harp*, as well as her CBSO commission, *Serenata Concertante*, which was moved to the 1962–3 season.[18] After devoting so much time to working on her operas, Maconchy found returning to writing chamber and orchestral works 'a very different cup of tea'.[19] While her situation improved somewhat after Stephen Dodgson succeeded her as Chairman of the Composers' Guild, Maconchy remained busy as a member of the Executive Committee, with various Guild meetings and activities, which included the visit of two delegate composers from the Soviet Union – Kirill Moltchanov (1922–82) and Boris Lyatoshinsky (1895–1968) – in May.[20] Following their visit, Maconchy travelled to Prague for a week. The invitation for this trip came from the President of the Czech Guild of Composers, Václav Dobiáš (1909–78), whom Maconchy had met during her trip to Canada.[21] During her visit, Maconchy attended the Prague Spring Festival, with all her expenses for the visit covered.

In addition to her continued work with the Composers' Guild, Maconchy joined the BBC's Central Music Advisory Committee in 1961, thus adding to

16 At the request of the Union's secretary, Maconchy agreed to approach Glock at the BBC to discuss Radio Moscow's proposal to include two hours of British music each month. Maconchy met with Glock for lunch on 1 December to discuss the proposal. According to a letter Glock sent to Maconchy on 2 February 1961, a similar issue had arisen after Bliss's trip to the Soviet Union in 1956. At the time Bliss was strongly against any proposal owing to the Soviet Union's refusal to pay royalties. William Glock to Elizabeth Maconchy, 2 February 1961, SHC.

17 Maconchy, 'Exchange visit with the Union of Soviet Composers'.

18 Elizabeth Maconchy to Grace Williams, 22 January 1961. Her work for the CBSO was eventually pushed back further to the 1963–4 season.

19 Ibid.

20 Moltchanov and Lyatoshinsky's visit took place from 8 to 24 May 1961. Maconchy hosted them on the 12th for a visit in Cambridge that featured a service at King's College Chapel. Following the service, they stayed the night at Shottesbrook, departing for London to visit the Royal Academy of Music the following day. Following Maconchy's year as Chairman of the Composers' Guild, she then moved into the position of Past Chairman, following the Guild's structure of leadership.

21 Václav Dobiáš to Elizabeth Maconchy, 10 April 1961, SHC.

her already busy schedule.[22] During her time as Chairman of the Composers' Guild, Maconchy had voiced concerns over the proportion of contemporary music on the BBC devoted to British composers, with an evident decline taking place in the 1959–60 season during which time the proportion of foreign works increased.[23] In her work on the BBC's Central Music Advisory Committee, Maconchy continued to advocate for British composers and urged the BBC to raise their commissioning fees, emphasising how the corporation's actions set a precedent for other organisations, using her own unpaid commission for the Thursday Invitation Concerts as an example.[24]

On 5 January 1961 Maconchy had the opportunity to hear her early Piano Concerto, which was featured in a BBC broadcast with pianist Liza Fuchsová (1913–77) and the London Symphony Orchestra, conducted by Raymond Leppard (1927–2019). Maconchy travelled to London to attend the broadcast, staying over with Ursula Vaughan Williams, attending a Guild meeting the following day. On the 7th she travelled to Aldeburgh to have lunch with Britten, discussing matters related to the Guild, details of which she relayed in a letter to Williams:

> [We had] a long talk about the Guild & his reasons for distrusting any sort of 'Union' which could restrict the liberty of the composer or try to 'regulate' the process of composition in any way. I was able to convince him that the Guild does not do this nor ever will (or if it ever did begin to lean towards it, he would be justified in resigning & I should do the same –) & he has definitely said he'll join. I'm very pleased about this – it will make a real difference to the Guild – it really has been an awful handicap not having him. He said he'd like to be a Vice-President, & to represent the Guild on delegations etc if we want him to.[25]

Britten subsequently joined the Guild, becoming a Vice-President along with William Walton.

During this period, Maconchy also contributed to an article on women composers that was published in the spring 1961 issue of the Guild's journal, *Composer*. Titled 'A Short Symposium of Women Composers', the article featured responses from Maconchy, Ruth Gipps (1921–99), Williams, and 'an anonymous composer's wife'. Before its publication the article generated some controversy amongst the Guild, as the editor's preface makes clear: 'Some of our lady members who were asked to contribute to this feel that some kind of discrimination was involved, which, of course, is very far from the truth. But surely women do have especial problems, and there is no harm in discussing this?'[26] Maconchy's thoughtful discussion of the challenges facing professional working women offers further insight into her own feelings on the subject matter:

[22] H. Carleton Greene to Elizabeth Maconchy, 7 February 1961, SHC.

[23] Elizabeth Maconchy, 'Meeting with the BBC', *Composer* 1 (October 1960): 12–14.

[24] Elizabeth Maconchy, prepared notes for meeting titled 'BBC Commissioning Fees', SHC.

[25] Elizabeth Maconchy to Grace Williams, 22 January 1961.

[26] 'A Short Symposium of Women Composers', *Composer* 6 (Spring 1961): 19.

When Ethel Smyth was in the right mood for composition she started on it first thing in the morning, shutting herself into her studio, away from household cares, obtrusive noises and other interruptions.

In due course a footman brought breakfast on a tray, which he deposited discreetly on a table outside the door. When Ethel Smyth found a poached egg on the tray, she rang the bell indignantly and demanded instead a 'grilled bone', saying that she could not write music on slops. The grilled bone was brought to her without delay.

She could shut herself into the studio whenever she wished and remain in it as long as she pleased: and everyone would say how wonderfully hard she worked.

And so she did. But all the same, she had not got a husband and children to look after, and cooking, washing, cleaning, shopping and much more to get through every day. If the footman was ill, a housemaid did his work: if her family were ill, there was someone to look after them: she could even be ill herself if she wanted to.

So if women have achieved 'emancipation' on the one hand, on the other they are more heavily handicapped than before. They now have to do everything.

It is perfectly true that no male composer now enjoys Ethel Smyth's advantages either – he has a living to get (and possibly also takes a part in domestic affairs, such as washing-up). But there is one great difference: he does not have the children.

It is not impossible to write music if one has children – though difficult enough: but rearing them comes just at the time when one ought to be making a career, and it is almost impossible to combine the two, if one takes one's children seriously, as any intelligent person must. Unfortunately, the experience and stimulus of performance are an essential part of the growth and development of a composer, – it is not only a matter of 'getting known'.

This, and not inferior capacity, accounts I believe for the relatively small number of women composers who have so far established themselves.

I think myself that it is a mistake to divide composers into men and women – as if the music they write is necessarily different. If there is a difference, it is something far more subtle than the conventional idea of 'masculine' or 'feminine' music. Can any honest and intelligent listener who does not know already tell which is which?[27]

On 27 April 1961, the work Maconchy had composed for the BBC's Thursday Invitation Concerts, *Reflections for Oboe, Clarinet, Viola, and Harp* (1960–1), was premièred by the Melos Ensemble.[28] Maconchy's invitation from Glock to write a work for the BBC series had come as a surprise as she had 'assumed

[27] Ibid. Maconchy's description of Smyth here is derived not from Smyth's own habits, but rather from E.F. Benson's novel *Dodo* (1893) which features a character based upon Smyth.

[28] The Melos Ensemble was formed in 1950 by clarinettist Gervase de Peyer (1926–2017), flautist Richard Adeney (1920–2010), violist Cecil Aronowitz (1916–78), and cellist Terence Weil (1921–95) to perform chamber works of varying size. The group comprised twelve players who could perform works requiring a string quartet, wind quintet, harpist, and pianist. For the première, Maconchy's *Reflections* was played by the following members of the Melos Ensemble: oboist Peter Graeme (1921–2012), de

he would invite only the young avant-garde'.[29] Started by Glock not long after he took over as Controller of Music, the series was inspired by some of his experiments at Dartington. While the series certainly favoured particular composers and schools over others, it was by no means entirely devoid of variety, as the diversity of programmes, which were often a blend of works both old and new, attest.[30]

Reflections is cast in four contrasting movements with the opening of the first movement, Poco lento, revealing the thematic material each movement builds upon: perfect fifths separated by a tritone in the harp, accentuated by the clarinet's emphasis on tritones, which is achieved through both leaps and scalar movement (Example 10.1). True to its title, the work's introspective nature is exemplified through the ways in which the key melodic and harmonic material undergoes continual transformation throughout all four movements. While the lyrical phrasing and rhythmic vitality bear some influence from Maconchy's work on her operas, one of the most notable aspects of the work is her exploration of colour.

The broadcast yielded a few reviews in the press, with the critic in the *Times* finding the work 'delightful if unpretentious', further adding that it demonstrated Maconchy's 'most sympathetic and attractive musical imagination'.[31] In further recognition of the work's merits, Maconchy was notified in the spring that it had been awarded Second Prize by the GEDOK International Contest for Women Composers. Maconchy travelled to Mannheim in September to receive the prize and hear a performance of the work at the Mannheimer Musiktage on 28 September. The work was subsequently published by the OUP. Some other promising news towards the end of the year came from Ricordi, who had decided to publish her cantata, *Christmas Morning* (1960–1), a new setting of *The Armado*, as well as some educational works for piano.[32]

Throughout the year, Maconchy continued working on *Serenata Concertante*, 'scrapping volumes' along the way.[33] By April 1962, she had finished the majority of the work, aside from the full score. Of its trajectory, and her frustrations with how long it was taking, Maconchy lamented in a letter to Williams, 'I seem to work very slowly now, with endless discardings. I've turned it into a Serenata concertante for violin & orchestra – it began as something in the nature of a concerto grosso with a group of solo-instruments – but the

---

Peyer, Aronowitz, and harpist Osian Ellis (1928–2021). The programme also featured Iain Hamilton's *Pharsalia*, as well as works by Ravel, Haydn, and Brahms.

[29] Elizabeth Maconchy to Grace Williams, 29 August 1960.

[30] See Carpenter, 202–3. The series included composers ranging from Bach and Beethoven to Berio, Britten, Cage, Carter, and Stockhausen, among others.

[31] 'An Indictment of War', *Times*, 28 April 1961.

[32] *The Armado* was premièred on 26 February 1963 at a Park Lane Group concert by the Singers in Consort – a choral group directed by Richard Wood. Maconchy's short piano pieces for Ricordi were published in the educational series *Modern Festival Pieces for Piano*, edited by Lionel Salter.

[33] Elizabeth Maconchy to Grace Williams, 31 December 1961.

Example 10.1. Maconchy, *Reflections*, mvt. I, opening.

solo violin got more & more important as I went along.'[34] After completing the work in June, Maconchy began work on a clarinet quintet as well as a work for harpsichord and wind ensemble. She also felt the pull towards writing another string quartet.[35]

Despite her initial enthusiasm for these new works, Maconchy remained deeply discouraged, as she detailed in a letter to Williams:

> I get brought up short very often by this awful feeling – what is the good of doing it? no-one wants to hear it & no-one is going to play it – it would be far better not to write at all. It is the lack of stimulation of performances that is worst I think: (aggravated by the numerous performances & commissions that a handful of serial composers get! – & not all good ones – & most of them writing too much, I suspect.) However it is very selfish of me to complain.[36]

Given the infrequency of performances and broadcasts of her works, with Maconchy averaging roughly six performances a year between 1960 and 1962, she was certainly justified in her frustrations. Sadly, she was also far from alone, with the Composers' Guild compiling a list of neglected composers, with two members submitting Maconchy's name.[37] Yet, compared with others, she was doing slightly better, as she remarked in a letter to Williams: 'It is frightening how many people are practically not broadcast at all – or rather how few have

[34] Elizabeth Maconchy to Grace Williams, 17 April 1962.

[35] Elizabeth Maconchy to Grace Williams, 24 June 1962. According to a subsequent letter Maconchy sent to Williams, much of the work for harpsichord was discarded. Elizabeth Maconchy to Grace Williams, 30 September 1962.

[36] Ibid.

[37] Williams was one of the individuals who named Maconchy. Elizabeth Maconchy to Grace Williams, 30 September 1962.

Figure 11. Maconchy and Anne Macnaghten at Shottesbrook, 1960 (reproduced by permission of the Maconchy Estate).

Figure 12. Maconchy with Zoltán Kodály and Ursula Vaughan Williams, 1961 (reproduced by permission of the Maconchy Estate).

any decent representation.'[38] Nevertheless, the BBC's figures for 1961 reveal just how vast the gulf between Maconchy and some of her male contemporaries truly was: Britten had 152 works broadcast, Berkeley had 29, Rubbra had 26, Rawsthorne came in with 20, and Tippett had 17. [39]

Maconchy did, however, have at least a couple of broadcasts early in 1962, with the BBC including a recording of *Duo: Theme and Variations* in a broadcast on 16 January, followed by a broadcast recording of *Divertimento* on 30 May.[40] In Europe, her Concertino for Bassoon and String Orchestra was featured in a programme on East Germany's DDR on 18 May. Beyond broadcasts, there were also a handful of concert performances of Maconchy's quartets, including a performance of String Quartet No. 1 by the Macnaghten Quartet in the Macnaghten Concerts' Thirtieth Anniversary Concert on 19 January held at the Arts Council's Great Drawing Room, St James's Square.

With the ISCM Festival held in London in 1962 from 31 May to 6 June, Maconchy attended a few of the concerts. She brought along Nicola, who was already developing her skills as a composer at St Mary's Calne where she was studying for her A levels with music as one of her subjects.[41] In late summer, Maconchy was busy with preparations for the upcoming wedding of her eldest daughter to Francis Dunlop, which took place on 1 September. Though an operation that required a two-week stay in hospital put a damper on her work in October, following her return home, she was to resume the scoring of *Serenata Concertante*.[42]

In November, the Allegri String Quartet recorded Maconchy's String Quartet No. 5, sponsored by the British Council. After a disastrous first recording earlier in the year, this second attempt went much more smoothly.[43] The record was eventually released by Argo Records in 1964 along with the Allegri's recording of Walton's String Quartet in A Minor.

Maconchy had further good news later in November when she was informed that the New Opera Workshop at Sadler's Wells had decided to stage a production of *The Departure* (1959–61) as part of a double bill with Buxton Orr's *The Wager* on 16 December. Ahead of the première, Williams came to visit on 5 December. The following day they travelled to Westminster Abbey for a

38 Ibid.

39 William Glock, *Notes in Advance: An Autobiography in Music* (Oxford: Oxford University Press, 1991), 203. Britten's high number is due in part to the large number of his songs that were broadcast.

40 The recording of *Duo: Theme and Variations* was made the previous summer with Robert Masters and Muriel Taylor. The recording of *Divertimento* featured George Isaac (cello) and Mary Kendall (piano).

41 Elizabeth Maconchy to Grace Williams, 24 June 1962.

42 Elizabeth Maconchy to Grace Williams, 30 September 1962; and Elizabeth Maconchy to Grace Williams, 9 November 1962.

43 For details of the first recording, see Elizabeth Maconchy to Grace Williams, 17 April 1962.

performance of Britten's *War Requiem*. Then on Saturday 8 December, they attended a rehearsal of *The Departure* at Sadler's Wells.[44]

Ahead of the première, Maconchy wrote a brief article about the opera that appeared in the December issue of *Musical Events*:

> The Opera is a new treatment of the theme of Death and the Lady – not the traditional expostulation of the Lady with Death, but the expression of her struggle to accept her death.
>
> It is in more than one sense a woman's opera. It seeks to express through music the emotional history of a woman's life – youth, love, the shared joy of marriage, and children and then death. The death which she must go to alone.[45]

The Departure opens with a theme that consists of two central motifs: a dotted rhythm played in unison on the pitch of D, followed by the introduction of a descending major seventh from D to E-flat. In addition to the intervallic relationship between D and E-flat, later in the opera Maconchy introduces the interval of a major third from D to F-sharp, which serves as another important motif. As the opera begins, Julia is at her dressing table, busy getting ready. She observes that she's paler than usual and finds herself struggling to grip the items she places her hands on. Deeply perplexed, she then hears the music of a funeral procession in the background with an off-stage chorus singing a setting of Psalm 120. Julia then turns to look out of the window where she sees her husband, Mark, in the procession. When Mark returns, he walks right past her, kneeling next to the bed. Confused, Julia calls out to him. He briefly turns his head and calls her name. At that moment, the memory of her death in a car accident comes flooding back. The two recall their lives together with a nostalgic waltz followed by a lullaby as Mark tries to convince Julia to stay. Julia, however, recognises that she must leave, and now having processed the events of her life and death, she is ready to depart alone. The off-stage chorus returns, and the emphasis on D and E-flat with which the opera began re-emerges as Julia repeatedly sings the word 'depart', oscillating between D and F-sharp, bringing the work to a close. While the work is typical of Maconchy's economic style and her use of recurrent motifs, such as the rhythmic figure and the importance of D, E-flat, and F-sharp, this economy never comes at the expense of the profound lyricism at the heart of the work.[46]

The workshop production, which featured mezzo-soprano Catherine Wilson as Julia and baritone Neil Howlett as Mark, was conducted by Alan Boustead and produced by Brian Trowell with set design by Rosemary Flegg. While the opera was warmly received by the audience, with Maconchy's friends praising the work highly, the critics were far less enthusiastic. As detailed in the *Times*,

[44] Williams was only able to attend part of the rehearsal. Grace Williams to Elizabeth Maconchy and William LeFanu, 9 December 1962.

[45] Elizabeth Maconchy, 'The Departure', *Musical Events* 17/12 (December 1962): 8.

[46] For further discussion of this work, see Mathias, *Lutyens, Maconchy, Williams and Twentieth-Century British Music*, 212–15; and Danielle Sofer, 'Death Becomes Him: Elizabeth Maconchy's One-Act Opera *The Departure*', in *Elizabeth Maconchy: Music as Impassioned Argument*, 181–97.

one particularly glaring mishap occurred when the bed on stage broke as Julia sat on it:

> It was unfortunate that the bed broke when the lady in the blue négligé sat on it, for she was meant to be a newly dead disembodied spirit. … [*The Departure*] might conceivably succeed operatically if presented in highly stylized stage form, with electronic or similarly advanced experimental music. But when treated conventionally and realistically the result can serve only as a reminder that the sublime and the ridiculous lie closer in opera than in any other art form.[47]

Reviews from Aprahamian in the *Sunday Times* and Philip Hope-Wallace in the *Guardian* offered more nuanced and thoughtful assessments of the work, if still finding some faults. Hope-Wallace remarked, '"The Departure" is a fraction overlong but her freshness of invention and her real talent for operatic craft serve Anne Ridler's eerie little *scena* very acutely.'[48] Aprahamian described the work as 'a kind of Western variant of Holst's "Savitri". … Her imaginative score with its offstage chorus accomplishes exactly what it sets out to do, and, within its far more modest proportions, shows a better sense of theatrical timing than Mr Orr's.'[49] Though Maconchy was left deeply disheartened by the reviews, the production did at least help her reassess the work by highlighting places where revisions were needed, such as in the pacing and build-up of dramatic tension in the second half of the opera.[50] Nevertheless, Maconchy lamented to Williams, 'the notices will certainly have killed any chance of life The Departure had – so it will never be heard again.'[51]

Maconchy began January 1963 with a trip to London to see the popular comedy revue *Beyond the Fringe* with her family on the 3rd, returning to the city the following week to take in a performance of *King Lear* at the Aldwych Theatre with Nicola and LeFanu.[52] Throughout the year, Maconchy remained busy with work on the Composers' Guild's Executive Committee, continuing her frequent travels to London as she finished up her final year of service. Despite her busy schedule, she still found time to deliver occasional lectures, giving an illustrated talk about her life as a composer to the Goodmayes Gramophone and Music Society on 31 January.

On 5 February, String Quartet No. 5 was featured in a Third Programme broadcast. Performed by the English String Quartet, the work was pre-recorded in December.[53] Though the group was familiar with the quartet, having previously played the work at an SWM concert in 1961, Maconchy

47 'Beggar's Opera in New Terms', *Times*, 17 December 1962.

48 Philip Hope-Wallace, 'Two New Operas', *Guardian*, 17 December 1962.

49 Felix Aprahamian, 'Singing Scrooge', *Sunday Times*, 23 December 1962.

50 Elizabeth Maconchy to Grace Williams, 30 December 1962.

51 Ibid.

52 Elizabeth Maconchy to Grace Williams, 30 December 1962.

53 At the time of the recording, the English String Quartet consisted of Nona Liddell (1st violin), Eleanor St George (2nd violin), Marjorie Lempfert (viola), and Helen Just (cello).

had been unable to attend a rehearsal, thus leading to some apprehension as the broadcast date drew near.[54] To Maconchy's relief, the group's playing had improved greatly, with the quartet's playing even exceeding the Aeolian Quartet in some sections.[55]

In the early months of the year Maconchy devoted much of her energy to scoring and revising *Serenata Concertante*. By mid-February, an initial full-score draft was nearing completion, with suggestions made by Williams aiding her greatly.[56] She also continued to work on her new Quintet for Clarinet and Strings. Progress, however, was not coming along as swiftly as she had hoped, as she wrote to Williams: '[the work] comes very slowly, but I hope is going to turn out as I want. (I scrap volumes.)'[57]

As frustration continued to mount over the slow progression of her works, in May, Maconchy took a much-needed break, travelling to Montreal to join her husband who had been in Canada since the end of March for work. They spent time there with Mima Bala (née Löwenbach), who had settled in Quebec with her husband, Karel Bala. Following a short trip to Jay Peak in Vermont before returning to Montreal, Maconchy and LeFanu flew to New York, where they stayed at the Shoreham Hotel in mid-town Manhattan. In New York, they attended a New York Philharmonic concert and visited several museums, including the Metropolitan Museum of Art, the Guggenheim, and the Frick Museum. They also visited Vilma and Jan Löwenbach, who, along with Mima, had been extraordinarily helpful in aiding them with all the arrangements for their trip.[58] They also found time to see a couple of plays, attending a production of Jean Genet's *The Blacks*, directed by Gene Frankel, at the St Marks Playhouse on 31 May, and *Who's Afraid of Virginia Woolf* at the Billy Rose Theatre on 4 June. On 3 June, Maconchy also met with Iain Hamilton, who had moved to New York the previous year. The following day, Maconchy met with publisher Franco Colombo, who, after acquiring the New York arm of Ricordi in 1960, had renamed the firm Franco Colombo, Inc. Later that evening Maconchy met with composer Jean Retí (1911–72) for dinner.[59]

On 7 June, Maconchy and LeFanu departed for San Francisco via Chicago. During their lay-over, she met with Jirák, who, after immigrating to the US in 1947, was now teaching at Roosevelt University. Maconchy and LeFanu then continued with their journey, spending the next two days in Napa, which included a trip to a winery, before they returned to San Francisco, staying at the Worth Hotel. During their brief stay in the city, they visited Fisherman's Wharf, dining at the Italian seafood restaurant Alioto's overlooking the Golden Gate Bridge. On the 11th they departed for Los Angeles. The following day they visited the Huntington Library in San Marino with LeFanu delivering a lecture

54 Elizabeth Maconchy to Grace Williams, 12 February 1963.
55 Ibid.
56 Ibid.
57 Elizabeth Maconchy to Grace Williams, 12 February 1963.
58 Ibid.
59 This meeting is listed in Maconchy's appointment diary on 4 June 1963.

at UCLA later that evening. According to LeFanu's appointment diary, there may have been a brief trip to Disneyland in Anaheim on the 13th, followed by a tour of the MGM Studios on the 14th.[60] The following day they departed for Washington DC. While LeFanu was busy attending a conference, Maconchy visited the National Gallery of Art, the Folger Library, and took a tour of the White House.

After returning to England on 23 June, Maconchy and LeFanu departed the following morning for Aldeburgh to attend a performance of *Reflections*. Maconchy was deeply pleased with the performance, believing it to be the best of the work thus far.[61] Although the trip to Canada and the US had offered some much-needed inspiration, by the end of August, the steady flow of ideas from her trip abroad appears to have slowed to a trickle, with some of her outstanding projects, such as a transcription of her Bassoon Concertino for Lengnick, and work on a string quartet for Chappell's educational series, leaving her with limited time to focus on more fulfilling projects.[62]

On 16 October 1963, Maconchy and LeFanu drove up to Birmingham for a rehearsal of what would be the most important performance of the year: the première of *Serenata Concertante* by the City of Birmingham Symphony Orchestra. The rehearsal took place at the local YMCA. Prior to the rehearsal, Maconchy worked through the score with the orchestra's conductor, Hugo Rignold (1905–76), and violinist Manoug Parikian (1920–87) in London. Though the first rehearsal with the orchestra was disappointing, the rehearsal on the morning of the 17th proved much more encouraging. While the orchestra's playing for the concert that evening did not quite match the level of their morning rehearsal, Parikian played the work beautifully, with Maconchy confessing to Williams, 'I doubted if it would "get across" as a result – but it amazingly did – & the audience really seemed very enthusiastic which was nice.'[63]

The *Serenata Concertante* is arranged in four movements, with the material for each derived from five themes presented at the outset. The work opens with theme a in the trumpets (Example 10.2a), which is followed by the introduction of theme b in the harp (Example 10.2b). The oboe then joins with theme c, anchored by the horns playing theme d (Example 10.2c). The solo violin then enters with theme e (Example 10.2d). This is followed by a slightly altered version of theme a, which leads into a sparsely scored allegro section with woodwind and pizzicato in the strings derived from themes b and c, followed by a

[60] Maconchy's appointment diary mentions the tour of MGM Studios but not Disneyland.

[61] Elizabeth Maconchy to Grace Williams, 6 July 1963. The performance featured oboist Janet Craxton (1929–81), clarinettist Thea King (1925–2007), violist Margaret Major, and harpist Osian Ellis.

[62] In her letter to Williams on 6 July, Maconchy noted that 'musical ideas seem to have started flowing – which they hadn't for some time!' See Elizabeth Maconchy to Grace Williams, 6 July 1963, 7 August 1963, and 30 August 1963. The string quartet was titled Sonatina for String Quartet.

[63] Elizabeth Maconchy to Grace Williams, 27 October 1963.

Example 10.2a. Maconchy, *Serenata Concertante*, mvt. I, opening.

Example 10.2b. Maconchy, *Serenata Concertante*, mvt. I, bars 3–4.

Example 10.2c. Maconchy, *Serenata Concertante*, mvt. I, bars 8–10.

Example 10.2d. Maconchy, *Serenata Concertante*, mvt. I, bars 10–13.

passage for the violin and xylophone with periodic interruptions by the brass section playing a variation of theme d, with a new derivative theme introduced by the trombones. An expanded section for solo violin and cor anglais follows, as the movement then builds to a climax featuring further variations of the primary themes before the energy dies down and the solo violin, accompanied by muted horns and harp glissandi, delicately concludes the movement.

The second movement, Scherzo, opens with a vigorous rhythmic figure in 5/8 which remains a driving force throughout. The third movement, Andante con moto, is lush and lyrical, opening with an E pedal with muted brass playing chords shifting back and forth. The movement also features extended passages for the soloist, as well as a canon for the woodwinds, before the E pedal and shifting chords return, gradually bringing the movement to a close. The fourth movement is an expanded rondo. Rhythmically dynamic, its character is closely aligned with the spirit of the second.[64]

In her programme notes, Maconchy described the *Serenata Concertante* as being written in 'chamber-music style rather than in the grand orchestral manner'.[65] Throughout the work, one can detect traces of Vaughan Williams, with hints of *Flos campi* and *Job* appearing in various guises, yet they are deftly woven into the fabric of the score. Maconchy's exploration of a broad range of textures and colours, combined with the successful fusion of her contrapuntal style now transformed into her orchestral writing establishes the *Serenata Concertante* as a significant advance in her evolving musical style.

Following the concert, Maconchy experienced her usual post-première misgivings, though she was cheered by a glowing review by Percy Cater in the *Daily Mail* who declared the work 'a complete success … It is clever, smart, busy, often exhilarating. … She knows exactly the sounds she wants, and exactly how to get them.'[66] Following the performance, Maconchy set about making some minor alterations ahead of the work's recording on 31 December for a BBC Home Service broadcast on 7 February 1964.

Aside from the première of the *Serenata Concertante*, Maconchy had some other pleasant news to celebrate in the autumn of 1963 with the birth of Anna's first child, Christopher, on 28 October. Maconchy, who was an ever-enthusiastic new grandmother, travelled to Lincoln on 4 November, spending two weeks with her daughter and new grandson. The following month brought the première of her cantata *Christmas Morning* (1960–1) on the 6th. For Christmas, Maconchy's sister Maureen and brother-in-law Bill visited for luncheon and tea. Then on the 27th, the Maconchy-LeFanu household travelled to Lincoln for Christopher's christening. Anna, her husband, and Christopher then returned with them the following day, staying at Shottesbrook for two and half weeks,

[64] See Elizabeth Maconchy, 'Serenata Concertante – an analytical note', in Peter Dickinson (ed.), *Twenty British Composers* (London: Chester Music, 1975), 50–3.

[65] Ibid.

[66] Percy Cater, 'Composer Maconchy Scores a Triumph', *Daily Mail*, 19 October 1963.

enabling Maconchy to be the 'doting grandmother' to her first grandchild, whom she described as 'a heavenly baby'.[67]

In the early months of 1964, Maconchy devoted much of her time to a number of her recently commissioned works. This included a commission in the amount of fifty guineas for a new setting of *How Samson bore away the Gates of Gaza* for the Chelmsford Grammar School. Based upon her earlier 1937 setting of the work for voice and piano, Maconchy expanded and adapted the piece to accommodate chorus and orchestra, with the school performing the new arrangement later in the year on 10 October.[68] Maconchy was also busy with two settings of poems by Gerard Manley Hopkins, 'The Starlight Night' and 'Peace', as well as a Proms commission for the 1965 season. For the latter, she settled on writing a work for oboe, clarinet, bassoon, horn, and strings to serve as a 'companion piece' for Mozart's *Sinfonia Concertante*, which had first been suggested by Glock. The work-in-progress initially bore the title *Dibattimenti* before Maconchy changed it to *Variazioni Concertante*.[69]

On 7 March, the *Serenata Concertante* had its first London performance in a CBSO concert at the Royal Festival Hall in London, once again featuring Parikian with Rignold conducting. Maconchy travelled to London for a rehearsal ahead of the performance. Both LeFanu and Nicola, who had come down from St Mary's, were in attendance for the concert and party that followed later in the evening, with the three of them then staying over at Ursula Vaughan Williams's home. The next day, Maconchy attended a performance of one of Humphrey Searle's operas, followed by *Fidelio* at Covent Garden on the 9th.

The following day, Maconchy made her first visit to Dartington, travelling by car with clarinettist Gervase de Peyer ahead of the première of her Quintet for Clarinet and Strings on 12 March. Given de Peyer's reckless driving, which at times reached upwards of 90 mph, it was perhaps a miracle that they made it to their destination in one piece.[70] Maconchy found her visit to Dartington enjoyable, and it also gave her an opportunity to catch up with an old friend from her RCM days, composer and pianist Helen Glatz (1908–96), who taught at Dartington Hall.

On the 11th, Maconchy attended a rehearsal of her quintet with de Peyer and the Dartington String Quartet. Later that evening, she delivered a pre-concert talk to the Minehead Concerts Society. In the Quintet for Clarinet and Strings, the major seconds in the strings and the melodic fragments introduced by the clarinet at the outset serve as the foundational building blocks for all four movements (Example 10.3). According to Maconchy, this was not an entirely

67 Elizabeth Maconchy to Grace Williams, 26 February 1964.

68 The new version included additional material which Maconchy detailed in a letter to Williams. After the performance, Maconchy set about making minor alterations to the work, which was subsequently published by Chappell. Elizabeth Maconchy to Grace Williams, 26 February 1964 and 14 October 1964.

69 Elizabeth Maconchy to Miss Evans, 24 May 1964, BBC WAC EM5. Maconchy received £100 for the work.

70 Elizabeth Maconchy to Grace Williams, 20 April 1964.

Example 10.3. Maconchy, Quintet for Clarinet and Strings, mvt. I, opening.

conscious act on her part as it was not until she began to analyse the work for her talk that she discovered how profound the connection was. In discussing this work a few years later, she remarked,

> I think a composer's mind works at two levels: while his conscious mind is working away at the complex process of constructing a piece of music, there is at the same time a sort of active underground movement going on in his unconscious. I came on an unexpected instance of this with my Clarinet Quintet. … I had a lot of trouble with it. I wrote the first page or so straight away, & liked it; but after that nothing went right: & I scrapped a great deal, including a whole Scherzo: but I never scrapped that first page: I always came back to that. Eventually the work went ahead as I wanted it to: I wrote a new Scherzo with no trouble – & the piece got finished.[71]

Though the rehearsal with de Peyer and the Dartington Quartet had gone well, she found the performance the following day disappointing. She subsequently set about revising the work, adding more material for the clarinet as well as a new coda to the Scherzo and a new ending to the fourth movement.[72] The BBC also recorded the performance, which was then broadcast later in the year on 23 June with Peter Pirie praising the work in the *Musical Times*: 'I had not heard anything from [Maconchy] for ages, and this came as something of a surprise. Without being in any way pretentious, it was a delicious little work.'[73]

Sadly, Maconchy had to miss the broadcast of her Clarinet Quintet as it conflicted with a trip to Berlin. Earlier in the year she had been invited by Berlin Radio to attend a concert of symphonic works by women composers which included her Concerto for Oboe, Bassoon, and String Orchestra to complement an international women's congress taking place that month. Maconchy departed England on the afternoon of the 23rd, and travelled to Berlin via Prague. The following day, she recorded two interviews for Berlin Radio prior to the performance of her work at the Volksbühne, or People's Theatre, in the evening.[74]

Maconchy's trip was filled with a number of concerts and receptions in addition to the opening session of the Women's Congress on the 25th, with approximately 1,000 delegates in attendance.[75] Over the course of her visit, she met German composer Ruth Zechlin (1926–2007), and also found time to walk through the city along the Karl-Marx-Allee, visiting some of the local shops. Of

[71] Maconchy, 'Conversation between Anne Macnaghten and Elizabeth Maconchy'.

[72] Elizabeth Maconchy to Grace Williams, 20 April 1964.

[73] Peter Pirie, 'Broadcasting', *Musical Times* 105/1458 (August 1964): 610.

[74] Maconchy's Concerto for Oboe, Bassoon, and String Orchestra was played by the Berlin Radio Symphony Orchestra conducted by Rolf Kleinert with oboist Hans-Werner Wätzig and bassoonist Erwin Kretzschmar as soloists. The programme also included Grazyna Bacewicz's Overture for Orchestra (1943), Alexandra Pakhmutova's Concerto for Trumpet and Orchestra (1955), and Ruth Zechlin's Violin Concerto (1963).

[75] While Maconchy mentions the number of delegates as approximately 1,500 in her notes from her trip held at SHC, according to other sources, the number of registered delegates was slightly lower, at around 1,000. See Martin McCauley, *The German Democratic Republic Since 1945* (London: Palgrave Macmillan, 1983), 106.

her impressions of the city, Maconchy remarked to Williams, 'E. Berlin looks awful – shattered & only partially rebuilt. Everything scarred & great huge bombed sites still empty.'[76] This short trip left her thankful for her own good fortune that enabled her to live a much more comfortable life in England.[77]

For the remainder of the summer Maconchy devoted her time and energy to her Proms commission. She did, however, find time for at least one enjoyable diversion when she served as an accompanist for a production of Mozart's *The Marriage of Figaro*. This production was produced by Nicola, who was home studying for exams, later gaining entrance to St Hilda's College.[78] Nicola took on the role of Cherubino in the production, which was staged by a group she had formed called the Shottesbrook Youth Players. Jeremy Dale-Roberts served as the troupe's conductor, with the production's designs by Ursula Vaughan Williams.[79]

In the late summer, one of Maconchy's much older works, *Theme and Variations for String Orchestra* (1942–3), was played by the Jacques Orchestra, conducted by Samuel Rosenheim, at the Wigmore Hall on 15 September. The following month saw the première of her new version of *Samson and the Gates of Gaza* on the 10th. After the performance, Maconchy set about making minor alterations to the work, which was subsequently published by Chappell.[80]

October also featured the first performance of her recently completed settings of Hopkins's *The Starlight Night* and *Peace*.[81] The première, which took place on the 22nd at Chelmsford Cathedral in a Jubilee Orchestra concert, featured the Jacques Orchestra conducted by Philip Ledger (1937–2012), with soprano Mary Wells serving as the soloist. Of seeking poetic inspiration, and the significance of Hopkins's words in particular, Maconchy later wrote the following:

> In searching for words to set every composer must have experienced that magic moment of recognition – 'This is it – this is what I have been looking for' – a sort of love-at-first-sight reaction. It may not in fact be one's first sight of the poem, but suddenly there is an instinctive sense of possession: the poem becomes as it were part of oneself.
>
> This for me, in any case, is how the writing of a song starts, or a choral work or any setting of words.
>
> This initial impulse starts the piece going and the sense of complete identification with the words continues to grow as the work takes shape, and persists to the end. When it is finished the mystic marriage is dissolved, and one may forget the words again almost completely, – as, alas, often happens in cases of love at first sight. [...]
>
> Gerald Manley Hopkins has meant more to me than almost any other poet.[82]

[76] Elizabeth Maconchy to Grace Williams, 5 July 1964.

[77] Ibid.

[78] Elizabeth Maconchy to Grace Williams, 7 January 1965.

[79] The opera was sung in English, using Dent's translation.

[80] Elizabeth Maconchy to Grace Williams, 4 November 1964.

[81] This work later bore the title *Settings of Poems by Gerard Manley Hopkins*, with Maconchy adding a setting of 'The May Magnificat' in 1970.

[82] Elizabeth Maconchy, draft of talk on 'Three Hopkins Settings' for Radio 3 programme that aired on 3 and 15 March 1977, SHC.

Example 10.4. Maconchy, *The Starlight Night*, opening.

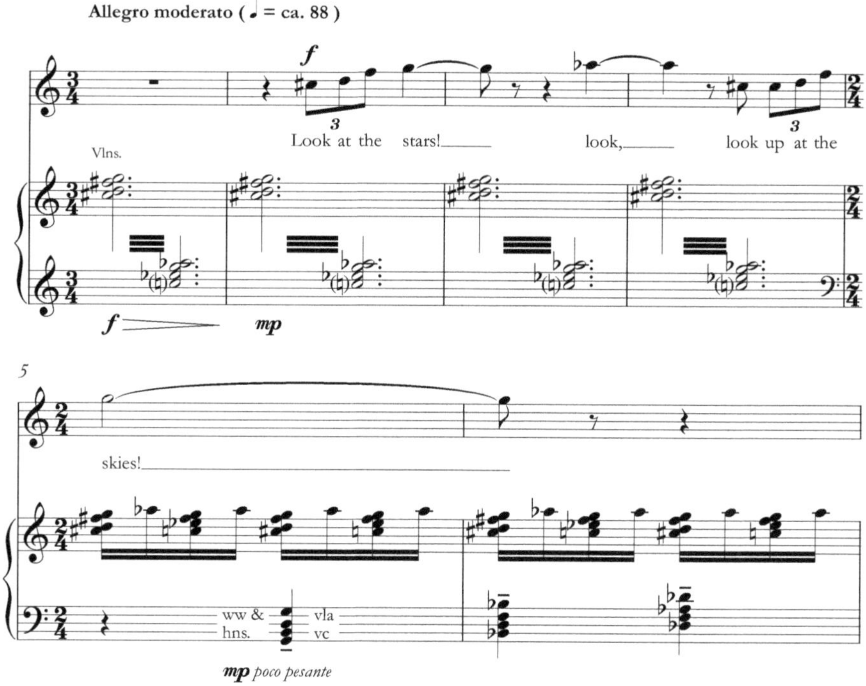

The Starlight Night begins with tremolos in the strings, vividly evoking the glistening of the stars as the soprano draws attention to them (Example 10.4). Maconchy's exploration of colour, combined with the skilful word-painting with descriptions of the woods, the wind, and floating doves vividly echoed by the orchestra highlights the ever-expanding range of Maconchy's artistic prowess.[83]

By the beginning of January 1965, Maconchy had largely completed her *Variazioni Concertante*, aside from the scoring. During the year she embarked upon a number of new works, including two for harpsichord, three songs set to texts by Shakespeare, and settings of John Donne's *A Hymn to Christ* and *The Sun Rising*, as well as three choral works: *Nocturnal*, which had been commissioned for the Cork International Festival; *Go, Penny, Go* for Maud Karpeles; and *Propheta Mendax* for the Vienna Boys' Choir.[84] She also began work on a commission

[83] For further discussion of this work, see Mathias, *Lutyens, Maconchy, Williams and Twentieth-Century British Music*, 223–6.

[84] Maconchy's three Shakespeare settings – *Take, oh take those lips away*; *The wind and the rain*; and *King Stephen* – were later published along with *Come away, Death* (1956)

from Morley College for her *Music for Woodwind and Brass*, which was completed the following year.

Performances were not neglected in the first half of 1965, with the *Divertimento* included at a Wigmore Hall Lunchtime Recital on 21 January; *Duo: Theme and Variations* at a concert devoted to works by English women composers on 18 March; a performance of the Quintet for Clarinet and Strings in Oxford on 6 May; as well as a performance of the Sonata for Violin and Piano at an SWM concert on 14 May.[85] Two of Maconchy's works were also broadcast, with her Quintet for Clarinet and Strings included in a programme on 26 March and the Allegri Quartet's recording of the String Quartet No. 5 featured on 21 April.

In April, Maconchy and LeFanu took a holiday to Italy. The following month, she travelled to Ireland along with her husband and Nicola to attend the International Choral Festival in Cork. In addition to the première of her work for the festival, Maconchy also served as an adjudicator. *Nocturnal* was written for conductor Graham Treacher (b. 1932) and the Morley College Choir. When Treacher became too busy with his conducting engagements with the BBC Scottish Orchestra, Michael Howard took over the responsibilities for the choir, which included rehearsing Maconchy's score, even though Treacher still planned to conduct the première.

Several months prior to the festival, Maconchy sent the work to Treacher, who informed her that it looked suitable and he would rehearse it with the choir in Cork ahead of its première. Maconchy subsequently sent all the parts in March; however, it was not until mid-April that Howard bothered to look over the piece.[86] In a letter to Williams, Maconchy detailed the events that transpired:

> On May 1st he rang me up to say it was absolutely impossible for the choir to sing it: he suggested as the only possibility that they might be able to get through the first & third sections – but the central (scherzo) section was quite impossible. … I said I couldn't agree to that – & he washed his hands of it. At that time he had never got beyond p. 2 of the first piece! … [I]t would have been a terrible let-down for the Cork festival at the last minute – which made it v. difficult to call off the performance … So I took the next (short) rehearsal myself, & Jeremy Dale-Roberts took 3 more short ones & Graham Treacher got down from Glasgow for a Sunday evening one. He then met them in Cork the day before they had to sing my piece & they continued to work there. On Sat. afternoon they sang it twice at a Seminar about the piece – & still didn't really know it … but somehow Graham T. worked a miracle (they were very keen – & also devoted to him) & they sang it really well, expressively & beautifully in the evening – & it really did sound nice! So it all ended happily.[87]

In contrast to some of her previous choral works, *Nocturnal* exemplifies Maconchy's extreme economy now transferred to her choral writing. It comprises

as *Four Shakespeare Songs for Voice and Piano.*

[85] Maconchy's Quintet for Clarinet and Strings was featured in an Oxford Subscription concert with de Peyer and the Melos Ensemble.

[86] Elizabeth Maconchy to Grace Williams, 9 June 1965.

[87] Ibid.

Example 10.5. Maconchy, *Nocturnal*, I, 'Come!', opening.

three poems: 'Come!' by William Barnes, 'Will you come?' by Edward Thomas, and 'To the Night' by Percy Bysshe Shelley, which Maconchy links through a series of three motifs expressed at the beginning of 'Come!' (Example 10.5). In the sopranos' opening two bars, two of the key motifs are highlighted: motif a, which consists of a whole-tone step and a perfect fourth ('Will you come'), and motif b, which introduces the notes of A and E ('in early Spring'). Beyond the intervallic relationships, Maconchy also uses the rhythm of the motifs for further development. In bar 2, she introduces a third motif in the tenor, which, combined with the bass, comprises two trichords. Though the opening bars establish a tonal centre of F-sharp, her penchant for chromatic alteration, inversion, and transposition destabilises this centre, highlighting her gradual move away from more traditional sonorities, in favour of a technique focused on a series of chords and intervals, with the pull towards particular pitches and intervals serving as stabilising forces.[88]

Following the festival, Maconchy had a few days of vacation with LeFanu and Nicola, exploring the Cork coast and nearby mountains. LeFanu and Nicola then returned to England, with Maconchy visiting Boyle at her home, Bushey Park, Enniskerry, for a few days before flying home on the 31st. In early June, Maconchy was busy taking care of Christopher to give Anna, who was expecting her second child, a brief respite while she and her husband Francis took a trip to Norfolk. Later in the month, Maconchy travelled to Aldeburgh to attend a performance of her *Hymn to God the Father* (1959) by Peter Pears and Viola Tunnard at the Aldeburgh Festival on the 22nd.

[88] For further discussion of *Nocturnal*, see Catherine Roma, *The Choral Music of Twentieth-Century Women Composers* (Lanham, Maryland: Scarecrow Press, 2006), 70–8.

Though Maconchy was staying with Anna in Rugby in August, she was able to travel to Glasgow for a rehearsal of her Proms commission, *Variazioni Concertante*, on the 3rd, ahead of its première at the Royal Albert Hall on the 10th. The work was performed by the BBC Scottish Orchestra conducted by James Loughran (b. 1931), with Terence MacDonagh (oboe), Jack Brymer (clarinet), Geoffrey Gambold (bassoon), and Douglas Moore (horn) as soloists.

For the concert, Maconchy contributed a detailed programme note, highlighting key thematic material for each of the work's eight variations:

> The work opens with a slow Introduction, almost an improvisation rather than a theme, but it contains all the material from which the ensuing variations are made. The opening chords for divided strings, the decorative phrases for oboe, clarinet, and horn, and the expressive dialogue for bassoon and oboe (who has the 'key-phrase') are all germinal themes. A repetition of the horn phrase closes the brief Introduction.
>
> Var. i, *andante con moto*, in a gentle 3/4 metre, takes its material mainly from the oboe and bassoon dialogue of the Introduction.
>
> Var. ii, *presto*, is a swift scherzo, *leggiero*, in 6/8 time with strings muted at first. A final crescendo, with a vigorous 3/4 passage in strings, leads into
>
> Var. iii, *molto moderato*, which opens with big repeated string chords, *ff con forza*. They give way to a calmer horn tune: long melodic phrases for the wind soloists are counterpointed with long string phrases and a five-note 'ground' in the bass, (the oboe's 'key-phrase'). The movement dies away with the calm horn-tune against widely spaced strings.
>
> Var. iv, *allegro*, is a lively 4-part fugue. The wind soloists enter in turn with the subject, which derives from a clarinet phrase in the Introduction: the counter-subject is the oboe key-phrase inverted. The fugue gathers momentum and ends *f* leaving behind a quiet diminished fifth in the violins, which links it to the pianissimo string glissandi of
>
> Var. v, *andante, tempo libero*. Expressive improvisatory passages in the soloists are punctuated by quiet repeated string chords, with a throbbing pizzicato figure in the double-bass.
>
> Var. vi, *allegro molto*, opens with a brief animated canon for oboe and clarinet: the rest join in and reach an *f*. As this subsides, oboe and clarinet are left playing their little canon inverted, and the brief movement grows to a bigger climax, ending *ff*.
>
> Var. vii, *andante con moto*, is by contrast a quiet colloquy in free rhythm between the four wind soloists with solo violin and cello added. Soon the winds in unison play a plainsong-like stanza against which the strings weave free melodic phrases. These phrases gradually become more urgent, the five-note ground reappears, and a crescendo leads into the final variation.
>
> Var. viii. This is an *allegro vivo* in 5/8 time and forms a fairly extended finale. The boisterous syncopated theme with which it opens gives way to a quieter middle section, which begins with a horn solo. The vigorous rhythms return, and then recede into the distance, with wind passages, *leggiero*, against a background of widely spaced string chords – and we are back to the music of the Introduction. The original material is re-stated, though transformed by what

> has happened in between, and the work ends very quietly, with the key-phrase fading out in the clarinet.[89]

Reviews of the concert, which was also broadcast, were mixed. In the *Guardian*, Edward Greenfield praised the lyricism of the fifth variation while also alleging the work bore some resemblance to Walton's *Portsmouth Point* overture, which, he argued, proved to be one of its weaknesses.[90] Martin Cooper, however, thought highly of the work, praising Maconchy's skilful craftsmanship, particularly in the seventh variation.[91] The unnamed critic in the *Times* criticised the work for being 'too fragmentary' while nevertheless conceding that it was at times 'felicitously imaginative'.[92]

Following the première, Maconchy stayed over with Ursula Vaughan Williams before returning to Rugby the following day. Her second grandchild, Sarah, arrived a few days later on the 15th. Maconchy subsequently set about revising *Variazioni Concertante*, which she completed shortly after returning home from Rugby in September. A broadcast of the revised version took place with the BBC Scottish Orchestra, conducted once again by Loughran, and featuring Valerie Taylor (oboe), Henry Morrison (clarinet), Barry Morris (bassoon), and Farquharson Cousins (horn) on 28 October.

Beyond the October broadcast of *Variazioni Concertante*, the autumn also featured a number of performances, including *Reflections* at a Macnaghten concert on 24 September at the Wigmore Hall, a Third Programme broadcast of *A Hymn to God the Father* on 28 September, a performance of the String Quartet No. 7 by the Arriaga Quartet at an SPNM concert on 4 October, and the première of the Sonatina for Harpsichord (1965) by Alan Cuckston (b. 1940) in Birmingham at a Birmingham University Musical Society concert on 26 November. The following month, Cuckston gave the first London performance of the work at a Park Lane Group concert on the 13th. Maconchy was also busy towards the end of the year composing incidental music for a play by Anne Ridler titled *Witnesses*, which Maconchy completed the following year.[93]

January 1966 began with the première of *Propheta Mendax* on the 3rd by the Vienna Boys' Choir. Though Maconchy was not in attendance as the concert took place in Salzburg, she was able to attend the choir's performance of the work on 3 February at the Royal Albert Hall. In March, Maconchy completed her commission for Morley College, *Music for Woodwind and Brass*, which was later premièred by the Morley College Symphony Orchestra, conducted by Treacher, on 25 June in a concert at Thaxted Parish Church as part of the Thaxted Midsummer Festival.

[89] Elizabeth Maconchy, programme note accompanying Proms concert programme, 10 August 1965.

[90] Edward Greenfield, 'Elizabeth Maconchy's Variazioni Concertanti [*sic*] and the Proms', *Guardian*, 12 August 1965.

[91] Martin Cooper, 'Happy skill of Maconchy variations', *Daily Telegraph*, 12 August 1965.

[92] 'Beguiling New Music', *Times*, 11 August 1965.

[93] *Witnesses* was premièred in Leeds in 1967.

Maconchy also started up her frequent trips to London for Composers' Guild meetings, having recently rejoined the Executive Committee. On 22 April, she joined Adrian Cruft (1921–87), who was then serving as Chairman of the Composers' Guild, as well as Tristram Cary (1925–2008), Stephen Dodgson, and Joseph Horovitz (1926–2022) as a participant in a discussion on the art of composition. This event, which was held at the Holborn Central Library, was organised by the London Symphony Orchestra Club.

Throughout the year, Maconchy remained busy with a number of choral works, which included *I Sing of a Maiden* and *This Day* for Faber, and *Down with the Rosemary and Bays: Twelfth Night Carol*, as well as *Nowell, sing we Nowell*. The latter two carols were commissioned for *The Cambridge Hymnal*, which was published the following year. In addition to completing the incidental music for Ridler's play, Maconchy also composed *Six Miniatures for Solo Violin* for Grinke and began work on *An Essex Overture*, which had been commissioned by the Essex Youth Orchestra. The itch to write a new quartet also became too hard to ignore as she commenced work on her String Quartet No. 8. Her progress, however, was initially impeded by time consumed by revisions to *The Sofa* ahead of its performance at the 1967 Camden Festival.

Broadcasts were not neglected early in the year, with the première of Maconchy's *Four Shakespeare Songs*, which was featured on Network Three in a programme of English songs with soprano Noelle Barker (1928–2013) accompanied by pianist Wilfrid Parry, on 20 April. A concert performance of the work followed on 16 May, with Barker accompanied by Robert Sherlaw Johnson. On 4 June, the songs received another performance, this time by tenor Peter Birts accompanied by Maconchy's cousin Giles Swayne (b. 1946) at a Cambridge University Musical Club concert.

On 8 May, Maconchy and LeFanu travelled to Venice for a holiday, returning on the 24th. Prior to leaving for Italy, Maconchy recorded an interview with Macnaghten on 4 May for the BBC's *Composer's Portrait* series, which was broadcast the following month on 15 June. In addition to the interview, the broadcast also included Maconchy's Quintet for Clarinet and Strings as well as three of her Shakespeare songs: *The wind and the rain*, *Come away, death*, and *King Stephen*. Later in the summer, Peter Pears and Viola Tunnard premièred *A Hymn to Christ* in a Network Three broadcast of English songs on 13 July. Another première took place in the autumn, with Grinke giving the first performance of *Six Miniatures for Solo Violin* at a University of Edinburgh chamber concert. Then in November, *Music for Woodwind and Brass* received its first London performance by Morley College on the 22nd. Despite a performance that lacked the nuance of more skilled, professional musicians, the work garnered praise from both the *Times* critic and Aprahamian, who went so far as to declare that the quality of the playing 'did not prevent the revelation of Elizabeth Maconchy's recent Music for Brass and Wind as one of her finest scores: taut in construction, distinguished in expression, with telling contrast of mood and colour, and a real mastery of the idiom'.[94]

[94] Felix Aprahamian, 'Divine Rollers', *Sunday Times*, 27 November 1966.

11

Of Ageing and Critics, 1967–73

One of the greatest advantages to a composer no longer in the throes of youth is the resurgence of interest that each decade and demi-decade brings as they approach particular milestone years. For Maconchy, her sixtieth year would be the first of several landmark birthdays that were especially advantageous, with a deluge of performances and speaking engagements filling her calendar throughout the year.

It was the first half of 1967 that proved to be the busiest. On 31 January, she delivered a talk at Morley College as part of a series of public lectures titled 'The Composer Speaks'. The series, which ran from mid-January to the beginning of March, featured Humphrey Searle, Nicholas Maw (1935–2009), Anthony Milner (1925–2002), Malcolm Williamson (1931–2003), Wilfred Josephs (1927–97), Edmund Rubbra, and Tristram Cary. A particular emphasis of the series was the relationship between the composer and the contemporary music scene. Maconchy focused her talk on the perils facing composers of serious music:

> [W]hat has all this preoccupation with serious music got to do with the world to-day? If one had to justify it – to make out a case for serious music – one would say, I think, that it gives intellectual and emotional satisfaction of the highest order to those who play & those who listen to it. And that its values and standards are absolute – self-interest, compromise, commercialism & money-values are irrelevant to it.
>
> But one must accept music on its own terms. If you try to harness it to serve some extra-musical purpose – however lofty – you degrade it. [...]
>
> Many people sincerely ask – 'Why can't you write to please the public?' But if you are consciously trying to please, you are not thinking exclusively of the music, you are thinking about what might please & what might not – & so inevitably you begin to 'write down'. (I don't mean that music that pleases is automatically inferior – of course not: but it is only good if the composer's instinct & whole hearted inclination was to write that way – & not if he has consciously been writing to please.)
>
> Well – if you do not write to please the public who do you write for? we are asked.
>
> A composer writes for the person who expects most from him, & is his severest critic; who has no illusions about him, & sets him impossibly high standards, & who nearly drives him to death. In fact he writes for himself.[1]

As for performances, on 22 January, Frederick Grinke played *Six Miniatures* at an Oxford Ladies' Musical Society concert. A couple of weeks later, a concert Nicola helped to organise with the Oxford University Musical Club and Union

[1] Maconchy, draft of talk titled 'The Composer Speaks', SHC.

on 7 February featured *The Garland*, *Nocturnal*, the Sonatina for Harpsichord, and the Quintet for Clarinet and Strings. The following day, Maconchy travelled to London for the recording of a BBC *Music Magazine* profile on her music by Williams. This also gave Maconchy a much-needed opportunity to catch up with Williams. The following day, they attended a performance of Janáček's opera *From the House of the Dead* at Sadler's Wells.

On 28 February, Maconchy's revised version of *The Sofa* was featured at the Camden Festival in a programme of three comedic one-act operas opening with Holst's *The Wandering Scholar*, followed by Hindemith's *There and Back*, with *The Sofa* concluding the programme. After an encouraging rehearsal on the 26th at the Royal Festival Hall, Maconchy was optimistic about the production. Sadly, this optimism was short-lived as the following evening's rehearsal at St. Pancras proved disastrous:

> at the evening rehearsal at St. Panc. none of the words came across & it was hell! It was hard to believe the difference. Joe Horovitz sat up that night taking out anything that could be taken out from the score (& bracketing in the parts). The only way to get it done was for him to do it, as it had to be ready for rehearsal the next day, & he had to know just what had been done. He did it excellently, & it made a lot of difference though it was still difficult to get the words across, & always will be at St. Panc. I fear.[2]

Shortly before the performance, the opera's librettist, Ursula Vaughan Williams, took a nasty fall, resulting in a black eye and a badly bruised arm. This was, perhaps, a foreshadowing of what would ultimately prove to be a disappointing performance. While Maconchy greatly enjoyed working with Horovitz, the same could not be said for the producer, Dennis Arundell, whom she found to be 'tyrannical', and tenor Joseph Ward, who played the role of Prince Dominic:

> Joe W. just could not learn & memorise his part correctly – & was wrong half the time on the 1st night. At the end of the evening Dennis A. was absolutely infuriated with him (but mainly because he had not obeyed producer's instructions! not because of musical mistakes) & said appalling things to him in front of the whole cast.[3]

Unsurprisingly, most of the reviews of the performance noted that it was nearly impossible to hear the words. This problem was likely made worse by the lack of a synopsis of the opera in the programme. Nevertheless, a number of critics praised the music, with Stephen Walsh lauding Maconchy's 'powers of light, operetta-like invention' in his review for *Music and Musicians*.[4] In the *Financial Times*, Ronald Crichton, who was disappointed in the opera's ending, quipped, 'The lame ending didn't matter so much because Miss Maconchy's music was otherwise delightfully fluent, gay and tuneful in a way one doesn't normally associate with such a serious

2 Elizabeth Maconchy to Grace Williams, 12 March 1967.

3 Ibid.

4 Stephen Walsh, 'Well produced laughs', *Music and Musicians* 15/9 (May 1967): 40.

and thoughtful composer.'[5] Fortunately for Maconchy, a recording the BBC made of the opera on 6 March went much more smoothly, with the broadcast of the work taking place later in the year on 1 October.[6]

Following the recording, Maconchy flew to Ireland on 7 March to see Ina Boyle. In late January, Boyle had written to Maconchy about her declining health, initially believing that she was struggling with an ulcer.[7] A barium X-ray, however, confirmed something much worse: cancer, most likely of the stomach, for which there was nothing the doctors could do.[8] Maconchy visited Boyle, who was receiving care at Castle Clare Nursing Home in Greystones.[9] Though incredibly weak, Boyle was coherent on Tuesday and the two discussed the recent production of *The Sofa*. Following Maconchy's first visit, she declined rapidly.[10] Maconchy said her goodbyes to Boyle on Thursday, returning to England on the afternoon of Friday 10 March. On Saturday, she received a phone call from Boyle's cousin, informing her that Boyle had died on Friday evening.[11]

Boyle's death was a tremendous loss for Maconchy as she had been not only a dear friend but also an astute colleague, routinely offering insightful feedback on scores and serving as an advocate for performances of Maconchy's music in Ireland. At the beginning of August, Maconchy and LeFanu returned to Ireland for a week to help sort out Boyle's estate. Maconchy went through Boyle's music at Bushey Park, the large country estate where Boyle had spent her entire life. She left all of her books on music as well as her collection of music periodicals and scores to Maconchy.[12] With the help of Brian Boydell (1917–2000), Maconchy arranged for Boyle's manuscripts to be placed in a collection at Trinity College, Dublin.[13] Maconchy later wrote an appreciation of her dear friend that was published along with a list of Boyle's works.[14]

In March, the BBC broadcast several of Maconchy's works, beginning on the 3rd with the Sonatina for Harpsichord and String Quartet No. 5 featured in a *Music of our Time* programme.[15] On the 14th, a recording by the Melos Ensemble and

5 Ronald Crichton, 'Comic operas', *Financial Times*, 1 March 1967.

6 Elizabeth Maconchy to Grace Williams, 12 March 1967.

7 Ina Boyle to Elizabeth Maconchy, 27 January 1967, private collection.

8 Ina Boyle to Elizabeth Maconchy, 9 February 1967, private collection. While Boyle does not state outright that the diagnosis was stomach cancer, references in the letter to her stomach and previous surgeries, combined with the barium X-ray, are highly suggestive.

9 Beausang and de Barra, 51.

10 Elizabeth Maconchy to Grace Williams, 12 March 1967.

11 Ibid.

12 Elizabeth Maconchy to Grace Williams, 10 August 1967.

13 Beausang and de Barra, 58. Also see Elizabeth Maconchy, *Ina Boyle: An Appreciation with a Select List of Her Music* (Dublin: Printed for the Library of Trinity College Dublin at the Dolmen Press, 1974).

14 Maconchy, *Ina Boyle*.

15 The Sonatina for Harpsichord was played by Valda Aveling; the String Quartet No. 5 was played by the English String Quartet.

de Peyer of the Quintet for Clarinet and Strings was broadcast. Then, on the 19th, the BBC aired the previously recorded *Music Magazine* profile, marking a triumphant sixtieth birthday for the composer. Beyond performances and broadcasts, Maconchy was occupied with more educational pieces for Faber, as she finished up her work for the Essex Youth Orchestra, *An Essex Overture*, and her new string quartet, which the Macnaghten concerts had commissioned.

The première of the String Quartet No. 8 (1966–7) took place on 5 April at a Macnaghten Concert held at the Purcell Room in London, featuring the Aeolian Quartet. While the work embodies Maconchy's established musical idiom, with each of the four movements linked to an idea presented at the first movement's opening, this quartet represents a stark departure from Maconchy's earlier quartets, particularly in her play with timbre. The unifying material upon which all four movements are based is the opening chord of the first movement, Lento: two perfect fifths separated by a diminished fifth (Example 11.1). As the movement proceeds from this initial chord, a contrasting idea is presented in an invigorating allegro section with the pace accelerating as this secondary theme is developed contrapuntally. In the ensuing poco lento section, minor thirds and a cantabile theme first introduced in the cello take prominence as the incorporation of the opening material brings the movement to a quiet but invigorating close.

The second movement, Scherzo, begins with a pattern of repeated eighth notes interspersed with sections of pizzicato. Though the second movement has an acidic bite, it is tempered by a rich theme in the viola based upon thematic material in the allegro section of the first movement. The viola's theme then leads into a tranquillo section, offering a respite from the movement's earlier intensity before the opening material returns with ferocity in a final section replete with double stops. The movement ends with the return of the opening pattern of repeated eighth notes, which Maconchy has inverted.

The third movement, also titled Lento, is written in a free tempo and exemplifies Maconchy's penchant for expansive melodies and intricate counterpoint. Indeed, she later remarked that this movement perfectly illustrated her approach to writing music as 'an impassioned argument', which is brilliantly expressed in the exchanges between the first violin and viola.[16]

The fourth movement, Allegro, opens with a syncopated rhythm as double stops, minor thirds, and a dotted rhythm first introduced in the viola serve as the predominant thematic material.

Maconchy's return to writing for string quartet after an eleven-year hiatus was met with universal acclaim, with the critic in the *Times* writing:

> Although the music of Elizabeth Maconchy has maintained over the years a remarkably consistent level of achievement it has never quite received the kind of attention which her qualities as a composer seem to merit. In her impressive series of string quartets especially she has devoted herself with a rigorous self-control and an admirable integrity to what are fundamental problems of growth and form. And her latest addition to the series … takes one step further

[16] Maconchy, 'Elizabeth Maconchy On Writing String Quartets'.

Example 11.1. Maconchy, String Quartet No. 8, mvt. I, opening. Copyright © 1970 by Faber Music Ltd. Reproduced by permission of the publishers. All rights reserved.

> her 'impassioned pursuit of an idea'. Like its predecessors, it is concise in form, severe in tone and extremely economical. … Indeed in its refusal to make any concessions to the more sensuous character of the instruments it sounds at times almost too bare and arid, and yet this very discipline becomes in the end its own self-justification.[17]

In the *Sunday Times*, Felix Aprahamian remarked: 'Having been present at the public birth of most of its predecessors over a period of more than thirty years, I find this the finest of the series.'[18]

[17] R.L.H., 'Disciplined composer', *Times*, 6 April 1967.

[18] Felix Aprahamian, 'Barenboim, Maconchy, and Mimi', *Sunday Times*, 9 April 1967.

Though Maconchy had lamented over a lack of commissions earlier in the year, her fortunes soon changed when she received a letter from Ernest Warburton, Head of Music at Bishop's Stortford College, regarding a commission for an opera to mark the school's centenary in 1968. Several years prior, Maconchy had played portions of *The Three Strangers* to Warburton when he was considering mounting a production of the opera in Oxford. With limited time to compose a two-act opera on such short notice, they settled on a plan to première *The Three Strangers* along with a new work to accompany it.[19] For the new work, Maconchy settled on *The Birds*, an ancient Greek comedy by Aristophanes, which she began later in the year. Beyond the commission from Bishop's Stortford College, she also received a commission from composer Richard Rodney Bennett (1936–2012) and pianist Susan Bradshaw (1931–2005) for a piano duet, *Preludio, fugato e finale*. Maconchy had known Rodney Bennett for quite some time with the two becoming acquainted during his childhood when he wrote to her seeking advice on some of his early string quartets.[20] Later in the year another commission arrived from the Cheltenham Festival for an orchestral work, *Cloudscapes*, which was premièred at the following year's festival.

On 9 May, Maconchy and LeFanu departed England for a holiday in Ireland. Though Maconchy received a couple of broadcasts in Ireland, with a performance of her Violin Sonata also taking place later in the year, the influx of performances she received remained largely confined to England. Following her return to England on 25 May, Maconchy quickly found herself back at work, attending a Composers' Guild Executive Committee meeting the following day. Maconchy's work on the Executive Committee would come to an end a few months later when she decided to step down owing to her disagreement with the Guild's decision to give the organisation greater collective power over its members.[21]

On 3 June, *Propheta Mendax* was featured in a concert at the Aldeburgh Festival, performed by the Vienna Boys' Choir. The performance, which was also recorded, left Maconchy deeply dissatisfied. Following the broadcast of the work on 19 October, Maconchy lamented in a letter to Williams,

> the V.B.C seem to concentrate exclusively on making a beautiful sound – no attack or variety of expression. How I longed for accents & attack & humour! & enjoyment. – I chose those words because I thought boys would enjoy singing them – but if they did, it didn't sound like it, did it? After hearing it I felt that as usual I'd missed the bus – that it was far too difficult, & that it is useless to write dramatic counterpoint (a thing I specially like trying to do; in opera most, of course – I feel it is the essence of opera...) & how much, much more simply Ben makes his effects, & how much more effective they are. ... It's disheartening never to have a good performance – isn't it? [W]hen one does have a performance at all![22]

[19] Elizabeth Maconchy to Grace Williams, [after 9 but before 22] April 1967.

[20] Rodney Bennett discusses this in Margaret Williams's 1985 documentary on Maconchy.

[21] Elizabeth Maconchy to Grace Williams, 2 August 1967.

[22] Elizabeth Maconchy to Grace Williams, 24 October 1967.

Given the high level of difficulty of some of her choral works during this period, it is unsurprising that performances would suffer. A broadcast recording of *Nocturnal* by the BBC Chorus on 25 July suffered a similar fate:

> I was rather disappointed in the perf. of 1st & 2nd parts – particularly the lack of freshness & spontaneity in No 1 – but thought the 3rd (Shelley) very good. ... It really sounded better & more as I meant it to when the Schola Cantorum at Oxford did it for my birthday concert. No – there never seems to be enough rehearsal for good professionals to get inside the music & let their own natural musical feeling (in phrasing, rhythm etc) come out in the music.[23]

Towards the end of the year, Maconchy primarily devoted her time to revising *The Three Strangers* and working on *The Birds*. However, performances were not neglected in the final months of the year, with a recording of *Music for Woodwind and Brass*, played by the BBC Scottish Symphony Orchestra and conducted by Graham Treacher, featured in a BBC broadcast on 2 November. Shortly thereafter, on 12 November, her *Theme and Variations* was included in a concert at the Victoria & Albert Museum featuring the Jacques Orchestra. Despite the work now being over twenty years old, it was praised in the press, demonstrating the ability of Maconchy's music to stand the test of time. Further performances also took place abroad, with her Sonatina for String Quartet performed by the Ringelberg-Quartett at a concert at the Mannheim Music Festival in Germany on 5 December. Her carols also received an increasing number of performances around Christmas time, both at home and abroad, with a performance of *Christmas Morning* in New York, thus ending the year on a triumphant note.

On 3 January, the String Quartet No. 8 was featured in a Radio 3 programme, the first installment of a new weekly series titled *British String Quartets*. In addition to Maconchy's quartet, the programme also featured Egon Wellesz's String Quartet No. 5 (1943) with pre-recorded introductions from both Maconchy and Wellesz.[24] The broadcast left Maconchy disheartened, as she detailed in a letter to Williams:

> I felt detached & un-moved & cold & hard towards it when I heard the broadcast – which made me feel it is perhaps cold & hard & un-moving itself. I've liked it better again listening to a recording – but think perhaps it is too tightly constructed, & not spontaneous enough. I do still like the slow mvt – & am so overjoyed that you do. ... I am in course of correcting the proofs... & must have a real heart-search & see if it must be changed at this 11th hour, before it's quite too late.[25]

[23] Elizabeth Maconchy to Grace Williams, 2 August 1967.

[24] Both of the quartets were played by the Aeolian String Quartet. Despite the series title, the programme was not strictly limited to British string quartets, as Richard Rodney Bennett's Sonatina for Flute was also featured in the programme, along with Mozart's Quartet in D Major, K. 285.

[25] Elizabeth Maconchy to Grace Williams, 8 January 1968.

In addition to the String Quartet No. 8, the first half of 1968 also included a number of broadcasts, with the Quintet for Clarinet and Strings featured in a Radio 3 programme on 14 February, followed by a broadcast of the Sonatina for Harpsichord on 22 April, and a repeat broadcast of *The Sofa* on 12 May.

Premières were not neglected during this period, as Bennett and Bradshaw premièred *Preludio, fugato e finale* (1967) on 16 February at a Macnaghten concert held at the Wigmore Hall. The work received a typically mixed response from critics. In the *Times*, Stephen Walsh stated that the work 'showed an accomplished hand in its fugue but rambled opaquely elsewhere'.[26] Writing in the *Sunday Times*, Aprahamian remarked, 'Miss Maconchy showed her usual sound sense of structure and continuity … where a brittle centre prefaced by gentler strains was followed by an ingenious yet expressive and dramatic conclusion.'[27] A broadcast of the work followed later in the year on 14 July.

In March Maconchy travelled to Wales for the rehearsal and recording of *Variazioni Concertante* featuring the BBC Welsh Orchestra, conducted by John Carewe (b. 1933), which took place on the 13th at BBC Llandaff, with a broadcast of the work taking place on 17 September. The recording had been largely due to the advocacy of Williams. Although Maconchy's stay was short, following the recording Maconchy and Williams found time to visit Llandaff Cathedral before she returned home to Essex.

On 5 June, Maconchy's *The Birds: An Extravaganza in One Act* (1967–8) was premièred as a part of a double bill along with the long-awaited first performance of *The Three Strangers* (1957–8, rev. 1967) at Bishop's Stortford College as part of their centenary celebrations. The programme was produced and directed by one of the College's teachers, John Cole, with Christopher Rees conducting *The Birds* and Ernest Warburton, who was now working for the BBC, conducting *The Three Strangers*.[28] The designer for the production was Charles Dunlop, the brother of Maconchy's son-in-law.

Maconchy composed the music and words for *The Birds* simultaneously, working with both Gilbert Murray's translation and a literal translation by LeFanu. The work opens with two birdwatchers, Pithetaerus and Euelpides, searching for the Birds. They first encounter the Hoopoe, King of the Birds. Pithetaerus convinces the Hoopoe that he sees 'a great future for the race of the birds' with a 'Bird Kingdom' in their future if they only do as he instructs.[29] The Hoopoe then calls to the Birds. Those who respond are suspicious of the two humans, fearing that the Hoopoe has betrayed them. The chorus of Birds then proceeds to attack Pithetaerus and Euelpides, who are barely able to escape. The

[26] Stephen Walsh, 'Unlucky duet', *Times*, 17 February 1968.

[27] Felix Aprahamian, 'The latest thing', *Sunday Times*, 18 February 1968.

[28] From 1977-82, Ernest Warburton (1937-2001) served as Head of Music Programmes at the BBC. From 1982-6 he served as Editor of Music at BBC Radio 3. As a musicologist he was noted for his scholarship on J.S. Bach. See 'Ernest Warburton', *Musical Times* 142/1877 (Winter 2001): 8.

[29] Elizabeth Maconchy, 'The Birds', *Music in Education* 33/335 (January-February 1969): 24.

Hoopoe, however, is eventually able to get the birds to listen and they are soon seduced by Pithetaerus's promises to build a great wall to protect their new city, Cloudcuckooland, with Pithetaerus serving as its dictator.

The work, which is interspersed with spoken dialogue, also features additional solo parts for Robin, the leader of the Birds, and the Nightingale, as well as other visitors to Cloudcuckooland which include a Beat-poet with a guitar and a Schoolmaster who is given a patter song. The satirical work also delves into the tragedy of the human condition through the events that follow Pithetaerus's inspection of the wall's progress. The Woodpeckers are rewarded handsomely for their efforts and are selected to serve as his bodyguards. Along with SS badges to wear, he urges them to sharpen their beaks. As for the Blackbirds, who toiled just as hard, they are segregated from the others, with the Woodpeckers urged to carry out Pithetaerus's orders.

As is evident from the overview of the work above, Maconchy allowed herself substantial liberties with Aristophanes's comedy, details of which she elaborated upon in an article for *Music in Education*:

> The traditional form of the Greek comedy could be kept: the opening scene, with the entry of the Chorus, and the combat scene that follows: then the series of unwelcome visitors who get kicked out in turn.
>
> In the final section the tie-up with Aristophanes could not be so close. The descent of the goddess Basileia and the mystic marriage between her and the opportunist dictator, Pithetaerus, to the acclamation of the Birds simply would not do. Pithetaerus would have been left in triumph to lord over the Birds, with a beautiful bride into the bargain.
>
> My Birds simply would be far too intelligent to let this happen; they might accept Pithetaerus and obey his commands in order to create a great Bird Kingdom, but when he began to show himself in his true colours, to bully the Blackbirds and restrict the freedom of the air, they would throw him out. The piece has a moral which is a plea for freedom.[30]

Maconchy also structured *The Birds* so that a topical issue could be inserted into the work. For the première, the topical episode was written by the producer, John Cole. Cole, who also taught at the school, selected the heavily contested building of nearby Stansted Airport with the visit of a Speculator to Cloudcuckooland. Pithetaerus is in favour of the speculator's plans to build the airport; however, he soon faces a revolt from the Birds, with the Robin declaring, 'We don't want power if it means power to destroy. We want to live our lives in peace', which is followed by a chorus in which the Birds urge the audience to 'have nothing to do with Dictators'.[31]

The Three Strangers was performed after the intermission. The work opens on a stormy night as the Shepherd and his wife celebrate their daughter's birth with a party at their cottage. Owing to inclement weather, the guests decide to stay until the morning. Over the course of the storm and party, three strangers arrive. Seeking shelter from the storm, the First Stranger, Timothy Sommers,

[30] Ibid.

[31] Ibid.

knocks on the door and is welcomed. The Second Stranger is decidedly less amiable than the first, demanding food and drink. He is revealed as The Hangman, who is to hang a man convicted of stealing sheep the next morning. The Third Stranger, Joseph Sommers, then arrives. Shocked to recognise his brother, he makes a quick exit. A gunshot is then heard in the distance, coming from the prison, indicating that a prisoner has escaped. A search party is then formed, capturing Joseph. Eventually, the facts come to light: it is not Joseph but his brother Timothy who is the escaped convict. Joseph is released, with Timothy already long gone.

While the opera is based on *The Three Wayfarers*, Maconchy also incorporated three poems by William Barnes, taken from Thomas Hardy's edition – 'The Gre't Woak Tree that's in the Dell', 'Angels by the Door', and 'Christmas Invitation' – as well as Hardy's poem, 'Not only I'.[32] In looking for inspiration, Maconchy also turned to traditional folk songs, incorporating *The Devil and the Farmer* and *Gaol Song*, which are deftly woven into her atmospheric score. As Maconchy had initially written the work with professional musicians in mind, for her revisions ahead of the première, she made several alterations to reduce the work's difficulty owing to concerns that it would simply be too challenging for the students of Bishop's Stortford College.

Though Maconchy's fears about *The Three Strangers* were realised, reviewers kept a surprisingly open mind. Of her inventive score, Porter wrote in the *Financial Times*,

> To call it a 'folk opera' would be misleading, and might not suggest the skill and resource of Miss Maconchy's score, the unelaborate but telling instrumentation, the sure sense of dramatic incident. *The Three Strangers* … has the directness, the powerful simplicity, the honesty of Hardy's own work. It is certainly an opera which some professional company should take up.[33]

Porter's sentiments were echoed in a review by Blyth in the *Times*: 'Its vocal requirements are well beyond schoolboys' capabilities but the performance was adequate enough to show what a finely atmospheric and subtley [*sic*] poetic piece it should become in fully professional voices and hands. Let us hope it is soon given to them.'[34]

As for *The Birds*, while Blyth as well as Antony Payne in the *Daily Telegraph* praised the satirical work,[35] Porter, a gay man, saw the work and a particularly offensive portion of the dialogue in a much different light:

> Racial hatred is hardly a subject that lends itself comfortably, or amusingly, to 'good-humoured guying.' Nor, perhaps, drug-addiction among the young. A patter-song with the refrain 'from ABC to GCE' was cunningly written and neatly

[32] Thomas Hardy (ed.), *Select Poems of William Barnes* (London: Henry Frowde, 1908).

[33] Andrew Porter, 'Two new operas', *Financial Times*, 7 June 1968.

[34] Alan Blyth, 'Opera for children', *Times*, 6 June 1968.

[35] A.E.P. [Anthony Payne], 'Rare School Double Bill', *Daily Telegraph*, 6 June 1968.

> versified, but indecisive in its satirical attitudes (it is sung by a schoolmaster who one of the birds described, rather surprisingly, as 'a fussy old faggot').[36]

This portion of dialogue, which occurs at the beginning of the topical episode, was written by Cole. While Maconchy did not include the derogatory term in her published score, Porter's arguments as to the suitability of the work are compelling.

On 5 July, *Three Cloudscapes for Orchestra* was premièred at the Cheltenham Festival by the Budapest Symphony Orchestra, conducted by György Lehel. Initially, Maconchy contemplated writing a concerto for de Peyer. However, owing to the geographical challenges and limited rehearsal time, she wisely decided to write a work for orchestra instead. As a result of *The Birds* taking up so much of her time, it was not until early 1968 that she was able to begin the work, which she ultimately felt was rushed.[37] As the work's title implies, *Three Cloudscapes* evokes the atmosphere of changing skies and floating clouds through harsh winds and calm lulls through both the day and night. The work's structure is born out in the opening material, with two chords and a triplet figure serving as the basis for the development of the first movement (or cloudscape), Lento. The second cloudscape, Scherzo, evokes shifting clouds in the wind, accentuated by cadenzas in the woodwind, with Maconchy's extensive use of glockenspiel and celeste adding an ethereal quality and brightness. The second cloudscape leads directly into the third, which begins with a solemn sustained chord in the brass, accented by a theme in the horns as the strings shift between chords supported by the brass with periodic interjections derived from the theme in the horns. As the third cloudscape progresses, a moment of calm serenity is provided in the guise of a sparsely scored section featuring solo violin, followed by the reintroduction and integration of previously introduced thematic material before the movement gradually begins to drift into quietness, evoking the stillness of the skies.

Reception of the work fell along the usual lines. In the *Daily Telegraph*, Gerald Abraham noted that Maconchy 'has not had quite the recognition she deserves'.[38] Words of praise also came from Aprahamian in the *Sunday Times*.[39] In the *South Wales Argus*, Ken Loveland declared Maconchy's ability to evoke picturesque images of the everchanging skies as 'one of the most successful works of its kind to have been brought out at Cheltenham in recent years, and should be assured of a permanent place in the repertory'.[40] Chissell's discussion of the work's 'Lazy string glissandos' was dismissive and condescending, though not quite as scathing as Larner's review in the *Guardian*: 'Perhaps it was wrong to expect too much of a work with a title like that, when a little cynicism and experience might have prepared one for the guileless impressionism that was to

36 Andrew Porter, 'Two new operas', *Financial Times*, 7 June 1968.

37 Elizabeth Maconchy to Grace Williams, 8 May 1968.

38 Gerald Abraham, '"Cloudscapes" shows assured touch', *Daily Telegraph*, 6 July 1968.

39 Felix Aprahamian, 'Hungarian entente', *Sunday Times*, 6 July 1968.

40 Kenneth Loveland, 'Cloud pictures by a late impressionist', *South Wales Argus*, undated clipping, SHC.

come.'[41] Though the work was briefly available for hire from the OUP, Maconchy later decided to have it withdrawn.

Following the disappointment of *Three Cloudscapes*, Maconchy focused her energies on her String Quartet No. 9 (1968–9), which the Radcliffe Trust had commissioned. In late September, Maconchy and LeFanu, who had recently retired from his librarianship at the Royal College of Surgeons, left for a two-week holiday in Italy. This trip, however, nearly didn't happen, as the events of the Prague Spring left Maconchy deeply distressed.[42] She did have at least some pleasant news to celebrate in the autumn when she received word that she had been selected for the Walter Willson Cobbett Medal from The Worshipful Company of Musicians. Suspecting that it was Herbert Howells who was behind the nomination, she wrote to Williams, 'I think he only thought of it because he happened to meet me in the corridor of the R.C.M. with Nicola one day!'[43] The ceremony for this quite unexpected honour took place the following year on 28 January 1969.

Maconchy devoted the early months of 1969 to work on the String Quartet No. 9, which she completed later in the spring. During this time, she was also busy with another work she had begun the previous year: a setting of Dylan Thomas's *And Death Shall Have No Dominion*, which had been commissioned by the Three Choirs Festival. Maconchy also embarked on several new projects in the year, which included a Sonata for Clarinet and Viola, Three Preludes for Violin and Piano, and a setting of Gerard Manley Hopkins's *The May Magnificat* to accompany her settings of *The Starlight Night* and *Peace*, as well as a meagre opera for young children titled *Johnny and the Mohawks*. For a composer who publicly voiced her views against colonial imperialism – in 1966, she lent her name to a list of signatories to a document titled 'The Declaration on Rhodesia' in support of the anti-apartheid campaign – the subject matter of her children's opera, which plays into harmful stereotypes, reveals a blind spot in her political activism.[44]

In the summer, Maconchy began making occasional trips to Dorchester to discuss a new collaboration with Anne Ridler on a masque titled *The Jesse Tree*. Despite enormous enthusiasm on the part of the Dorchester Abbey Festival, a lack of money made the prospect appear dire, as Maconchy wrote in a letter to Williams:

> it is all rather in the melting pot, as they may not be able to get hold of enough money to put it on: they are asking for an Arts Council grant, of course, (& another grant for commissioning it) but don't think they'll get nearly enough! So perhaps it won't come off after all. I've done no work on it yet – just had a few ideas, but I'd like to do it, & hope it will materialise.[45]

On 24 August, Maconchy and her husband travelled to Worcester for the Three Choirs Festival where they stayed with Canon Davies and his wife near

[41] Joan Chissell, 'Maconchy Cloudscapes', *Times*, 8 July 1968; Gerald Larner, 'The Cheltenham Festival', *Guardian*, 6 July 1968.

[42] William LeFanu to Grace Williams, 14 September 1968, private collection.

[43] Elizabeth Maconchy to Grace Williams, 9 January 1969.

[44] 'Declaration on Rhodesia', *Anti-Apartheid News* (July 1966): 1.

[45] Elizabeth Maconchy to Grace Williams, 5 September 1969.

Figure 13. Maconchy with Luigi Dallapiccola, Jonathan Harvey, and Peter Dickinson, at the Three Choirs Festival, 1969 (reproduced by permission of the Maconchy Estate).

the cathedral.[46] The following afternoon, Maconchy attended a rehearsal of her commissioned work. Though she was pleased with the three cathedral choirs' singing, the same could not be said of the Birmingham Brass Consort's playing. Fortunately, some improvements were made throughout the rehearsal, resulting in a performance on the afternoon of the 26th that she was largely satisfied with.[47]

And Death Shall Have No Dominion won praise from Aprahamian in the *Sunday Times*, with a slightly less enthusiastic but nevertheless positive review from Kenneth Dommett in the *Birmingham Post*. Loveland's review in the *Times* was less kind: 'one missed both the consolation and the lyricism of Dylan Thomas's verses but the structural unity of the poem was given strong expression'.[48] Williams suspected that Loveland's radical change in tone was due to outward influences, namely a young woman journalist who covered the poetry section and often accompanied him to concerts.[49]

[46] Ibid.

[47] Ibid.

[48] Kenneth Loveland, 'Cathedral tames imperious Mass', *Times*, 27 August 1969.

[49] Elizabeth Maconchy to Grace Williams, 16 November 1969. Loveland (1915–98), who had no formal musical training, enjoyed a long career in music journalism, writing for the *South Wales Argus*, the *Times*, and *Opera*, among other publications.

On the morning of the 27th, Maconchy participated in a Composers' Forum as part of the Festival's activities. Organised by the Extra-Mural Department of the University of Birmingham with Peter Dickinson (b. 1934) serving as chair, the Forum also featured two other composers who had works featured at that year's Festival: Jonathan Harvey (1939–2012) and Luigi Dallapiccola. Following the Composers' Forum, Maconchy had lunch with Dickinson, returning home to Essex in the evening. In September, Maconchy's time was partially taken up with writing some reflections on Vaughan Williams ahead of her contribution to a film directed by Stanley Williamson. Titled *Omnibus: Ralph Vaughan Williams – A Portrait of an English Composer*, the film was broadcast on BBC1 the following year on 1 March. Shortly after filming, Maconchy and LeFanu took a two-week holiday in Ireland, offering some much-needed rest and relaxation.

October began with a Radio 3 broadcast of the Concertino for Bassoon and String Orchestra on the 2nd featuring the BBC Scottish Symphony Orchestra conducted by James Loughran, with Gwydion Brooke as soloist. Three days later, the work was featured in a concert at the Royal Festival Hall with Brooke and Loughran conducting the New Philharmonia Orchestra. The programme at the Royal Festival Hall also featured Alexander Goehr's *Little Symphony*, Britten's *Serenade*, and Hindemith's *Mathias de Maler*. Owing to a time conflict with a rehearsal at Maida Vale for a recording of *The Three Strangers*, which took place on 12 October with the BBC Northern Singers and Symphony Orchestra conducted by Myer Fredman, Maconchy was able to attend only the second half of the programme, featuring her Bassoon Concertino followed by the Hindemith.

While the majority of attention in reviews of the concert was devoted to the works of Goehr and Hindemith, Maconchy's Bassoon Concertino received some modest praise from Mason in the *Daily Telegraph*, who described the work as 'a typically compact, serious and attractive Concertino'.[50] In the *Times*, Blyth simply described the work as a 'well-made score'.[51] A particular emphasis in the press was the concert's low attendance, with Mason suggesting that the programme's strong emphasis on contemporary works was 'possibly laudable in intention', but 'deterred great numbers of the normally large audience for Sunday night concerts and also imposed a heavy strain on the orchestra'.[52] Blyth was much more scathing in his discussion of the programme, writing,

> Whoever planned last night's New Philharmonia programme ... obviously has a starry-eyed view of what present-day concert-goers are like – or else had decided, masochistically, that he would see just how small an attendance he could get. Four twentieth-century works, none of them with news or curiosity value, whatever their other merits ... was bound to spell box-office disaster. Audiences, who obstinately know what they like, do not owe orchestras, or anyone else, a living.[53]

[50] Colin Mason, 'Music of four decades strain on players', *Daily Telegraph*, 6 October 1969.

[51] Alan Blyth, 'Brilliance of Goehr', *Times*, 6 October 1969.

[52] Mason, 'Music of four decades strain on players'.

[53] Blyth, 'Brilliance of Goehr'.

On 30 October, Maconchy had a visit from Dallapiccola ahead of a performance of his works at the University of Essex.[54] The following day, Maconchy travelled to Sussex for the much-anticipated Radcliffe Music Award competition. The rehearsals and judging took place at the University of Sussex in the morning and afternoon of the 31st, with the selection jury, advisory panel, and judges invited to attend along with a select number of students and other guests.[55] On 1 November, Maconchy's quartet along with the quartets of the three other competitors – Peter Schulthorpe's String Quartet Music, Robert Sherlaw Johnson's String Quartet No. 2, and Sebastian Forbes's String Quartet No. 1 – was performed by the Allegri String Quartet over the course of a morning and afternoon session.

The String Quartet No. 9 (1968–9) opens with the strings in unison. The opening paragraph of the first movement, Allegro, reveals the central motifs of the work: major and minor thirds, major sevenths, diminished fifths, and a four-note motif consisting of C-sharp, D, F-sharp, and D-sharp, in addition to a rising third grace-note figure (Example 11.2). Dynamic and brief, the first movement nevertheless covers a great deal of ground, with frequent changes in tempo and exploration of texture. The second movement, Scherzo and Trio, is arranged in ternary form. Featuring lyrical sections interspersed with lively pizzicato and playful back-and-forth exchanges among the players, the opening of the movement is characterised by ascending and descending minor thirds, which dominate the Scherzo. At the beginning of the Trio, the intervals of a major seventh and diminished fifth are highlighted, thus linking it to the first movement. After the return of the Scherzo, a brief pizzicato coda brings the movement to a close.

Maconchy composed the emotive third movement as a lament to Prague in August 1968. It opens with a freely written section for viola (Example 11.3). Deeply lyrical and passionate with long, weaving melodic lines, sections of the third movement bear a striking resemblance to her String Quartet No. 3, which she wrote for the Hungarian String Quartet. The fourth movement offers a drastic change in mood, opening with a bold statement in the first violin. Syncopated rhythms add dramatic contrast and flair, as material from the previous movements returns, with the work ending on a series of vigorous, repeated minor seventh chords.

The competition was judged by Britten, Thea Musgrave (b. 1928), and Searle, with the announcement of the winner taking place shortly after a tea break in the afternoon. In what was likely a surprise to the competitors, the judges decided that all four composers would share the inaugural Radcliffe Music Award. In a concert of the prizewinning works presented by the Macnaghten

[54] According to a letter Maconchy sent to Williams prior to Dallapiccola's visit, the Italian composer 'likes to sleep for 2 hours before conducting, it seems! So we are going to meet him at Chelmsford, give him lunch, put him to sleep & take him on to Colchester!' Elizabeth Maconchy to Grace Williams, 9 October 1969.

[55] Programme of events provided to Maconchy, SHC.

Example 11.2. Maconchy, String Quartet No. 9, mvt. I, opening. Copyright © Chester Music Ltd. International Copyright Secured. All Rights Reserved. Reproduced by permission of Hal Leonard Europe Ltd.

Example 11.3. Maconchy, String Quartet No. 9, mvt. III, opening. Copyright © Chester Music Ltd. International Copyright Secured. All Rights Reserved. Reproduced by permission of Hal Leonard Europe Ltd.

Concerts in coordination with the Radcliffe Trust, Britten provided the following explanation for the jury's decision:

> We, the Jury, assembled to judge this Competition, organised over a long period with great seriousness and intelligence, have had a fascinating time, reading the scores and listening to the fine playing of the Allegri Quartet. … We have listened carefully and sympathetically to the rehearsals and performances these last two days, and have come to the following conclusion: In spite of, in one case, a brilliantly intelligent gift; in another, a passionate and dedicated career; in the third, a most exciting promise; and lastly, a vivid and original personality, we do not feel that one work stands high above the others, a 'flawless masterpiece'; nor do we feel that any of them lags way behind: a 'ghastly flop'. We would therefore like to divide the prizes equally between the four competitors. We all feel that this has been a most worthwhile occasion to have produced such remarkable compositions – that is, real works of art, and not just 'competition entries'.[56]

Ever the humble composer, Maconchy felt that 'the Solomon judgement was the right one, & given all the circumstances, & the fact that all four really are good 4tets (though I say it) it was the best thing they could do'.[57] Williams, however, would have none of Maconchy's reasoning, believing that Maconchy's demonstrable mastery of the chosen medium of the competition should have put her in the place of an adjudicator as opposed to a competitor. In a letter sent a couple of weeks after the announcement of the jury's decision, Williams wrote, 'I'm sure you should have won it outright. … Just wait till the public performances!'[58]

The performance of the work on 15 January may not have had quite the effect that Williams was so confident it would. In the *Daily Telegraph*, Mason felt that Maconchy's was the quartet that 'impressed as the most purposeful and surest work of the four' despite what he felt was too close a link to Bartók.[59] While the other critics were not as bold as to declare the superiority of Maconchy's quartet over those of her competitors, the piece still received praise in the *Financial Times* and the *Sunday Times*. Reviews in both the *Times* and the *Observer* were less glowing, but still positive. Maconchy's quartet also won considerable praise from her peers, with Lennox Berkeley writing in his diary, 'I have for some time much admired Betty Maconchy and consider her one of the best living English composers – sadly underrated and far too little known.'[60] A recording of the concert was broadcast later in the summer on 5 August on Radio 3.

Following the performance of the Radcliffe Award-winning quartets, the Allegri Quartet played the works at a series of sixteen workshops and

[56] 'Decision of the Jury', published in concert programme, 15 January 1970, SHC.

[57] Elizabeth Maconchy to Grace Williams, 11 November 1969.

[58] Grace Williams to Elizabeth Maconchy, 16 November 1969.

[59] Colin Mason, '4 Quartets in Bartok's Footsteps', *Daily Telegraph*, 16 January 1970.

[60] Lennox Berkeley, January 1970 diary entry in Peter Dickinson (ed.), *Lennox Berkeley and Friends* (Woodbridge: Boydell, 2012), 187.

concerts held at several universities between 19 January and 17 June.[61] Some of these events featured one or more of the composers present, with Maconchy delivering talks at the University of Southampton on 28 January and at the Holywell Music Room in Oxford on 30 January. Listening to additional performances soured her view of the work as she wrote to Williams: 'I'm not all that pleased with my No 9. 4tet (I think 8 is better, – also 5, & 7 probably.) I haven't heard an entirely satisfactory performance yet – the 1st mvt troubles them a lot – they hate the acciaccaturas which somehow put them off & they don't play the mvt. convincingly.'[62]

The early months of the year were filled with performances and broadcasts, including the première of *Conversations for Clarinet and Viola* at a Huddersfield Music Society concert on 12 January, the long-awaited BBC Radio 3 broadcast of *The Three Strangers* on 8 February, and a BBC Midlands broadcast of *And Death Shall Have No Dominion* on 9 February.[63] A week prior, on 2 February, Maconchy also delivered a talk about her chamber music at the Birmingham and Midlands Institute, followed by a talk at the University of Warwick in Coventry on the 3rd.[64] Owing to apprehensiveness on her part, Maconchy ultimately ended up spending more time than she ideally would have liked crafting her talks in January and February. Though she initially found the talks intimidating, the positive reception from the audiences reassured her greatly, and by the time she delivered her final talk in Coventry, she had even begun to enjoy them somewhat.[65] Later in the month, on the 21st, her forty-year-old Piano Concerto was featured in a Cheltenham Chamber Orchestra concert.

Further broadcasts and performances continued in the late winter and spring, beginning with the first broadcast of *An Essex Overture* on 5 March. A couple of weeks later, Maconchy was back in Birmingham for a performance of a slightly revised version of *And Death Shall Have No Dominion* by the University Musical Society at Birmingham Cathedral on the 18th. Later in the spring, *The May Magnificat* (1970) – a setting of another poem of Gerard Manley Hopkins to accompany her settings of *The Starlight Night* and *Peace* – was fittingly premièred on 29 May in a University of East Anglia Choral and Orchestral concert featuring the English Chamber Orchestra conducted by Philip Ledger, with tenor Robert Tear as soloist.[66] The following month, *The Three Strangers* was performed at the Royal College of Music from 10 to 12 June.

[61] The concerts did not feature all four works together as the programmes usually included one or two of the winning quartets along with a quartet by Haydn, Mozart, Beethoven, Schubert, and/or Dvořák.

[62] Elizabeth Maconchy to Grace Williams, 27 January 1970.

[63] *Conversations for Clarinet and Viola* was originally titled Sonata for Clarinet and Viola. Maconchy wrote the work especially for clarinettist Martin Ronchetti and violist John White, who were members of the Stadler Trio.

[64] Maconchy's talks were part of a series titled *British Composers Today*, which was devised by Peter Dickinson as an exploration of twentieth-century British music.

[65] Elizabeth Maconchy to Grace Williams, 21 February 1970.

[66] The concert was repeated the following day in London at the Queen Elizabeth Hall.

Though the calibre of the performers and orchestra did not match the quality of the recording by the BBC Northern Singers, Maconchy was relieved to have an opera that was at last receiving more than two performances.[67]

In the summer and early autumn, most of Maconchy's time was occupied with her collaboration on *The Jesse Tree* with Ridler, which was premièred at the Dorchester Abbey Festival on 7 October 1970. The Abbey's fourteenth-century Tree of Jesse window, comprising stained glass, tracery, and sculpture, inspired Ridler's libretto, for which she provided the following synopsis:

> The Jesse tree of this Masque is something more than the traditional family tree of Christ (as seen in the stone tracery here in the Abbey): it is also the Norse tree Yggdrasil, linking earth and heaven, and it is the tree of the Crucifixion. (There is an ancient tradition connecting the Rood with the death of the Norse god, Balder).
>
> Peregrine comes into the church to rest, and sees the Jesse Tree. Although her name means 'pilgrim', she has no goal, and feels that she belongs nowhere. She falls asleep, and a voice off-stage (Mary's) sings lines about the Tree which introduce the visionary part of the drama, a waking dream in which Jesse, the figure at the root, is interpreter. Peregrine sees first the creation of the world out of fire, then the green growth of the tree, and the drama of Balder, god of brightness. All living things (represented here by the four Elements) take an oath not to harm him, and the other gods hurl sticks at him as a game, thinking him to be safe. But the evil god Loki, knowing that the mistletoe can harm him, puts a shaft of it into the hand of Hodur, the blind god, and Balder is killed.
>
> Then goodness is renewed in Christ, seen in Mary's arms, and the three Kings, whose homage recalls the Elements' pledge to Balder, bring their gifts. But almost at once, Christ's life is threatened, and the children are massacred in his place.
>
> When Christ has grown to manhood, the world waits for him to take possession of his kingdom, but instead, he is dragged in by the Destroyers to be crucified on the World Tree. He mounts his throne, the Cross, and in his suffering we see the agony of the persecuted, of those destroyed by the atom bomb, burnt by napalm. Peregrine at this point tries to intervene in the action, but she is powerless. It is evil that destroys the Son, and yet, because he is the Creator and those whom he created suffer, there is justice (as men see it) in his death.
>
> Men and women come to kneel at the foot of the Tree, and Peregrine speaks for them in her prayer that all things may start afresh, as at the seed-time of the Tree. But the vision fades, and she starts again on her travels, not, now, as 'belonging nowhere', but as 'Actor in some great mystery,
> Branch of a growing tree'.[68]

As the synopsis demonstrates, to state that Ridler's conception was ambitious would be an understatement. Sadly, neither Maconchy's music nor John Piper's beautifully crafted tree for the set could save the work from its overwrought symbolism. Porter's perspective review summed up some of the work's most problematic elements:

[67] Elizabeth Maconchy to Grace Williams [after 18] June 1970. As per her usual practice, she made some additional alterations to the score.

[68] Synopsis of *The Jesse Tree* accompanying the concert programme, SHC.

> During Christ's agony, Jesse invokes Auschwitz, Hiroshima, Vietnam ('He has been burnt with a special fire that clings … they call it napalm'), and Miss Ridler seems to be throwing the whole doctrine of Redemption into question: who is suffering for whom? […]
>
> Miss Ridler's sincerity is not in question; but there is something almost distasteful, very nearly glib, in the result. She invokes terrible things too easily. The most potent images of our age – such as the shadow on a Hiroshima wall which was once a man – are diminished by her treatment. How can she and Miss Maconchy contemplate such things, one asked, and keep the emotional temperature so low? They are not matter for a mild High Anglican pageant.[69]

Fortunately, Ridler, Maconchy, and the producers recognised this as the constructive criticism it was, and alterations were subsequently made to the work, strengthening it significantly.

Following *The Jesse Tree*, Maconchy was busy with her next commission: a work for the 1971 King's Lynn Festival. As part of the festival's celebrations to mark its twenty-first year, King's Lynn commissioned a series of new works. In addition to Maconchy, other composers taking part included Berkeley, Nicholas Maw, and Gordon Crosse. After some contemplation and early sketching of a new setting of Hopkins's *The Leaden Echo and the Golden Echo*, Maconchy decided to embark on a work for mezzo-soprano and orchestra based on Cecil Day-Lewis's poem *Ariadne on Naxos*.[70]

On 14 January 1971, Maconchy's *Music for Double Bass and Piano* was premièred at a Park Lane Group concert at the Purcell Room. That same month, she was about halfway done with her score of *Ariadne*, which she composed with its intended soloist, famed mezzo-soprano Janet Baker (b. 1933), in mind. Later in the spring, Maconchy was informed that Baker had decided that she could not commit to *Ariadne* on account of the level of difficulty of the work.[71] Raymond Leppard then arranged for soprano Heather Harper (1930–2019) to replace Baker. While this was indeed a blow to Maconchy, as replacing Baker with Harper required substantial revisions to the work, a rehearsal in mid-June with Leppard and Harper set her mind at ease.[72]

The première of *Ariadne* took place at the King's Lynn Festival on 30 July 1971 in a programme that also featured the première of Berkeley's *Dialogue for Cello Solo and Chamber Orchestra*. The performance took place in St Nicolas Chapel with The English Orchestra. Like her settings of Hopkins's poems for voice and orchestra, *Ariadne* brilliantly captures the drama of Day-Lewis's poem. Maconchy's score vividly evokes Ariadne's changes of moods of anger and distress after having woken up to discover that Theseus has abandoned her on the island of Naxos. Though the scoring is much more economical than

69 Andrew Porter, 'The Jesse Tree', *Financial Times*, 9 October 1970.

70 Elizabeth Maconchy to Grace Williams, [after 18] June 1970 and 25 September 1970.

71 Elizabeth Maconchy to Grace Williams, 24 June 1971. Maconchy states that, according to Raymond Leppard, Baker's apprehension towards contemporary music was likely the reason she declined it after looking over the score.

72 Ibid. According to Maconchy's appointment diary, a rehearsal occurred on 15 June.

some of her previous orchestral works, it never comes at the price of exploring a vast array of dramatic imagery, as exemplified in Ariadne's desire to strangle Theseus for his betrayal (Example 11.4). The work received marks of high praise in the press, with Stewart Deas declaring in *Country Life*, 'I should be inclined to consider Miss Maconchy's *Ariadne* as one of her major works.'[73]

Though Day-Lewis was able to attend a rehearsal, sadly he was not in attendance for the performance owing to illness. Maconchy did have the support of her husband and daughters in what was surely a busy few days that were also filled with a number of parties. Of the performance, Maconchy wrote to Williams,

> it was all rather exciting. … Heather Harper was superb – produced a beautiful sound & is so intelligent – & Ray Leppard & the orchestra also very good: a nice thing was that the orchestra were very keen & enthusiastic about it. … Harper is v. enthusiastic too, which is nice – & the audience were too! including the Q. Mother, who was full of questions & praises etc.[74]

Following the concert, Maconchy made some slight alterations to the score, which she later dedicated to Harper.

In October, Williams came to visit, giving Maconchy an opportunity to go over some of the new works she was writing, which included *Faustus: Scena for Tenor and Piano*, as well as her String Quartet No. 10, which had been commissioned by the Cheltenham Festival.[75] Shortly after Williams's visit, a talk Maconchy had recorded in September for BBC Radio 3's *The Composer Speaks* series aired on 17 October. The invitation had come from Hans Keller, which came as quite a surprise for Maconchy.[76] In her twenty-minute talk, Maconchy discussed her musical idiom and how she continued to forge on with her music, as well as the pitfalls of ageing:

> Growing old is very unpleasant and the attacks of depression to which a creative artist is subject all through his life become more frequent and formidable – 'Have I still got anything worthwhile to say? – or have all my ideas dried up? – is any of my work any good anyway? Why go on trying?' Most composers go through this sort of thing, I believe, and perhaps it really would be better to retire and leave it to the younger generation.
>
> But despite my interest in the young and in the music they write I do not yet feel I want to stop writing it myself. After a blank patch now and then the urge to write has up till now returned again with its old compulsion – ideas begin to come, and one is off again, planning, writing, scrapping, – with a mounting pile of sheets of manuscript on the floor. Being a composer is a life-sentence from which there is no escape.[77]

73 Stewart Deas, 'When is a Concerto not a Concerto?', *Country Life* (12 August 1971): 376.

74 Elizabeth Maconchy to Grace Williams, 18 September 1971.

75 Grace Williams to Elizabeth Maconchy, 13 October 1971; and Elizabeth Maconchy to Grace Williams, 11 November 1971.

76 Elizabeth Maconchy to Grace Williams, 18 September 1971.

77 Maconchy's talk was subsequently printed in *Composer*. See Elizabeth Maconchy, 'A Composer Speaks – I', *Composer* 42 (Winter 1971–2): 25–9.

Example 11.4. Maconchy, *Ariadne*, bars 86–95.

—(*continued*)

Example 11.4—*concluded*

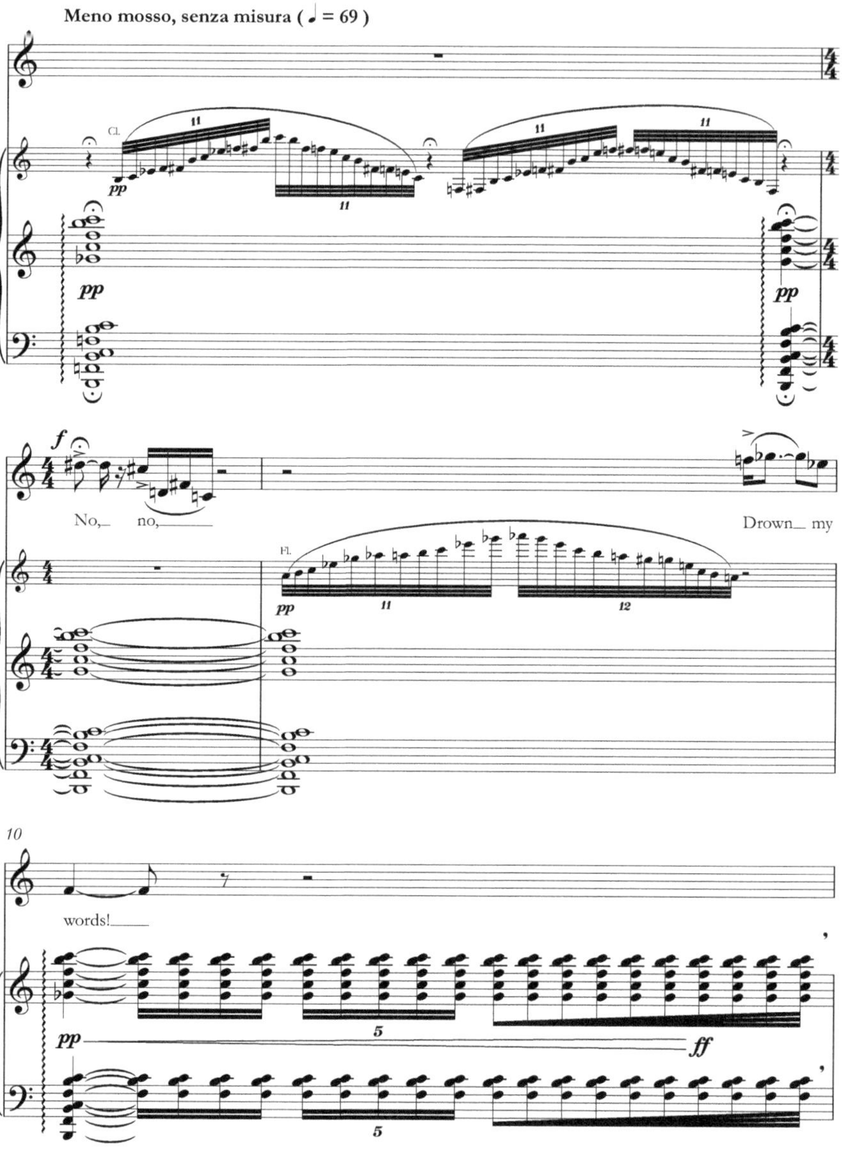

The following month, on 23 November, Maconchy's works along with those of her daughter, Nicola, who was establishing herself as a musical force to be reckoned with, were featured in a *Music in Our Time* broadcast.[78]

By the end of 1971, Maconchy's busy schedule was beginning to take its toll. On the advice of Williams, she took a short break, resigning herself to only copying work.[79] Williams's advice seems to have proved beneficial, and in February 1972 Maconchy was back to work on two new works for oboe: *Three Bagatelles* and Quartet for Oboe, Violin, Viola, and Cello, both of which were completed and premièred later in the year.

On 12 January 1972, Maconchy's newly composed *Faustus: Scena for Tenor and Piano* (1971) was premièred at a Park Lane Group concert. Set to words from the final scene of Christopher Marlowe's play *The Tragical History of the Life and Death of Doctor Faustus*, the dramatic flair of Maconchy's score received praise in the press despite a less than stellar performance from tenor Neil Page.[80] Five days later, *Nocturnal* was featured in a Radio 3 broadcast by the BBC Chorus.

The most exciting performance scheduled for Maconchy in the early months of 1972 was the first London performance of *Ariadne*, which was slated to take place on 11 February at the Queen's Hall, featuring Harper and the English Chamber Orchestra, as in the original première. Unfortunately, disaster struck when a blackout occurred during the second half of the programme, mid-way through Britten's *Six Metamorphoses after Ovid*, op. 49. Though the orchestra was able to continue through Britten's work, they had to forgo the programme's last item: *Ariadne*. This was surely a blow to Maconchy as the second half of the programme was to be simultaneously broadcast. While a concert performance of the work would have to wait until May 1973, a recording of the work made on 13 February was issued later in the year in December by Decca's subsidiary label, L'Oiseau Lyre, along with a recording of Walton's *A Song for the Lord Major's Table* and *Three Songs after Edith Sitwell*.[81]

In the early spring, *Serenata Concertante* was featured in a series of public rehearsals of British music held at the Round House in Camden on 24 April, played by the London Philharmonic Orchestra conducted by Vernon Handley (1930–2008), with violinist Levon Chilingirian. Shortly thereafter, Maconchy travelled to Ireland with her husband for a holiday during which she also attended the première of a work for women's chorus, *Prayer Before Birth*, on 6 May, which had been commissioned by Messrs. Player and Wills (Ireland) Ltd. for the Cork International Choral and Folk Dance Festival. The work was performed by its dedicatees, the Lindsay Singers and their conductor, Ethna

[78] The programme featured Maconchy's String Quartet No. 5, Nicola's Variations for Oboe Quartet and *Il Cantico Dei Cantici II* for unaccompanied voice, as well as works by Robert Sherlaw Johnson, Richard Stoker, and Gilbert Amy Jeux.

[79] Elizabeth Maconchy to Grace Williams, 24 February 1972.

[80] Joan Chissell, 'Park Lane Group', *Times*, 13 January 1972; Robert Henderson, 'Modest scale of oboe and tenor music', *Daily Telegraph*, 13 January 1972.

[81] This recording was largely made possible by financial support from the RVW Trust.

Barror (1915–2011). On their way back from Ireland, Maconchy and LeFanu travelled to Wales for a visit with Williams before returning home to Essex on 22 May. A few days later, on the 28th, *Reflections* and *Conversations* were featured at the Bath Festival in a concert that was recorded for a broadcast that took place on 30 July. Unfortunately the performances were both quite poor, leaving Maconchy disappointed.[82]

On 15 July 1972, Maconchy's String Quartet No. 10 (1971–2) was premièred at the Cheltenham Festival by the Alberta String Quartet. Arranged in a single, continuous movement, the work is cyclical in form with a series of repeated chords at the opening of the work, along with a motif introduced by the viola serving as the primary thematic material that the work builds upon (Example 11.5). Though the work is not a radical advancement upon her individual style, its deeply lyrical nature, combined with contrasting sections that all offer their own variation of the viola's motif, highlight Maconchy's evident mastery of her chosen medium. On the whole, reception of the work was favourable.

Throughout the summer, Maconchy remained busy with her *Three Bagatelles* and Quartet for Oboe, Violin, Viola, and Cello. August turned into a particularly eventful month when Dallapiccola, who was giving a lecture at the SPNM Composer's Weekend in Durham which Nicola had helped to organise, suffered a heart attack. He was first discovered by soprano Jane Manning (1938–2021), who quickly called for an ambulance. After being released from the hospital, he travelled to Shottesbrook where he stayed for a week to recuperate.[83]

As the première of her *Three Bagatelles* approached, Maconchy went through the work with its dedicatees, Valda Aveling (1920–2007) and Evelyn Barbirolli (1911–2008). Despite their enthusiasm for the work, Maconchy had concerns about Barbirolli's playing, as she remarked in a letter to Williams: 'I was rather non-plussed by Evelyn's playing! Really incompetent at times. I think she must have let it go a bit, & I hope can pick up again.'[84] The work was premièred on 23 October 1972 in a concert at the Purcell Room. In spite of Barbirolli's weak playing, the work was recorded along with Aveling and was released by EMI in 1973. The première of the Quartet for Oboe, Violin, Viola, and Cello (1972) by the London Oboe Quartet took place later in the year on 17 December in a concert at the Wigmore Hall, earning positive reviews.[85]

In the latter part of the year, Maconchy began work on a new piece titled *Genesis* for the English Chamber Orchestra to accompany the forthcoming London performance of *Ariadne*. Early in 1973, Maconchy started a new Halloween-inspired choral work titled *Fly-By-Nights* for the Finchley Children's Music Group. Beyond work on her new compositions, Maconchy was also becoming increasingly busy with administrative work, serving

[82] Elizabeth Maconchy to Grace Williams, 4 September 1972.

[83] Nicola LeFanu, interview by author.

[84] Elizabeth Maconchy to Grace Williams, 4 September 1972.

[85] The London Oboe Quartet comprised Janet Craxton (oboe), Perry Hart (violin), Brian Hawkins (viola), and Kenneth Heath (cello).

Example 11.5. Maconchy, String Quartet No. 10, opening.

as Chairman of the SPNM Council. Maconchy's work for the SPNM in the months leading up to the organisation's thirtieth anniversary took up a great deal of her time. In addition to recording a talk on 24 January about the organisation for the BBC's *Music Magazine*, she also wrote an article on the SPNM which appeared in the 29 April issue of the *Listener*.[86]

On 11 March, Maconchy and Nicola were featured in a BBC broadcast titled *Composers on Criticism*.[87] The series, which was broadcast on Radio 3 between August 1972 and April 1973, featured a number of composers discussing their general thoughts on music criticism and its impact on their careers.[88] The points Maconchy raised in her talk – namely, the importance of a critic truly being competent musically – is a vital one as Maconchy knew all too well:

> When I was young I was proof against the expressed opinion of critics, good or bad. It simply didn't matter – had very little impact emotionally and made no conceivable difference to what one was writing. One had no doubt whatever that what one was doing was right – right for oneself, that is –, and no outside view had any relevance.
>
> But slowly as we get older that unquestioning certainty – assurance, if you like – changes. We become less single-minded, see both sides of a question, in life in general or in politics, as well as in art. We acquire what middle-aged people call tolerance, the balanced view. This is giving a flattering name to something that to me is deplorable – the loss of the conviction, the certainty of aim of youth, for the doubts and misgivings of middle-age. Without the armour of unconscious self-assurance, we become vulnerable to the shafts of criticism. It is still true that they do not make any direct impact on one's work, or indeed seem to have much bearing on it – but they do make some impact on one's emotions, the good notices as well as the bad: and since a depression of spirits inhibits the creative faculty and a raising of the spirits seems to release it, one cannot be said to remain totally unaffected by criticism. You have only to read Virginia Woolf's diary to taste the effects of adverse or ill-informed criticism: it is an extreme case, but not an isolated one.
>
> The assumption I am making is that criticism is of no help to a composer in his work, and he is happiest if he can simply ignore it; and of the hastily written day-to-day reports of which reviews of our work almost wholly consist I am afraid this is true. Musical journalism is a condition of life, like the weather, which one simply puts up with. And of course one can never protest or argue, even when, as once happened to me, a critic chose to discuss my flute-writing when there wasn't a flute in the piece.

86 Elizabeth Maconchy, 'Music: Elizabeth Maconchy writes about the Society for the Promotion of New Music', *Listener* (26 April 1973): 561. The programme for *Music Magazine* aired on 4 February 1973.

87 Maconchy and Nicola recorded their contributions to the programme on 14 December 1972.

88 In addition to Maconchy and her daughter, contributors to the series included composers Milton Babbitt, Berkeley, Alan Bush, Justin Connolly, Aaron Copland, Martin Dalby, Iain Hamilton, Alun Hoddinott, John Joubert, Lutyens, Roger Smalley, Tim Souster, and Karlheinz Stockhausen. The final broadcast in the series featured a response from critic Jeremy Noble.

How many of us have ever received a constructive suggestion or piece of critical advice that would be of help to us from any critic? Benjamin Britten once said he hadn't, and most of us would agree. I think the only piece of public criticism that has ever been helpful to me in the craft of composition was a remark by a fellow-composer, Matyas Seiber, many years ago at an S.P.N.M. discussion, when he said he thought I got stuck for too long on the open C string of the cello in one of my string quartets.

It goes without saying that informed and constructive criticism can be extremely valuable and is necessary to a composer. But it must be from someone who knows our previous work and who understands what we is [*sic*] aiming at in the work under discussion. From someone in fact who sees the work from the inside outwards, as a composer does – rather than from the outside inwards, which is how a critic or performer has to look at it. Isn't this the difference between any creative artist and everyone else who isn't? So a fellow-composer is usually the most helpful critic – but it must be someone we can trust to be candid: a mutual admiration party is useless.[89]

On 6 May, *Ariadne* received its delayed first London performance along with the première of *Genesis* at a concert by the English Chamber Orchestra, conducted by Leppard at the Queen Elizabeth Hall in a programme that also featured selections from Mendelssohn's *A Midsummer Night's Dream* and Piano Concerto No. 2 in D Minor, op. 40. The performance of *Ariadne*, which once again featured Harper, was highly praised, with Martin Cooper going so far as to title his review 'Faultless taste in chamber cantata'. The same, sadly, could not be said of *Genesis*, which was largely panned by the critics for failing to live up to expectations wrought by its ambitious subject.[90] As the concert was recorded, the works were featured together in a BBC broadcast on 21 July 1974. Owing to her deep dissatisfaction with *Genesis*, and its poor critical reception, Maconchy ultimately decided to withdraw the work from her catalogue.

[89] Maconchy, draft of 'Composers on Criticism', SHC.

[90] Martin Cooper, 'Faultless taste in chamber cantata', *Daily Telegraph*, 7 May 1973.

12

Recognition at Last, 1973–7

Following a holiday in Italy from 8 to 18 June, Maconchy hit the ground running upon her return to England, attending a concert followed by a supper party at Windsor Castle with Queen Elizabeth II in attendance on the 19th.[1] A couple of days later, Maconchy and LeFanu travelled to Aldeburgh for the première of Nicola's *Paysage* for baritone solo. During her time in Aldeburgh, Maconchy had the opportunity to see a production of Britten's *Death in Venice*, as well as a rehearsal of a work by Lutosławski and a recital by Pears. Then, on the morning of the 25th, she attended rehearsals of her Oboe Quartet, which was performed that evening in an SPNM concert.

Maconchy returned home from Aldeburgh later that night, giving her a day to prepare before her trip to Wales on the 27th to attend a rehearsal and recording by BBC Wales of her Symphony for Double String Orchestra, conducted by Vernon Handley, which was surely due to Williams's continued advocacy. The following month, Maconchy attended the final day of the SPNM Composers' Weekend. Begun in 1967 by composers Don Banks (1923–80), Anthony Gilbert (b. 1934), and Maconchy's future son-in-law, David Lumsdaine (b. 1931), the Composers' Weekend was held annually in the summer and featured a number of lectures, masterclasses, and concerts, as well as a number of discussions.[2]

On 27 July, Maconchy was at the Royal Academy of Music to receive her honorary membership – a gesture that had left her somewhat perplexed as to the reasoning behind it.[3] Following the ceremony, she then travelled to Salisbury for a rehearsal of *And Death Shall Have No Dominion* on the morning of the 28th, with a performance taking place later in the evening as part of the final concert of that year's Southern Cathedrals Festival.

On 7 August, Maconchy was in London for the première of Nicola's *The Hidden Landscape*, which had been commissioned for the Proms. Of the four Proms commissions for 1973, three went to women.[4] Unsurprisingly this drew a great deal of attention in the press, with Edward Greenfield going so far as to declare, 'Sir William Glock denies that he is a convert to Women's Lib!'[5]

1 Elizabeth Maconchy to Grace Williams, 20 June 1973.

2 Elizabeth Maconchy, 'Elizabeth Maconchy writes about the Society for the Promotion of New Music', *Listener* (26 April 1973): 561.

3 Elizabeth Maconchy to Grace Williams, 26 July 1973.

4 The other commissions were Thea Musgrave's Viola Concerto, Priaulx Rainier's *Ploërmel*, and Lennox Berkeley's *Sinfonia Concertante*.

5 Edward Greenfield, 'Proms have own flavor', the *Ottawa Citizen*, 21 July 1973.

While sexism remained a stubborn thorn in every woman composer's side, the barriers facing them were beginning to gain more sustained critical attention, with the second wave of the women's movement bringing about a renewed interest in the topic among historians and musicologists. On 30 September 1973, BBC Radio 3 aired part one of a programme titled *Women as Composers*, featuring Thea Musgrave, Phyllis Tate (1911–87), Williams, Maconchy, and Nicola. Maconchy and Nicola recorded their contributions to the programme on 24 July. In her draft, Maconchy wrote the following:

> That one special day is being devoted to Women in the Arts only shows how widely held is the view that art created by women is in a different category to that created by men.
>
> As a follow-up to this single day's programmes I should like the BBC to put on a concert of anonymous works, and to discover if anyone could tell by listening to them which were by men and which by women.
>
> I'm not trying to say that there is no difference between men and women. The differences are sufficiently obvious, and this division into two sexes conditions our lives physically, psychologically and emotionally from the start. (To say nothing of our practical living conditions.) [...]
>
> But when it comes to the creation of works of art or literature, can conditions ever be equal? Or is the fact of being a woman and of having children, with all the emotional and physical involvement that that entails, too great a handicap? The gross inequality of social conditions in the past, the weighing of the scales against women, is such an old story that one doesn't want to go over it again. It is a story familiar to most people by now.
>
> The fact that in the past no woman composer, painter, sculptor or architect has come near to achieving what the greatest men have achieved seems to me inevitable, taking into account the handicaps women have laboured under. In fields where the handicaps have not been quite so crippling, something has been achieved. There have been great women novelists and a few great poets.
>
> Many of the physical and social handicaps of the past have now disappeared: an intelligent and gifted girl can now get a good education and the technical training she needs, she can earn her own independence, and thanks to the pill she can have her children when she wants them, or not if she doesn't.
>
> There is still a lot to fight for and to fight against; the idea of masculine superiority takes an unconscionable time a-dying. And while a woman has still to fight for equality she can't achieve the detachment and serenity – the wholeness – necessary to the creation of a work of art. [...]
>
> There have certainly been times in the past when I have felt 'If only I was a man'. The lack of recognition, lack of performances and consequent lack of practical experience of the orchestra, and above all, once one had children, always, always the lack of time (because children's needs must come first): those are some of the things one has been up against.
>
> All the same I do like being a woman.[6]

By the time the talk aired, Nicola was in the US, having started a Harkness Fellowship earlier in the month. In her absence, Maconchy attended rehearsals of her works on her behalf in the autumn.

6 Elizabeth Maconchy, draft of talk titled 'Women in the Arts', 14 July 1973, SHC.

In the latter half of the year, Maconchy was also busy finishing up an arrangement of *Samson and the Gates of Gaza* for brass band and chorus, which was performed at a National Federation of Music Societies concert held at the Royal Albert Hall on 13 January 1974.[7] Another work that occupied her time in the final months of the year was a setting of *The Isles of Greece* for The Byron Society's celebrations of the 150th anniversary of Lord Byron's death in 1974. Maconchy was initially apprehensive when The Byron Society first approached her about the commission. However, after reading the poem they had suggested, she found herself deeply inspired and simply unable to say no to the project. While she sketched out the work quickly in the autumn of 1973, scoring took up a substantial amount of her time, forcing her to postpone work on her new composition for cello and strings, *Epyllion*, that she had desperately wanted to devote time to earlier in the year.

Despite the delays for *Epyllion*, Maconchy nevertheless found time to write two songs for voice and harp, which she sent to Peter Pears in December. Any further work was likely hampered by renovations on her house that began in November, as Maconchy remarked in a letter to Williams that the forthcoming disruption would result in her 'making endless trays of tea'; both the dining room and stairs were to be redecorated along with the creation of a new bathroom and work on the garage.[8] Fortunately, Maconchy had a brief respite from the disruption, travelling to Norwich to spend Christmas with Anna and her family, before returning to Shottesbrook to endure more trays of tea as work on the interior of the house continued well into the new year. At the beginning of 1974, Maconchy remained busy with frequent trips to London for SPNM meetings, with her travels made all the more difficult by frequent rail disruptions.[9] Beyond her new arrangement of *Samson and the Gates of Gaza*, some notable performances and broadcasts early in the year included a BBC broadcast of *Prayer Before Birth* on 21 February by the Cantamus Ensemble, a performance of her Oboe Quartet on 9 March by the London Oboe Quartet at an Ipswich Chamber Music Society concert, and a Radio 3 broadcast on 22 March of a recording of the work's performance at the Aldeburgh Festival the previous year. In Ireland, two of her *Six Miniatures for Solo Violin* were featured in a new series of programmes dedicated to twentieth-century works by Irish composers on RTÉ, with 'Lullaby' broadcast on 29 April and 'Roundabout' on 6 May. Maconchy was also busy attending some rehearsals ahead of a series of forthcoming broadcasts of her quartets.[10]

On 21 April, *The Isles of Greece* received its première. Ahead of the event, Maconchy met with Bernard Herrmann in the afternoon of 11 April, presumably to go over the score ahead of rehearsals that took place on the 18th and the morning of the 21st. Exactly whose idea it was to approach Maconchy for the

[7] Elizabeth Maconchy to Grace Williams, 26 July 1973 and 10 December 1973.

[8] Elizabeth Maconchy to Grace Williams, 10 December 1973.

[9] Elizabeth Maconchy to Grace Williams, 11 February 1974.

[10] Ibid.

commission remains unclear: though it was The Byron Society who formally asked her, Herrmann, who was reportedly a fan of Maconchy's music, was heavily involved in the planning, suggesting that he may have had a role to play.[11] The première took place at Drury Lane's Theatre Royal, and in addition to Maconchy's work, the concert also featured Bliss's *Fanfare for Heroes*, Berlioz's *Harold in Italy*, Rossini's *Il Pianto delle Muse in Morte di Lord Byron*, Richard Arnell's *Symphonic Portrait – Lord Byron*, and Liszt's *Tasso, Lamento e Trionfo*, in addition to Byron's speech at the re-opening of the theatre on 10 October 1812, which was spoken by actor Robert Hardy, who also read the poem 'On this day I complete my 36th year'. Herrmann conducted the entire programme.

Of the inspiration behind *The Isles of Greece*, Maconchy provided the following programme note:

> This setting for Chorus and Orchestra is of five stanzas from Byron's 'Don Juan'. They are among his best-known and best-loved poems, and embody his deepest feelings: the consummation of his love for Greece and his passionate concern for liberty. I hope the depth and conviction of his feeling has in some degree communicated itself to the music.
>
> It is a straightforward setting. The character of the musical ideas, the overall shape of the work, and the changes of mood are all suggested by the words. The variety of mood gives plenty of scope, within a tightly constructed framework, for variety in the music. The impassioned invocation of the opening, the lyrical musing of Marathon, the change to 'Standing on the Persians' grave, I could not deem myself a slave' (which gives rise to a resolute tune, echoed later at 'And there, perhaps, some seed is sown, The Heracleidan blood might own') – and the final cry of the liberator: 'A land of slaves shall ne'er be mine – Dash down you cup of Samian wine!'[12]

At the time Maconchy wrote her score, Greece was still in the throes of military dictatorship. According to Nicola, her mother's strong commitment to socialism and liberation likely influenced her eager commitment to the project.[13]

Sadly, this concert served as Herrmann's last public conducting engagement. Though he had envisioned the concert as 'an attempt to recreate the living presence of Byron in music which grew out naturally from his influence and ambience',[14] as Herrmann's biographer, Steven C. Smith has discussed, Herrmann's vision fell far from its intended target and proved to be more of 'an autopsy' than a triumph, due in part to Herrmann's poor health:

> Herrmann's increasing lack of strength … rendered his rudimentary baton technique almost invisible. His entrance that evening was that of a feeble old man who reached the podium long after the applause had ended. From the rostrum

[11] Irving Kolodin, 'The Wide Screen World of Bernard Herrmann', *Saturday Review*, 6 March 1976.

[12] Elizabeth Maconchy, programme note on *The Isles of Greece*, SHC.

[13] Email from Nicola LeFanu to author.

[14] Steven C. Smith, *A Heart at Fire's Center: The Life and Music of Bernard Herrmann* (Berkeley: University of California Press, 1991), 337.

> Herrmann took a labored bow, which elicited a second pathetic smattering of applause from the audience.[15]

With the exception of *The Isles of Greece*, which won praise for its skilful writing that aptly captured the spirit of Byron's poetry, the concert was widely panned by the critics.[16] Though the work was available on hire from Chappell, no records of further performances have been traced.

On 29 April, Maconchy and LeFanu flew to the US, arriving in Boston to visit Nicola who was still on her Harkness Fellowship. In addition to touring various museums, Maconchy visited the music department at Harvard, dining with Earl Kim and his wife Martha at the Acropolis in Cambridge.[17] After approximately a week in Massachusetts, Maconchy and LeFanu spent about a week in New York, making visits to the Metropolitan Museum of Art, the Cloisters, and the Pierpont Morgan Library, as well as a visit to Vilma Löwenbach. Maconchy also fitted in a trip to Alice Tully Hall for a concert of Schönberg's works. After New York they travelled on to Washington DC where they spent several days, before making a day trip to Shenandoah Ridge in Virginia, which was hampered by inclement weather. They then made their way to Baltimore, followed by a trip to New Haven. Finally, they returned briefly to Boston before departing on a three-day trip to Nantucket.

Following her return to England on 29 May, Maconchy attended a rehearsal of *Fly-By-Nights* on the 31st ahead of its semi-staged première that evening in a concert at St George's Church, Hanover Square, London, by the Finchley Children's Music Group, conducted by John Andrews and featuring harpist Osian Ellis. Then in June, Maconchy was busy looking over scores for the Cobbett Prize, which she was judging that year, in addition to serving as an adjudicator for the Radcliffe Music Award.

Notably, performances and broadcasts of Maconchy's works were becoming increasingly frequent, with no fewer than twenty-five known to have taken place in 1974.[18] Ahead of the BBC's forthcoming series on her string quartets, Maconchy rehearsed String Quartet No. 5 with the Lindsay Quartet on 8 June, with the group recording the work later in the summer. She then made a brief trip to Aldeburgh for the première of Thea Musgrave's opera *Voice of Ariadne* on the 11th. Then, on the 13th, she was at Broadcasting House for the Gabrieli Quartet's recording of String Quartet No. 1, returning once again on the 18th

15 Ibid.

16 See Martin Cooper, 'Eloquence of Maconchy and Byron Concert', *Daily Telegraph*, 22 April 1974; Ronald Crichton, 'Byron Concert', *Financial Times*, 22 April 1974; Keith Horner, 'Irony for poet's ghost', *Times*, 22 April 1974.

17 Earl Kim (1920–98) was a distinguished composer and pedagogue who enjoyed a long teaching career at both Princeton (1952–67), and Harvard (1967–90). Martha Potter is a noted violinist. See Anthony Tommasini, 'Earl Kim, 78, Noted Composer of Austere and Dazzling Works', *New York Times*, 26 November 1998.

18 This includes broadcasts and concerts that also took place in the US and in Ireland. Between 1975 and 1977, Maconchy continued to average around two dozen performances of her works a year.

Figure 14. LeFanu and Maconchy during their trip to the US, 1974 (reproduced by permission of the Maconchy Estate).

for the Lindsay Quartet's recording of String Quartet No. 5. The following day, Maconchy was back in Aldeburgh to rehearse her *Three Songs for Tenor and Harp* with Pears and Ellis, which included the two songs she had sent to Pears in December – a setting of Shelley's *A widow-bird sate mourning* and Byron's *So we'll go no more a-roving* – along with a newly composed song set to Thomas Campbell's *The knot there's no untying* which she had written at the request of Pears.[19] Maconchy's *Three Songs* was premièred later that evening by Pears in a recital at the Snape Maltings Concert Hall as part of that year's Aldeburgh Festival.

In September, Maconchy and LeFanu departed on a four-week holiday, beginning with a visit to Hamburg to see Anna and her children who were briefly living there. They then travelled to Italy, where they spent their time exploring Florence, Pisa, Mazzola, Volterra, Assisi, and Siena. They also visited

[19] After going through *A widow-bird sate mourning* and *So we'll go no more a-roving* with Ellis, Pears felt that the two songs would benefit from a third more melancholic song. Peter Pears to Elizabeth Maconchy, [1974], private collection.

Example 12.1. Maconchy, *Sirens' Song*, rehearsal number 1.

Dallapiccola and his wife on 1 October before returning home on 3 October. Maconchy spent the autumn working on *Epyllion*, as well as settings of two part songs for the Cantamus Ensemble, titled *Two Epitaphs*, in November.[20] Later that month, on the 23rd, a work Maconchy had completed earlier in the year titled *Sirens' Song* was premièred by the Louis Halsey Singers.

The text for the piece comes from William Browne's poem, 'Steer, hither steer your winged pines, All beaten mariners', taken from his 1614 masque, *Circe and Ulysses*. Maconchy's setting opens with the sirens trying to lure the mariners, who eventually answer their call (Example 12.1). As Roma has observed, Maconchy's scoring for when the sirens sing the word 'steer' bears a resemblance to Debussy's *Sirènes*, a score that Maconchy was familiar with during her RCM days. In the years to come, earlier influences would start to creep in once more, becoming increasingly frequent features of Maconchy's works.[21]

[20] In the summer of 1973, Maconchy mentioned in a letter to Williams that she wanted to write part songs for a choir in Mansfield, which was most likely a reference to Pamela Cook's Cantamus Ensemble, which was based in Mansfield. Maconchy initially referred to the work as *Two Elegies*, later changing the title to *Two Epitaphs*. In a letter to Williams, Maconchy remarked that she wrote the work over one or two days. Elizabeth Maconchy to Grace Williams, 27 May 1976.

[21] See Catherine Roma, *The Choral Music of Twentieth-Century Women Composers: Elisabeth Lutyens, Elizabeth Maconchy, and Thea Musgrave* (Lanham, MD: Scarecrow Press, 2006), 78–81.

As Chairman of the SPNM's Council, Maconchy continued to make frequent trips to London. On 3 February, her String Quartet No. 10 was featured in a concert as part of a new SPNM series titled *The String Quartet Today*. Held at the Waterloo Room at the Royal Festival Hall, Maconchy's work was introduced by Hugh Wood and played by the Gabrieli Quartet.[22] Maconchy was apprehensive about the focus on her given what she felt was an inherent conflict of interest owing to her position as Chairman. Wood, however, was apparently adamant about the matter, with Maconchy eventually relenting.[23] As an administrator, those who worked with Maconchy found her to be a very effective leader. While known for her kindliness and soft-spoken nature, she was straightforward without being authoritarian, allowing others to be heard. She undoubtedly had a gift for diplomacy, and Gilbert credited her open-mindedness for encouraging ideas to be developed, even if she disagreed with the feasibility of proposals initially. Above all, she was a staunch supporter of young composers and made a concerted effort to ensure that people felt welcome and included.[24]

In the spring, Maconchy revisited the topic of women composers, delivering a talk at the Incorporated Society of Musicians' 77th Annual Meeting, which was held in Bristol on 3 April. Titled 'A Woman Composer in a Man's World', Maconchy's talk delved into issues she had brought up years earlier in her contribution to *Composer*, as well as in her more recent BBC talk. A draft reveals she was markedly more forceful in expressing her disdain for the term 'woman composer': 'I don't like this term Woman Composer: it bolsters up the view that Art created by women is in a different category to that created by men. (It would be equally logical, wouldn't it? to have a special category for homosexual composers?)'[25]

After devoting much of her time to the SPNM over the previous two years, Maconchy stepped down as Chairman of the Council in the spring. This gave her some much-needed time to devote to her own compositions, many of which she had had to neglect. In addition to continued work on *Epyllion*, Maconchy also had a new large-scale project on the horizon: another collaboration with Ridler, this time on a children's opera titled *The King of the Golden River*, after Ruskin's well-known novel.[26]

On 5 May, an updated talk Maconchy had recorded on her string quartets aired on Radio 3 ahead of a series of six programmes featuring her works alongside string quartets by Schubert. This series took place on Friday afternoons, running from 9 May to 13 June, beginning with String Quartet No. 1 on the 9th (Gabrieli String Quartet), String Quartet No. 5 on 16 May (Lindsay String

[22] The series consisted of four programmes with illustrated talks held on Mondays from 20 January to 10 February.

[23] See Elizabeth Maconchy to Grace Williams, 29 January 1975.

[24] Anthony Gilbert, interview by author.

[25] Elizabeth Maconchy, draft of talk titled 'A Woman Composer in a Man's World', 3 April 1975, SHC.

[26] Maconchy completed a rough draft of *The King of the Golden River* in mid-June. Elizabeth Maconchy to Grace Williams, 18 June 1975.

Quartet), String Quartet No. 7 on 23 May (Alberni String Quartet), String Quartet No. 8 on 30 May (Aeolian String Quartet), String Quartet No. 9 on 6 June (Allegri String Quartet), and concluding with String Quartet No. 10 on 13 June (Gabrieli String Quartet).[27] Of the groups, Maconchy felt that the Alberni String Quartet were the weakest, struggling in particular with the first movement of String Quartet No. 7.[28]

The series received scant notice in the press with Desmond Shawe-Taylor writing in the *Sunday Times*,

> Her logical, often elliptical, designs and keen feeling for the medium afford continual pleasure, especially in the toughly argued, somewhat Bartókian No. 7 and the boldly exploratory No. 8, with its structure ingeniously based on a pair of harmonically distant super-imposed fifths.
>
> Time was when such a series would have enjoyed one of those invaluable introductory articles that used to adorn the pages of The Listener; but the decline in musical coverage and standards in that journal is a sad story. While the BBC's range of transmitted music continues to compare favourably with that of any other country in the world, there can be few of them, if any, which do so little as the Corporation now does to help the intelligent public with the printed work. Both Radio Times and [The] Listener have abandoned this attempt.[29]

Shawe-Taylor further grumbled about the BBC's decision to feature the series in the afternoons, arguing that the programme 'deserves an evening repeat'.[30]

The neglect of promotion in the *Listener* is perhaps not surprising, echoing general biases in their coverage. Aside from a brief notice on 3 April, no detailed discussion of the series appeared, aside from a glib remark by Christopher Driver.[31] It was not until the end of the year that the series garnered any further discussion. In an article summing up the BBC's music programming, Hugo Cole praised the organisation's diversity of programmes while also, perhaps unwittingly, acknowledging much of Shawe-Taylor's criticism: 'Six of Elizabeth Maconchy's quartets were played on Friday afternoons in May and June for no apparent reason except that she is an excellent and neglected composer (in fact, the best of reasons).'[32]

A few days after the broadcast of String Quartet No. 10, a commissioned work Maconchy wrote for Janet Craxton and Alan Harveston – *Touchstone for Oboe and Chamber Organ* (1975) – was premièred by its dedicatees at the

[27] The Gabrieli String Quartet was established in 1966 and consisted of Kenneth Sillito (1st violin), Brendan O'Reilly (2nd violin), Ian Jewel (viola), and Keith Harvey (cello). The Alberni String Quartet was formed in 1962 and featured Howard Davis (1st violin), Peter Pople (2nd violin), Roger Best (viola), and David Smith (cello). The Lindsay String Quartet comprised Paul Cropper (1st violin), Ronald Birks (2nd violin), Roger Bigley (viola), and Bernard Gregor-Smith (cello).

[28] Elizabeth Maconchy to Grace Williams, 18 June 1975.

[29] Desmond Shawe-Taylor, 'The classical touch', *Sunday Times*, 8 June 1975.

[30] Ibid.

[31] Christopher Driver, 'Violinists', *Listener* (12 June 1975): 785.

[32] Hugo Cole, 'A year of discovery', *Listener* (25 December 1975): 886.

Queen Elizabeth Hall in London as part of the Greater London Council's series of chamber organ concerts. The concert, which took place on 17 June, also included works by Krebs, Telemann, Scheidemann, Kerll, Badings, Boëly, Cherubini, Haydn, Britten, and J.S. Bach. The short, five-minute work was inspired by the character Touchstone in Shakespeare's *As You Like It*. True to the work's namesake, Maconchy described the work as embodying 'the quips and quirks of the fool' while also delving into some contemplative themes.[33]

Beyond the broadcasts of Maconchy's string quartets, the two most important performances for Maconchy in 1975 were the premières of *Epyllion* and *The King of the Golden River*. *Epyllion* (1973–5) was premièred at the final concert of that year's Cheltenham Festival on 13 July. Arranged for cello and strings, *Epyllion* was inspired by the Greek word for a short, narrative epic poem. Given that Maconchy began the work a couple of years after *Ariadne*, one may wonder if the work could have taken some of its inspiration from Catullus's Hellenistic epyllion, *Ariadne*. According to Nicola, however, much of the inspiration for the work came from a trip to Venice:

> [Maconchy] said the wonderful sound early in the morning of … all the deep, deep sounding bells, and then the screaming of the swifts as the birds flew high in the sky … got into her ears, and you can hear the orchestral strings being the deep bells and the cellist, very high with harmonics – the screaming swifts.[34]

As Mathias has explored, the repetitive tritone chords can be seen as embodying the tolling chords, with the first entrance of the cello representing what Nicola describes as the swifts flying overhead (Example 12.2). In terms of Maconchy's compositional approach, there is, as Mathias discusses, some similarity to *Serenata Concertante* in regard to the relationship between the soloist and strings.[35] Another work in which Maconchy explored this relationship was in her *Dialogue for Piano and Orchestra* (1940–1). *Epyllion* itself is deeply expressive, combining the brilliance of Maconchy's deft orchestration as exemplified in *Nocturne* with the intensity and exploratory play with texture and timbre in her quartets, exemplified in her use of free writing and abundant use of harmonics as the interval of a tritone binds the work together.[36]

In the *Sunday Times*, Aprahamian praised the work highly:

> [*Epyllion*] should prove a godsend to string orchestras wishing to set a cellist in relief. … The score shows the ever-youthful and open-minded composer using several present-day techniques. Happily, they are completely integrated in music which sounds as personal as ever, with the familiar tritonal tensions and eloquent harping on repeated-note formulae. This is a work both useful and beautiful.[37]

[33] Elizabeth Maconchy, programme note on *Touchstone*, SHC. A recording of the concert was broadcast later in the year on 3 November on Radio 3.

[34] Quoted in Mathias, *Lutyens, Maconchy, Williams and Twentieth-Century British Music*, 235.

[35] See Ibid., 235–9.

[36] LeFanu, 'Elizabeth Maconchy DBE (1907–1994)'.

[37] Felix Aprahamian [untitled clipping], *Sunday Times*, 20 July 1975.

Example 12.2. Maconchy, *Epyllion*, mvt. I, opening.

—(*continued*)

Example 12.2—*concluded*

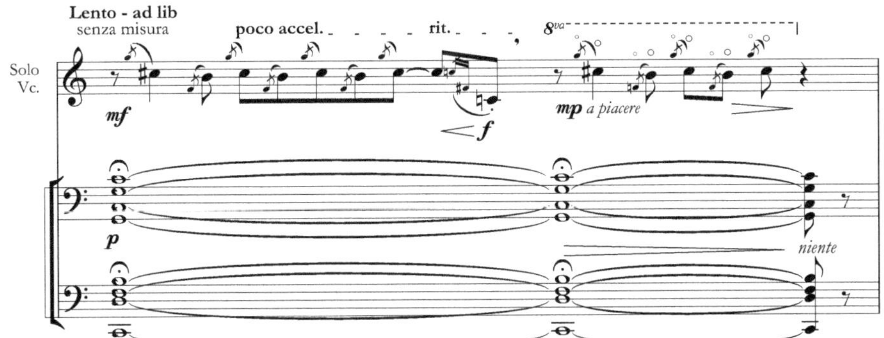

Though Stephen Walsh's review in the *Times* was less generous, praise of the work also came from Gillian Widdicombe in the *Financial Times* and Gerald Larner in the *Guardian*, with the latter remarking, 'So Elizabeth Maconchy, who is one of the senior composers on the British musical scene, still has ears and a mind open to new sounds. That, combined with her long experience in scoring for strings and her imaginative resources, should have Epyllion a regular item on Academy programmes.'[38] Maconchy summed up her own thoughts about the première in a letter to Williams:

> it was a good performance, Ken Heath (though not one's ideal of a cellist) did play remarkably well – & the strings, who were most disappointing at the rehearsal, late on the Friday evening, came on very well at the Sunday rehearsal & even more at the performance – though they could play it better, if more familiar with it: but will they ever play it again, I wonder? Neville M. really hates doing anything new, I'm afraid – & is quite at sea as to how to conduct even a mild 'free' passage![39]

As always, Maconchy subsequently made some slight adjustments to the score.

Though Maconchy remained busy in the summer with *The King of the Golden River*, during a short break while the parts were being prepared, she found time to set two of Gerard Manley Hopkins's poems – 'Pied Beauty' and 'Heaven-haven' – for the Salisbury Cathedral Choir.[40] Arranged for chorus and brass, these two settings, which came to bear the title *Two Settings of Poems by Gerard Manley Hopkins*, were premièred the following year at the Southern Cathedrals Festival.

In the autumn, Maconchy was in Oxford for rehearsals ahead of the première of *The King of the Golden River*, which ran from 29 October to 1 November at the University Church of St Mary the Virgin, which had commissioned the

38 Gerald Larner, 'Academy of St Martin in the Fields', *Guardian*, 14 July 1975.

39 Elizabeth Maconchy to Grace Williams, 17 November 1975.

40 Maconchy completed her short score of *The King of the Golden River* on 17 June, later finishing the full score in August.

work. The opera is arranged in seven scenes, with Ridler's libretto loosely adapted from Ruskin's story of the same title. Though Ridler took some liberties in her adaptation – for instance, all the characters are renamed – the general outline and themes remain largely the same.

The opera, which is not entirely sung but also features spoken dialogue, was conducted by David Whittington and produced by Katherine Ross, with set designs by Peter Pelz. The cast comprised amateurs with the exception of the role of the King, which was taken on by baritone Peter Reynolds. Maconchy's music for the opera, which she scored for strings, oboe, flute, clarinet, bassoon, horn, percussion, trumpet, organ, and recorders, is playful and enchanting, particularly the Schoolmistress's rhyming ABCs lesson.

The production was not without its challenges, however, with many disagreements among the project's collaborators. Though Maconchy wanted to include a part for harp, a harpist was unable to be procured, despite securing additional funding for the production from the Vaughan Williams Trust and the George Butterworth Memorial Trust. Maconchy also objected to the casting of Sheila Southern, the wife of Richard Southern, President of St John's College, in the role of the Schoolmistress, whom she felt did not have the adequate technique to project her voice.[41] Maconchy was far from thrilled with the performances, but they did at least manage to exceed her expectations after an especially disastrous dress rehearsal.[42]

Fortunately, the collaborators eventually arrived at a compromise, with a professional, Carol Lethaby, replacing Southern for the BBC's recording of the work. By the time the recording took place on Sunday 29 October, the cast also had a much firmer grasp of the work, which helped tremendously. The broadcast of *The King of the Golden River*, which took place on 19 April 1976, garnered positive reviews in the press, with Chissell, who was often quite critical of Maconchy, praising the atmospheric score.[43] Following the broadcast, Ridler and Maconchy set about making substantial alterations to the score, which they completed later in the year.

Towards the end of 1975, Maconchy was dealt a blow when one of her publishers, Chappell, decided to downsize its classical music division. Maconchy had signed a three-year contract with the publisher in 1974, which gave them the right of first refusal for her scores. Though Chappell offered to continue to honour their agreement, they also gave Maconchy the option to be released from her contract. Maconchy opted for the latter and had the copyrights of nearly twenty works returned to her in early 1976. She was understandably upset by this change in circumstances and the substantial disruption it brought to lending her works. Not long after the debacle with Chappell, Chester Music expressed an interest in taking up some of her scores, initially agreeing to publish six of the works that Chappell had relinquished. While Maconchy did not

41 Extensive letters detailing the trajectory of the opera are held at SHC.

42 Elizabeth Maconchy to Grace Williams, 17 November 1975.

43 Joan Chissell, 'Children's Opera', *Times*, 20 April 1976.

sign an exclusivity contract with Chester, all of her works from 1976 onwards would be published by the firm.

Throughout the year, Maconchy continued to be busy with a number of recent commissions, which included a Sinfonietta (1975–6) for the Essex Youth Orchestra; her String Quartet No. 11 (1976–7) for the City Music Society; *Morning, Noon and Night* for Pears and Ellis; and *Héloïse and Abelard* (1975–8) for the Croydon Philharmonic Society. In the summer, she was forced to take a break from the latter in order to rescore *The Three Strangers* ahead of its performance, along with her other two one-act operas, which were being mounted in a triple bill by Opera Nova in 1977. Performances and broadcasts were also not neglected, with the Cantamus Ensemble's première of *Two Epitaphs* in a Radio 3 broadcast on 4 May and a repeat of Maconchy's series of quartets that ran from September to the end of November. While the majority of works that received performances during this period were confined to smaller-scale works, a performance of *Proud Thames* was featured in a concert on 29 October by the London Chanticleer Orchestra, conducted by Gipps.

In November, Maconchy received exciting news from Kenneth Stowe, Prime Minister James Callaghan's principal private secretary, that Callaghan intended to submit Maconchy's name to the Queen with a recommendation for the appointment of CBE.[44] Maconchy wrote back to Stowe, letting him know that she would be glad to have her name forwarded, further noting that she wished to have her maiden name used as opposed to her legal name, LeFanu, if the honour was to be conferred.[45]

On 1 January, Maconchy's name was included in the Queen's New Year Honours list, heralding a wonderful start to the many birthday celebrations that would mark her seventieth year. Maconchy spent part of the day at Ursula Vaughan Williams's home, spending the night before travelling to Manchester for a recording of *Music of our Time*, to be broadcast in March. Any early celebrations, however, were marred the following month by Williams's death on 10 February. Though she had been in poor health for some time as she underwent treatment for a malignant cyst, the loss of Maconchy's closest confidante for the past fifty years was immense. Later in the year, Maconchy contributed to an issue of *Welsh Music* which featured a memorial to Williams.[46]

Maconchy's investiture ceremony took place at Buckingham Palace on 8 March. For the ceremony and reception, she was accompanied by her husband and two daughters. Seven days later, her *Music of Our Time* broadcast was aired on Radio 3. In addition to an introduction she provided, the programme also featured her *Settings of Poems by Gerard Manley Hopkins* and *Epyllion*, as well as

[44] Kenneth Stowe to Elizabeth Maconchy, 23 November 1976, SHC. The nomination appears to have been organised by Maconchy's sister's husband, Colonel William Charles Palliser Dawson (1896–1977).

[45] Copy of letter from Elizabeth Maconchy to Kenneth Stowe, 27 November 1976, SHC.

[46] See Maconchy, 'Grace Williams: A Symposium'.

Berg's *Lyric Suite*. A birthday concert that aired on the 19th featured *The Land*, *Ariadne*, and *Variazioni Concertante*.

Birthday tributes were not restricted to the BBC, with the BMIC (the British Music Information Centre) featuring an exhibition on Maconchy in March and a number of retrospective articles delving into her career and status as an accomplished but much-underrated composer appearing in the press. In the *Guardian*, Cole included excerpts of an interview with Maconchy in an article that bore the provocative question 'Why can't a woman?' in its title. Cole's article touched on a number of issues, ranging from Maconchy's struggles with balancing her career with motherhood, as well as some of her regrets:

> 'It's quite extraordinary how often one is interrupted; all the way through a struggle to get enough time.' But somehow, all claims were met. Of course there are regrets: 'I haven't ever mixed or worked enough with other musicians, or heard enough music.'
>
> Maybe that is part of the price paid for being a woman. Women cannot, like arrogant males, assume their right to spare time and frivolous, non-productive, re-creative activities. [...]
>
> Was her enforced retirement perhaps a blessing in disguise? 'No, it was not a good thing. I have never heard enough music, and have a bad musical memory, so I can't remember what I do hear.'[47]

Cole further asked whether Maconchy felt that she had succeeded in her goals and aspirations. She responded,

> 'No, not at all. I feel terribly diffident. And after the first enthusiasm of writing a work has gone, you look at it and ask: God – is it really any good?'
>
> But the urge to compose never goes. 'I still feel I always want to write rather than play or read a score.' And she need not worry – her music will perhaps never appeal to mass audiences; but there is no questioning its quality, or the fact that in the eyes of the serious musicians of her day she has undoubtedly made it to the top.[48]

Maconchy spent her seventieth birthday at home, where she had a tea party with family and friends. Though she admitted to no longer having the same energy of her youth, it could hardly be perceptible given the busy schedule she maintained, as a brief glimpse at her appointment diary on 22 March attests: in the morning, she was at Chester's offices in London before delivering a talk on her string quartets at the Royal Academy of Music, then later attending a concert at St Paul's Girls School. As a member of the SPNM's Council, Maconchy also continued to attend meetings. Later in the month, she received a letter from John Woolf, the SPNM's administrator, informing her that the Executive Committee had unanimously endorsed a proposal for Maconchy to succeed Britten as President of the SPNM, following Britten's death the previous year.[49]

[47] Hugo Cole, 'Why can't a woman?: Hugo Cole meets composer Elizabeth Maconchy, 70 today', *Guardian*, 19 March 1977.

[48] Ibid.

[49] According to her appointment diary, Maconchy attended Britten's memorial service at Westminster Abbey, which was held on 10 March.

Figure 15. Nicola LeFanu with her mother, Maconchy, 1977 (reproduced by permission of the Maconchy Estate).

On 26 May, the Park Lane Group organised a birthday concert for Maconchy as part of a series of concerts marking important anniversaries. The programme consisted of works selected by Maconchy, opening with the String Quartet No. 10 played by the Gabrieli String Quartet, followed by her three Donne settings for tenor and piano with Philip Langridge (1939–2010) and John Constable (b. 1934), as well as Beethoven's String Quartet in F Minor, op. 95. Following a brief intermission, two choral works – *Nocturnal* and *Sirens' Song* – were performed by the Saltarello Choir, with the Quintet for Clarinet and Strings finishing off the programme with Thea King as soloist. The concert, which was heavily attended by critics, led to a substantial number of reviews in the press, garnering perhaps the most reviews from a single concert she had received in years, if not decades. Echoing what had become a common theme in discussions of her works, Shawe-Taylor wrote in the *Sunday Times*, 'Miss Maconchy's music, though greatly admired by fellow musicians and composers, remains too little known to the wider public.'[50]

The year 1977 was also filled with a number of premières of newly completed works. On 23 April, the Essex Youth Orchestra premièred Maconchy's Sinfonietta at the Chelmsford Festival, which they played once again on 18 September at the Aldeburgh Festival. The Sinfonietta was not the only work to be heard at that year's festival, as her commissioned work for harp, *Morning, Noon and Night* (1976), was premièred by its dedicatee, Osian Ellis, on 17 June. The concert, which

[50] Desmond Shawe-Taylor, 'Music', *Sunday Times*, 29 May 1977.

was themed 'anniversaries', also included Maconchy's *Three Songs for Tenor and Harp*, performed by Pears accompanied by Ellis, along with works by Imogen Holst, who was also celebrating her seventieth birthday that year.[51]

From the 6th to the 8th of October, *The Sofa*, *The Three Strangers*, and *The Departure* were featured in a triple bill presented by Opera Nova at Middlesbrough Little Theatre. Opera Nova was founded in 1968 to support amateur opera in the Cleveland area. The triple bill was conducted by Opera Nova's artistic director, Iris Lemare, and produced by John Morton, who also managed scene design and lighting. Maconchy and LeFanu drove to Middlesbrough to attend rehearsals as well as the performances. While she had long envisioned her three one-act operas to be performed together, sadly, Opera Nova's production would mark the first and last time Maconchy's vision would be realised. As with all opera productions, the greatest barrier was cost, and the triple bill was no exception as Lemare and Morton struggled to scrape together enough funding.[52] The production was far from flawless, with Paul Dewhirst noting in the *Daily Telegraph* that the singing was at times lacking; however, he offered words of praise for *The Sofa*, which he described as 'witty and eclectic'.[53]

On 13 December the String Quartet No. 11, which she had completed earlier in the year, was premièred by the Lindsay String Quartet at Goldsmiths' Hall in a City Music Society concert in a programme that also included Haydn's Quartet in C Major, op. 54, and Beethoven's Quartet in F Major, op. 135.[54] Like its predecessor, String Quartet No. 11 is cast in one movement. It opens with a lento section in which Maconchy reveals the key motifs of the work: the interval of a minor seventh and a three-note motif consisting of B, D-flat, and C (Example 12.3). Though more acidic than its predecessor, its deeply contrapuntal texture remains true to her style, with references to some of her earlier works, most notably her String Quartet No. 3 creeping in. The performance yielded praise from Cole in the *Guardian* and Paul Griffiths in the *Times*. Griffiths's review was nothing short of glowing:

> One of the most quietly reassuring features of British musical life in our time has been the series of string quartets on which Elizabeth Maconchy has been engaged for the past four-and-a-half decades. She has, of course, a large and varied output to her credit, but it is her quartets, I suspect, that she had [*sic*] made her most lasting contribution, for the medium seems particularly to suit her style of tough, thematic argument and expressive power. [...]
>
> Miss Maconchy can hardly have hoped for a more earnest and impassioned performance than this first one by the Lindsay Quartet. ... Now we must look forward to the twelfth.[55]

[51] The concert also featured works by Britten and H. Balfour Gardiner, as well as songs by Thomas Dunhill, Graham Peel, and Roger Quilter.

[52] The triple bill was eventually funded in part by Cleveland County Council, the Arts Council, the Vaughan Williams Trust, and Northern Arts.

[53] Paul Dewhirst, 'Middlesbrough: Maconchy', *Daily Telegraph*, 8 October 1977.

[54] The City Music Society commissioned Maconchy's quartet as part of its celebration of the 650th anniversary of its charter to the Worshipful Company of Goldsmiths.

[55] Paul Griffiths, 'Lindsay Quartet: Goldsmiths' Hall', *Times*, 14 December 1977.

Example 12.3. Maconchy, String Quartet No. 11, opening.

13

Sunset before Twilight, 1978–94

With the flood of performances and broadcasts celebrating Maconchy's seventieth year, it is hardly surprising that this momentum did not continue into 1978. However, her music was not entirely neglected, with a handful of BBC broadcasts, in addition to several performances of String Quartet No. 11 by the Lindsay String Quartet taking place over the course of the year. On the international stage, Jane Manning and Richard Rodney Bennett premièred her song cycle *Sun, Moon and Stars* (1977) in Hong Kong in February, later performing the work in England at Hull University on 13 October.[1]

Throughout the year, Maconchy was busy with several commissioned works, which included continued work on *Héloïse and Abelard*, which she completed on 25 July. She also revisited Hopkins's *The Leaden Echo and the Golden Echo*, writing a new setting of the work for the William Byrd Singers at the request of their conductor Stephen Wilkinson. Maconchy also found time to compose two additional works during the year: *Contemplation for Cello and Piano*, and *Four Miniatures* for unaccompanied chorus, both of which received premières the following year.

Of Hopkins's poetry, Maconchy described *The Leaden Echo and the Golden Echo* as the poem of his 'that has haunted me most vividly, and which seems to me to cry out for music'.[2] Arranged for mixed choir and alto flute, viola, and harp, the William Byrd Singers and members of the Lontano Ensemble premièred the work on 25 November 1978 at a concert held at the Royal Northern College of Music in Manchester.[3] Of her approach to the poem, she wrote the following in a programme note:

> Much has been written about Hopkins's 'sprung rhythm', both by himself and by later commentators, but another rhythmical quality of his verse, very important for a musical setting, seems to have gone almost unnoticed. This is the variety of pace – of *tempi* – within a poem, and particularly this poem. There are lines that hurry forward, propelled by an almost aggressive alliteration, followed by lines

[1] For further discussion of this work, see Jane Manning, *Vocal Repertoire for the Twenty-First Century*, vol. 1 (Oxford: Oxford University Press, 2020), 186–9.

[2] Elizabeth Maconchy, programme note for *The Leaden Echo and the Golden Echo*, SHC. For a detailed discussion of this work, see Roma, 88–95; and Mathias, *Lutyens, Maconchy, Williams and Twentieth-Century British Music*, 226–9.

[3] The Lontano Ensemble was founded in 1976 by Cuban-American composer and conductor Odaline de la Martínez (b. 1949) and flautist Ingrid Culliford. Dedicated to contemporary music, the Lontano Ensemble is also well known for its commitment to promoting works by women composers.

of slowly drawn out syllables. And, of course, in music the two things can happen at the same time – something music can do which words alone cannot.

The St Winefred's Well of Hopkins's poem is, I am sure, one with a spring bubbling up into a little pool (not a bucket-and-chain affair). The watery music of the spring and the echoes sounding from the rocks round the well have suggested the musical ideas: as in the poem, the echoing of the voices chimes all through the piece.

The Leaden Echo introduces these two elements at once – the watery sounds and the echoing of the women's intertwining voices. The men enter with more sinister words 'O no, there's none', and the women affirm 'No, nothing can be done to keep back beauty from vanishing away'. *The Leaden Echo* ends 'So be beginning to despair, despair, despair'; but a solo soprano voice answers 'spare', leading to *The Golden Echo*, with its happier mood – 'Somewhere elsewhere I do know such a place'. The ideas contrast, combine and intermingle, now racing along, now lingering, while echoes chime through the texture all the way. Finally the voices recede into the distance: 'follow, follow, we follow – yonder, yonder, yonder'.[4]

With its varied rhythm, intricate counterpoint, and vivid word-painting, *The Leaden Echo and the Golden Echo* embodies Maconchy's 'impassioned argument' brilliantly translated to her choral writing, especially her play with Hopkins's alliterative text (Example 13.1). While the work does not have a stable tonal centre in the traditional sense, her recurrent use of particular intervals, as well as the use of a modified octatonic scale, creates a pull towards particular notes and intervals, creating a sense of stability in spite of the work's chromaticism.[5] Though the work poses challenges, particularly with its high tessitura, Maconchy's score was praised in the press, with Paul Dewhirst writing in his review for the *Daily Telegraph*, 'the sustained radiance of the work … makes the deepest impression'.[6]

On 3 March, *Héloïse and Abelard* (1975–8) was premièred by the English Symphony Orchestra and Croydon Philharmonic Choir at Fairfield Hall in Croydon, conducted by James Gaddarn with soprano Hannah Francis, tenor Philip Langridge, and baritone Tom McDonnell taking on the parts of Héloïse, Abelard, and Fulbert (Héloïse's uncle). When Maconchy was approached by the Croydon Philharmonic about a commission in 1975, she was given a tremendous amount of freedom in the selection of subject matter. She eventually settled on the controversial twelfth-century love affair between Héloïse and Abelard – a story which she later remarked had 'always fascinated me'.[7] The work was initially projected to be thirty to forty minutes in duration. The final

4 Ibid.

5 See Roma, 88–95.

6 Paul Dewhirst, 'William Byrd Singers', *Daily Telegraph*, 27 November 1978. The work received its first London performance on 19 February 1981, performed by the BBC Singers and members of the Nash Ensemble, conducted by John Poole.

7 Elizabeth Maconchy, draft of talk on *Héloïse and Abelard*, SHC.

Example 13.1. Maconchy, *The Leaden Echo and the Golden Echo*, bars 25–7. Copyright © Chester Music Ltd. International Copyright Secured. All Rights Reserved. Reproduced by permission of Hal Leonard Europe Ltd.

result after some substantial cuts was seventy-five minutes, making the cantata Maconchy's longest extant work.

Though it is unclear as to when Maconchy first became familiar with the story of the ill-fated lovers, three books on the lovers published in the 1920s and 1930s kept their story firmly in the public consciousness. In the early 1970s, renewed interest in Héloïse and Abelard was sparked, first with the reissue of Enid McLeod's 1938 biography of Héloïse in 1971, followed by new translations of the lovers' letters by Régine Pernoud and Betty Radice. The story of Abelard and Héloïse's love affair begins in Paris, where Fulbert approaches the well-known philosopher and theologian Pierre Abelard to tutor his brilliant young niece, Héloïse, who, despite her young age, was already developing a reputation as a noted scholar. Abelard accepts Fulbert's proposal and decides to seduce his pupil, who soon becomes infatuated with her tutor. The two embark on a love affair which becomes known to everyone except Fulbert. Once the affair is revealed, Fulbert attempts to separate the lovers. His attempt, however, comes to no avail, as Héloïse soon finds herself pregnant. At Abelard's urging, the lovers move to Brittany in an effort to minimise the scandal. Once there, Héloïse gives birth to a son, Astrolabe. To pacify Fulbert, Abelard agrees to marry Héloïse. Héloïse is firmly against the marriage, fearing professional repercussions for Abelard owing to his position in the Church. She eventually gives in to Abelard's demands and marries him under the condition that it remains a secret. In order to protect Abelard, Héloïse returns to Fulbert's home, where she is sorely mistreated. To get away from Fulbert, Abelard arranges for Héloïse to be sent to the Benedictine convent Argenteuil, which appears to confirm Héloïse's denial that the marriage ever took place. Outraged, Fulbert has Abelard castrated in retaliation. Following this, Abelard decides to become a monk. Though Abelard and Héloïse never meet again, they exchange letters, through which the story of their love affair survives.

In a programme note, Maconchy stated that she avoided the use of any fictionalised accounts, developing the libretto entirely from the following: the letters exchanged between the lovers; Abelard's 'Letter to a Friend' contained in his *Historia Calamitatum*; two hymns written by Abelard; his *Planctus*, a tenth-century love song, and a setting of a popular Latin song.[8] In the initial planning stages, however, she expressed an interest in using George Moore's fictionalised account published in 1921.[9] While this idea was later abandoned, in addition to Pernoud and Radice's translations, Maconchy also relied on McLeod's biography.

Maconchy's cantata is arranged in nine sections. Section I comprises a setting of Abelard's Easter hymn *Veris grato tempore*, arranged for chorus, which Maconchy described as 'a sort of twentieth-century chorale'.[10] In Section II, the scene shifts to the cloisters of Notre-Dame where Abelard is finishing a session with his students. Héloïse sings of her desire to study philosophy and Fulbert makes his arrangement with Abelard. A trio ensues in which they each voice their thoughts on the arrangement, with Héloïse already expressing her feelings of love for Abelard. Section III takes place in Fulbert's house. Fulbert tells Abelard that he must not be too easy on Héloïse to ensure that she realises her full intellectual potential. As Fulbert makes his exit, the chorus, representing Abelard's students, are heard singing *O admirabile Veneris idolum* – a twelfth-century love song, which Maconchy adapted from *Oxford Early Medieval Music*.[11] Abelard then joins the chorus, praising Héloïse and his love for her, which then leads to the consummation of their relationship. A short orchestral interlude follows, with Section IV taking place in Brittany where Héloïse has given birth. She sings a lullaby accompanied by a women's chorus, with Maconchy's scoring in this section particularly ravishing. Section V is divided into two sections: the first takes place in Fulbert's house, while the second is outside Abelard's house in the cloister, featuring the wailing of the students and townspeople over Abelard's castration. In Section VI, some time has passed and Héloïse is now in the convent. This section opens with the nuns in a plainsong chant, followed by words of praise for Héloïse, while she voices her longing for Abelard, asking, 'Abelard, Abelard, why have you forgotten me?' Section VII consists of Maconchy's setting of Abelard's hymn *O Quanta Qualia* sung by the chorus. 'Abelard's Lament' follows in Section VIII. Section IX features the chorus's funeral chant at Abelard's grave as Héloïse sings a final farewell to her lover.

8 Ibid.

9 Elizabeth Maconchy to James Gaddarn, 29 September 1975, ACGB/50/457, V&A Theatre and Performance Archives.

10 Maconchy, draft of talk on *Héloïse and Abelard*.

11 Maconchy's extensive notes on the work are held at SHC.

In placing the focus of the cantata primarily on Héloïse, Maconchy's interpretation certainly offers a contrast to previous accounts that diminished her role. Her interpretation remains in line with viewing the relationship between Hèloïse and Abelard as romantic and consensual, sidestepping the question of consent. Her scoring of the choral sections as well as the lullaby in Section IV highlight Maconchy at her best; however, the same cannot be said for much of the score and the libretto, which come across as disjointed. It is unfortunate that Maconchy did not appear to consult either Ursula Vaughan Williams or Ridler, who could have offered some much-needed feedback. The première received a handful of notices in the press. In the *Advertiser*, David Squibb offered substantial praise.[12] Roger Harris's review in *Music and Musicians* offered a much more reasoned assessment, both acknowledging the accomplished choral writing as well as the libretto's weaknesses.[13] As the performance was recorded, a broadcast of the work followed later in the year on 2 November. After the première, Maconchy made some further alterations to the score.

Shortly after the première of *Héloïse and Abelard*, Maconchy celebrated Nicola's marriage to Australian composer David Lumsdaine. During this time, Maconchy was also attending a number of rehearsals and concerts of Nicola's works, including *Deva*, which was premièred at the Camden Festival on 24 March. On 4 April, Maconchy flew to Holland along with Sheila MacCrindle for a brief three-day trip consisting of rehearsals and a recording of *Epyllion* at Algemene Vereniging Radio Omroep Studios in Hiversum. MacCrindle, who had worked in publishing since the 1960s, arrived at Chester Music's promotions office a couple of years before Maconchy began working with the firm.[14] This recording was likely due in part to MacCrindle's advocacy, as she had made earlier trips to Holland to promote composers.

Epyllion was recorded by the Radio Chamber Orchestra, conducted by Ernest Bour (1913–2001) and featuring cellist Max Werner. A change in the rehearsal schedule made without Maconchy and MacCrindle's knowledge added to some confusion; however, Maconchy was pleased overall and the work was broadcast later in the year on 27 July.[15]

Maconchy returned from Holland on 6 April. The following day, she took a train to Birmingham, attending a performance of her String Quartet No. 11 by the Lindsay String Quartet at the Birmingham Art Gallery. The following day, she attended a recording of the work at the BBC's studios in Birmingham. The recording was broadcast later in the year on 6 June, marking the work's first broadcast. Throughout the year, Maconchy was busy with several new commissions, including *Colloquy for Flute and Piano*, String Quartet No. 12, *Creatures* for unaccompanied chorus, and *Romanza for Viola and Chamber*

[12] David Squibb, 'Maconchy cantata has striking impact', *Advertiser*, 9 March 1979.

[13] Roger Harris, 'Héloïse and Abélard', *Music and Musicians* (May 1979): 58.

[14] Caroline Heslop, 'The Middle Person', *Classical Music* (14 March 1987): 39.

[15] Sheila MacCrindle, report titled 'Trip to Holland, 4th – 6th April 1979', June 1979, SHC.

Ensemble. *Colloquy*, which Maconchy had written at the request of flautist Ingrid Culliford, was premièred on 2 June in a concert at the Wigmore Hall with pianist Shelagh Sutherland.

October featured the premières of three works, with *Four Miniatures* (1978) performed by the Broadland Singers at the Norfolk & Norwich Festival on the 17th, String Quartet No. 12 by the Lindsay String Quartet in Sheffield on the 21st, and *Contemplation for Cello and Piano* (1978) premièred by cellist Rohan de Saram and pianist Douglas Young in a concert at the Huddersfield Contemporary Music Festival on 31 October.

Maconchy's String Quartet No. 12 (1979) was commissioned by the University of Sheffield as part of the university's centenary celebrations. In contrast to her previous two quartets, which were cast in a single movement, this work is arranged in four movements. Meticulously well-crafted and beautifully written, the first movement, Allegro moderato, opens with the introduction of a dotted rhythm that dominates much of the movement, with the chords introduced in bars 2–3 also playing a key role as the work progresses (Example 13.2). To balance the dominance of the dotted rhythm in the first movement, Maconchy adds contrasting lyrical sections heavily derived from the two chords previously introduced.

The second movement, Scherzo, is in 5/8 and dominated by pizzicato. Maconchy makes ample use of harmonics and glissandi, which add a further dimension to the work's colour and texture. The third movement, Lento non troppo e flessibile, is characteristically lush and lyrical, opening with an expressive melody in the viola. The movement features long, weaving contrapuntal melodic lines, as well as references to the two chords introduced in the first movement.

Maconchy begins the fourth movement, Molto moderato, with stark and piercing glissando chords that dominate the movement's opening bars. This is followed by the introduction of the movement's primary theme, with the movement also featuring a brief canon for the first violin and viola. Maconchy then begins to reintroduce thematic ideas from the previous movements, as the work concludes 'with a bang not a whimper'.[16] Though the performance was not heavily attended by the press, it received a few pleasant notices, with a recording of the performance featured in a broadcast the following year on 22 April.

Throughout the early 1980s, Maconchy continued to maintain a busy and full schedule, making frequent trips to London for SPNM meetings, and attending various rehearsals and performances of her music that took place in England. On 12 March 1980, her *Romanza* (1979) was premièred at the Queen Elizabeth Hall. Written for the John Bates Orchestra with funding provided by the Arts Council, Maconchy composed the work for viola and a small ensemble comprising wind and string quintets. The work opens with viola (Paul Silverthorne served as the soloist), oscillating back and forth between double stops comprising F and E-flat and D-flat and A-flat. Following the entrance of the ensemble, the viola's melodic lines begin to flow, developing contrapuntally. A section dominated by a dotted rhythm offers a contrast, before the sweeping

[16] Maconchy, 'Elizabeth Maconchy On Writing String Quartets'.

Example 13.2. Maconchy, String Quartet No. 12, mvt. I, opening.

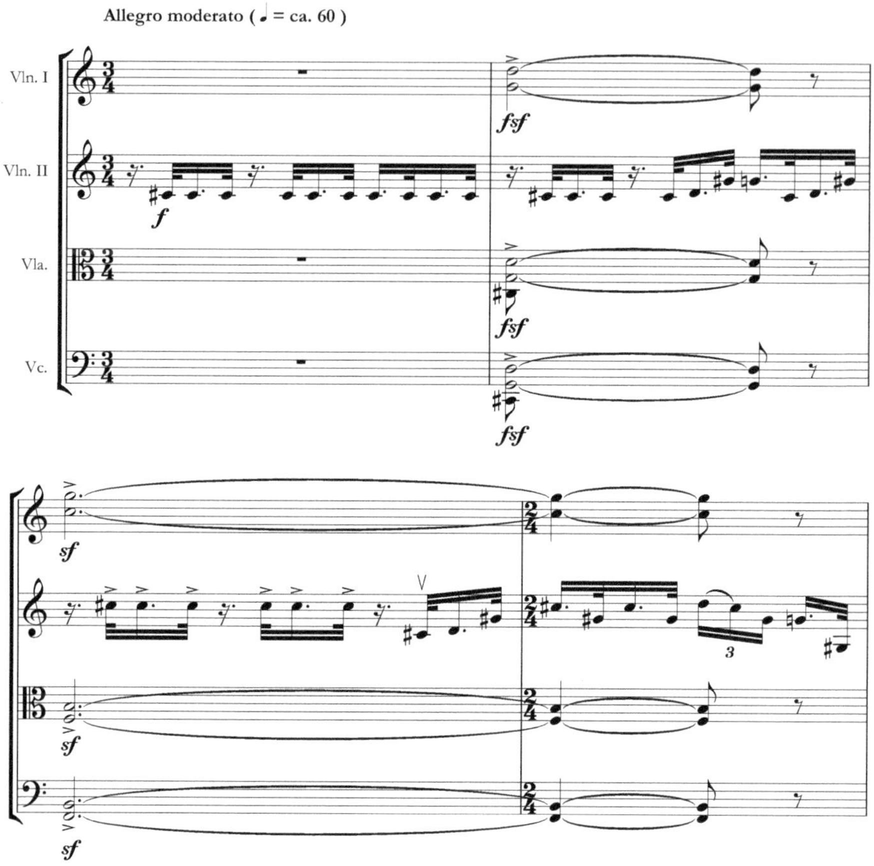

melodic lines return as the work builds to a climax, followed by the return of the opening with the viola gradually becoming softer, bringing the work to a close. Notably, Maconchy's writing for the viola is reminiscent of Vaughan Williams's *Flos campi*. It remains unclear as to whether the links to his score were intentional. As Maconchy revisited many of her early scores that were performed during her birthday celebrations in 1977, the echoes of *Flos campi* present in *Romanza* may have been filtered through her own early works.

The summer of 1980 yielded further premières, with her playful choral work, *Creatures* (1979), premièred by the BBC Northern Singers conducted by Wilkinson at the Chester Summer Music Festival on 23 July, followed by the première of her recently completed *Fantasia for Clarinet and Piano*, which was performed at the International Clarinet Congress in Denver, Colorado by its dedicatee, Thea King, on 12 August.[17] Throughout the year, Maconchy also had a handful of new commissions to keep her occupied, with her *Piccola Musica* (1980), which was premièred at the Cheltenham Festival on 13 July 1981, as well as her *Trittico* (1980), which was premièred the following day at the City of London Festival. A couple of weeks later, a work she had written for the Norfolk County Youth Orchestra titled *Little Symphony* (1980–1) received its first performance at St Andrew's Hall in Norwich.

Maconchy's seventy-fifth birthday in 1982 led to a number of performances and renewed interest in her music, with concerts held in her honour at the RCM, which featured the première of her deeply evocative work for soprano and six players, *My Dark Heart* (1981), as well as a concert at King's College, London, featuring *Romanza*, String Quartet No. 1, and *The Land*. This latter birthday concert, which featured the King's College Orchestra, was conducted by Lumsdaine.[18] Later in the year, her Wind Quintet (1981), which she had written for the Albion Ensemble, was premièred at the Cricklade Arts Festival on 29 September.

Though a prolonged illness in 1982 depleted much of her energy, she was nevertheless able to continue composing, completing a number of chamber and choral works in the ensuing years, as well as a commissioned work for the Proms, *Music for Strings* (1981–2). Initially, she doubted her ability to finish *Music for Strings*, going so far as to call the BBC to suggest that the commission be withdrawn.[19] They did not relent, and Maconchy completed the work, which was premièred by the BBC Philharmonic conducted by Edward Downes (1924–2009) at the Royal Albert Hall on 26 July 1983, with Maconchy delivering a pre-concert talk.[20]

Music for Strings is arranged in four movements, with the opening featuring repeated chords in the low strings (Example 13.3).[21] This first movement is characteristically contrapuntal, and while the opening chords offer clues to thematic links throughout the work, these themes are not as tightly woven as in her quartets. The second movement, Scherzo, consists largely of alternating sections of pizzicato and arco in 5/8 and 6/8. Though the Scherzo is dominated by pizzicato, an arco section featuring a luxurious descending melody offers contrast to the light-hearted and playful character of the movement (Example 13.4). The third movement, Mesto, opens with a solo viola whose sombre character pervades throughout. The finale is rhythmically dynamic as melodic gestures are played back and forth between the strings. Music from the Scherzo briefly returns as it is absorbed into the rhythmic fabric of the movement, which ends rather abruptly.

On the day of the première, the *Guardian* ran an article by Fiona Maddocks titled 'The composer breaks her silence', chronicling some of the challenges,

[17] For a detailed discussion of *Creatures*, see Roma, 82–6.

[18] For a discussion of *My Dark Heart*, see Mathias, *Lutyens, Maconchy, Williams and Twentieth-Century British Music*, 224–7.

[19] Fiona Maddocks, 'The composer breaks her silence', *Guardian*, 26 July 1983.

[20] A draft of Maconchy's talk is held at SHC.

[21] As Mathias has observed, the opening chords of *Music for Strings* are the same that end *My Dark Heart*.

Example 13.3. Maconchy, *Music for Strings*, mvt. I, opening.

Example 13.4. Maconchy, *Music for Strings*, mvt. II, bars 42–9.

namely sexism, Maconchy had long faced, as well as Maconchy's optimism in seeing conditions improve, even if they remained far from perfect.[22] The performance of the work, which received favourable reviews in the press, marked another triumph for Maconchy, with Max Harrison declaring the work 'a distinguished (and also enjoyable), contribution to a tradition that goes back, in modern times, to Elgar's *Introduction and Allegro*. Not that it was ever, despite its frequently ellegiac [*sic*] tone, self consciously English.'[23] Similar comparisons were made in Cole's review for the *Guardian*: 'Maconchy's Music for Strings, both spacious and lyrical, was a fine piece to demonstrate the qualities of the Philharmonic's string section. Like Elgar's Introduction and Allegro, the work plays off the full orchestra against solo strings, making the former sound all the more impressive in the process.'[24]

One of the most significant works Maconchy completed in her later years was her *Quartetto corto* (String Quartet No. 13), which was written for the 1985 Portsmouth String Quartet Competition, which took place at the end of March. The work, which is arranged in three movements, was used as the test piece that the finalists performed for the competition. *Quartetto corto* is significantly shorter than its predecessors, lasting approximately eight minutes. The work opens abruptly with a series of repeated tremolo chords followed by the introduction of a short motif (Example 13.5). The slow movement is a vivid contrast as it opens with an expansive melody, with motific material from the first movement's opening playing a supporting role (Example 13.6). The third and final movement is characterised by its rhythmic vitality with frequent changes in metre, as Maconchy characteristically interweaves the thematic material previously introduced with a slight variation of the work's opening chords, bringing the work to a vigorous close. Owing to its concise and powerful nature, *Quartetto corto* was a superb fit for the demands of a chamber music competition.

While the competition was taking place, Maconchy was preparing for a trip to Australia with Anna. They departed on the 29th, and throughout the three and half week visit, Maconchy spent much of her time with Nicola and her son-in-law, as well as her young grandson, Peter. In spite of frail health, these weeks were filled with a number of activities, including a trip to Manly Beach, where she had fish and chips, a visit to Kangaroo Valley, a performance of Stravinsky's *The Rite of Spring* at the Sydney Opera House, as well as a reception held at the Australian Music Centre in her honour.[25]

Beyond *Quartetto corto*, the spring of 1985 also included the première of a choral work she had written for the Chelmsford Cathedral Festival, *Still Falls the Rain* (1984), which took place on 22 May. Later in the year, her Concertino for Clarinet and Small Orchestra (1984) was premièred by its dedicatee Janet Hilton and the BBC Scottish Symphony Orchestra, conducted by Nicholas Kraemer, at the Henry Wood Hall in Glasgow. Like *Romanza*, the Concertino

[22] Maddocks, 'The composer breaks her silence'.

[23] Max Harrison, 'Promenade Concert: Invented space', *Times*, 27 July 1983.

[24] Hugo Cole, 'Downes/BBCPO', *Guardian*, 27 July 1983.

[25] These activities are detailed in Maconchy's appointment diary.

Example 13.5. Maconchy, String Quartet No. 13, opening.

for Clarinet and Small Orchestra revisits a work from the past, with the first movement bearing a striking resemblance to *The Land*.

As Maconchy's health declined, she slowly began to recede from public life. Her eightieth year, however, brought in a flood of performances and broadcasts. In addition to several honours, the most notable being a DBE, making her the second female composer after Smyth to hold the honour,[26] the year also saw the première of a documentary on her life on Channel 4, directed by Margaret Williams. Filmed in the spring of 1984, Maconchy was already appearing frail, and sadly her health only continued to deteriorate as the decade drew to a close. Nevertheless, she still made it to occasional concerts and performances, and gave some occasional interviews. Her final work, a choral setting titled *On St Stephenses Day* for women and chorus to mark Stephen Wilkinson's seventieth birthday, was completed in 1989. That same year, her cycle of thirteen string quartets finally received the much overdue recordings they deserved. Arranged in three volumes, Unicorn-Kanchana Records released Vol. 1 in 1989, followed by Vol. 2 in March 1990, and Vol. 3 in the autumn of 1990.[27] The final years of her life were marred by illness, with a series of transient ischemic attacks, as well as glaucoma that eventually led to blindness. She died at St Clements Nursing Home in Norwich on 11 November 1994.

[26] The investiture ceremony took place on 8 December 1987.

[27] Volume 1 featured nos. 1–4, played by the Hanson String Quartet. Volume 2 covered nos. 5–8, played by the Bingham String Quartet. Volume 3 comprised nos. 9–13, played by the Mistry String Quartet.

Example 13.6. Maconchy, String Quartet No. 13, bars 115–23.

—(*continued*)

Example 13.6—*concluded*

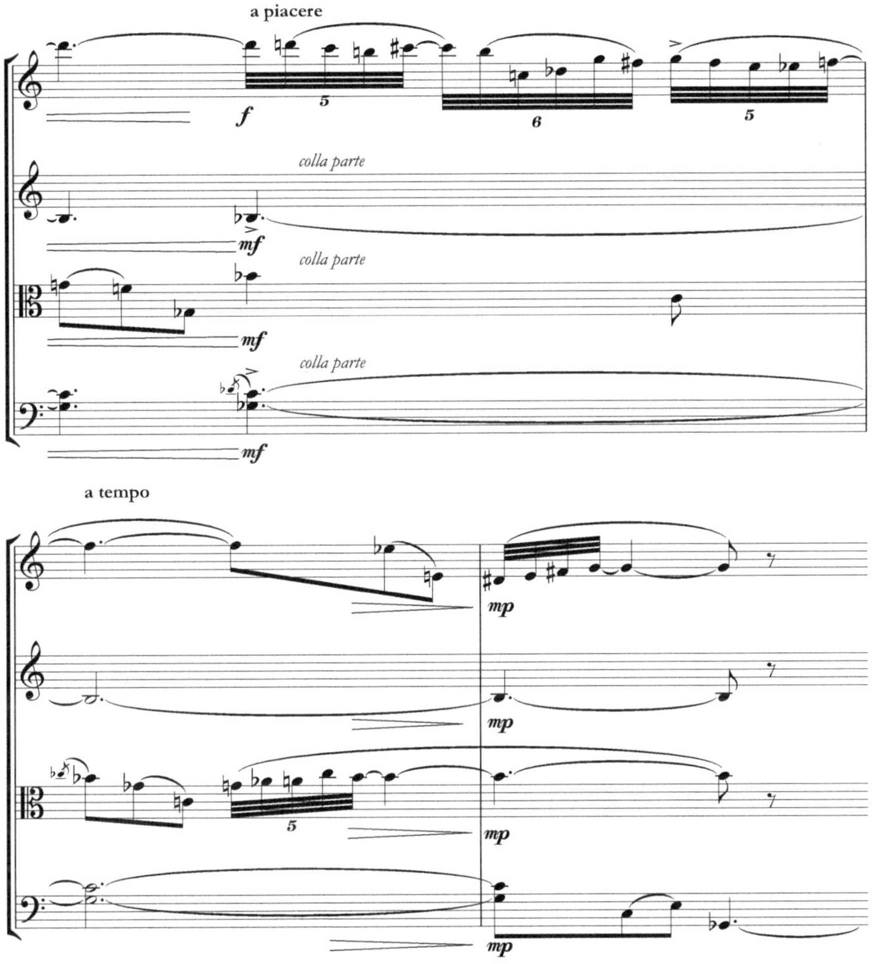

Figure 16. Maconchy at her eightieth birthday concert with Ursula Vaughan Williams, daughter Anna Dunlop, and grandchildren Sarah and Christopher Dunlop, 1987 (reproduced by permission of the Maconchy Estate).

Epilogue

In 2007, a series of concerts to mark Maconchy's centenary sparked a renewed interest in her music. In a review of *The Sofa*, which was revived as part of a double bill with *The Departure*, Andrew Porter wrote the following:

> In my early days as a critic, Maconchy was not prominent. Her contributions to the 1951 Festival of Britain, the Sixth String Quartet and the Theme and Variations for String Orchestra, are but passing references in the *Times* volume of reviews recording the events of that year of British musical achievement. But I like to think that I heard and hailed Maconchy's merits when I reviewed her operas a half-century ago. The Independent Opera revivals provided confirmation. I won't put her beside Bartók – not yet, not till I've heard more of her music. But maybe that's where she should be ranked.[1]

For so long, the story of Maconchy's career has been viewed as simply a tale of neglect. And yet, at times during her career, this was not always the case. In the years before Porter became a critic, she was able to achieve a remarkable level of success in spite of her sex and changing attitudes towards her music. Maconchy was far from an outlier in the early 1930s when she was routinely viewed as one of the best and brightest of the younger generation of emerging composers, beating Britten in the *Daily Telegraph* Chamber Music Competition in 1933. While Britten had three works performed at ISCM Festivals in the 1930s, Maconchy was not far behind with two. Even Constant Lambert could not deny Maconchy's importance when he declared in 1933, 'There are regrettably few young composers to-day, but in Miss Elizabeth Maconchy and Mr. Benjamin Britten we have two whose future development should be of the greatest interest.'[2]

There were, however, several factors that ultimately impeded the expansion of her career within Britain and abroad, which did indeed lead to the neglect of her works. The increased scrutiny of modernist works combined with the growth of anti-intellectualism in the 1930s created a cultural climate that was disadvantageous to Maconchy's music. In this regard, her modernism arrived at an inopportune time, as interest in continental modernism had peaked in the 1920s with the BBC's heavy promotion of modernist – and predominately foreign – music. By the latter part of the decade, musical modernism was widely perceived to be in decline, if not already dead.[3] The declining popularity of chamber music, for example, combined with its continued association with overtly intellectual music of foreign origin was yet another hindrance to the

1 Andrew Porter, 'Are you sitting comfortably?', *Times Literary Supplement*, 23 November 2007.

2 Constant Lambert, 'Musical Matters', *Sunday Referee*, 12 November 1933.

3 Ernest Newman, 'The Gathering of the Tide', *Sunday Times*, 6 May 1928.

acceptance of Maconchy's growing corpus of string quartets. In this climate, which peaked around the mid-1950s, much of Maconchy's music was distinctly out of favour.

Maconchy's success during the interwar years was due to the coalescence of several factors: she had access to musical education with teachers such as Ralph Vaughan Williams, who treated his pupils equally regardless of gender, and she had supportive colleagues such as Grace Williams. Within the context of the principal educational institution in which she matriculated, the RCM, she was encouraged by her teachers to compose in a variety of genres. However, the harsh realities in the professional musical world were far less welcoming. Although Maconchy did not have powerful connections with music publishers, she did, however, have the advantage of several individuals within the musical establishment willing to champion her music, such as Vaughan Williams, Tovey, Wood, and even Hugh Allen. Tovey's death in 1940, followed by Wood in 1944 and Allen in 1946, however, severed her most powerful connections and strongest advocates. As Vaughan Williams's own reputation declined during the 1950s, his power to assist her lessened considerably. While her career had a resurgence beginning in the 1960s, she never fully regained the same level of fame she had enjoyed in the 1930s.

It has never been easy for a composer to make their way in the world, but one cannot deny that, historically, it has been significantly easier for male composers to raise capital and find publishers for their works. In this regard, Maconchy was at a marked disadvantage throughout her career. As her relationship with publishers was precarious, she often had to handle all aspects of negotiations for performances herself, as well as bearing the burden of all the costs of paper and copying. All too often she was her own copyist, which was a tiresome, messy, and time-consuming task. For the majority of her career, she also had to handle promotional aspects of her career herself until Chester took a vested interest in her in the 1970s. Their interest in supporting and promoting her works enabled her music to become known to wider audiences, and unsurprisingly, many more performances followed. Nevertheless, a majority of her orchestral works have never been typeset and remain available for hire only.

Perhaps one of the most significant disadvantages Maconchy faced was the fact that in order to succeed in the music profession, one has to be a tireless self-promoter. Of this aspect of her personality, Hugh Wood aptly surmised,

> Typical of Betty Maconchy that one's very first contact with her should reveal her in her truest light. She put up – on the strength of one piece – a very young composer for membership of the Composers' Guild: I still have the kind, encouraging note she wrote to me then. The second memory is perhaps more significant. Long ago, I used to sit on an SPNM committee, and attendance would vary from meeting to meeting. But one person, I noted, was always there: Betty Maconchy would always conscientiously turn up. And she had the longest journey of any of us – up to London from the depths of Essex.
>
> Awareness of other people – particularly one's juniors – and conscientiousness over duty undertaken are extremely uncharacteristic qualities of most composers. Add to these habits of behaviour what I suspect may be a naturally

> self-effacing personality, and you have all the reasons why we do not hear of her music more than we do; and not half so much as we should. [...]
>
> In a corrupt world where the exploitation of personality and talent for public relations has replaced any attempt at the evaluation of one's work – in that world Elizabeth Maconchy remains more interested in doing her work, and doing it well.[4]

Though Maconchy may not have achieved the widespread popularity enjoyed by her male peers and even some of her female colleagues, her ability to triumph over adversity is a testament to her tenacity, resolve, and, whatever her occasional misgivings, her belief in her own gifts as a composer. And as interest continues to grow, with more performances of her works and recordings becoming available, her music is at last beginning to gain the recognition and reevaluation it has long deserved.

[4] Hugh Wood, tribute to Maconchy accompanying seventieth birthday concert programme, SHC.

Chronological List of Works

The first comprehensive chronological list of Maconchy's works was compiled by Jennifer Doctor and published in volume 3 of *A Dictionary-Catalog of Modern British Composers*, edited by Alan Pulton in 2000. In 2018, this list was republished in *Elizabeth Maconchy: Music as Impassioned Argument* with additions by Annika Forkert.

In her later years, Maconchy maintained a handwritten list of works. Though incomplete, a great deal of the information she provided is correct. In some instances, however, the dates she attributed to her compositions and first performances are not. While this substantially truncated list offers further updates to reflect new information that has come to light, many details regarding exact dates of various works, first performances, and firm dates of publication remain murky or unknown.

The majority of Maconchy's music manuscripts are held at SHC, with some additional manuscripts available at the British Library, RCM, and the Britten-Pears Archive. Over the years, Maconchy worked with a number of publishing firms, namely, OUP, Hinrichsen, Lengnick, and Chester. Nearly all recordings of Maconchy's music can be found with a simple Google search.

***Impetuous heart* (1924)**
For voice and piano, set to text by W.B. Yeats

Suite for Strings in E Minor (1924)
1. Allegretto vivace 2. Allegro 3. Andante sostenuto 4. Animato
First performance: 25 November 1924, RCM Informal Concert (No. 72), Mary Gladden (1st violin), Mabel Weller (2nd violin), Gwendolen Windsor (viola), Ruth Riley (cello)

***Three Short Pieces for Piano* (1924)**
1. Allegro con brio 2. Andante cantabile 3. Allegro moderato, giocoso

***There is a lady sweet and kind* (1924–5)**
For voice and piano, text anon
First performance: 11 March 1926, RCM College Concert (No. 825), Muriel Nixon (soprano), Audrey Piggott (piano)

***O to have a little house* (c. 1925)**
For voice and piano, set to text by Padraic Colum

***The Wife a-lost* (c. 1925)**
For voice and piano, set to text by William Barnes

***The Piper* (1925)**
For voice and piano, set to text by Seamus O'Sullivan

Grace **(1925)**
For SSAA, set to text from Psalm 145:15

Beauty **(1925)**
For voice and piano, set to text by John Masefield

Baby Lou or The Bonnie Banks of Fordie **(1925)**
For SATB, text trad.

Mamble **(1925)**
For voice and piano, set to text by John Drinkwater

The Poet-Wooer **(1925)**
For voice and piano, set to text by Ben Jonson

Deirdre **(1925)**
For SATB and bass solo with optional harp, set to text by James Stephens

Martin said to his man **(c. 1926)**
For voice and piano, text trad.
First performance: 13 October 1927, Repton, Steuart Wilson (tenor), Phyllis Arnott (piano)

O mistress mine **(c. 1926)**
For voice and piano, set to text from Shakespeare's *Twelfth Night*
First performance: 13 October 1927, Repton, Steuart Wilson (tenor), Phyllis Arnott (piano)

There were three ravens **(c. 1926)**
For voice and piano, text trad.
First performance: 13 October 1927, Repton, Steuart Wilson (tenor), Phyllis Arnott (piano)

Once I loved a maiden fair **(c. 1926)**
For voice and piano, text trad.
Note: incomplete

The Call **(1926)**
For voice and piano, text anon.
First performance: 11 March 1926, RCM College Concert (No. 825), Muriel Nixon (soprano), Audrey Piggott (piano)

My sweet sweeting **(1926)**
For voice and piano, text anon.
First performance: 11 March 1926, RCM College Concert (No. 825), Muriel Nixon (soprano), Audrey Piggott (piano)

Ophelia's Song **(1926, arr. 1962)**
For voice and piano, set to text from Shakespeare's *Hamlet*
First documented performance: 3 March 1936, Grotrian Hall, London, Audrey Langford (soprano), George Reeves (piano)
Publication: OUP, 1930
Arranged: for soprano, unison chorus, optional descant recorder, and piano in 1962
Publication (arrangement): OUP, 1962

Holiday Time **(1926)**
For flute and piano
Dedication: for Robin [Robert Vere Darwin]

Allegro for Flute and Strings **(1926)**
First performance: 7 May 1927, Eton (School Subscription Concerts), Guildford Orchestra, R.V. [Robert 'Robin' Vere] Darwin (flute), conducted by Claud Powell

The Sign of the Bonny Blue Bell **(1926)**
For voice and piano, text trad.

O waly, waly **(1926)**
For voice and piano, text trad.

The Passionate Shepherd to his Love **(1926)**
For voice and piano, set to text by Christopher Marlowe

The Hundred and Fourth Psalm **(1926)**
For SATB and orchestra

Fantasy for Flute, Harp, and String Orchestra **(1926)**
First performance: 23 July 1926, RCM College Concert (No. 834), College Orchestra, conducted by W.H. Reed

Elegy for Flute, Horn, and String Orchestra **(1926)**
First performance: 3 December 1926, RCM College Concert (No. 841), College Orchestra, conducted by Adrian Boult

Untitled opera (1926)
Note: incomplete

Four Pieces for String Quartet **(1926–7)**
1. Tempo giusto 2. Molto moderato – quasi lento 3. Allegretto 4. Allegro molto

All the flowers **(1927)**
For voice and piano, text unidentified
First performance: 18 June 1929, RCM College Concert (No. 904), Muriel St. C. Green (voice)

Falling asleep **(1927)**
For tenor, 2 flutes, oboe, clarinet in B-flat, horn in F, viola, and piano, set to text by Siegfried Sassoon

Andante con moto for Flute and Strings **(1927)**
First performance: 7 May 1927, Eton (School Subscription Concerts), Guildford Orchestra, R.V. [Robert 'Robin' Vere] Darwin (flute), conducted by Claud Powell

Untitled works for piano (1927)
1. Allegro (fuga a tre voci) 2. Allegro moderato [possibly replaced by 2. Scherzo] 3. Allegretto (Rondo)

Laudamus Te **(1927)**
For double chorus

Sonata for Violin and Piano (1927)
1. Molto moderato, e marcato 2. Allegro scherzando 3. Lento 4. Allegro molto
First performance: 18 October 1932, Ballet Club Theatre, London (Macnaghten-Lemare Concerts), Anne Macnaghten (violin), Helen Perkin (piano)

Ward the Pirate **(c. 1927)**
Educational arrangement of folk song for orchestra
First performance: 10 November 1927, Kensington Town Hall, London (Kensington Musical Festival Competition), all participating boys, conducted by Keith Falkner

Willow, Willow **(1927)**
For SATB, set to text from Shakespeare's *Othello*

He that hath a little tiny wit **(1927)**
For SATB, set to text from Shakespeare's *King Lear*

Harp Song of the Dane Woman **(1927, arr. 1962)**
For voice and harp, set to text from Rudyard Kipling's *Puck of Pook's Hill*
Arranged: for voice(s) and piano, May 1962
First performance (arranged): 4 February 1976, St Paul's Girls School, London, Senior Choir
Publication: Chester

What Shall he have that kill'd the Deer? **(1927)**
For SATB and soprano solo, set to text from Shakespeare's *As You Like It*

Bluebeard and Fatima **(1927)**
Ballet for chamber orchestra

Fantasy for Children **(1927–8)**
For chamber orchestra
First performance: 17 January 1929, Pump Room, Bath (Pump Room Concerts), Pump Room Orchestra, conducted by Jan Hurst

Theme and Variations for Orchestra **(1928)**

O summer sun **(1928)**
For voice and piano, set to text by Laurence Binyon

Under the Greenwood Tree **(1928)**
For voice and piano, set to text from Shakespeare's *As You Like It*

Music Box and Jig **(1928)**
For piano

A Meditation for His Mistress **(1928)**
For voice and piano, set to text by Robert Herrick
First performance: 18 June 1929, RCM College Concert (No. 904), Muriel St. C. Green (voice), unnamed pianist
Publication: OUP, 1930

In Fountain Court **(c. 1928)**
For voice and piano, set to text by Arthur Symons
First performance: 18 June 1929, RCM College Concert (No. 904), Muriel St. C. Green (voice), unnamed pianist

Concerto (Concertino) for Piano and Chamber Orchestra (1928, rev. 1929)
First performance: 30 November 1928, RCM Patron's Fund Rehearsal, New Symphony Orchestra, Gwendo Paul (piano), conducted by Adrian Boult
First performance (revised): 30 March 1930, Smetana Hall, Prague, Prague Philharmonic, Erwin Schulhoff (piano), conducted by K.B. Jirák
Publication: OUP, 1937; transferred to Lengnick, 1953

***The Knight's Tale* (1928)**
Opera, based upon Chaucer's *The Canterbury Tales*
Note: incomplete

Untitled work for string quartet (1928)
1. Allegro molto 2. Andante

***The Cloths of Heaven* (1929)**
For voice and piano, set to text by W.B. Yeats

***Have you seen a bright lily grow?* (1929)**
For voice and piano, set to text by Ben Jonson
First performance: 17 June 1930, 2 Mansfield Street, London, Thomas Dance (voice), E. Warr (piano)
Publication: OUP, 1930

***The Land* (1929)**
For chamber orchestra
1. Winter 2. Spring 3. Summer 4. Autumn
First performance: 30 August 1930, Queen's Hall, London (BBC Promenade Concerts), conducted by Henry Wood
Publication: OUP, 1937; transferred to Lengnick, 1953
Note: based on Vita Sackville-West's *The Land*

Quintet for Strings (1929)
1. Poco lento 2. Allegro molto
First performance: 11 July 1931, 74 Grosvenor Street, London (SWM), Kendall String Quartet, Winifred Stiles (viola)

Symphony (1929–30)
1. Allegro molto 2. Presto 3. Poco lento 4. Presto
First performance: 30 March 1930, BBC Studio 10, London (BBC play-through rehearsal), BBC Orchestra, conducted by Aylmer Buesst
Note: withdrawn by composer

Suite for Chamber Orchestra (1930)
1. Allegro molto 2. Allegretto 3. Allegro moderato 4. Andante con moto 5. Allegro
First performance: 10 February 1931, Aeolian Hall, London (New English Music Society), London Chamber Orchestra, conducted by Anthony Bernard
Publication: OUP, 1937; transferred to Lengnick, 1953
Note: withdrawn by composer

***The Woodspurge* (1930)**
For voice and piano, set to text by D.G. Rossetti
First performance: 15 November 1932, Ballet Club Theatre, London (Macnaghten-Lemare Concerts), Muriel Herbert (soprano), Alannah Delias (piano)

The Leaden Echo and the Golden Echo **(1930–1)**
For chorus (SSAATB) and chamber orchestra, set to text by Gerard Manley Hopkins
Note: withdrawn by composer. Another setting of the work was done in 1978

The Willow Plate **(1931)**
Opera in three acts, based upon Ernest Bramah's 'The Story of Wong T'sin and the Willow Plate Embellishment' in *Kai Lung's Golden Hours*
Note: incomplete

Quintet for Oboe and Strings (1932)
1. Moderato 2. Poco sostenuto 3. Allegro non troppo
First performance: 13 May 1933, Concert Hall, Broadcasting House, London (BBC London Regional broadcast), Griller String Quartet, Helen Gaskill (oboe)
Publication: Hinrichsen; Chester, 1996

Two Motets for Double Chorus **(1932)**
1. A Hymn to Christ (John Donne) 2. A Hymn to God the Father (John Donne)
First performance: 11 December 1933, Ballet Club Theatre, London (Macnaghten-Lemare Concerts), unnamed choir, conducted by Iris Lemare
Publication: Hinrichsen

Comedy Overture **(1932–3)**
For chamber orchestra
First performance: 7 March 1934, The Pavilion, Bournemouth, Bournemouth Municipal Orchestra, conducted by Dan Godfrey
Note: concert was broadcast in a BBC National Programme

Great Agrippa, or the Inky Boys **(1933)**
Ballet based upon Heinrich Hoffmann's *Der Struwwelpeter*
First performance: 4 February 1935, Mercury Theatre, London (Macnaghten-Lemare Concerts), unnamed orchestra, conducted by Iris Lemare (concert performance only)
Publication: OUP, 1937; transferred to Lengnick, 1953

String Quartet No. 1 (1933)
1. Allegro feroce 2. Scherzo 3. Andante sostenuto 4. Presto
First performance: 6 November 1933, Ballet Club Theatre, London (Macnaghten-Lemare Concerts), Macnaghten String Quartet
Publication: Hinrichsen; Lengnick, 1956

Deborah **(c. 1934)**
Oratorio
Note: incomplete

The Thrush **(1934)**
For voice and piano, set to text by John Keats
First performance: 17 August 1935, BBC National Programme broadcast, Sophie Wyss (soprano), Adolph Hallis (piano)
Publication: Hinrichsen

Prelude, Interlude and Fugue for Two Violins **(1934)**
First performance: 24 June 1935, BBC Regional Programme broadcast, André Mangeot (violin), Anne Macnaghten (violin)
Publication: Hinrichsen

Divertissement for Twelve Instruments **(1935)**
1. Moderato 2. Andante sostenuto – allegro scherzando
First performance: 18 October 1935, Prague Radio broadcast, Prague Radio Orchestra, conducted by Otakar Jeremiáš
Publication: OUP, 1937; transferred to Lengnick, 1953

Little Red Shoes **(1935)**
Ballet for children, based upon Hans Christian Andersen's *The Red Shoes*
Publication: Hinrichsen
Note: withdrawn by composer

The Arab **(1935)**
For voice and piano, set to text by George Meredith
First performance: 17 August 1935, BBC National Programme broadcast, Sophie Wyss (soprano), Adolph Hallis (piano)

Toccata for Piano (1935)
First performance: 17 August 1935, BBC National Programme broadcast, Adolph Hallis

String Quartet No. 2 (1936)
1. Molto lento 2. Poco presto 3. Lento sostenuto 4. Allegro
First performance: 1 February 1937, Mercury Theatre, London (Lemare Concerts), Brosa String Quartet
Publication: Hinrichsen; transferred to Lengnick, 1955

Concerto for Viola and Orchestra (1937)
1. Molto moderato 2. Allegro 3. Allegro molto
First performance: 4 February 1938, Concert Hall, Broadcasting House, London (BBC Contemporary Music Concerts broadcast), BBC Orchestra, Bernard Shore (viola), conducted by Constant Lambert
Publication: OUP, 1937; transferred to Lengnick, 1953
Note: withdrawn by composer

I made another song **(c. 1937)**
For voice and piano, set to text by Robert Bridges
First performance: 12 October 1937, Grotrian Hall, London, Norah Scott Turner (soprano), Gerald Moore (piano)

Sleep brings no joy to me **(1937)**
For voice and piano, set to text by Emily Brönte
First performance: 12 October 1937, Grotrian Hall, London, Norah Scott Turner (soprano), Gerald Moore (piano)

Five Pieces for Viola **(1937)**
1. Prelude 2. Lament 3. Lullaby 4. Etude 5. Passacaglia

***How Samson bore away the Gates of Gaza* (1937–8, arr. 1938, rev. 1963-4, arr. 1973)**
Scena for voice and piano
First performance: 8 February 1938, Cowdray Hall, London (LCMC), Sophie Wyss (soprano), Adolph Hallis (piano)
Publication: Hinrichsen
Arranged: for soprano (or tenor) and orchestra, 1938
Revised: for chorus and orchestra as *Samson and the Gates of Gaza*, 1963–4
First performance (revised): 10 October 1964, King Edward VI School, Chelmsford, school choir and orchestra, conducted by John Jordan
Arranged: for choir and brass band, 1973
First performance (arranged): 13 January 1974, Royal Albert Hall, London (National Federation of Music Societies), participating choirs, conducted by David Willcocks
Publication (revised and arranged): Chappell

Sonata for Viola and Piano (1937–8)
1. Allegro 2. Lento moderato 3. Presto
First performance: 15 February 1938, Wigmore Hall, London (Adolph Hallis Chamber Music Concerts), Frederick Riddle (viola), Adolph Hallis (piano)
Publication: Hinrichsen; Chester, 2015

***The Mothers* (1938)**
For SSAA, set to text by Sylvia Townsend Warner

***The Garland* (1938)**
Song cycle set to Anacreontic text, translated by William LeFanu
1. The Garland 2. The Swallow 3. Old and Young 4. Love knocks at the door 5. No end to Love
Dedication: 'For Sophie Wyss'
First performance: 14 February 1939, Wigmore Hall, London (Adolph Hallis Chamber Music Concerts), Sophie Wyss (soprano), Adolph Hallis (piano)
Publication: Hinrichsen; Chappell, 1974, copyright returned to Maconchy, 1976; Chester, 1984
Note: published score includes nos. 1, 3, 5 and *I would I were a mirror* placed between nos. 3 and 5

String Quartet No. 3 (1938)
In one movement
Dedication: 'For the New Hungarian Quartet'
First performance: 4 October 1938, Cowdray Hall, London (LCMC), New Hungarian String Quartet
Publication: Hinrichsen; transferred to Lengnick, 1956

***Impromptu* (1938)**
Fantasia on one note for piano
Dedication: 'For Harriet Cohen'
First documented performance: 6 November 1941, Birmingham (University Musical Society), Eric Hope
Publication: Hinrichsen, 1939
Note: an earlier performance may have occurred at Wigmore Hall

The Ribbon in her Hair **(1939)**
For men's chorus and piano, set to text by Sean O'Casey
Publication: WMA, 1939

The People Advance **(1939)**
For chorus
First performance: 1 April 1939, Royal Albert Hall, London (Festival of Music for the People)
Note: this work was episode 9 of the musical pageant *Music for the People*

A Country Town: Suite for Piano **(1939, arr. 1950, c. 1956)**
1. The Fair 2. The Beggar 3. The Quarrel 4. Lament 5. The Knifegrinder 6. The Singer 7. Bells 8. The Recruit 9. Goodnight
First performance: 1 June 1944, Wigmore Hall, London, Eric Hope
Publication: Hinrichsen, 1945
Arranged: for String Quartet in eight movements, 1950
1. The Fair 2. The Beggar 3. The Quarrel 4. The Singer 5. Bells 6. Lament 7. The Knifegrinder 8. Goodnight
First documented performance (arranged): 16 October 1960, Gunfield, 19 Norham Gardens, Oxford (Oxford Ladies' Musical Society), Macnaghten String Quartet
Note: arrangement made for the Macnaghten Quartet
Arranged: for Small Orchestra in six movements, c. 1956
1. The Fair 2. The Beggar 3. Bells 4. Lament 5. The Knifegrinder 6. Goodnight
First documented performance (arranged): 12 July 1972, Francis Holland School, London, School Orchestra
Note: arrangement made for Miss Mundlak and the Orchestra of St Mary's Calne

Puck Fair **(1939–40, arr. 1943, 1950, rev. 1953)**
Ballet in five scenes
First performance: 9 February 1941, Gaiety Theatre, Dublin, Irish Ballet Club
Choreography: Cepta Cullen
Designer: Mainie Jellett
Musicians: Charles Lynch (piano) and Miles Rumbold (piano)
Note: the work was originally scored for two pianos
Arranged: for small orchestra by Ina Boyle in the mid 1940s
First performance (arranged): 10 May 1948, Opera House, Cork, Cork Ballet Group with Cork Symphony Orchestra, conducted by Aloys Fleischmann
Choreography: Joan Denise Moriarty
Designer: Frank Sanquest
Revised: orchestration revised by Maconchy in 1953
First performance (revised): 19 April 1953, Opera House, Cork Ballet Group with Cork Symphony Orchestra, conducted by Aloys Fleischmann
Publication: Hinrichsen
Arranged: as *Puck Fair Suite* in 1943
1. The Goat 2. The Priest 3. The Lovers 4. The Policemen 5. Evening 6. Tinkers
First performance (arranged): 5 August 1944, BBC General Forces Programme broadcast from Bedford (BBC Promenade Concerts), BBC Symphony Orchestra, conducted by Adrian Boult
Publication: Lengnick
Arranged: as *Two Dances from Puck Fair* in 1950
First performance (arranged): 30 September 1950, BBC Home Service broadcast, BBC Welsh Orchestra, conducted by Mansel Thomas
Publication: Lengnick

The Winkle Woman **(1940)**
For mezzo-soprano and piano set to text by Sigerson Clifford
Publication: WMA, 1940

Dies Irae **(1940–1)**
For contralto, chorus, and orchestra
Dedication: 'In memory of my mother'
Note: withdrawn by composer

The Disillusion **(1941)**
For voice and piano, set to text by Sheila Wingfield
First performance: 7 January 1942, BBC Home Service broadcast, Sophie Wyss (soprano), unnamed pianist
Publication: Hinrichsen

Sailor's Song of the Two Balconies **(1941)**
For voice and piano, set to text by Sheila Wingfield
First performance: 15 February, 1942, BBC Home Service broadcast, Sophie Wyss (soprano), unnamed pianist
Publication: Hinrichsen

Dialogue for Piano and Orchestra **(1939–41)**
I. Lento moderato 2. Allegro molto 3. Sostenuto 4. Presto
First performance: 16 July 1942, Royal Albert Hall, London (Promenade Concerts), London Philharmonic Orchestra, Clifford Curzon (piano), conducted by Basil Cameron
Publication: Hinrichsen; Lengnick

Contrapuntal Pieces for Piano **(c. 1941)**
1. Prelude 2. Fugue: Allegro ben marcato 3. Fugue: Allegro vigoroso

String Quartet No. 4 (1939–41)
1. Allegro 2. Allegro molto 3. Lento, molto espressivo 4. Presto
First performance: 19 April 1943, BBC Latin American Service broadcast, Blech String Quartet
Publication: Hinrichsen; Lengnick, 1949

Variations on a Well-Known Theme **(1942)**
For orchestra
First performance: 12 October 1942, BBC Maida Vale Studio, BBC Home Service broadcast, London Symphony Orchestra, conducted by Clarence Raybould
Note: written for Vaughan Williams's seventieth birthday at the request of Arthur Bliss
Publication: Hinrichsen

The Shark and the Whale **(c. 1942)**
For unison voices and piano, set to text by Isidor Schneider
Publication: WMA, 1942

Divertimento for Cello and Piano **(1941–3)**
1. Serenade (Preamble) 2. Golubchick 3. The Clock 4. Vigil 5. Masquerade
First documented performance (Serenade only): 10/11 March 1943, BBC Latin American Service broadcast, Sela Trau (cello), John Willis (piano)

First documented performance (entire work): 11 December 1952, BBC Home Service broadcast, Arnold Ashby (viola), Ernest Lush (piano)
Publication: Lengnick, 1954

How ye **(1943)**
For chorus and orchestra

By the Waters of Babylon **(c. 1943)**
For chorus and orchestra

Sonata for Violin and Piano (1943)
1. Molto moderato – Allegro moderato 2. Allegro molto 3. Lento 4. Presto
First performance: 3 May 1945, Cowdray Hall, London (LCMC), Maria Lidka (violin), Anthony Hopkins (piano)

Theme and Variations for String Orchestra **(1942–3)**
First performance: 13 January 1946, Capitol Theatre, Dublin, Radio Éireann concert and broadcast, Radio Éireann Orchestra, conducted by Michael Bowles
Publication: Lengnick

The Voice of the City **(1943)**
For SSA, set to text by Jacqueline Morris
First documented performance: 1944, London, WMA
Publication: WMA, 1943

Pioneers of Rochdale **(1944)**
For unison or mixed chorus, set to text by Frank Crome
Publication: WMA, 1944
Note: 'Specially written and composed for the Co-Operative Centenary 1944'

A Song of Freedom **(1944)**
For men's chorus
Note: written for the WMA

Concertino for Clarinet and String Orchestra (1945)
1. Allegro molto 2. Lento 3. Allegro
Dedication: 'For Frederick Thurston'
First performance: 2 June 1947, Large Hall, Concert Palace, Copenhagen (ISCM Festival), unnamed orchestra, Frederick Thurston (clarinet), conducted by Anthony Bernard
Publication: Chester, 1993

Sonnet Sequence **(1946–7)**
For soprano and nine instruments, set to text by Kenneth Gee
First performance: 29 April 1947, Wigmore Hall, London (Gerald Cooper Concerts), Kathleen Merritt Orchestra, Joan Cross (soprano), conducted by Kathleen Merritt
Note: written at the request of Gerald Cooper

String Quartet No. 5 (1948)
1. Molto lento 2. Presto 3. Lento espressivo 4. Allegro
First performance: 5 April 1959, RBA Galleries, London (LCMC/BBC Third Programme broadcast), Hurwitz String Quartet
Publication: Lengnick, 1950

Symphony (1945–8)
1. Allegro moderato 2. Lento moderato 3. Allegro scherzando 4. Allegro molto
First performance: 27 April 1950, Maida Vale Studio 1, London (LCMC/BBC Third Programme broadcast), BBC Symphony Orchestra, conducted by Adrian Boult
Publication: Lengnick
Note: withdrawn by composer

***A Winter's Tale* (1949)**
For soprano and string quartet, set to text by Kenneth Gee
First performance: 21 January 1959, BBC Third Programme broadcast, Amici String Quartet, April Cantelo (soprano)

Concertino for Piano and String Orchestra (1949)
1. Allegro molto 2. Lento, serioso 3. Allegro con brio
First performance: 21 February 1951, BBC Third Programme broadcast, Kathleen Merritt Orchestra, Margaret Kitchin (piano), conducted by Kathleen Merritt
Publication: Lengnick

String Quartet No. 6 (1949–51)
1. Passacaglia 2. Allegro scherzando 3. Lento espressivo, rubato 4. Allegro molto, con brio
First performance: 22 May 1951, RBA Galleries, London (LCMC), Martin String Quartet
Publication: Lengnick, 1951

***Nocturne for Orchestra* (1950–1)**
First performance: 13 May 1952, Maida Vale Studio 1, London (LCMC/BBC Third Programme broadcast), Royal Philharmonic Orchestra, conducted by John Pritchard
Publication: Lengnick

***Duo: Theme and Variations for Violin and Violoncello* (1951)**
Dedication: 'For Anne and Arnold Ashby'
First performance: 12 February 1952, Mercury Theatre, London, Anne Macnaghten (violin), Arnold Ashby (viola)
Publication: Lengnick, 1954

***Six Settings of Poems by W.B. Yeats* (1951)**
1. O do not love too long 2. Fasten your hair 3. The old, old men 4. The Shadowy Horses 5. The heart of the woman 6. Penny, brown penny
First performance: 5 April 1952, Christchurch School, Ipswich, Northgatean Singers, Sophie Wyss (soprano), conducted by Peter Burges

Concertino for Bassoon and String Orchestra (1952)
1. Moderato 2. Lento espressivo, intimo 3. Presto giocoso
Dedication: 'For Gwydion Brooke'
First performance: Maida Vale Studio 1, London (LCMC/BBC broadcast concert), Goldsbrough Orchestra, Gwydion Brooke (bassoon), conducted by Edric Cundell
Publication: Lengnick, 1952

Educational piano pieces (c. 1952)
Sad Story;. The Bell; Conversation; Cradle Song; Nodding; The Dancing Bear; The Sewing Machine; Spring Waters; The Ice-Cream Man; Perpetual Motion; Drums
Note: several were published by Lengnick in various educational series

Proud Thames (1952–3)
Coronation Overture
First performance: 14 October 1953, Royal Festival Hall, London, BBC Symphony Orchestra, conducted by Adrian Boult
Publication: Lengnick

Symphony for Double String Orchestra (1952–3)
1. Allegro molto 2. Lento 3. Scherzo 4. Passacaglia
First performance: 30 November 1954, London (ICA/BBC Third Programme broadcast) Royal Philharmonic Orchestra, conducted by Walter Goehr
Publication: Lengnick

Suite on Irish Airs (1953, arr. 1954)
Suite of arrangements from the Feis Ceoil and Petrie Collections for small orchestra
1. Dirge (air: 'The Death of Staker Wallace', Feis Ceoil) 2. Lullaby (airs: 'Lullaby', Petrie; and 'O rouse yourself as cold you've got', Petrie) 3. Goodnight & joy be with you (airs: 'When the cock crows it is day', Feis Ceoil; 'Danity Down was a lad', Joyce; and 'Goodnight and joy be with you', Petrie)
Arranged: for full orchestra, 1954
First performance (arranged): 2 July 1954, Radio Éireann Symphony Orchestra broadcast
Note: commissioned by Radio Éireann

Five Hungarian Tunes (1954)
For clarinet and piano
1. Allegro moderato, vigoroso 2. Moderato 3. Corrente 4. Allegretto grazioso 5. Allegro deciso
Arranged: for piano duets (four hands) for beginners, c. 1954

Four Improvisations for Solo Double-Bass (1954)
1. Moderato 2. Tempo comodo, rubato 3. Lento meditativo 4. Allegro
Note: written for Eugene Cruft

Toombeola (1954)
For solo violin and string orchestra
Note: withdrawn by composer

Suite on Irish Airs for Violin and Piano (c. 1955)
1. The sail around the rocks (airs: 'The sail round the rocks' and 'Limerick Road'); 2. Lament (air: 'Lament for Hugh Reynolds'); 3. Old Peadar Carthy (airs: 'The Irishman's Toast' and 'Old Peadar Carthy from Clonmore')
Arranged: for flute and piano, c. 1955
1. Lament 2. The sail round the rocks 3. The Irishman's toast
Arranged: for orchestra, 1955
Dedication: 'For King Edward VI Grammar School, Chelmsford'
First performance: 13 April 1955, Hoffman Social Hall, Chelmsford, Essex, Combined German and English Orchestras, conducted by Francis Jackson

Movement for Viola and Piano (1955)
Dedication: 'For Margaret Major'
First performance: 21 November 1955, Arts Council Great Drawing Room, London (Macnaghten Concerts), Margaret Major (viola), Dorothy Manley (piano)

Where's my little basket gone? **(1955)**
Variation V: con passione based on Alfred Scott-Gatty's tune
First performance: 16 May 1955, Arts Council Great Drawing Room, London (Macnaghten New Music Group), conducted by Iris Lemare

String Quartet No. 7 (1954–5)
1. Allegro 2. Scherzo 3. Lento, tempo libero 4. Pizzicato 5. Allegro molto
First performance: 8 January 1958, BBC Third Programme broadcast, Aeolian String Quartet
Publication: Lengnick

Three Pieces for 2 Clarinets **(1955)**
1. Pastoral 2. Lament 3. Dance
Dedication: 'To Anna'

Concerto for Oboe, Bassoon, and String Orchestra (1955–6)
1. Allegro moderato 2. Lento 3. Vivo
First performance: 8 June 1959, BBC Third Programme broadcast, Welbeck String Orchestra, Evelyn Rothwell (oboe), Archie Camden (bassoon), conducted by Maurice Miles
Publication: Lengnick
Note: written for Evelyn Rothwell and Gwydion Brooke

Suite for Oboe and String Orchestra **(1955–6)**
1. Lento 2. Allegro vivo 3. Lento espressivo 4. Allegro grazioso
Dedication: 'For Gerald Finzi and the Newbury String Players'

Part Songs for St Mary's School **(1955–6)**
1. The Bellman (Robert Herrick) 2. The Armado 3. Tony O! (Colin Francis) 4. Polly Pillicote
First performance: 17 November 1956, St Mary's School, Calne, Wiltshire, School Choir (Nos. 1, 2, and 3 only)

The Exequy **(1956)**
For voice and piano, set to text by Henry King

Come away, death **(1956)**
For voice and piano, set to text from Shakespeare's *Twelfth Night*
First performance: 1966; see ***Four Shakespeare Songs*** (1956, 1965)
Publication: Chappell, 1974; copyright returned to Maconchy, 1976; Chester, 2007

String Trio (1956)
1. Allegro moderato, risoluto 2. Scherzo 3. Poco lento 4. Allegro, con gaiezza
Dedication: 'For Watson Forbes and the London String Trio'
First performance: 22 May 1957, BBC Third Programme broadcast, London String Trio
Note: withdrawn by composer

Life is a dream **(c. 1956)**
Opera based upon Pedro Calderón de la Barca's play *Life is a Dream* (*La vida es sueño*, 1635) with a libretto translated and adapted by William LeFanu
Note: incomplete

The Sofa **(1956–9, rev. 1966, 1977)**
Opera in one act after Crébillion, with libretto by Ursula Vaughan Williams
First performance: 13 December 1959, Sadler's Wells Theatre, London, New Opera Workshop, New Opera Company, New Opera Chorus, conducted by Keith Darlington
Principals: Jack Irons, Anne Abbott, Anne Pashley, Delme Bryn Jones, Heather Goddin
Producer and designer: Michael Geliot
First performance (revised): 28 February 1967, Town Hall, Euston Road, London (Camden Festival), Irwell Opera, Irwell Chamber Orchestra, conducted by Joseph Horovitz
First performance (revised): 6 October 1977, Little Theatre, Middlesbrough, Opera Nova, Lemare Orchestra, conducted by Iris Lemare
Publication: Chester, 1978

Variations on a Theme from Vaughan Williams's Job **(1957)**
For unaccompanied cello
Dedication: 'For dear Uncle Ralph on his 85th birthday'
First performance: 23 January 1959, Arts Council Great Drawing Room, London (Macnaghten Concerts), Arnold Ashby (cello)
Publication: Lengnick, 1960

The Three Strangers **(1957–8, rev. 1967, 1969, 1977)**
Opera in one act after Thomas Hardy
First performance: 5 June 1968, Bishop's Stortford, Hertfordshire, Bishop's Stortford College, conducted by Ernest Warburton
First performance (revised): 8 February 1970, BBC Radio 3 broadcast, BBC Northern Singers, BBC Symphony Orchestra, conducted by Myer Fredman
First performance (revised): 6 October 1977, Little Theatre, Middlesbrough, Opera Nova, Lemare Orchestra, conducted by Iris Lemare
Publication: Chester, 1978

A Hymn to God the Father **(1959)**
For tenor and piano, set to text by John Donne
First performance: 12 April 1964, BBC Third Programme broadcast, Peter Pears (tenor), Viola Tunnard (piano)
Publication: Chappell, 1974 (*Three Donne Songs*); copyright returned to Maconchy, 1976; Chester

The Departure **(1959–61, rev. 1977)**
Opera in one act with libretto by Anne Ridler
First performance: 16 December 1962, Sadler's Wells Theatre, London, New Opera Workshop, London Opera Sinfonietta, conducted by Alan Boustead
Principals: Catherine Wilson, Neil Howlett
Producer: Brian Trowell
Designer: Rosemary Flegg
First performance (revised): 6 October 1977, Little Theatre, Middlesbrough, Opera Nova, Lemare Orchestra, conducted by Iris Lemare
Publication: Chester, 1978

Reflections for Oboe, Clarinet, Viola, and Harp **(1960–1)**
1. Poco lento 2. Allegro molto 3. Lento 4. Con allegrezza
First performance: 27 April 1961, Maida Vale Studio 1, BBC Third Programme broadcast (Thursday Invitation Concerts), featuring the following members of the Melos Ensemble: Peter Graeme (oboe), Gervase de Peyer (clarinet), Cecil Aronowitz (viola), Osian Ellis (harp)
Publication: OUP, 1962; Chester, 1988
Note: Commissioned by the BBC

Christmas Morning: A Carol Cantata **(1960–1)**
Six carols for soprano solo, girls', boys' or women's chorus, and piano or organ, as well as optional woodwind and percussion
First performance: 6 December 1963, Church of the Holy Sepulchre, Holborn, London, Trinity College of Music Vocal Ensemble Class, conducted by James Gaddarn
Publication: Ricordi, 1963

The Yaffle **(c. 1961)**
For piano
Publication: Ricordi, 1961 (*Modern Festival Pieces for Piano*)

Conversation **(c. 1962)**
For piano
Publication: Lengnick, 1988 (*The Guildhall School of Music and Drama Piano Book, Vol. I*)

Mill Race **(1962)**
For piano
Publication: Ricordi, 1963 (*Modern Festival Pieces for Piano*)

Moonlight Night **(1962)**
For piano

The Armado **(1962)**
For chorus (SATB) and piano, text anon.
First performance: 26 February 1964, Arts Council Great Drawing Room, London (Park Lane Group), Richard Wood Singers, conducted by Richard Wood
Publication: Ricordi, 1963

Serenata Concertante **(1961–3)**
1. Lento 2. Scherzo 3. Andante con moto 4. Allegro vigoroso
For violin and orchestra
First performance: 17 October 1963, Town Hall, Birmingham, City of Birmingham Symphony Orchestra, Manoug Parikian (violin), conducted by Hugo Rignold
Publication: OUP, 1963; Chester, 1988
Note: commissioned by the City of Birmingham Symphony Orchestra under the auspices of the Feeney Trust

Quintet for Clarinet and Strings (1963)
1. Poco lento 2. Scherzo 3. Lento 4. Allegro molto
Dedication: 'For Gervase de Peyer'

First performance: 12 March 1964, Grammar School, Minehead, Dartington String Quartet, Gervase de Peyer (clarinet)
Publication: OUP, 1966; Chester, 1985
Note: commissioned by the Minehead Concerts Society

Sonatina for String Quartet (1963)
Publication: Chappell, 1964
Note: educational work

***The Starlight Night* and *Peace* (1964)**
Note: see ***Settings of Poems by Gerard Manley Hopkins***

***When that I was and a little tiny boy* (1964)**
For high voice and piano, set to text from Shakespeare's *Twelfth Night*
Note: based on the date of composition, it's possible that this work may have been initially considered for inclusion in ***Four Shakespeare Songs***

***Variazioni Concertante* (1964–5, rev. 1965)**
For oboe, clarinet, bassoon, horn, and string orchestra
First performance: 10 August 1965, Royal Albert Hall, London (BBC Promenades Concerts), BBC Scottish Orchestra, conducted by James Loughran
Note: commissioned by the BBC for the Proms

***Nocturnal* (1965)**
For mixed chorus (SATB)
1. Come! (William Barnes) 2. Will you come? (Edward Thomas) 3. To the Night (Shelley)
First performance: 22 May 1965, Staff House, University College, Cork (Cork International Choral Festival), Morley College Choir, conducted by Graham Treacher
Publication: OUP, 1966; Chester, 1984
Note: commissioned for the Cork International Festival

***A Hymn to Christ* (1965)**
For tenor and piano, set to text by John Donne
First performance: 13 July 1966, BBC Network Three broadcast, Peter Pears (tenor), Viola Tunnard (piano)
Publication: Chappell, 1974 (*Three Donne Songs*); copyright returned to Maconchy, 1976; Chester, 2007

***The Sun Rising* (1965)**
For tenor and piano, set to text by John Donne
Dedication: 'For Peter Pears'
First performance: 24 December 1971, BBC Radio 3 broadcast, Philip Langridge (tenor), Mark Elder (piano)
Publication: Chappell, 1974 (*Three Donne Songs*); copyright returned to Maconchy, 1976; Chester, 2007

Sonatina for Harpsichord (1965)
1. Allegro moderato 2. Allegro 3. Lento compassione 4. Allegro con brio
First performance: 26 November 1965, Birmingham University (Birmingham University Musical Society), Alan Cuckston (harpsichord)
Publication: Lengnick, 1972

Four Shakespeare Songs **(1956, 1965)**
For voice and piano
1. Take, oh take those lips away (*Measure for Measure*) 2. The Wind and the Rain (*Twelfth Night*) 3. Come away, Death (*Twelfth Night*) [1956] 4. King Stephen (*Othello*)
First performance: 20 April 1966, BBC Network Three broadcast, Noelle Barker (soprano), Wilfrid Parry (piano)
Publication: Chappell, 1974; copyright returned to Maconchy, 1976; Chester, 2007

Go, Penny, Go **(1965)**
Round for four equal voices
Dedication: 'For Maud Karpeles in homage and affection'

Notebook for Harpsichord **(1965)**
1. Allegro 2. Con allegrezza 3. Tempo libero, poco lento espressivo 4. Allegro molto
Dedication: 'For Zuzana Ruzickova'
First performance: 4 October 1974, Purcell Room, London, Margaret Philips
Publication: Chappell, 1974; copyright returned to Maconchy, 1976; Chester, 1977

Propheta Mendax **(1965)**
For unaccompanied boys' or women's voices, set to text from eleventh-century collection of Latin poems titled *Cambridge Songs*, translated by William LeFanu
Dedication: 'For the Vienna Boys' Choir'
First performance: 3 January 1966, Salzburg, Austria, Vienna Boys' Choir
Publication: Faber, 1966; copyright returned to Maconchy, 1978; Chester, 1989

Music for Woodwind and Brass **(1965–6)**
First performance: 25 June 1966, Thaxted Parish Church, Essex (Thaxted Midsummer Festival), Morley College Symphony Orchestra, conducted by Graham Treacher
Publication: Chester, 1986
Note: commissioned by Morley College

Down with the Rosemary and Bays **(1966)**
Twelfth Night carol for two-part chorus, set to text by Robert Herrick
First documented performance: 9 December 1972, Wangford Parish Church, Wangford Singers, conducted by Marguerita Chilvers
Publication: Cambridge University Press, 1967 (*The Cambridge Hymnal*)

An Essex Overture **(1966)**
For orchestra
Dedication: 'Dedicated to the Essex Youth Orchestra'
First performance: 1968 Bath Music Festival, Essex Youth Orchestra, conducted by Graham Treacher
Publication: British and Continental Music Agencies, 1967

I sing of a Maiden **(1966)**
Carol for soprano or treble solo and unaccompanied three-part chorus, text anon.
Publication: Faber, 1966

Witnesses **(1965–6)**
Incidental music for play by the same title by Anne Ridler premièred in Leeds on 13 July 1967

Nowell, sing we nowell **(1966)**
Carol for three-part unaccompanied choir
First documented performance: 9 December 1972, Wangford Parish Church, Wangford Singers, conducted by Marguerita Chilvers
Publication: Cambridge University Press, 1967 (*The Cambridge Hymnal*)

Six Miniatures for Solo Violin **(1966)**
1. Preamble 2. Meditation 3. Dialogue 4. Lullaby 5. Badinage 6. Roundabout
Dedication: 'For Frederick Grinke'
First performance: 27 October 1966, University of Edinburgh Frederick Grinke

This Day **(1966)**
Carol for soprano or treble solo and unaccompanied two-part chorus, text anon.
First documented performance: 6 January 1969, BBC Music Programme, Lindsay Singers, conducted by Ethna Barror
Publication: Faber, 1966

String Quartet No. 8 (1966–7)
1. Lento 2. Scherzo 3. Lento 4. Allegro
First performance: 5 April 1967, Purcell Room, London (Macnaghten Concerts), Aeolian String Quartet
Publication: Faber, 1967
Note: commissioned by the Macnaghten Concerts

Preludio, fugato e finale **(1967)**
Duet for piano
Dedication: 'For Susan Bradshaw and Richard Rodney Bennett'
First performance: 16 February 1968, Wigmore Hall, London (Macnaghten Concerts), Susan Bradshaw and Richard Rodney Bennett
Publication: Chappell, 1974; copyright returned to Maconchy, 1976

Conversations for Clarinet and Viola **(1967–8)**
1. Tempo libero, poco lento 2. Sostenuto 3. Allegro molto ritmico 4. Moderato
First performance: 12 January 1970, Major's Reception Room, Town Hall, Huddersfield (Huddersfield Music Society), Martin Ronchetti (clarinet), John White (viola)
Publication: Chappell, 1974, copyright returned to Maconchy, 1976; Chester, 1987

Three Cloudscapes for Orchestra **(1968)**
1. Lento 2. Scherzo 3. Trio
First performance: 5 July 1968, Town Hall, Cheltenham (Cheltenham Festival), Budapest Symphony Orchestra, conducted by György Lehel
Note: commissioned by the Cheltenham Festival and later withdrawn by composer

The Birds **(1967–8)**
Extravaganza in one act
First performance: 5 June 1968, Bishop's Stortford, Hertfordshire, Bishop's Stortford College, conducted by Christopher Rees
Publication: Boosey & Hawkes, 1978

And Death Shall Have No Dominion **(1968–9)**
For mixed chorus (SATB) and brass ensemble, set to text by Dylan Thomas
First performance: 26 August 1969, Worcester Cathedral (Three Choirs Festival), Cathedral Choirs, Birmingham Brass Ensemble, conducted by Christopher Robinson
Publication: Chester, 2006

String Quartet No. 9 (1968–9)
1. Allegro 2. Scherzo 3. Mesto, tempo libero 4. Allegro
First performance: 1 November 1969, The Meeting House, University of Sussex (Radcliffe Music Award Competition), Allegri String Quartet
Publication: Chappell, 1974; copyright returned to Maconchy, 1976; Chester

Johnny and the Mohawks **(1969)**
Opera for children 7–9
Note: written for Francis Holland School in London and performed in the summer of 1971
Publication: OUP, 1970

Three Preludes for Violin and Piano (1969)
1. Tempo libero, senza misura 2. Andantino quieto 3. Con allegrezza
Dedication: 'For Antonietta and Felicity Notariello'
First performance: 1970, Dublin
Publication: Chappell, 1974; copyright returned to Maconchy, 1976

Settings of Poems by Gerard Manley Hopkins **(1964, 1970)**
1. The Starlight Night (1964) 2. Peace (1964) 3. The May Magnificat (1970)
Dedication: 'For Mary Wells and Philip Ledger' (Nos. 1 and 2)
First performance (Nos. 1 and 2): 24 October 1964, Chelmsford Cathedral, Jacques Orchestra, Mary Wells (soprano), conducted by Philip Ledger
First performance (all three): 29 May 1970, St Andrew's Hall, Norwich, English Chamber Orchestra, Robert Tear (tenor), conducted by Philip Ledger
Publication: Chester

The Jesse Tree **(1969–70, rev. 1970)**
Masque with libretto by Anne Ridler
First performance: 7 October 1970, Dorchester Abbey (Dorchester Abbey Festival), Choir of Culham College of Education, unnamed orchestra, conducted by Henry Ward
Principals: Rosanne Creffield, Bryan Drake, Philip Langridge, Anne Pashley
Producers: Daphne Marshall and Alan Kitching
Designer: John Piper
Choreography: Sylvia Demmery
Note: Maconchy also made arrangements for voice and piano of Mary's Song and Carol with the former published along with an arrangement of the Trio and Chorus in Anne Rider, *The Jesse Tree with Drawings by John Piper* (London: Lyrebird Press, 1972).

Music for Double-Bass and Piano **(1970)**
Dedication: 'For Rodney Slatford'
First performance: 14 January 1971, Purcell Room, London (Park Lane Group), Rodney Slatford (double bass), Clifford Lee (piano)
Publication: Yorke, 1971

Ariadne **(1970–1)**
Dramatic monologue for soprano and orchestra, set to text by Cecil Day-Lewis
First performance: 30 July 1971, St Nicholas Chapel, King's Lynn, English Chamber Orchestra, Heather Harper (soprano), conducted by Raymond Leppard
Publication: Chester, 1976
Note: commissioned by the King's Lynn Festival

Prayer before Birth **(1971)**
For women's chorus, set to text by Louis MacNeice
Dedication: 'For Ethna Barror and the Lindsay Singers'
First performance: 6 May 1972, Staff House, University College, Cork (Cork International Choral and Folk Dance Festival), Lindsay Singers, conducted by Ethna Barror
Publication: Chester, 1987

Doubt that the stars are fire **(1971)**
Round for four voices, set to text by Shakespeare
Dedication: 'To Arthur Bliss in homage and affection for his 80th birthday'

Faustus **(1971)**
Scena for tenor and piano
First performance: 12 January 1972, Purcell Room, London (Park Lane Group), Neil Page (tenor), Clifford Lee (piano)
Publication: Chappell, 1974; copyright returned to Maconchy, 1976
Note: commissioned by the Park Lane Group

String Quartet No. 10 (1971–2)
In one movement
First performance: 15 July 1972, Pitville Pump Room, Cheltenham (Cheltenham Festival), Alberta String Quartet
Publication: Chappell, 1974; copyright returned to Maconchy, 1976; Chester, 1976
Note: commissioned by the Cheltenham Festival

Quartet for Oboe, Violin, Viola, and Cello (1972)
Dedication: 'For Janet Craxton and the London Oboe Quartet'
First performance: 17 December 1972, Wigmore Hall, London, Janet Craxton (oboe), Perry Hart (violin), Brian Hawkins (viola), Kenneth Heath (cello)
Publication: Chappell, 1974; copyright returned to Maconchy, 1976; Chester 1984

Three Bagatelles **(1972)**
For oboe and harpsichord
1. Allegro 2. Poco lento, tempo libero 3. Vivo
Dedication: 'For Evelyn Barbirolli and Valda Aveling'
First performance: 23 October 1972, Purcell Room, London, Evelyn Barbirolli (oboe), Valda Aveling (harpsichord)
Publication: OUP, 1974

3 Easy Duets for Two Violas (c. 1972)
1. Mimic 2. Dialogue 3. Threnody
Publication: Faber, 1972
Note: also arranged for two cellos

3 Easy Pieces for Violin and Viola (c. 1972)
1. Lullaby 2. Moto perpetuo 3. The Waterwheel
Publication: Faber, 1972

4 Easy Trios for Two Violins and Violas (or Violin and Two Violas) (c.1972)
1. Musette 2. Waltz 3. Elegy 4. Serenade
Publication: Faber, 1972

Four Canons (in the first position) for Two Violins (1972)
Note: educational work

Four Easy Pieces for Two Violins (1972)
Note: educational work

Lament for Two Violins (1972)
Note: educational work

Genesis (1972–3)
For chamber orchestra
First performance: 6 May 1973, Queen Elizabeth Hall, London, English Chamber Orchestra, conducted by Raymond Leppard
Note: withdrawn by composer

Fly-by-Nights (1973)
For women's or children's chorus with harp or piano
1. Hey-how for Hallowe'en 2. All the Night Over 3. The Owl's Song 4. Witches 5. Bell Song 6. The Ghosts's Song 7. When Larks 'gin sing
Dedication: 'For Osian Ellis, John Andrewes and the Finchley Children's Music Group'
First performance: 31 May 1974, St George's, Hanover Square, London, Finchley Children's Music Group, Osian Ellis (harp), conducted by John Andrewes
Publication: Boosey & Hawkes, 1977

The Isles of Greece (1973)
For chorus (SATB) and orchestra, set to text by Lord Byron
First performance: 21 April 1974, Drury Lane Theatre, London, Royal Philharmonic Orchestra, Louis Halsey Singers, conducted by Bernard Herrmann
Publication: Chappell, 1973; copyright returned to Maconchy, 1976
Note: commissioned by the Byron Society

Three Songs for Tenor and Harp (1973–4)
1. A widow-bird sate mourning (Shelley) 2. So we'll go no more a-roving (Byron) 3. The knot there's no untying (Thomas Campbell)
Dedication: 'For Peter Pears and Osian Ellis'
First performance: 19 June 1974, Snape Maltings Concert Hall, Aldeburgh (Aldeburgh Festival), Peter Pears (tenor), Osian Ellis (harp)
Publication: Chappell, 1974; copyright returned to Maconchy, 1976; Chester, 1976

Sirens' Song (1974)
For soprano solo and unaccompanied chorus, set to text by William Browne
First performance: 23 November 1974, Queen Elizabeth Hall, London (Thames Concerts Society), Louis Halsey Singers, conducted by Louis Halsey

Publication: Chester, 1977
Note: commissioned by the Louis Halsey Singers with funding provided by the Arts Council of Great Britain

Two Epitaphs (1974)
Two part songs for SSA chorus
1. Our life is nothing but a winter's day (Francis Quarles) 2. As the tree falls (anon.)
Dedication: 'For the Cantamus Ensemble'
First performance: 4 May 1976, BBC Radio 3 broadcast, Cantamus Ensemble, conducted by Pamela Cook
Publication: Chester, 1976

***Christmas Night* (1974)**
A carol in four parts, a *cappella*
Dedication: 'For James Gaddarn and the Croydon Philharmonic Choir'
First performance: 14 December 1974, St John's, Smith Square, London, BBC Singers, conducted by John Poole
Publication: Chappell, 1974

***Chant for Bishop's Stortford Parish Church* (1975)**

Touchstone for Oboe and Chamber Organ (1975)
Dedication: 'For Janet Craxton and Alan Harverson'
First performance: 17 June 1975, Queen Elizabeth Hall, London, Janet Craxton (oboe), Alan Harverson (organ)

***Epyllion* (1973–5)**
For solo cello and string orchestra
1. Lento moderato 2. Scherzo 3. Lento 4. Moderato
Dedication: 'For Kenneth Heath and the Academy of St Martin-in-the-Fields'
First performance: 13 July 1975, Town Hall, Cheltenham (Cheltenham Festival), Academy of St Martin-in-the-Fields, Kenneth Heath (cello), conducted by Neville Marriner
Publication: Chappell, 1975; copyright returned to Maconchy, 1976; Chester, 1976

***The King of the Golden River* (1974–5, rev. 1976)**
Opera for children after Ruskin's tale with libretto by Anne Ridler
First performance: 29 October 1975, University Church of St Mary the Virgin, Oxford, pupils of Headington School and New College School, Oxford, conducted by David Whittington
Note: commissioned by the University Church of St Mary the Virgin, Oxford, with funding provided by the Arts Council of Great Britain

***Two Settings of Poems by Gerard Manley Hopkins* (1975)**
For choir and brass
1. Pied Beauty 2. Heaven-haven
Dedication: 'To Richard Seal and the choir of Salisbury Cathedral'
First performance: 24 July 1976, Salisbury Cathedral (Southern Cathedrals Festival), Choirs of Salisbury, Winchester, and Chichester Cathedrals, Philip Jones Brass Ensemble, conducted by Richard Seal
Publication: Chester, 1982

Morning, Noon and Night **(1976)**
For harp
Dedication: 'For Osian Ellis'
First performance: 17 June 1977, Jubilee Hall, Aldeburgh (Aldeburgh Festival), Osian Ellis
Publication: Chester, 1978

Sinfonietta (1976)
For orchestra
First performance: 23 April 1977, Civic Centre, Chelmsford, Essex Youth Orchestra, conducted by Graham Treacher
Publication: Chester, 1976
Note: commissioned by the Essex Youth Orchestra with funding provided by the Arts Council of Great Britain

String Quartet No. 11 (1976–7)
In one movement
First performance: 13 December 1977, Goldsmiths' Hall, London (City Music Society), Lindsay String Quartet
Publication: Chester, 1982
Note: 'commissioned by the City Music Society to celebrate the 650th anniversary of the granting of its charter to the Worshipful Company of Goldsmiths'

Sun, Moon and Stars **(1977)**
For soprano and piano, set to text by Thomas Traherne
1. Sun, Moon and Stars 2. The Hill 3. Solitude
Dedication: 'For Jane Manning and Richard Rodney Bennett'
First performance: 19 February 1978, Hong Kong Performing Arts Centre, Hong Kong, Jane Manning (soprano), Richard Rodney Bennett (piano)
Publication: Chester, 1978

The Leaden Echo and the Golden Echo **(1978)**
For mixed choir, alto flute, viola, and harp, set to text by Gerard Manley Hopkins
First performance: 25 November 1978, Royal Northern College of Music, Manchester, William Byrd Singers, Christine Malkin (soprano), Ingrid Culliford (alto flute), Robin Grice (viola), Barry Cheshire (harp), conducted by Stephen Wilkinson
Publication: Chester, 1981
Note: commissioned by Wilkinson for the William Byrd Singers with funding provided by the Arts Council of Great Britain

Héloïse and Abelard **(1975–8)**
Dramatic cantata arranged in nine sections for soprano, tenor, baritone, chorus, and orchestra
First performance: 3 March 1979, Fairfield Hall, Croydon, Croydon Philharmonic Choir, English Symphony Orchestra, Hannah Francis (soprano), Philip Langridge (tenor), Tom McDonnell (baritone), conducted by James Gaddarn
Publication: Chester, 1978
Note: commissioned by the Croydon Philharmonic Society with funding provided by the Arts Council of Great Britain

***Contemplation for Cello and Piano* (1978)**
Dedication: 'For Rohan de Saram and Douglas Young'
First performance: 31 October 1979, Recital Hall, University of Huddersfield (Huddersfield Contemporary Music Festival), Rohan de Saram (cello), Douglas Young (piano)
Publication: Chester, 1978

***Four Miniatures* (1978)**
For unaccompanied chorus (SATB), set to texts by Eleanor Farjeon
1. Light the lamps, lamplighter 2. For Snow 3. The night will never stay 4. For a Mocking Voice
Dedication: 'For Angela Dugdale and the Broadland Singers'
First performance: 17 October 1979, Marble Hall, Surrey House, Norwich (Norfolk & Norwich Triennial Festival), Broadland Singers, conducted by Angela Dugdale
Publication: Chester, 1979
Note: commissioned with funds provided by the Arts Council of Great Britain

***Colloquy for Flute and Piano* (1979)**
1. Allegro 2. Scherzando 3. Poco lento 4. Vivo
Dedication: 'For Ingrid Culliford'
First performance: 2 June 1979, Wigmore Hall, London, Ingrid Culliford (flute), Shelagh Sutherland (piano)
Publication: Chester, 1980
Note: commissioned with funds provided by the Arts Council of Great Britain

String Quartet No. 12 (1979)
1. Allegro moderato 2. Scherzo 3. Lento non troppo e flessibile 4. Molto moderato
First performance: 21 October 1979, Crucible Theatre, Sheffield, Lindsay String Quartet
Publication: Chester, 1979
Note: commissioned by the University of Sheffield for the Lindsay String Quartet with funds provided by the Arts Council of Great Britain as part of the university's centenary celebrations of Firth College

***Creatures* (1979)**
For unaccompanied chorus (SATB)
1. The Hen and the Carp (Ian Serraillier) 2. The Snail (James Reeves) 3. Rendezvous with a Beetle (E.V. Rieu) 4. Tiger! Tiger! (William Blake) 5. Cat's Funeral (E.V. Rieu) 6. The Dove and the Wren (trad.) 7. Cat! (Eleanor Farjeon)
Dedication: 'For Stephen Wilkinson & the BBC Northern Singers'
First performance: 23 July 1980, Chester Town Hall (Chester Summer Music Festival), BBC Northern Singers, conducted by Stephen Wilkinson
Publication: Chester, 1980
Note: commissioned by the Chester Summer Music Festival with funding provided by the Arts Council of Great Britain

***Romanza* (1979)**
For solo viola and ensemble (wind quintet and string quintet)
First performance: 12 March 1980, Queen Elizabeth Hall, London, John Bate Orchestra, Paul Silverthorne (viola), conducted by John Bate
Publication: Chester, 1979

Fantasia for Clarinet and Piano **(1980)**
Dedication: 'For Thea King'
First performance: 12 August 1980, Denver, Colorado (International Clarinet Congress), Thea King (clarinet), Paula Fan (piano)
Publication: Chester, 1981
Note: commissioned by Thea King with funding provided by the Arts Council of Great Britain

Piccola musica **(1980)**
For string trio
I. Allegro moderato 2. Andante 3. Moderato 4. Poco lento 5. Allegro moderato
First performance: 13 July 1981, Pittville Pump Room, Cheltenham (Cheltenham Festival), Nash String Trio
Publication: Chester, 1981
Note: commissioned by the Cheltenham Festival with funding provided by South West Arts and Cheltenham Arts Festival Ltd

Trittico **(1980)**
For two oboes, bassoon, and harpsichord
I. Preludio 2. Ninna-nanna (Lullaby) 3. Finale
Dedication: 'For Sheba Sound'
First performance: 14 July 1981, London (City of London Festival), Catherine Smith (oboe), John Macintyre (oboe), Richard Skinner (bassoon), Sharon Gould (harpsichord)
Publication: Chester, 1981
Note: commissioned by Sheba Sound with funding provided by the Arts Council of Great Britain

Little Symphony **(1980–1)**
1. Moderato 2. Scherzo 3. Andante sostenuto 4. Allegro moderato
Dedication: 'For Lawrence Leonard and the Norfolk CYO'
First performance: 28 July 1981, St Andrew's Hall, Norwich, Norfolk County Youth Orchestra, conducted by Lawrence Leonard
Publication: Chester, 1981
Note: commissioned by the Norfolk County Youth Orchestra with funding provided by the Eastern Arts Association

My Dark Heart **(1981)**
For soprano and six players, set to text from Petrarch's Sonnets, translated by J.M. Synge
1. Andante 2. Comodo, flessibile 3. Andante
First performance: 19 March 1982, Recital Hall, RCM (Maconchy's seventy-fifth birthday concert), Anne Richards (soprano), Shaun Sellings (flute), Alan Garner (oboe), Stephen Bell (horn), Stephen Bryant (violin), Russell Thackeray (viola), Caroline Dearnley (cello), conducted by John Forster
Publication: Chester, 1981
Note: commissioned by the RCM for its centenary with funding provided by the Arts Council of Great Britain

Wind Quintet (1981)
For flute, oboe, clarinet, horn, and bassoon
1. Allegro 2. Poco lento 3. Vivo e leggiero 4. Andante 5. Allegretto

Dedication: 'For the Albion Ensemble'
First performance: 29 September 1982, St Sampson's Church, Cricklade (Cricklade Arts Festival), Albion Ensemble
Publication: Chester, 1982

Music for Strings **(1981–2)**
1. Molto moderato 2. Scherzo 3. Mesto 4. Allegro
First performance: 26 July 1983, Royal Albert Hall, London (Promenade Concert and broadcast), BBC Philharmonic Orchestra, conducted by Edward Downes
Publication: Chester, 1983
Note: commissioned by the BBC for the Proms

For Bonny, Sweet Robin **(1982)**
For solo voice and unaccompanied chorus, set to text by Shakespeare

L'horloge **(1982)**
For soprano, clarinet, and piano, sext to text by Charles Baudelaire
First performance: 21 May 1983, Rosslyn Hill Chapel, London, Sylvia Eaves (soprano), Thea King (clarinet), Courtney Kenny (piano)
Publication: Chester, 1983
Note: written for Anthony Friese-Greene

Three Songs for Baritone and Piano **(1982)**
1. Abelard's Lament (adapted from *Héloïse and Abelard*) 2. The Hangman's Song (from *The Three Strangers*) 3. Not only I (from *The Three Strangers*)
Publication: Chester, 1982
Note: arranged for Brian Rayner Cook

Tribute **(1982)**
For solo violin and double woodwind
Dedication: 'For Iris Lemare'
First performance: 10 April 1983, Civic Centre, Darlington (Iris Lemare eightieth birthday concert), Nicholas Ward (violin), John Barrow (flute), Clare Jordan (flute), Chris Knowles (oboe), Valerie Taylor (oboe), Ruth Ellis (clarinet), Anthony Houghton (clarinet), Richard Jackson (bassoon), Roy Walmsley (bassoon), conducted by Iris Lemare
Publication: Chester, 1983

Quartetto corto **(String Quartet No. 13) (1982–3)**
In one movement
First performance: 28 March 1985, Menuhin Room, County Library, Portsmouth (Third Portsmouth International String Quartet Competition), played by all semifinalists
Publication: Chester, 1984
Note: commissioned specially for the competition with funding provided by the Southern Arts Association

Five Sketches for Viola **(1983)**
1. Molto moderato 2. Allegro deciso 3. Andantino 4. Poco lento 5. Presto
Dedication: 'For Nicholas Logie'
First performance: 31 May 1984, Wigmore Hall, London, Nicolas Logie
Publication: Chester, 1987

***The Bellman* (1983)**
Carol for mixed voices (SATB), set to text by Robert Herrick
Publication: Chester (*The Chester Book of Carols*), 1985
Note: Maconchy initially titled the work *My masters, all good day to you!*

***There is no Rose* (1983)**
Carol for mixed voices (SATB), text anon.
Dedication: 'For the Witham Choral Society'
First performance: 5 December 1984, St Nicholas Church, Witham, Witham Choral Society, conducted by George James
Publication: Chester (*The Chester Book of Carols*), 1985

***O time turn back* (1983–4)**
For chorus (SATB), wind quintet, and cello. Set to words by Shakespeare, Henry Vaughan, William Blake, Walter Raleigh, Robert Herrick
First Performance: 20 May 1985, BBC Radio 3 broadcast, BBC Singers, Albion Ensemble, conducted by Stephen Wilkinson
Publication: Chester, 1984
Note: commissioned by the BBC

Concertino for Clarinet and Small Orchestra (1984)
I. Poco lento 2. Vivo 3. Allegro Ritmico
Dedication: 'For Janet Hilton'
First performance: 6 December 1985, Henry Wood Hall, Glasgow, BBC Scottish Symphony Orchestra, Janet Hilton (clarinet), conducted by Nicholas Kraemer
Publication: Chester, 1984

***Narration* (1984)**
For solo cello
First performance: 13 February 1985, Town Hall, Huntingdon (Huntingdon Music Society), Steven Isserlis
Publication: Chester, 1984
Note: commissioned by the Huntingdon Music Society with funding provided by the Arts Council of Great Britain

***Still Falls the Rain* (1984)**
For unaccompanied double choir, set to text by Edith Sitwell
First performance: 22 May 1985, Chelmsford Cathedral (Chelmsford Cathedral Festival), BBC Singers, conducted by John Poole
Publication: Chester, 1985
Note: commissioned by the Chelmsford Cathedral Festival with funding provided by the Eastern Arts Council

***Excursion* (c. 1984)**
For solo bassoon
Publication: Chester, 1986
Note: written for Maconchy's grandson, Christopher Dunlop

***Life Story* (1985)**
For string orchestra
First performance: 4 June 1986, Sawtry Village College, Cambridgeshire, Peterborough String Orchestra, conducted by Paul Manley

Publication: Chester, 1985
Note: commissioned by the Peterborough String Orchestra with funding provided by the Eastern Arts Association

Three Songs for Tracy Chadwell **(1985)**
For voice and piano
1. In Memory of W.B. Yeats (W.H. Auden) 2. In Memory of W. B. Yeats II (W.H. Auden) 3. It's No Go (Louis MacNeice)
First performance: 26 October 1985, Folkestone, Kent (Folkestone and Hythe Music Club), Tracy Chadwell (soprano), Pamela Lidiard (piano)
Publication: Chester, 1985
Note: commissioned by Tracy Chadwell with funding provided by Southern Arts

Butterflies **(1986)**
For voice and harp, set to text by John Ray
First performance: 4 October 1986, Braintree, Essex, Betty Beal (mezzo-soprano), Meriel Barclay (harp)
Publication: Chester, 1986
Note: commissioned by the Braintree District Arts Council with funding provided by the Eastern Arts Association

Bagatelle for Piano **(1986)**
Dedication: 'For Richard [Rodney Bennett] on his 50th birthday'

On St Stephenses Day **(1989)**
For women's chorus
First performance: BBC Northern Singers, conducted by Stephen Wilkinson
Publication: Chester, 1989
Note: written for Stephen Wilkinson's seventieth birthday. The première, which was scheduled to take place at The Studio in Manchester on 9 September, had to be postponed.

Undated Works

Chicane **(c. 1950s)**
For two clarinets
Note: educational work

Golden hair
For voice and piano

Not I
Round in four parts, set to text by Robert Stevenson

Petite Suite
For piano quintet

Seven Little Inventions for Clavicord (in seven metres) **(c. 1960s)**
Dedication: 'For Valda Aveling'
Note: incomplete

Seven O'Clock
For piano

When I was one and twenty (c. 1920s)
For voice and piano, set to text by A.E. Housman

Where are you going my pretty maid?
For voice and piano

Zodiac Book
For piano
1. Taurus 2. Gemini 3. Sagittarius 4. Pisces 5. Libra or Aquarius 6. Aries

Select Bibliography

Primary Archives Consulted

National Archives, Kew
BBC Written Archives Centre, Caversham
British Library, London
Royal College of Music Archives, London
St Hilda's College, Oxford
V&A Theatre and Performance Archives, London

Newspapers and Periodicals

Advertiser
Birmingham Post
Bohemia
Chesterian
Classical Music
Country Life
Daily Express
Daily Mail
Daily Telegraph
Dublin Evening Mail
Edinburgh Evening News
Evening News
Financial Times
Gentlewoman
Guardian
Irish Independent
Irish Press
Irish Times
Leader
Listener
Liverpool Daily Post
Liverpool Post and Mercury
Manchester Guardian
Monthly Musical Record
Morning Post
Music and Musicians
Musical Opinion
Music Lover
Musical Events
Musical Times
Národni Osvobozeni

New Statesman
News Chronicle
Observer
Ottawa Citizen
Penguin Music Magazine
Prager Presse
Prager Tagblatt
R.C.M. Magazine
Rocky Mountain Telegraph
The Queen: The Lady's Newspaper and Court Chronicle
Radio Times
Saturday Review
Scotsman
Spectator
Sunday Referee
Sunday Times
Times
Venkov
Weekly News
Western Daily Press
Western Morning News

Published Sources

'The Late Dr. Charles Wood: An Appreciation by a Friend', *R.C.M. Magazine* 22/3 (1926): 71–7.

Adams, Byron, and Robin Wells (eds), *Vaughan Williams Essays* (Aldershot: Ashgate, 2003).

Aldgate, Anthony, *Censorship and the Permissive Society: British Cinema and Theatre 1955–1965* (Oxford: Clarendon Press, 1995).

Aldgate, Anthony, and James C. Robertson, *Censorship in Theatre and Cinema* (Edinburgh: Edinburgh University Press, 2005).

Aldridge, Maisie, 'Arthur Alexander, 1891–1969', *R.C.M. Magazine* 65/3 (1969): 33–5.

Anderson, W.R., 'Tobias Matthay (1858–1945)', *Musical Times* 87/1235 (January 1946): 9–13.

Armstrong, Thomas, 'Sir Hugh Allen', *Musical Times* 87/1237 (March 1946): 73–6.

Bacharach, A.L. (ed.), *British Music of Our Time* (Harmondsworth: Pelican Books, 1946).

Bailey, Cyril, *Hugh Percy Allen* (London: Oxford University Press, 1984).

Banfield, Stephen (ed.), *Music in Britain: The Twentieth Century* (Oxford: Blackwell, 1995).

Banner, Barbara, 'Charles Herbert Kitson', *R.C.M. Magazine* 40/2 (1944): 57–8.

Beausang, Ita, and Séamas de Barra, *Ina Boyle (1889–1967): A Composer's Life* (Cork: Cork University Press), 2018.

Beckwith, John, and Udo Kasemets (eds), *The Modern Composer and His World* (Toronto: University of Toronto Press, 1961).

Bingham, Adrian, *Gender, Modernity, and the Popular Press in Inter-war Britain* (Oxford: Oxford University Press 2004).

Blunnie, Ailie, 'Passion and Intellect in the Music of Elizabeth Maconchy DBE (1907–1994)' (Master's thesis, National University of Ireland, Maynooth, 2010).
Blyth, Ian, 'A Sort of English Georgics: Vita Sackville-West's *The Land*', *Modern Language Studies* 45/1 (2008): 19–31.
Bullivant, Joanna, *Alan Bush, Modern Music, and the Cold War* (Cambridge: Cambridge University Press, 2017).
———, 'Modernism, Politics, and Individuality in 1930s Britain: The Case of Alan Bush', *Music & Letters* 90/3 (August 2009): 432–52.
Burke, Bernard, *A genealogical and heraldic history of the landed gentry of Great Britain & Ireland,* 6th edn with supplement, vol. II (London: Harrison and Sons, 1882).
Bush, Alan, 'The I.S.C.M. Festival at Prague', *Musical Times* 76/1112 (October 1935): 940–1.
Carpenter, Humphrey, *The Envy of the World: Fifty Years of the BBC Third Programme and Radio 3* (London: Weidenfeld and Nicolson, 1996).
Chapman, Ernest, 'The Macnaghten Concerts', *Composer* 57 (Spring 1976): 13–18.
Charterhouse Register, 1872–1910, vol. I (London: Proprietors at the Chiswick Press, 1911).
Clark, Walter, 'Vaughan Williams and the "night side of nature": Octatonicism in *Riders to the Sea*', in Byron Adams and Robin Wells (eds), *Vaughan Williams Essays* (Aldershot: Ashgate, 2003), 55–71.
Cobbe, Hugh (ed.), *Letters of Ralph Vaughan Williams 1895–1958* (Oxford: Oxford University Press, 2008).
Cole, Hugo, *The Changing Face of Music* (London: Victor Gollancz Ltd, 1978).
Colles, H.C., 'Directors of the R.C.M.: Sir Hugh Allen and Dr. George Dyson', *Musical Times* 78/1136 (October 1937): 861–3.
———, *The Royal College of Music: A Jubilee Record, 1883–1933* (London: Macmillan, 1933).
Columb, Frank, *The Lough Gowna Valley* (Oxford: Gasan Academic Publishing Company, 2002).
Commanday, Robert P., 'In Memoriam Sandor Salgo', *San Francisco Classical Voice*: http://www.sfcv.org/arts_revs/sandor_tribute_1_23_07.php [accessed 2 May 2014].
Copley, Ian A., *The Music of Charles Wood: A Critical Study* (London: Thames, 1978).
Cox, David, *The Henry Wood Proms* (London: British Broadcasting Corporation, 1980).
Craig, Tina, Eustace Cornelius, and Ian Lyle, 'Obituary: William Richard Lefanu (1904–1995)', *Health Libraries Review* 13 (1996): 179–81.
De Burgh, U.H. Hussey, *The Landowners of Ireland* (Dublin: Hodges, Foster, and Figgis, 1878).
Dibble, Jeremy, 'Wood, Charles', *Grove Music Online*, 2001, https://doi.org/10.1093/gmo/9781561592630.article.30536 [accessed 15 July 2020].
Dickinson, Peter (ed.), *Lennox Berkeley and Friends* (Woodbridge: Boydell, 2012).
Doctor, Jennifer, 'Maconchy's String Quartet No. 7 and the BBC', *Musical Objects* 1 (1995): 5–8.

———, '"Working for her own Salvation": Vaughan Williams as teacher of Elizabeth Maconchy, Grace Williams, and Ina Boyle', in Lewis Foreman (ed.), *Vaughan Williams in Perspective* (London: Albion, 1998), 181–201.

———, 'Intersecting Circles: The Early Careers of Elizabeth Maconchy, Elisabeth Lutyens, and Grace Williams', *Women & Music* 2 (1998): 90–109.

———, 'Maconchy, Dame Elizabeth Violet (1907–1994)', in H. C. G. Matthew and Brian Harrison (eds), *Oxford Dictionary of National Biography* (Oxford: Oxford University Press, 2004).

———, *The BBC and Ultra-Modern Music, 1922–1936* (Cambridge: Cambridge University Press, 1999).

Doctor, Jennifer, and Sophie Fuller (eds), *Music, Life, and Changing Times: Selected Correspondence Between Composers Elizabeth Maconchy and Grace Williams, 1927–77*, vols. I and II (London: Routledge, 2019).

Doctor, Jennifer, and Nicholas Kenyon (eds), *The Proms* (London: Thames & Hudson, 2007).

Dodd, John, 'The growth of the Pollard Wood area', http://www.chalfonthistory.co.uk/pollards_wood_recent_history.html [accessed 30 March 2021].

Dunlop, Anna, 'Personal Recollections of my Mother, Elizabeth Maconchy', in Christa Brüstle and Danielle Sofer (eds), *Elizabeth Maconchy: Music as Impassioned Argument* (Vienna: Universal Edition, 2018), 14–20.

Ehrlich, Cyril, *The Music Profession in Britain since the Eighteenth Century: A Social History* (Oxford: Clarendon Press, 1985).

Elias, William Y., 'Partos, Oedoen', *Grove Music Online*, 2001, https://doi.org/10.1093/gmo/9781561592630.article.20985 [accessed 6 September 2020].

Evans, Edwin, 'Then and Now', *Musical Times* 85/1219 (September 1944): 269–71.

Fauser, Annegret, 'The Scholar behind the Medal: Edward J. Dent (1876–1957) and the Politics of Music History', *Journal of the Royal Musical Association* 139/2 (2014): 235–60.

Fuller, Sophie, *The Pandora Guide to Women Composers* (London: Pandora, 1994).

——— ,'"Putting the BBC and T. Beecham to Shame": The Macnaghten-Lemare Concerts, 1931–7', *Journal of the Royal Musical Association* 138/2 (2013): 377–414.

———, 'The Maconchy-Williams Correspondence, 1927–1977', in Christa Brüstle and Danielle Sofer (eds), *Elizabeth Maconchy: Music as Impassioned Argument* (Vienna: Universal Edition, 2018), 38–62.

———, 'Women Composers during the British Musical Renaissance, 1880–1918' (PhD thesis, King's College, University of London, 1998).

Garside, W.R., *British Unemployment, 1919–1939: A Study in Public Policy* (Cambridge: Cambridge University Press, 1990).

Gershon, Leoine, 'The String Quartets of Elizabeth Maconchy C.B.E.' (thesis, University of Bristol, 1983–4).

Gilbert, Susie, *Opera for Everybody: The Story of English National Opera* (London: Faber and Faber, 2009).

Gillett, Paula, *Musical Women in England, 1870–1914: 'Encroaching on All Man's Privileges'* (New York: St. Martin's Press, 2000).

Glendinning, Victoria, *Vita: The Life of Vita Sackville-West* (London: Penguin Books, 1984).

Glock, William, *Notes in Advance: An Autobiography in Music* (Oxford: Oxford University Press, 1991).

Gottlieb, Julie V., and Richard Toye (eds), *The Aftermath of Suffrage: Women, Gender, and Politics in Britain, 1918–1945* (Basingstoke: Palgrave Macmillan, 2013).

Gray, Cecil, *A Survey of Contemporary Music*, 2nd edn (London: Oxford University Press, 1928).

Grogan, Christopher (ed.), *Imogen Holst: A Life in Music*, revised edn (Woodbridge: Boydell, 2010).

Halstead, Jill, *Ruth Gipps: Anti-Modernism, Nationalism and Difference in English Music* (Aldershot: Ashgate, 2006).

———, *The Woman Composer: Creativity and the Gendered Politics of Musical Composition* (Aldershot: Ashgate, 1997).

Hardy, Thomas (ed.), *Select Poems of William Barnes* (London: Henry Frowde, 1908).

Heward Rees, A.J., 'Views and Revisions. The Composer Grace Williams talks with A.J. Heward Rees', *Welsh Music* 5/4 (Winter 1976–7): 7–18.

Holst, Imogen, 'Grace Williams: A Symposium (Part I)', *Welsh Music* 5/6 (1977): 19–21.

———, *The Music of Gustav Holst* (Oxford: Oxford University Press, 1969).

Howes, Frank, 'Sir Hugh Allen', *Monthly Musical Record* 60/711 (1 March 1930): 65–7.

———, 'Sir Hugh Allen, 1869–1946', *R.C.M. Magazine* 65/3 (1969): 25–6.

———, 'The Young English Composers – III. Elizabeth Maconchy', *The Musical Monthly Record* 68/798 (July-August 1938): 165–8.

———, *The English Musical Renaissance* (New York: Stein and Day, 1966).

Isaac, Susan, 'Evacuating the Library in World War II', *Royal College of Surgeons Library Blog*, 12 May 2017, https://www.rcseng.ac.uk/library-and-publications/library/blog/evacuating-the-library-in-world-war-ii/ [accessed 27 May 2019].

Jacobs, Arthur, 'Robinson, Stanford', *Grove Music Online*, 2002, https://doi.org/10.1093/gmo/9781561592630.article.O007148 [accessed 6 September 2020].

Jacobs, Arthur, *Henry J. Wood: Maker of the Proms* (London: Methuen, 1994).

Kenyon, Nicholas, *The BBC Symphony Orchestra* (London: British Broadcasting Corporation, 1981).

Kildea, Paul, *Selling Britten: Music and the Market Place* (Oxford: Oxford University Press, 2002).

Kingsley, Nick, '(418) Barry of Santry Court, Barons Barry of Santry', *Landed families of Britain and Ireland* (blog), 27 May 2020, https://landedfamilies.blogspot.com/2020/05/418-barry-of-santry-court-barons-barry.html [accessed 5 June 2019].

Kuna, Milan, 'Jirák, K(arel) B(oleslav)', *Grove Music Online*, 2001, https://doi.org/10.1093/gmo/9781561592630.article.14315 [accessed 5 September 2020].

Lachendro, Jacek, 'The Orchestras in KL Auschwitz', *Auschwitz Studies* 27 (2015): 5–174.

Laity, Paul (ed.), *The Left Book Club Anthology* (London: Victor Gollancz, 2001).

LeFanu, Elizabeth, 'The Harpsichord', in *The Times Anthology of Ghost Stories* (London: Jonathan Cape, Ltd, 1975), 59–71.

LeFanu, Nicola, 'Elizabeth Maconchy', *Contemporary Music Review* 11/1 (1994): 201–4.
———, 'Elizabeth Maconchy DBE (1907–1994): some biographical and musical notes by her daughter Nicola LeFanu. Part 1: 1907–1945' (Programme notes, 2007).
———,'Elizabeth Maconchy DBE (1907–1994): some biographical and musical notes by her daughter Nicola LeFanu, Part II', (Programme notes, 2007).
———,'Elizabeth Maconchy – A Life in Music', in Christa Brüstle and Danielle Sofer (eds), *Elizabeth Maconchy: Music as Impassioned Argument* (Vienna: Universal Edition, 2018), 21–9.
Lewis, John, *The Left Book Club: An Historical Record* (London: Victor Gollancz, 1970).
Lloyd, Stephen, *Constant Lambert: Beyond the Rio Grande* (Woodbridge: Boydell, 2014).
Lutyens, Elisabeth, *A Goldfish Bowl* (London: Cassell, 1972).
McCauley, Martin, *The German Democratic Republic Since 1945* (London: Palgrave Macmillan, 1983).
Macnaghten, Anne, 'Elizabeth Maconchy', *Musical Times* 96/1348 (June 1955): 298–302.
———, 'The Story of the Macnaghten Concerts', *Musical Times* 100/1399 (September 1959): 460–1.
Maconchy, Betty, 'The New Year', *Little Folks* 21/1 (May 1918): 13.
Maconchy, Elizabeth, 'A Short Symposium on Women Composers', *Composer* 6 (1961) 19–21.
———-, 'Book Review – The Modern Composer and His World', *Composer* 10 (Winter 1962): 4–5.
———-, 'The Birds', *Music in Education* 33/335 (January-February 1969): 24–5.
———-, 'Vaughan Williams as a Teacher', *Composer* 2 (March 1959): 18–20.
———-, *Ina Boyle: An Appreciation with a Select List of Her Music* (Dublin: Printed for the Library of Trinity College Dublin at the Dolmen Press, 1974).
———, 'Elizabeth Maconchy On Writing String Quartets', programme notes to *Elizabeth Maconchy Complete String Quartets*. Unicorn-Kanchana, CD DKP 9080, 1989.
———, 'Elizabeth Maconchy writes about the Society for the Promotion of New Music', *Listener* (26 April 1973): 561.
———, 'Grace Williams: A Symposium', *Welsh Music* 5/6 (Summer 1977): 18–19.
———, 'Serenata Concertante – an analytical note' in Peter Dickinson (ed.), *Twenty British Composers* (London: Chester Music, 1975), 50–3.
———, 'The Birds', *Music in Education* 33/335 (January-February 1969): 24–5.
———, 'The Image of Greatness: Ralph Vaughan Williams', *Composer* 15 (April 1965): 10–12.
———, 'Who is your favourite Composer?', *Composer* 24 (Summer 1967): 20–1.
———,'A Composer Speaks', *Composer* 42 (Winter 1971–2): 25–9.
———,'Ralph Vaughan Williams', *R.C.M. Magazine* 55/1 (1959): 33–4.
Manning, Jane, *Vocal Repertoire for the Twenty-First Century*, vol. 1 (Oxford: Oxford University Press, 2020).
Mathias, Rhiannon, *Lutyens, Maconchy, Williams and Twentieth-Century British Music: A Blest Trio of Sirens* (Farnham: Ashgate, 2012).

———, 'Maconchy's Late String Quartets with particular reference to String Quartet No. 9' in Christa Brüstle and Danielle Sofer (eds), *Elizabeth Maconchy: Music as Impassioned Argument* (Vienna: Universal Edition, 2018), 150–63.

McVeagh, Diana, 'Long, Kathleen', *Grove Music Online*, 2001, https://doi.org/10.1093/gmo/9781561592630.article.16947 [accessed 5 September 2020].

'The Myra Hess Concerts', *The National Gallery*, https://www.nationalgallery.org.uk/about-us/history/the-myra-hess-concerts [accessed 4 April 2019].

Morrison, Angus, 'Personal Appreciation', *R.C.M. Magazine* 65/3 (1969): 36.

Nagai, Kaori, 'Kipling and Gender', in Howard J. Booth (ed.), *The Cambridge Companion to Rudyard Kipling* (Cambridge: Cambridge University Press, 2011), 66–79.

Neighbour, Oliver, 'Ralph, Adeline, and Ursula Vaughan Williams: Some Facts and Speculation (with a note about Tippett)', *Music & Letters* 89/3 (2008): 337–45.

O'Brien, Victoria, *A History of Irish Ballet from 1927 to 1963* (Bern: Peter Lang, 2011).

O'Connor, Jennifer, 'The Role of Women in Music in Nineteenth-Century Dublin' (PhD thesis, National University of Ireland, Maynooth, 2010).

O'Higgins, Rachel, *The Correspondence of Alan Bush and John Ireland* (Aldershot: Ashgate, 2006).

Pomeroy, Elizabeth W., 'Within Living Memory: Vita Sackville-West's Poems of Land and Garden', *Twentieth Century Literature* 28/3 (Autumn 1982): 269–89

Pugh, Martin, *Women and the Women's Movement in Britain*, 2nd edn (London: Macmillan Press, 2000).

Roma, Catherine, *The Choral Music of Twentieth-Century Women Composers: Elisabeth Lutyens, Elizabeth Maconchy, and Thea Musgrave* (Lanham, MD: Scarecrow Press, 2006).

Roth, Ernest, *The Business of Music* (London: Cassell, 1966).

Rupprecht, Philip, *British Musical Modernism: The Manchester Group and their Contemporaries* (Cambridge: Cambridge University Press, 2015).

Sackville-West, Vita, *The Land & The Garden* (London: Webb & Bower, 1989).

Seddon, Laura, *British Women Composers and Instrumental Chamber Music in the Early Twentieth Century* (Farnham: Ashgate, 2013).

Shreffler, Anne C., 'The International Society for Contemporary Music and Its Political Context (Prague, 1935)', in Jessica C.E. Gienow-Hecht (ed.), *Music and International History in the Twentieth Century* (New York: Berghahn, 2015), 58–90.

Siek, Stephen, *England's Piano Sage: The Life and Teachings of Tobias Matthay* (Lanham: The Scarecrow Press, 2012).

Skiba, John, 'Elizabeth Maconchy in Conversation with John Skiba', *Composer* 63 (Spring 1978): 7–10.

Smith, Steven C., *A Heart at Fire's Center: The Life and Music of Bernard Herrmann* (Berkeley: University of California Press, 1991).

Sofer, Danielle, 'Death Becomes Him: Elizabeth Maconchy's One-Act Opera *The Departure*', in Christa Brüstle and Danielle Sofer (eds), *Elizabeth Maconchy: Music as Impassioned Argument* (Vienna: Universal Edition, 2018), 181–97.

Spencer, William, *First World War Army Service Records*, 4th edn (Kew: National Archives, 2008).

Stone, Reynolds, and James Hamilton, 'Raverat, Gwendolen Mary (1885–1957)', *Oxford Dictionary of National Biography*, 2004, https://doi.org/10.1093/ref:odnb/35685 [accessed 6 September 2020].

Summerfield, Penny, and Corinna Peniston-Bird, *Contesting Home Defence: Men, Women and the Home Guard in the Second World War* (Manchester: Manchester University Press, 2007).

Talbot, Michael, 'Farewell to Arthur Alexander…', *R.C.M. Magazine* 57/2 (May 1961): 38–9.

Tovey, Donald, *The Classics of Music: Talks, Essays, and Other Writings Previously Uncollected*, edited by Michael Tilmouth (Oxford: Oxford University Press, 2010).

Tyrrell, John, 'Jan, Löwenbach', *Grove Music Online*, 2001, https://doi.org/10.1093/gmo/9781561592630.article.17064 [accessed 5 September 2020].

Vaughan Williams, Ralph, *National Music and Other Essays* (London: Oxford University Press, 1963).

Vaughan Williams, Ursula, *Paradise Remembered* (London: Albion, 2002).

––––––, *R.V.W.: A Biography of Ralph Vaughan Williams* (Oxford: Clarendon, 1964).

Warrack, Guy, *The Royal College of Music: The First Eighty-five Years*, typescript draft (British Library, c. 1977).

Webster, Alan, 'Obituary: William LeFanu', *Independent*, 7 April 1995.

White, Harry, *The Keeper's Recital* (Cork: Cork University Press, 1998).

Whittall, Arnold, 'British Music Thirty Years Ago', *Musical Times* 105/1453 (March 1964): 186–7.

Wiggins, Louise, '"Story of a friendship": Alan Bush, Grigorii Shneerson and cultural diplomacy before and during the Cold War', *Russian Journal of Communication* 8/3 (2016): 256–72.

Williams, Grace, 'A Letter from Vienna', *R.C.M. Magazine* 26/2 (June 1930): 64–6.

––––––, 'Ralph Vaughan Williams', *R.C.M. Magazine* 55/1 (1959): 36.

Williams, Margaret (dir.), *Elizabeth Maconchy*, DVD, produced by the Arts Council of Great Britain (Suffolk: Concord Media, 1985).

Witts, Richard, *Artist Unknown: An Alternative History of the Arts Council* (London: Little, Brown and Company, 1998).

Wood, Hugh, 'SPNM 20', *Musical Times* 104/1448 (October 1963): 708–10.

Woolf, Virginia, *A Room of One's Own*, Harbinger Books edn (New York: Harcourt, Brace & World, 1929).

Index

Numbers referring to photographs are given in italics. Numbers referring to musical illustrations are given in bold. Only those abbreviations that do not appear on page xiv are cross-referenced.

'EM' refers to Elizabeth Maconchy. Works listed are by EM unless otherwise stated.

Music in Britain, 1600–2000

ISSN 2053-3217

Series Editors:
BYRON ADAMS, RACHEL COWGILL AND PETER HOLMAN

This series provides a forum for the best new work in the field of British music studies, placing music from the early seventeenth to the late twentieth centuries in its social, cultural, and historical contexts. Its approach is deliberately inclusive, covering immigrants and emigrants as well as native musicians, and explores Britain's musical links both within and beyond Europe. The series celebrates the vitality and diversity of music-making across Britain in whatever form it took and wherever it was found, exploring its aesthetic dimensions alongside its meaning for contemporaries, its place in the global market, and its use in the promotion of political and social agendas.

Proposals or queries should be sent in the first instance to Professors Byron Adams, Rachel Cowgill, Peter Holman or Boydell & Brewer at the addresses shown below. All submissions will receive prompt and informed consideration.

Professor Byron Adams,
Department of Music – 061, University of California, Riverside, CA 92521–0325
email: byronadams@earthlink.net

Professor Rachel Cowgill,
Department of Music, University of York
Heslington, York, YO10 5DD
email: rachel.cowgill@york.ac.uk

Emeritus Professor Peter Holman MBE,
119 Maldon Road, Colchester, Essex, CO3 3AX
email: peter@parley.org.uk

Boydell & Brewer, PO Box 9, Woodbridge, Suffolk, IP12 3DF
email: editorial@boydell.co.uk

Titles listed here were originally published
under the series title *Music in Britain, 1600–1900*
ISSN 1752-1904

Lectures on Musical Life: William Sterndale Bennett
edited by Nicholas Temperley, with Yunchung Yang

John Stainer: A Life in Music
Jeremy Dibble

The Pursuit of High Culture: John Ella and Chamber Music in Victorian London
Christina Bashford

Thomas Tallis and his Music in Victorian England
Suzanne Cole

The Consort Music of William Lawes, 1602–1645
John Cunningham

Life After Death: The Viola da Gamba in Britain from Purcell to Dolmetsch
Peter Holman

The Musical Salvationist: The World of Richard Slater (1854–1939) 'Father of Salvation Army Music'
Gordon Cox

British Music and Literary Context: Artistic Connections in the Long Nineteenth Century
Michael Allis

New titles published under the series title *Music in Britain, 1600–2000*
ISSN 2053-3217

Hamilton Harty: Musical Polymath
Jeremy Dibble

Thomas Morley: Elizabethan Music Publisher
Tessa Murray

The Advancement of Music in Enlightenment England: Benjamin Cooke and the Academy of Ancient Music
Tim Eggington

George Smart and Nineteenth-Century London Concert Life
John Carnelley

The Lives of George Frideric Handel
David Hunter

Musicians of Bath and Beyond: Edward Loder (1809–1865) and his Family
edited by Nicholas Temperley

Conductors in Britain, 1870–1914: Wielding the Baton at the Height of Empire
Fiona M. Palmer

Ernest Newman: A Critical Biography
Paul Watt

The Well-Travelled Musician: John Sigismond Cousser and Musical Exchange in Baroque Europe
Samantha Owens

Music in the West Country: Social and Cultural History Across an English Region
Stephen Banfield

British Musical Criticism and Intellectual Thought, 1850–1950
edited by Jeremy Dibble and Julian Horton

Composing History: National Identities and the English Masque Revival, 1860–1920
Deborah Heckert

With Mornefull Musique: Funeral Elegies in Early Modern England
K. Dawn Grapes

Music for St Cecilia's Day: From Purcell to Handel
Bryan White

Before the Baton: Musical Direction
and Conducting in Stuart and Georgian Britain
Peter Holman

Organ-building in Georgian and Victorian England:
The Work of Gray & Davison, 1772–1890
Nicholas Thistlethwaite

Musical Exchange between Britain and Europe, 1500–1800:
Essays in Honour of Peter Holman
edited by John Cunningham and Bryan White

The Symphonic Poem in Britain, 1850–1950
edited by Michael Allis and Paul Watt

Music in North-East England, 1500–1800
edited by Stephanie Carter, Kirsten Gibson, Roz Southey

British Music, Musicians and Institutions, c. 1630–1800:
Essays in Honour of Harry Diack Johnstone
edited by Peter Lynan and Julian Rushton

John Gunn: Musician Scholar in Enlightenment Britain
George Kennaway

Exhibitions, Music and the British Empire
Sarah Kirby

Opera and Politics in Queen Anne's Britain, 1705–1714
Thomas McGeary